ISBN 978-1-332-77406-7
PIBN 10441361

# 1 MONTH OF
# FREE
# READING

at

## www.ForgottenBooks.com

By purchasing this book you are eligible for one month membership to ForgottenBooks.com, giving you unlimited access to our entire collection of over 700,000 titles via our web site and mobile apps.

To claim your free month visit:
www.forgottenbooks.com/free441361

English
Français
Deutsche
Italiano
Español
Português

# www.forgottenbooks.com

**Mythology** Photography **Fiction**
Fishing Christianity **Art** Cooking
Essays Buddhism Freemasonry
Medicine **Biology** Music **Ancient
Egypt** Evolution Carpentry Physics
Dance Geology **Mathematics** Fitness
Shakespeare **Folklore** Yoga Marketing
**Confidence** Immortality Biographies
Poetry **Psychology** Witchcraft
Electronics Chemistry History **Law**
Accounting **Philosophy** Anthropology
Alchemy Drama Quantum Mechanics
Atheism Sexual Health **Ancient History**
**Entrepreneurship** Languages Sport
Paleontology Needlework Islam
**Metaphysics** Investment Archaeology
Parenting Statistics Criminology
**Motivational**

# SELECT TREATISES

OF

# MARTIN LUTHER,

IN

# THE ORIGINAL GERMAN,

WITH

PHILOLOGICAL NOTES, AND AN ESSAY ON GERMAN
AND ENGLISH ETYMOLOGY.

## BY B. SEARS.

.

———

## ANDOVER:

PUBLISHED BY ALLEN, MORRILL AND WARDWELL.

BOSTON: JOHN P. JEWETT AND COMPANY.

NEW-YORK: M. H. NEWMAN AND CO.

1846.

# PREFACE.

THE volume here presented to the public, is designed for those who have already made a beginning in the study of the German language, and who wish to prosecute it with philological accuracy. Helps of this kind in English are very scarce, if indeed they exist at all. Explanations that may be found in the common grammars or in the smaller dictionaries are not repeated here. Particular attention has been paid to the peculiar structure and idioms of the language, to the exact signification of difficult words, to synonymes, to the connection existing between etymology and usage, and, in short, to everything which should tend to remove from the mind of the student vague generalities in respect to the meaning of words and phrases.

If the works of the German authors which are most in circulation, were provided with commentaries like the Greek and Roman classics, and the object of the present volume were to add one to the number, it might be objected to the plan of the work, that it embraces too much. But standing as it does alone, there is a demand that it should assume, as far as is practicable, the character of a manual of German philology, which may be used as a book of reference in reading other authors. With this object in view, the most idiomatic writer, the one who in great measure moulded the language to its present form, has been selected. Thus a text, of limited extent, has furnished occasion for ample commentary; and such is the number of idiomatic expressions occurring in the author, and of others introduced in connection with them in the notes, that no small portion, it is believed, of the difficult idioms to be met with in the current popular literature may find an explanation by a reference to the Index of this volume.

The synoptical view of German and English Etymologies is an addition to the plan of the work made at a late period, and containing a very few repetitions of what may be found in the Notes.

It is hoped that the intrinsic merits of the pieces here selected will add to the interest of the work. With the exception of the brief discourse on indulgences,—which is nevertheless important as giving us a view of Luther's early mode of thinking and style of composition,—the selections are among the richest and most eloquent, not only of the author's works, but of the whole body of literature to which they belong. The address to the German nobility will render it conceivable how he could so arouse the patriotic spirit of his countrymen. His high-minded and irresistible appeal to the civil authorities on the subject of establishing and supporting public schools, will place him, at least, side by side with the ablest and most philanthropic promoters of popular education at the present day. The specimens of practical commentary from his pen will furnish evidence of a religious character and of a degree of genius which some, in their ignorance, have felt disposed to deny him.

B. S.

*Newton Centre, Oct.* 1, 1846.

# CONTENTS.

A*

# CORRECTIONS.

Page 5, line 2, read **denn** for **den**.

6, note 2, strike out the period after **keiner**.

20, note 1, last line but one, read *admitted* for *omitted*.

21, note, line 8, read **er** for **es**.

27, note, line 3, read **greifen** for **griefen**.

29, line 4, read **Glauben** for **Glauden**.

31, notes, 1 and 2, for 6 and 7.

35, note 4, **Schanden** is not in the singular. See p. 56. n. 3.

46, line 1, strike out the comma after **müssen**.

46, note 4, line 3, insert *in* at the beginning of the line.

52, line 7, read **sein** for **fein**.

56, last line but two, read **Schanden** for **Schenden**.

81, note 3, line 1, read *has this* for *hast his*.

117, line 2, read **Urlaubs** for **Urlauds**.

199, note 3, read *colon,* for *semicolon.*

289, note 3, line 2, read *thine* for *their.*

# SYNOPTICAL VIEW

OF

# GERMAN AND ENGLISH WORDS

## HAVING THE SAME ETYMOLOGY.

---

THE manner in which words substantially the same are represented in cognate languages, or in the different dialects of any one language, is, to a very great extent, conformed to fixed laws. An exact comparison of the English language with the entire family of the Teutonic dialects, with this end in view, would be of great service to the critical English scholar. In the present outline, nothing more is attempted than a mere sketch of the principal classes of words corresponding to each other in the modern English and the modern German. Words that are so nearly the same as to be without organic changes, and those, which are either very dissimilar, or very irregular, are for the most part omitted, the chief object of the essay being to aid the memory of the student. It must not be supposed that the English is derived from the German, or the German from the English. The English is much the older form, resembling the old Saxon, the Gothic, and even the old high German, much more than it does the modern German. In those dialects, many words and forms of words common to them and to the English are found, which are not preserved in the modern German. It is to *etymological analogies*, rather than to *derivations*, that attention, in the following essay, is directed. The classification is made according to the leading characteristic of the word. Other characteristics are explained in the remarks to which the figures, appended to the words, refer.

1. The vowel a in German frequently corresponds to an e-sound in English; and the vowel e, when short, corresponds in a few instances to a.

Aal, eel

Abend, even(ing)[16]

Bank, bench[11]

Bart, beard[18]

dar, there[18]

Gast, guest

Hanf, hemp[22] and [17]

klar, clear

Knall, knell

mager, meager

Mahl, meal

Nacken, neck

Nadel, needle

Rast, rest

Saat, seed[18]

Schaf, sheep[17]

Schale, shell

Schlaf, sleep[23] and [17]

Stahl, steel

Stamm, stem

statt, stead[18]

Straße, street[14]

That, deed[18]

Waffen, weapon[17]

walten, wield[18]

———

Espe, asp

fern, far[21]

fest, fast (firm)

fet, fat

Kelch, chalice[11]

Lerche, lark[11]

Schmerz, smart[23] and [15]

sterben, starve[16]

Stern, star[21]

Theer, tar

Wespe, wasp

NOTE. The word Abend is explained under No. 16.—The word knell is much more restricted in its present signification than Knall, which means any quick sound.—Meager is now mostly used in a figurative sense, and the word *lean* corresponds more accurately to mager.—The termination en in Nacken is not an essential part of the word.—Saat corresponds to seed in etymology, but not in signification.—Schale signifies any dish or vessel in the form of a shell.—Walten is generally used of moral, and *wield*, of physical agency.—*Starve* is used in a more specific sense than sterben, and corresponds nearly to the cognate word darben.

2. In a certain class of words, and generally before the letters l and n, the vowel a in German corresponds to o in English. In a very few cases the vowel is o in German, and a, or an a-sound in English.

| | |
|---|---|
| Alt, old[18] | lang, long |
| behalten, behold[18] | Nase, nose |
| Drang, throng[18] | sanft, soft[21] |
| falten, fold[18] | schalten, scold[18] |
| (Ge)fang, song | Thaler, dollar[18] |
| Haaken, hook | Wald, woods[21] |
| halten, hold[18] | |
| Kaffee, coffee | Borke, bark |
| kalt, cold[1s] | horchen, hearken[11] |
| Kamm, comb[24] | roh, raw[19] |
| laden, load | Stroh, straw[19] |

NOTE. B e h a l t e n clears up the origin of our word *beholden*, (*bound*), which was such a puzzle to Dr. Campbell, and also of the word *behold* (*to see*) i. e. *to ho'd near*, or *before one's eyes.*—D r a n g means a *press* and *trouble*. See d r ä n g e n, No. 18. The prefix g e, is frequently dependent on usage alone, there being no uniform rule for its insertion or omission in certain derivative words.

3. In a few words, the vowel a long in German corresponds to i or ei in English.

| | |
|---|---|
| Acht, eight[11] | Nacht, night[11] |
| Bram, brim | nahe, nigh |
| Fracht, freight[11] | Sänger, singer |
| Macht, might[11] | Schlamm, slime[23] |
| Nachbar, neighbor[11] | Strange, string |

4. The vowel e in German, often corresponds to an i-sound in English, and i to an e-sound. The former is also represented by the diphthong ea in English.

| | |
|---|---|
| Es, it[14] | Feld, field |
| fechten, fight[11] | geben, give[16] |

leben, live[16]

Leber, liver[16]

lecken, lick

Pech, pitch

Recht, right[11]

Schwester, sister[23]

Schnepfe, snipe[23] and [13]

sechs, six

spähen, spy

stecken, stick

streben, strive[16]

welch, which[20] and [21]

———

Biber, beaver[16]

Bier, beer

dich, thee[18]

Fieber, fever[16]

Filz, felt[15]

frisch, fresh

Glimmer, gleam (mica)

glimmen, gleam

Grieche, Greek[11]

Hitze, heat[15]

Kiel, keel

Knie, knee

mich, me

Schlitten, sled[18]

schmieren, smear[23]

schwitzen, sweat[23] and [15]

sieben, seven[16]

Sitz, seat[15]

Strich, streak[11]

tief, deep[17]

wichtig, weighty[11] and [25]

wir, we[21]

———

Brechen, break[11]

bähren, bear

Erde, earth[18]

ernst, earnest

essen, eat[14]

Feder, feather[18]

heben, heave[16]

Herd, hearth[18]

Herz, heart[15]

kleben, cleave[16]

lecken, leak

lehnen, lean

scheren, shear

sprechen, speak[21] and [11]

stehlen, steal

treten, tread[18]

weben, weave[16]

Wetter, weather

Note. *Pitch* comes from the Anglo-Saxon *pic*, and these are connected with the Latin *pix*.—S p ä h e n is placed here on account of its analogy, the *a* being equivalent to *e*, and the *i* to *y*.—B ä h r e n. See s p ä h e n above.—E r n s t is an abridged form from E r n e s t.


5. The *o*-sound and the *e*-sound, (or in a few cases the *i*-sound) are used for each other.

Bohne, bean

Brod, bread

Floh, flea

Flotte, fleet

groß, great[14]

Hölle, hell

hören, hear

—los,—less

Noth, need[18]

Ohr, ear

Ost, east

Oster, easter

roth, red[18]

schwören, swear[23]

Strom, stream

Tod, death[18]

todt, dead

Woche, week[11]

wohl, well

Wolke, welkin

zwölf, twelve[15]

———

Erz, ore

gehen, go

Krähe, crow[19]

Klee, clover

Lehm, loam

Lehen, loan

Lehre, lore

mähen, mow[19]

mehr, more

Reh, roe

Rhede, road (of the sea)

säen, sow[19]

schelten, scold[18]

Schnee, snow[23]

Schwert, sword[23] and [18]

Seele, soul

wehe ! woe !

Werth, worth

Zehe, toe[15]

———

Lieben, love[16]

schieben, shove[16]

schießen, shoot[14]

———

ob, if[17]

Stock, stick

NOTE. The Dutch word *klewer* is intermediate between *clover* and Klee.—The derivation of *if*, from the imperative of the Anglo-Saxon verb *gifan*, is doubtless an error. Not only does that fail to explain the meaning of the word, but it leaves the cognate forms, in the Gothic *ibai*; in old German, *ibu*, *ube* and *obe*; in old Frisian, *jef*; in Icelandic, *ef*; in low Saxon, *of*; and in German, o b, unexplained. As these are all connected, no derivation can be satisfactory which does not explain them all.

6. The diphthong au in German, corresponds to the diphthong *ea* (or a long *e*-sound), to the vowels *o* and *u*, and sometimes to *i*, in English.

Auge, eye

Baum, beam

brauen, brew[19]

hauen, hew[19]

Haufe, heap[17]

Haupt, head[18]

kauen, chew[11] and [19]

Tau, tow[19]

Laube, leaf[17]

Taube, dove[16]

Lauch, leek[11]

trauen, trow[19]

laufen, leap[17]

_____

Pfau, pea(cock)[13]

Blau, blue

rauhen, reek[11]

dauern, (en)dure

Schaube, sheaf[17]

Daum, thumb[24]

Schraube, screw[19]

Maul(esel), mule

taub, deaf[17]

Maulbeere, mulberry

Thau, dew[19]

faugen, suck

Traum, dream[18]

schauder, shudder

traurig, dreary[18] and [25]

Schaum, scum

_____

_____

Rauben, rob

Braut, bride[18]

rauh, rough

Brautigam, bridegroom

Raum, room

Faust, fist

Schaufel, shovel[17]

Haut, hide[18]

stauen, stow[19]

schlau, sly

NOTE. A u g e, _eye_, is introduced here with a little license. As the _u_ in German, when it is the last letter of a diphthong, often becomes _w_ in English, the words, _brew, hew, chew, screw, dew, stow, tow,_ and _trow,_ may be regarded as coming under a modification of the rule, which cannot be more particularly specified here.—R a u h, _rough_, is a little irregular, and is mentioned here for the sake of convenience. The same may be said of R a u m, and b l a u.—D a u e r n, will remind one of the old English word _dure_, and the Latin _duro_.—M a u l (e s e l) and _mule_, come from the Latin _mulus_, the animal that works at the _mola_, or mill.— _Groom_ in _bridegroom_, is _gum_ in Anglo-Saxon. In the Gothic and Anglo-Saxon, _guma_ means _a man_.—_Sly_ is substantially conformed to the rule, the _y_ being equivalent to _i_.

7. The letter u in German, corresponds to an _o_-sound, mostly _oo, o,_ and _ou_ in English ; and _o_ short in German, to _u_ short, for the most part, in English.

Behuf, behoof

Brut, brood[18]

Blume, bloom

Bube, booby

Blut, blood[18]

Buch, book[11]

Fluth, flood[18]
Fuß, foot[14]
gut, good[18]
Huf, hoof
Stuhl, stool, etc. etc.

———

Bruder, brother[18]
Bund, bond
Busen, bosom[22]
Fuchs, fox
Furt, ford[18]
Füllen, foal
Futter, fodder
genug, enough
Kuh, cow[19]
Kupfer, copper[13]
Mutter, mother
Ruthe, rod[18]
Schuh, shoe
Sturm, storm
thun, do[18]
Wunder, wonder
Wurm, worm
Wurtz, wort[15]
zu, to[15]
Zunge, tongue[15]

———

Du, thou[18]
Grund, ground
Hund, hound
jung, young
Mund, mouth[21] and [18]
rund, round
Pfund, pound[13]
Puder, powder
Süd, south[18]
(ge)sund, sound
Schulter, shoulder[18]
Wunde, wound
Bock, buck
Donner, thunder
Mord, murder
(er)mordern, murder
Nonne, nun
Rost, rust
Sommer, summer
sondern, sunder
Sonne, sun
Stoff, stuff
Stoppel, stouble
Tonne, tun (cask)
Torf, turf
voll, full
Wolle, wool (wul)

NOTE. Füllen, genug, Schuh Puder, Stoppel, and Wolle only approximate the rule. In thun and zu, we see the reason of the peculiar pronunciation of *do* and *to*. The final *n* (for *en*) in thun, sondern and other verbs, being a mere ending, is not taken into the account. The few instances in which *i* in English corresponds to *u* in German, are Durst, thirst; Gurth, girth; Zunder, tinder, and perhaps some others.

8. Ue in German, corresponds sometimes to *i*, sometimes to *e*, and sometimes, though rarely, to *o*, in English.

Dünn, thin[18]

füllen, fill

fünf, five[21]

Fürst, first (prince)

Gürtel, girdle[18]

knütten, knit

küssen, kiss

lügen, lie[12]

Mühle, mill

Münze, mint[15]

Stück, stick

Sünde, sin

———

Brüder, brethren[18]

Büche, beech

blüten, bleed[18]

fühlen, feel

Füsse, feet[14]

grün, green

grüssen, greet[14]

Hülfe, help[17]

hüten, heed[18]

kühn, keen

füß, sweet[14]

übel, evil[16]

———

blühen, blow[19]

glühen, glow[19]

hüpfen, hop[13]

fühl, cool

Küste, coast

NOTE. Munze, *coin*; Stück, *piece*; huten, *guard*; and kühn. *bold*, vary somewhat in their signification from the English words of the same etymology as now used.

9. The diphthong ei in German, corresponds sometimes to an *e*-sound, sometimes to an *o*-sound, and less frequently to the vowel *a* in English.

(Be)reit, ready[18]

bleichen, bleach

Breite, breadth[18]

drei, three[18]

Fleisch, flesh

frei, free

Heide, heath and hea-

heilen, heal        [then[18]

leiten, lead[18]

meinen, mean

reichen, reach

Scheide, sheath[18]

Schweiß, sweat[14]

Theil, deal[18]

weich, weak[11]

Weißen, wheat[20]

———

Bein, bone

beide, both[18]

breit, broad[18]

Eiche, oak[11]

Eid, oath[18]

eigen, own

ein, one

Geist, ghost

Geiß, goat[14]

heilig, holy[12]

heim, home

heifer, hoarse[22]

heiß, hot[14]

kleiden, clothe[18]

Leim, loam

meist, most

Reihe, row[19]

Seife, soap[17]

Speiche, spoke[11]

Stein, stone

streichen, stroke[11]

Teig, dough[18]

Zeichen, token[15] and [11]

zwei, two[15]

———

Ein, an

Leisten, last

Leiter, ladder[18]

Meister, master

NOTE. Fleisch, *meat;* meinen, *to be of opinion;* Theil, *part;* weich, *soft;* and Zeichen, *a sign,* agree with their corresponding words better in etymology than in their present signification.

10. The diphthong eu in German, sometimes corresponds to an *i*-sound, or an *e*-sound in English.

Feur, fire

leuchten, lighten (light)[11]

neun, nine

scheu, shy

Freund, friend

streuen, strew[19]

steuern, steer

theur, dear[18]

———

11. Ch in German, corresponds sometimes to *gh* in English, and sometimes to *k*, and vice versa. In a few words cke goes into *dge*, and g into *k*.

Flucht, flight

Fracht, freight[3]

(Ge)lächter, laughter

lachen, laugh

leicht, light

Licht, light

Macht, might[3]

Nacht, night[3]

Nachbar, neighbor[3]

recht, right[4]

Schlacht, slaughter

Vorsicht, foresight

———

Brechen, break[4]

Buch, book[7]

Deich, dike

Lerche, lark[1]

machen, make

Milch, milk

Sichel, sickle

Storch, stork

sprechen, speak[21]

wachen, wake

———

Bank, bench[1]     strecken, stretch

Birke, birch     kühl, chill (and cool[8])

Kalk, chalk (lime)     kiesen, choose

Käfer, chafer     ————

Kammer, chamber[24]     Brücke, bridge[8]

Käse, cheese     Ecke, edge

kauen, chew[19]     Hecke, hedge

Kerl, churl     Mücke, midge[8]

Kinn, chin     Rücken, ridge[8]

Krucke, crutch     ————

Fink, finch     Klang, clank

Kirche, church     klingen, clink

Kiste, chest     Rang, rank

12. G final in German is frequently represented by *y* in English, or by *i*, if another letter or syllable be appended.

Betrügen, betray     Norwegen, Norway

belügen, belie[8]     Regen, rain

einig, any[3]     Roggen, rye[5]

Felge, felly     sagen, say

Flegel, flail     schlagen, slay[23]

fliegen, fly     Segel, sail[1]

Frucht, fruit     Siegel, seal

Hagel, hail     Stag-segel, stay-sail

Honig, honey     Steige, stair[3, 21]

Hügel, hill[8]     Tag, day[18]

Lager, lair and layer     Montag, Monday

legen, lay     Sonntag, Sunday

(ge)legen, lain     Freitag, Friday

liegen, lie     Werktag, work-day

Magd, maid     Fasttag, fast-day

manig, many     (Ge)burthstag, birth-day

Mergel, marl[1]     Mittag, mid-day     (noon)

mögen, may     vormittag, fore-midday

Nagel, nail     Neujahrstag, newyears-day

täglich, daily   Weg, way
wägen, weigh   Ziegel, tile[15]

NOTE. F r u c h t, and *weigh* (w ä g e n) are slight variations from the rule. In the Anglo-Saxon, the letter *g* performs the same office that it does in German, and corresponds to the same letters in English.

**13.** The letter p in German often has f appended to it, especially in words of foreign origin.

Apfel, apple   Pflanze, plant[15]
Hüpfen, hop[8]   Pflaume, plum[6]
Kampf, camp   Pflaster, plaster
Kropf, crop   Pfoste, post
Krampf, cramp   pflücken, pluck
Kupfer, copper[7]   Pflock, plug[7]
opfern, offer (sacrifice)   Pflug, plough[7]
Pfad, path[18]   Pfropf, prop
Pfahl, pale (palus)   Pfuhl, pool[7]
Pfanne, pan   Pfund, pound[7]
Pfarre, parish (paroisse)   Rumpf, rump
Pfeffer, pepper[17]   stampfen, stamp
Pfeife, pipe and fife   Sumpf, swamp
Pfeiler, pillar   stopfen, stop
Pfennig, peuny[12]   zapfen, tap[15]

NOTE. K a m p f means a *battle* rather than the *field*.

**14.** S, or ß at the end of a word or syllable in German, corresponds to the *t* in English.

Apricose, apricot   essen, eat[4]
aus, out   Floß, } float
beissen, bite   Flosse, }
besser, better   Faß, fat, or vat
das, that[18]   Fuß, foot[7]
daß, that[18]   (Ge)biß, bit
Drossel, throttle (thrush)[18]   Gries, grit
es, it[4]   Grüssen, greet[8]

B*

Haß, hate

Horniß, hornet[4]

Kessel, kettle

lassen, let[1]

Los, lot

messen, mete

müssen, must

Nessel, nettle

Mörser, mortar

Rassel, rattle[']

Schweiß, sweat[23] and [9]

Straße, street[1]

süß, sweet[8]

Spieß, spit

Wasser, water

was, what[20]

15. *T* initial in English, corresponds to z in German ; and *t* final, generally to ß. In some cases, the t before z is omitted.

Zahm, tame

Zange, tongs[2]

Zebe, toe[5]

Zeit, tide (time)

Zehn, ten

zieren, (at)tire

Zeichen, token[9]

Zinn, tin

Zipf, tip[13]

Zug, tug

zu, to[7]

zoll, toll

Zunder, tinder

zehren, } tear[4]
zerren, }

zwanzig, twenty[12]

Zweig, twig

Zunge, tongue[7]

———

Bolz, } bolt
Bolzen, }

Herz, heart[4]

Filz, felt[4]

Hitze, heat[4]

Katze, cat

Malz, malt

Münze, mint[8]

Netz, net

Pelz, pelt

Salz, salt[1]

schmelzen, smelt[23]

Schmutz, smut[23]

setzen, set

sitzen, sit

schmerz, smart[23]

Stelze, stilts[4]

strotzen, strut[7]

Witz, wit

NOTE. Zieren, corresponds to the old English *tire*, and to the Anglo-Saxon *tir.*—Zeichen, *a sign*, agrees only in etymology with *token* ; and so Zug, *the act of drawing*, with *tug* ; Münze, *coin*, with *mint*. Schmutz, *filth*, with *smut* ; and Schmerz, *pain*, with *smart*.

16. The letter *v* in English, often corresponds to its cognate *b* in German.

| | |
|---|---|
| Abend, even[1] | proben, prove |
| Biber, beaver[4] | Probst, provost |
| eben, even | Rabe, raven |
| Fieber, fever | Salbe, salve |
| Grab, grave | schaben, shave |
| haben, have | Sieb, sieve |
| heben, heave | sieben, seven |
| Herbst, harvest[1] | Silber, silver |
| kleben, cleave | streben, strive[4] |
| Knabe, knave | Taube, dove[6] |
| leben, live[4] | übel, evil[8] |
| Leber, liver[4] | weben, weave |
| Nabe, nave | Wissmuth, bismuth |
| Nabel, navel | |

NOTE. A b e n d is a participle from the verb a b e n, which is derived from a b. With T a g understood, it means *the departing day.* There can be but little doubt that *even*, which also has a participial form, *evening*, is of the same derivation, the letter *d* in A b e n d, being dropped.—K n a b e, *a boy*, agrees with *knave* only in etymology, or in the obsolete signification of the latter.—P r o b s t, or P r o p s t, is a corruption of the Latin, *praepositus.* The English form is nearer to the original, than the German.—W i s s m u t h is placed here, because *v* and *w* are often treated as the same letter in German.

17. The letters *b* and *v* are cognate with *f*; the former is also cognate with *p*, and this sometimes with *f*.

| | |
|---|---|
| Dieb, thief[18] | ———— |
| halb, half | Hafen, haven |
| Kalb, calf | Neffe, nephew |
| lieb, lief | Schaufel, shovel[6] |
| Karfunkel, carbuncle | Teufel, devil[10] |
| Probe, proof | Volk, folk |
| Stab, staff | |
| Tafel, table | ———— |
| Weib, wife | Börse, purse |

doppel, double

Krippe, crib

plappern, blabb

Pedell, beadle[4]

Polster, bolster

Pöbel, people

Rippe, rib

Stoppel, stubble

———

Affe, ape

offen, open

scharf, sharp

Streife, stripe

tief, deep[18]

Waffen, weapon[1]

Hanf, hemp

helfen, help

Harfe, harp

gaffen, gape

greifen, gripe

Hüfte, hip[8]

hoffen, hope

Schiffe, ship

reif, ripe

Note. Weib, *woman*, has a different meaning from what *wife* has come to have.—Neffe is placed here with *nephew*, partly because the *ph* in the latter is equivalent to *v* (in old German *nevo*), and partly because the English comes directly from the Anglo-Saxon *nefa*.—Both Teufel and *devil* have a common Greek origin. Neither is derived from the other. So the words Börse, and *purse*, come from the Greek word βύρσα. Börse has come to signify *the exchange*.—Pedell and *beadle* come from the Latin *pedellus*.—Pöbel, like *people*, and the French *peuple*, comes from *populus*.—Greifen signifies *to seize*.

18. The letter *d* is cognate both with *t*, and with *th*, and the two last with each other.

Aelter, elder

Bett, bed

bieten, bid

Blatt, blade

Blut, blood

Boden, bottom[22]

breit, broad[5]

Brut, brood

eitel, idle (empty)

Euter, udder

Futter, fodder[7]

gleiten, glide

Gott, God

Gürtel, girdle[8]

gürten, gird[8]

hart, hard

Hut, hood[7]

hüten, heed[8]

kneten, knead[4]

Mittel, middle

reiten, ride

Rettig, radish[1]

Sattel, saddle

Schatten, shade

Seite, side
selten, seldom[22]
siedeln, settle
Sinter, cinders
Spaten, spade
Statt, stead
Tanz, dance
Teufel, devil[10]
Tochter, daughter[11]
tragen, drag
treiben, drive[16]
treten, tread[4]
trinken, drink
Trommel, drum[7]
Tropf, drop[13]
waten, wade
—warts,—wards
unter, under

———

Bad, bath
Bruder, brother[7]
Bude, booth[7]
Christenthum, christen-
Dach, thatch        [dom
Dank, thanks
dar, there[1]
darein, therein[1]
Daum, thumb[24]
dein, thine
denken, think[4]
denn, then (and than)
derer, their
dick, thick
diese, these
Ding, thing
Distel, thistle

doch, though[11]
Dorn, thorn
drängen, throng
dreschen, thresh
drei, three[9]
du, thou[7]
Durst, thirst
dünn, thin[8]
Erde; earth[4]
Feder, feather[4]
fürder, further
Heide, heath and heathen
Herd, hearth[4]
Leder, leather[4]
Nord, north
Schmid, smith[23]
sieden, seethe
Süd, south

———

Fluth, flood[7]
Methe, mead[4]
Ruthe, rod and rood[7]
Thal, dale
Thaler, dollar[2]
That, deed[1]
Thau, dew[1, 19]
theur, dear
thun, do[7]
Thür, } door[8]
Thor, }
Wittwe, widow

———

Fort, forth
Latte, lath
Monat, month
Motte, moth

| | |
|---|---|
| taufenb, thousand | Vater, father |
| Trumm, thrumb[24] | Wetter, weather[4] |

NOTE. *Blade* does not commonly signify *leaf,* like B l a t t.—B o d e n *ground, soil,* and *bottom,* is but rarely used in this last signification.—E i t e l, *empty,* has not the sense of *idle.*—H u t corresponds to *hood* and *hat.*—R e t t i g is *radic* in Anglo-Saxon, *radichio* in Italian, and is derived from the Latin r a d i x.—S e l t e n has various forms in the different Teutonic dialects.—T r a g e n goes into *drag* and *draw.* Compare the Latin *traho.*—T r o m m e l takes the form of T r u m m e in low Saxon, and T r o m m e in Upper German.—W ä r t s, as a termination, not bearing the accent, corresponds exactly to the English termination *wards* in *towards, backwards,* etc.—Thatch has a more limited signification than D a c h, *roof.* The same is true of *feather,* as compared with F e d e r.—H e i d e, *a heath,* i. e. *a desert,* and then *a plant* that grows there; and finally, as a translation of *paganus,* an idolater living in the country or desert, a pagan, a heathen.—T h a l e r is a coin which was first struck in a certain T h a l, *dale,* (J o a c h i m s - t h a l, in Bohemia). It is an abbreviation of J o a c h i m s - t h a l e r.—W i t t w e is *widowo* in the Gothic, and *witawa* in old German.

19. *W*, at the end of a word in English, stands in the place of h, g, (or ch, or h) u and v in German, and of j in the old dialects, which is omitted in the modern German.

| | |
|---|---|
| Bellen, bellow | Sau, sow |
| blühen, blow[8] | Sehne, sinew[4] |
| brauen, brew[1] | ſtauen, stow[2] |
| glühen, glow[8] | ſtreuen, strew |
| hauen, hew[1] | Stroh, straw[2] |
| hohl, hollow | Tau, tow |
| kauen, chew[11, 1] | Thau, dew[18] |
| Klaue, claw | trauen, trow[2] |
| krähen, crow[5] | ——— |
| Kuh, cow[8] | (Blaſe) balg, bellows[1] |
| mähen, mow[5] | biegen, bow |
| Malve, mallow | Bogen, bow |
| nagen, gnaw | Borg, barrow[2] |
| Reihe, row[9] | borgen, borrow |
| ſäen, sow[5] | Burg, burrow (borough) |

Ellenbogen, elbow
folgen, follow
Furche, furrow
Galge, gallows
Hageborn, hawthorn[18]
heiligen, hallow[3]
Magen, maw
Mark, marrow

Morgen, morrow
sägen, saw
schwelgen, swallow[23]
Sorge, sorrow
tagen, dawn[18]
Talg, tallow
Vogel, fowl

NOTE. B e l l e n means properly *to bark*. Our words *bell* and *bull* are cognate with it. In this word there is no trace of the letter *j*.— H o h l is also irregular. The *w* may come from the *h* transposed. Compare S e h n e.—S ä e n is *sajan* in Gothic.—T r a u e n, *to trust*, old English *trow* —B a h r e, *barrow*, i. e. *bier*; perhaps belongs to this class of words.—*Hallow* comes from Anglo-Saxon *halgian* for *haligan*.—M a g e n properly means *stomach*.—S o r g e now means *anxiety*, *care*.— From s c h w e l g e n comes S c h w a l g, *the swallow*, or throat.

20. The letter *h* before *w*, which is of frequent occurrence in the old German dialects, and is retained and inserted after the *w* in English, is dropped in the modern German.

Wall(fisch), whale ; old German *hual*
Weißen, wheat; Gothic *hwaiteis*
Was, what; Dutch *wat* ; Swedish *hvas*
Weil, while ; old Saxon *huila*
Weiland, whilom
weinen, whine ; Gothic *guainon*
weiß, white ; Gothic *hveits* ; old German *huiz*
wenn, when ; old German *huenne*
wessen, whose ; Gothic *hvis* ; old German *hues*
wetzen, whet; old German *huezan ;* A. S. *hvettan*
Werft, wharf; Anglo-Saxon and Swedish *hvarf*
wispern, whisper

NOTE. It will be observed that though the *h* comes after the *w* in English, it is pronounced as if it preceded.

21. A liquid is frequently dropped in the English; less frequently in the German.

Als, as; low German *as*

ander, other; Gothic *anthar*; old Saxon *athar* and *othar*[2]

Biene, *bee*; old German *bine* and *bie*

dir, thee

fern, far; old German *verre* and *verren*[1]

fünf, five; Gothic *fimf*; Anglo-Saxon *fif*[8]

mir, me; old Saxon *mi*

Mund, mouth; Gothic *munths*; Anglo-Saxon *muth*[7]

Jugend, youth; Anglo-Saxon *jugudh*[7]

nun, now; in eight dialects *nu*

gestern, yester(day)[25]

Priester, priest; from *presbyter*; Anglo-Saxon *preost*

Pfortner, porter[13]

Rosmarin, rosemary; Lat. *ros maris*, or *ros marinus*

rechnen, reckon

sanft, soft[2]

solch, such; Anglo-Saxon *svilk*[7]

Sporn, spur; old German *sporo* and *spor*[7]

Stern, star: old German *sterro* and *sterno*[1]

sprechen, speak; Anglo-Saxon *sprecan* and *specan*[11]

Thurm, tower; old German *turre*; Anglo-Saxon *tor*

uns, us; old Saxon *us*

welch, which; Anglo-Saxon *hvilc*[4]

wir, we; old Saxon *we* and *wi*; Swedish *vi*

———

Bürde, burden

Brautigam, bridegroom[6]

Laterne, lantern

Luchs, lynx

Myrthe, myrtle

Pilger, pilgrim

Splitter, splinter

Steige, stair[1]

Welt, world; old German *werlt*[5]

22. The liquids are sometimes interchanged with each other ; and *r* is sometimes used for *s*, and is sometimes transposed.

Alaun, alum

Besen, bosom[5]

Boden, bottom[18]

Busen, bosom

Degen, dagger[1]

Dolch, dirk[5]

Fessel, fetter[14]

Kind, child[11]

Orden, order

Orgel, organ[1]

Purpur, purple

Zelt, tent[15]

———

Eisen, iron

frieren, freeze (A. S. frysan)

Hase, hare

(ver)lieren, loose[5]

war, was

———

Brennen, burn

Bürste, brush

Borste, bristle ?

Brette, board[5], [18]

dritte, third[18]

durch, through[16]

Furcht, fright[11]

hundert, hundred

Roß, (h)orse ; old German *hros* and *ors*

23. Sch in German, when it comes before *l, m, n*, or *w*, corresponds to *s* in English.

Schlaf, sleep[1] ·

schlagen, slay[12]

Schleim, slime

schlank, slank

schlau, sly[6]

schleissen, slice (split)

schlimm, slim

schlitten, slide[18]

Schlummer, slumber[24]

schlüpfen, slip[8], [13]

schmecken, smack[1]

schmeißen, smite[14]

schmelzen, smelt[15]

Schmertz, smart[1], [15]

Schmid, smith[18]

schmieren, smear

Schmutz, smut[15]

Schnee, snow[5]

Schnepfe, snipe[13]

Schnupfen, snuff[13]

Schwalbe, swallow[19] ?

Schwan, swan

Schwarm, swarm

schwartz, swart(hy)

Schwede, Swede

Schwein, swine

Schweiß, sweat[14]

schwellen, swell

c

| | |
|---|---|
| Schwert, sword[5], [18] | schwingen, swing |
| Schwester, sister[4] | schwitzen, sweat[4] |
| schwimmen, swim | schwören, swear |

**Note.** S c h generally corresponds to s h; in a few cases, to s c, as in S c h r a u b e, s rew; S c h r i f t, s ript. The words *smack, smut, swart* or *swarthy*, do not correspond exactly in sense with the German words.

24. *Mb* in English corresponds to mm or m in German.

| | |
|---|---|
| Daum, thumb[6] | Lamm, lamb |
| Hummel, humble(bee) | Nummer, number |
| Kamm, comb[2] | Schlummer, slumber |
| Kammer, chamber[11] | tummeln, tumble |
| Krume, crumb | |

25. The letter g in German sometimes corresponds to *y* in English.

| | |
|---|---|
| Gähnen, yawn | Gäscht, yeast |
| Garderobe, wardrobe | gällen, yell |
| Garn, yarn | Gestern, yester(day) |

---

# APPENDIX

It will be useful to add here a few of the most common words of Latin origin which have become so far Germanized as not always to be recognized by the student.

| | |
|---|---|
| Aurikel, auriculus | Brille, beryllus (chrystal) |
| Achse, axis | Buchs(baum), buxus |
| Acker, ager | Dechant. deeanus |
| Alaun, alumen | Eber, aper |
| Angst, angustia | Essig, acetum |
| Bakel, baculus | Fabel, fabula |
| Börse, bursa (purse) | Falke, falco |
| Brief, breve (epistle) | falsch, falsus |

Fasan, Phasianus (bird of Phasis)
Fenster, fenestra
Gestern, hesternus
Halm, calamus
Hans, Johannis
heute, hodie
Horn, cornu
irren, erro
kahl, calvus
Kammer, camera
Kanzel, cancelli
Karl, Carolus
Katheder, cathedra
Kastane, castanea
Käse, caseus
Kehle, gula
Kelch, calix
Kerker, carcer
Kette, catena
Kicher, cicer (chick-pea)
Kloster, claustrum
Kopf, caput
Körper, corpus
Krone, corona
Lor(beere), laurel
Lorenz, Laurentius (Lawrence)
Makel, macula
mahnen, moneo
malen, molo
Meer, mare
Mauer, murus
Münster, monasterium (minster)
Mühle, mola (mill)

Nahme, nomen
Pacht, pactum
Pedel, pedellus (beadle)
Pech, pix
Pendel, pendulum
Pfau, pavo
Pfalz, palatium (Palatinate)
Pfeil, pilum
Pforte, porta
Pokal, poculum
Pulver, pulvis
Punkt, punctum
Rad, rota
Ruin, ruina
schreiben, scribo
Schüßel, scutella
Senf, sinapi
sicher, securus
Siegel, sigillum
Spiegel, speculum
Sylbe, syllaba
Talar, talaris (long gown)
Tafel, tabula
Terzie, tertia (pars),
Thron, thronus
Tisch, discus
Uhr, hora
Ulm, ulmus
Unze, uncia, (ounce)
Veit, Vitus (Saint V.)
wahr, verus
Wilhelm, Guilielmus
Zins, census
Zirkil, circulus
Zither, cithera

Words are very commonly adopted from the Latin with no other important change than the omission of the final syllable; as, Abſolut, Achyl, Advocat, Apparat, caduc, Conſulat, Decret, Figur, frivol, Gran, Gyps, Koloß, Natur, Nerv, Officin, Präfekt, Primat, Quart, Senat, Tractat, Tyrann, Uſur, Vaſal, Vocal. See Gram. p. 56.

When the final syllable of words ending in *osus* is omitted, the vowel *o* is commonly changed into ö; as, Ambitiös, curiös, generös, ingeniös, luminös, ſkandalös, tuberös.

When the final syllable of words ending in *ulus*, *a*, *um*, or *ola* is dropped, the vowels, *u*, *a* and *o* in the penult are changed into e, that is, the words all end in el in German; as, Artikel, Epiſtel, Erempel, Fiſtel, Glandel, Inſel, Jubel, Kapitel, Makel, Manipel, Matrikel, Mirakel, Muskel, Drakel, Partikel, Regel, Spectakel, Tempel, Vehikel, Vocabel. The hard sound of the letter *c* before those Latin terminations is preserved by changing the letter into *k*.

When two syllables are dropped, *entia* goes into enz ; *itius*, *a*, *um*, into iz ; and *arius* sometimes into ar and sometimes into är ; as, Accidenz, Adoleſcenz, Appetenz, Audienz, Differenz, Eleganz, Eminenz, Ercreſcenz, Erperienz, Frequenz, Impertinenz, Impudenz, Incidenz, Incoherenz, Indulgenz, Influenz, Inherenz, Inſolenz, Inſtanz (instance, objection *urged*), Licenz, Munificenz, Reverenz ; — Horaz, Lucrez, Properz, Sulpiz, Terenz ; Juſtiz, Notiz, Solſtiz, Präjudiz ; — Denar, Emiſar, Notar, Seminar, Miſſionär, Secretär.

Substantives ending in *tas*, gen. *tatis*, change that termination into tät in German ; as, Bonität, Facultät, Humanität, Immunität, Impunität, Indignität, Infinität, Infirmität, Irregularität, Majeſtät, Mortalität.

When the letter *c* comes before *e*, *i* and *y*, it is commonly changed into z in German ; as, Kanzel, Prozeß, Rezeß, Unze, Zins, Zirkel, Zither, etc.

# SELECTIONS.

## SERMON ON INDULGENCES.

### PUBLISHED SEPTEMBER 4, 1517.[1]

---

Sermon vom Ablaß und Gnade.

Zum ersten[2] sollt ihr wissen, daß etliche[3] neue[4] Lehrer, als Magister Sententiarum, St. Thomas, und ihre Folger, ge-

---

[1] There is special propriety in beginning these selections with the sermon on indulgences, not only because it preceded the celebrated Ninety-Five Theses, but because, being written in German, it gives us a good specimen of Luther's early style of composition. It has not, indeed, the regularity, the ease and the richness of his later composi- tions, and is therefore more difficult to translate ; but it furnishes the most natural beginning, and is, moreover, so short that it may, with- out danger of being too repulsive, be placed before other more at- tractive pieces. This sermon was publicly burnt by Tetzel at Frank- fort on the Oder. The same person attempted to write a refutation of it, to which Luther replied in an elaborate defence.

[2] Zum ersten for zum ersten Male, *in the first place*, like the Latin *primo*. Am ersten is equivalent to zuerst, *first of all*. Fürs erste, means, *for the present*, or, *to begin with*, and is equiva- lent to für jetzt, or, vorläufig.

[3] Etliche, *some*, is obsolete. For etlicher (in the singular) irgend einer is now used; and for etliche (plural), einige is used.

[4] Neue, in comparison with the apostles and early fathers. By Magister Sententiarum, he means Peter of Lombardy or Lombardus; and by St. Thomas, Thomas Aquinas.

1

ben der Buße drei Theile,[1] nemlich:[2] die Reue, die Beichte, die Genugthuung.[3] Und wiewohl dieser Unterschied (nach ihrer Meinung) schwerlich[4] oder auch gar nichts gegründet erfunden wird in der heiligen Schrift, noch in den alten heiligen christlichen Lehren, doch wollen wir das jetzt so bleiben lassen, und nach ihrer Weise reden.

Zum andern fagen fie,[5] der Ablaß nimmt nicht hin den erften oder andern Theil,[6] das ist die Rene oder Beichte, fondern[7] den dritten nehmlich die Genugthuung.

---

[1] **Der Busse drei Theile.** Der Busse is in the dative case,—"assign to repentance three parts," i. e. divide it into three parts.

[2] **Nemlich**, more commonly written nämlich. Observe the use of the colon, which stands not only before quotations, but often before words in apposition.

[3] **Genugthuung**, *penance*, properly *satisfaction* made by submitting to the penalties imposed by the laws of the church.

[4] **Schwerlich**, like our word *hardly*, expresses, 1. difficulty, 2. a high degree of improbability. This latter is the more common signification. "And although this division according to their view (theory), is scarcely or rather in no wise found (to be) grounded in the Holy Scriptures, nor in the ancient holy Christian teaching, still we will for the present let that remain so (let that pass) and speak after their manner." Oder auch gar nichts (for nicht), *or even not at all.* In order to perceive the force of auch, *also, even,* it will be necessary to regard the phrase, not in the light of a contrast to the preceding word, but in that of a climax,—"probably not (schwerlich) or even not at all, or certainly not."

[5] **Sagen sie.** When a principal sentence begins with anything which has the nature of an adverb, whether it be a proper adverb, an adverbial phrase or an adverbial conjunction, the nominative commonly follows its verb.

[6] **Andern Theil.** Ander frequently stands for zweiter, like *alter* for *secundus* in Latin. Strictly speaking, it designates a thing *differing from the one first named.* "Secondly, they say indulgence does not remit (nimmt nicht hin) the first or the second part, i. e. repentance or confession, but the third, viz. penance."

[7] **Sondern**, *but,* is derived from the verb sondern, *to sunder, to separate,* and is therefore used only after negatives. Only in such

Zum dritten, die Genugthuung wird weiter[1] getheilet in drei Theile, das ist, Beten, Fasten, Almosen, also,[2] daß Beten, begreife[3] allerlei[4] Werk der Seelen eigen,[5] als lesen,

cases could it have its natural *antithetic* force. Aber, *but*, is a mere adversative, meaning originally, *again, but again*, as we see in the word abermal, *a second time*. So in the word Aberglaube, it signifies faith of a *secondary*, counterfeit, or spurious character, that is, *superstition*.

[1] Weit is of the same etymology as the English word *wide*, the *t* and the *d* being continually interchanged in the different Teutonic family of languages. The Germans use the word to represent *distance simply* without reference to form, as it respects length and breadth. Hence weiter means *farther*.

[2] Also, in German, never corresponds to the English word *also*. The second particle in the compound, *so*, is the significant one, and the first, or *all* (equivalent to ganz) simply gives intensity to the particle *so*, meaning *altogether so*. Out of the primary meaning *so* or *thus*, grows the derivative signification, *consequently*; though in this sense, it never expresses logical *necessity*, like folglich, but a looser connection of antecedent and consequent, which may be accidental.

[3] Begreifen means first and literally *to take hold of, to seize with the hand*, as in Gen. 27: 21. Tritt herzu, mein Sohn, dass ich dich begreife. Greifen is of the same origin as the English word *gripe*, *p* and *f* being often interchanged, and corresponds to the Latin *prehendo*. The second sense of begreifen is *to comprise, to comprehend*, as in this place. The third is *to apprehend*. Begriff, means a *simple conception*, or *notion*, or that which is expressed by a single word, and not by a sentence which would be Gedanke.

[4] Allerlei. Lei was formerly a substantive signifying *kind*, and governed such genitives as aller, vieler, mancher, zweier, but finally coalesced with them, forming what are now regarded as adverbs, as, allerlei, vielerlei, mancherlei, zweierlei, *all sorts of, many sorts of*, etc.

[5] Der Seelen eigen. Eigen now governs the dative; formerly it governed also the genitive, as the Latin adjectives *proprius, similis*, etc. govern sometimes the dative and sometimes the genitive. "Prayer comprehends every kind of act peculiar to the mind." Der Seelen, is here probably the genitive singular governed by eigen. So Luther uses the word eigen elsewhere, as des römischen Stuhls eigen. Formerly feminine nouns were declined in the

dichten,[1] hören Gottes Wort, predigen, lehren und berglei=
chen.[2] Faſten begreift allerlei Werk der Caſteiung ſeines
Fleiſches, als wachen, arbeiten, hart Lager,[3] Kleider ꝛc.
Almoſen begreift allerlei gute Werke der Liebe und Barm=
herzigkeit gegen den Nächſten.

Zum vierten iſt bei ihnen allen unbezweifelt, daß der Ab=

---

singular number as well as in the plural.  We find many remains of
such declension in hereditary forms of expression, as, a u f  E r d e n,
instead of a u f  d e r  E r d e, *on earth.*

[1] D i c h t e n  originally signified *to make, to produce,* as may be
seen in the works of the earliest German authors.  At a later period,
it came to be used only of *the productions of the mind,* 1. *to meditate*
or *think,* in a general sense, 2. *to compose works of imagination.*  Compare the Greek words ποιέω and ποίησις.  It is here used in the former of these two significations (to meditate), now obsolete, except in
such phrases as D i c h t e n  u n d  T r a c h t e n, *purposes and efforts.*
Its present prevailing signification is, *to write poetry or romance.*

[2] D e r g l e i c h e n.  In the early German, the word g l e i c h commonly governed the genitive.  Hence we have many compound
words, formed by the coalescence of g l e i c h and the genitive of the
word it governs.  D e r g l e i c h e n, for d e r e r  g l e i c h e n, is formed from the adjective g l e i c h and the relative pronoun d e r, which
both in the genitive plural and in the feminine of the genitive singular is d e r e r.  This form, therefore, was used, when the substantive
to which it referred was either in the plural or in the singular of the
feminine.  When a masculine or neuter singular was referred to,
d e s s g l e i c h e n for d e s s e n  g l e i c h e n was used. We find something very similar in the Latin words *ejusmodi* and *cujusmodi.*  This
will be best illustrated by a few examples; as, d e r g l e i c h e n
T h i e r e  k e n n e  i c h  n i c h t, *I am unacquainted with animals of
the kind.*  S a n f t m u t h, d e r e n  g l e i c h e n  m i r  i n  d e r  G e-
s c h i c h t e  n o c h  n i c h t  b e k a n n t  i s t, *a mildness the like of which
is not known to me in history.*  E r  i s t  e i n  M a n n, d e s s g l e i-
c h e n  i c h  n o c h  n i c h t  g e s e h e n  h a b e, *he is a man, the like
of whom I have never seen.*  D e s s g l e i c h e n, *likewise, also,* is a
conjunction.  D e r g l e i c h e n is not so used.

[3] H a r t [e s]  L a g e r.  Before neuter substantives, the nominative and accusative ending of the adjective e s is often omitted, especially in familiar language or where no particular stress is to be
laid upon the adjective.

laß hinnimmt dieselben Werke der Genugthuung, für die
Sünde schuldig¹ zu thun oder aufgesetzt.  Den so² er diesel=
ben Werke alle sollte hinnehmen, bliebe nichts Gutes mehr
da, das wir thun möchten.

Zum fünften ist bei vielen gewesen eine große und noch
unbeschloffene Opinion, ob der Ablaß auch noch etwas mehr
hinnehme, denn³ solche aufgelegte gute Werke, nemlich, ob
er auch die Pein, welche die göttliche Gerechtigkeit für die
Sünde fordert, abnehme.

Zum sechsten, laß⁴ ich ihre Opinion unverworfen⁵ auf

---

¹ S c h u l d i g with its dependent words, f ü r   d i e   S ü n d e   z u
t h u n, qualifies the substantive W e r k e.  The sentence is abrupt.
Regularly it would be, W e r k e   d e r   G e n u g t h u u n g, w e l c h e
f ü r   d i e   S ü n d e   s c h u l d i g   z u   t h u n   o d e r   a u f g e s e t z t
s i n d, "Indulgences release one from those works of satisfaction
which are due (s c h u l d i g   z u   t h u n) for sin, or which are imposed (by the laws of the church)."  A u f g e l e g t would now be
used instead of a u f g e s e t z t.  A l l e, which occurs twice in this
paragraph, is the only adjective that is declined, when placed after
its substantive.

² S o, *if*, as in old English.  "For if it should release from all
these works, nothing good (no good work) would remain which we
might perform."  In modern German, w e n n is used instead of s o,
which has become obsolete.

³ D e n n, in the old writers is the common word after comparatives,
for which a l s, *than*, is now employed, except in a few cases required by euphony, as m e h r   d e n n   a l l e, not a l s   a l l e.  "With
many there has been a great and still unsettled question, whether indulgences release from anything more than such good works imposed
(by the church), whether it remove also the penalty which divine
justice demands for sin."

⁴ L a s s, for l a s s e.  Such omissions of the final *e* in the first
person singular of the present, are frequent in the older language and
in colloquial style.  An elision in German, on account of the vowel
with which the following word begins is not required, nor even allowed, at present, except in familiar conversation and in poetry.  In
the very next line we meet with s a g e   i c h without any elision of
the final *e* of the verb.

⁵ U n v e r w o r f e n, *not reprobated*.  Though this is a participle,

1*

dießmahl;[1] das sage ich, daß man aus keiner Schrift[2] be=
währen kann, das göttliche Gerechtigkeit etwas Pein oder
Genugthuung begehre oder fordere von dem Sünder, denn
allein seine herzliche und wahre Reu[3] und Bekehrung, mit
Fürsatz,[4] hinfürder[5] das Kreuz Christi zu tragen, und die
obgenannten[6] Werke (auch von Niemand aufgesetzt)[7] zu

---

the verb, u n v e r w e r f e n is not, and could not be used. V e r-
w e r f e n, *to reject,* is used, but its participle, v e r w o r f e n, is often
used adjectively like our word *abandoned.* U n v e r w o r f e n is not
used adjectively.

[1] A u f  d i e s s m a h l, for the old grammatical form, a u f  d i e s e s
M a l, *for* this time, *for the present.* As an adverb, it is now used without the preposition, as d i e s m a l, from which even an adjective,
d i e s m a l i g, *pertaining to this time,* is formed. F ü r  d i e s m a l
is still in use.

[2] A u s  k e i n e r.  S c h r i f t, *from no passage of Scripture.* In
English, we also say, " this Scripture," for " this passage of Scripture " " This I say, that no one can prove from any passage of Scripture, etc.—except simply one's (his) hearty," etc.

[3] R e u, now written R e u e, *repentance,* is cognate with our word
*rue.* Compare n e u, *new,* t r e u, *true.*

[4] F ü r s a t z.  F ü r and v o r were originally the same word, and
hence in later times were often used for each other. V o r s a t z, is
now the settled orthography.

[5] H i n f ü r d e r.  F ü r d e r or f ö r d e r, an old comparative of the
word f o r t (as the English word *further* is a comparative of *forth*).
Instead of h i n f ü r d e r, *henceforth,* the words f e r n e r, w e i t e r
are now employed.

[6] O b g e n a n n t e n.  O b, in old German, was used in the sense
of o b e n, *above,* as may still be seen in such compounds as O b d a c h,
*a cover over something, a shelter ;* and O b h u t, *protection over one.*
In official and legal documents, such antiquated forms as o b b e m e l-
d e t, o b b e s a g t, o b b e r ü h r t, o b e r w a h n t and o b g e n a n n t
are still found for o b e n b e m e l d e t, o b e n b e s a g t, etc. *before-
mentioned, aforesaid,* etc.

[7] A u c h  v o n  N i e m a n d  a u f g e s e t z t, an elliptical or rather
pointed mode of expression, perfectly in character with Luther's terse
style.  In the smoother but more diffuse manner of the present age,
we should expect such an expression as, a u c h  w e n n  s i e  v o n

üben. Denn so spricht er[1] durch Ezechiel: Wenn sich
der Sünder bekehret, und thut recht, so will
ich seiner Sünde nicht mehr gedenken. Item,[2]
also hat er selbst alle die[3] absolvirt, Maria Magdalena, den
Gichtbrüchigen, die Ehebrecherin ꝛc. Und möchte wohl
gerne[4] hören, wer das anders[5] bewähren soll, unangesehen,[6]
daß etliche Doctores so gedäucht hat.[7]

---

Niemand aufgesetz (or rather aufgelegt) würden.
" With a determination henceforth to practise the abovementioned
works (Beten, Fasten, Almosen), though they should be imposed by no one," i. e. though not required by the discipline of the
church.

[1] So spricht er. Er is often so used by Luther, in quotations,
in which the pronoun does not refer to any preceding word, but to
the general idea, easily supplied in each instance, of God as the au
thor of the Scriptures. In the present case, er might, indeed, refer
to the word *Christi* in the preceding sentence. But it is altogether
improbable that Luther had that word in mind.

[2] Item, a Latin word much used by the old German authors, in
the sense of *likewise, also,* in enumerating particulars. In its Angli-
cised signification, where it stands for the *particulars themselves* (the
several *items*), it comes about as near to the original, as the word *tan-
dem* does when applied to the mode of harnessing horses *at length*, instead of abreast.

[3] Alle die, *all these*. As in Greek, so in German, that, which
came to be a definite article, was originally a demonstrative pronoun.
In the old writers, therefore, we must expect to meet with the demonstrative use of the word more frequently than in later writers.
In Luther's works, it is constantly occurring.

[4] Möchte gerne, an abrupt expression for ich mochte
gern. Luther often omits the personal pronouns in the nominative
in this way. Gerne is not now used in elevated style.

[5] Das anders, *that otherwise*, i. e. the contrary.

[6] Unangesehen, dass, *notwithstanding;* angesehen, dass,
*considering that.* Sometimes the genitive is used with the former,
dessen unangesehen, *no regard being paid to that.* This mode
of expres ion is now limited mostly to legal forms. Dessen ungeachtet is now in good use.

[7] Gedäucht hat. Dauchten, an impersonal verb, now, according to the grammarians, requiring the dative, according to usage

Zum siebenten, das findet man wohl, daß Gott etliche nach seiner Gerechtigkeit strafet, oder durch Pein bringet zu der Reu, wie im 89. Psalm: So seine Kinder werden sündigen, will ich mit der Ruthen ihre Sünde heimsuchen, aber doch meine Barmherzigkeit nicht von ihnen wenden. Aber diese Pein stehet in Niemandes Gewalt[1] nachzulassen, denn allein Gottes; ja er will sie nicht lassen, sondern verspricht, er wolle sie auflegen.

Zum achten, derhalben[2] so kann man derselben gedünkten Pein keinen Namen geben, weiß auch[3] Niemand, was sie ist, so sie diese Strafe nicht ist, auch die guten obgenannten Werke nicht ist.

Zum neunten sage ich, ob die christliche Kirche noch hent beschlösse und auserkläret, daß der Ablaß mehr denn die Werke[4] der Genugthuung hinnehme; so wäre es dennoch tausendmal besser, daß kein Christenmensch den Ablaß lö-

---

often governs the accusative; and so it does in this passage. "It has so appeared to some doctors."

[1] In Niemandes Gewalt nachzulassen. "In no one's power to remit, except God's alone (i. e. to remit this penalty stands or is in no one's power, etc.). Nay he will not let it go, but promises, he will inflict it."

[2] Derhalben, *therefore*, is an obsolete form, for which desshalben is used. Halben originally governed the particle prefixed to it in the genitive; at present it is treated as a single word. Desshalben so, *thus therefore*. Halber is now used instead of halben except in a few cases, mostly with a pronoun (as meinethalben) or where the substantive has the article.

[3] Auch, followed by a negative, means *neither*, or *nor*. Weiss auch Niemand, *nor does any one know;* auch die guten Werke nicht, *nor the good works above mentioned.*

[4] Mehr denn die Werke, etc. "that indulgences release from (take away) more than the works of satisfaction," i. e. release one not only from the necessity of performing the works of penance imposed by the church, but from suffering the penalty which God has affixed to sin. See paragraph fifth.

sete[1] oder begehrete, sondern daß sie lieber die Werke thäten und die Pein litten. Denn der Ablaß nichts anders ist noch mag werden,[2] denn Nachlassung guter Werke und heilsamer Pein, die man billiger sollte erwählen, denn verlassen. Wiewohl etliche[3] der neuen Prediger zweierlei Pein erfunden, Medicativas et Satisfactorias, das ist, etliche Pein zur Genugthuung, etliche zur Besserung. Aber wir haben mehr Freiheit zu verachten (Gott Lob)[4] solches und deßgleichen Plauderei, denn sie haben zu erdichten; denn alle Pein, ja alles, was Gott auflegt, ist besserlich und zuträglich dem Christen.

Zum zehnten, das ist nichts geredet,[5] daß der Pein und

---

[1] L ö s e t e. Etymologically, l ö s e n means to make l o s, *loose* or *free*. Next it signifies *to redeem*, or *to purchase one's release with money*, and then *to purchase*, or *obtain*. A b l a s s l ö s e n means *to purchase or obtain indulgence, or release from ecclesiastical penalty*.

[2] N o c h m a g w e r d e n, *nor may become*, i. e. be made anything else than the remission, etc. N a c h l a s s u n g g u t e n W e r k e is not *the omission of good works*, on the part of the individual, but a relaxation of the law which requires them of penitents.

[3] W i e w o h l e t l i c h e, etc., though some of the modern preachers have invented (e r f u n d e n, with h a b e n understood) two kinds of penalty, *medicativas et Satisfactorias*, i. e. " some penalties (penalty) as a satisfaction, some as a correction." This sentence is properly only a clause belonging to the preceding.

[4] G o t t L o b b for G o t t s e y L o b, *praise to God*. G o t t is dative. " But we have more liberty (thank God) to despise such nonsense (babblings) than they have to fabricate it; for all penalties, nay even everything which God imposes is corrective and profitable." B e s s e r l i c h is scarcely ever used now, and never, as here, in the sense of *corrective*. It me n , at present, *improvable, corrigible*.

[5] D a s i s t n i c h t s g e r e d e t. This turn of expression is peculiarly German. The Germans often use a passive, where it could not be used in English. " That is nothing said," means, " such an assertion (as that which follows) amounts to nothing, or is idle talk." N i c h t s must be carefully distinguished from n i c h t, which could hardly be used and would give a very different sense, viz. " that has not been spoken" (s o n d e r n a u s g e s c h r i e n, but screamed out).

Werke zu viel[1] sind, daß der Mensch sie nicht mag vollbrin=
gen, der Kürze halben[2] seines Lebens, darum ihm Noth sey
der Ablaß.  Antworte ich,[3] daß das keinen Grund habe und
ein lauter[4] Gedicht ist.  Denn Gott und die heilige Kirche
legen Niemand mehr auf,[5] denn ihm zu tragen möglich ist,

---

[1] Zu viel governs the genitives der Pein und Werke,
" too much of penalty and of works for a man to perform."  Instead
of dass, present usage would require als dass; it would require
nicht to be omitted, and mag to come after vollbringen; thus,
als dass der Mensch sie vollbringen mag. For an explanation of the idiom, zu viel als dass (too much for a man to
perform) see Gram. p. 378 infra.

[2] Halben always follows the genitive which it governs; consequently der Kürze is governed by halben, and governs Lebens, " on account of the brevity of his life."

[3] Ihm Noth sey der Ablass, is, on account of darum,
a grammatical or necessary inversion for der Ablass sey ihm
Noth (necessary is indulgence, for indulgence is necessary). According to present usage, the inverted sentence would be given thus : sei
ihm der Ablass Noth. But the words, Antworte ich,
in the beginning of the next sentence, are inverted optionally, merely for the sake of rhetorical effect.  The verb is rendered emphatic
by being placed before its nominative.

[4] Lauter, when declined, means pure, unmixed; when not declined, it means, nothing but, equivalent to nichts als.  Lautere Steine would mean pure stones, each one of which is free
from foreign admixture.  Lauter Steine, would mean nothing
but stones.  Lautere Weiber, neat, cleanly women; lanter
Weiber, nothing but women, i. e. a company of women without
any men.  Eitel, empty, mere, is used with a similar distinction
when declined and undeclined.  Eitele Menschen means,
vain men; eitel Menschen, nothing but men.  Lauter Gedicht, or eitel Gedicht means, nothing but a fiction, which
accidentally coincides nearly with a pure (unmixed) fiction, or a
mere (empty) fiction.

[5] Legen Niemand mehr auf.  Auflegen, when it
means, not to place one thing upon another (auflegen eine
Sache auf etwas), but to impose, in a metaphorical sense, some
obligation upon a person, as in the passage before us, requires the da-

als auch St. Paul sagt: daß Gott nicht läßt ver=
sucht werden Jemand,[1] mehr denn er mag
tragen. Und es langet[2] nicht wenig zu der Christenheit[3]
Schmach, daß man ihr Schuld giebt, sie lege mehr auf,[4]
denn wir tragen können.

Zum eilften, wenn gleich die Buße, im geistlichen Recht[5]

---

*tive* of the person (N i e m a n d). N i e m a n d is not declined generally in the old writers except in the genitive. Modern writers are
not uniform in respect to this, but more frequently form the dative
and accusative by adding e m and e n to the nominative.

[1] D a s s G o t t n i c h t l ä s s t v e r s u c h t w e r d e n J e m a n d,
is a construction that would hardly be allowed at the present time.
Not only does d a s s ordinarily require that the leading verb (l ä s s t)
be thrown to the end of the clause, but that the accusative (J e -
m a n d) stand immediately before the dependent verb (v e r s u c h t
w e r d e n) thus, dass G o t t nicht Jemand v e r s u c h t
w e r d a n l ä s s t, or for the sake of euphony, l ä s s t v e r s u c h t
w e r d e n.

[2] E s l a n g e t z u corresponds to the modern German e s g e-
r e i c h t z u. The literal translation, *it reaches to*, does not give the
sense. It is exactly of the same import as *sum* with the *dativus
commodi* in Latin, *est opprobrio, it is a disgrace*, (e s l a n g e t z u r
S c h m a c h).

[3] C h r i s t e n h e i t, properly means *Christians collectively*, C h r i s-
t e n t h u m, (etymologically the same as *Christendom*), means *Christianity*. Our word *Christendom*, therefore, does not correspond in
signification with C h r i s t e n t h u m, as we should expect, but with
C h r i s t e n h e i t. The old writers, however, frequently use C h r i s-
t e n h e i t in both senses.

[4] S i e l e g e m e h r a u f. For this construction with the subjunctive (l e g e, of the same form with the indicative) instead of the inversion of the clause with d a s s and the use of the indicative, (d a s s
s i e m e h r a u f l e g e), see Gram. p. 369, med.

[5] I m g e i s t l i c h e n R e c h t g e s e t z t, *established in the canonical law*. G e s e t z t, from s e t z e n, means *settled, established.*.
This participle was anciently used substantively (d a s G e s e t z t e)
in the sense of *law, lex*. Subsequently the form G e s e t z, *something
settled, law*, was adopted. Of the origin of this last word, we see a
clear trace in the passage before us; for a few lines below that which
was g e s e t z t is referred to, and called G e s e t z.

gefeßt, jeßt noch gienge,[1] daß für eine jegliche Todfünde
fieben Jahre Buße aufgelegt wäre; fo müßte doch die
Chriftenheit diefelben Gefeße laffen,[2] und nicht weiter auf=
legen, denn fie einem jeglichen zu tragen wären:[3] viel we=
niger nun fie jeßt nicht find,[4] foll man achten, daß nicht

---

[1] G i e n g e, *were current, were in force*, obsolete, for which g e l -
t e n is now more in use.

[2] L a s s e n, *let go*, i. e. relax or suspend. See the use of the word
in connection with n a c h l a s s e n, near the close of the 17th paragraph.

[3] E i n e m  J e g l i c h e n  z u  t r a g e n  w ä r e n, "than (they)
are possible to be borne by each one." In explaining this idiom of
the infinitive after the verb s e y n, we must not suppose that there
is an ellipsis of any such word as m ö g l i c h (m ö g l i c h  z u  t r a -
g e n  w ä r e n); for the infinitive itself, in such constructions, has
nearly the nature of the Latin participle in *dus* (*ferendae sint*), except that the German expression conveys the idea of *possibility* and
rarely that of *necessity*, which is implied in the Latin. *Urbs capien-
da est*, means, "the city *must* be taken;" whereas d i e  S t a d t  i s t
e i n z u n e h m e n means "the city *can* be taken." In other respects,
the constructions are similar. In sense, the infinitive (z u  t r a g e n)
may be represented nearly by Latin adjectives in *bilis* (*tolerabiles
sint*). See Gram. p. 258, infra.

[4] V i e l  w e n i g e r  n u n  s i e  j e t z t  n i c h t  s i n d, etc. W e -
n i g e r does not correspond with the rest of the sentence (which
would seem to require m e h r in its stead). There is probably an
anacoluthon in the words s o l l  m a n  a c h t e n  d a s s  n i c h t
m e h r  a u f g e l e g t  w e r d e. N u n, as an adverb, means *now*.
But as a conjunction, for which it is here used, it means *now that,
since*, and is nearly of the same import as w e i l. W o h l, near
the end of the paragraph, qualifies t r a g e n, as the emphasis rests
on it rendering it equivalent to g u t. In the sense of e t w a it cannot receive the emphasis. The whole paragraph may be translated
thus : " Even if the penance, laid down in the canonical law, were
now in force, (viz.) that for every mortal offence seven years' penance,
be imposed, still would the church (C h r i s t e n h e i t) be obliged to
relax those laws, and impose no more than each one should be able to
bear. Much less (should those laws be executed) now that they are
not (in force)—one should take care, that no more be imposed than
each one can well bear."

mehr aufgelegt werde, denn jedermann wohl tragen kann.

Zum zwölften, man sagt wohl,[1] daß der Sünder mit der übrigen Pein[2] in's Fegfeuer oder zum Ablaß geweiset soll werden ; aber es wird wohl mehr Dings[3] ohne Grund und Bewährung gesagt.

Zum dreizehnten, es ist ein großer Irrthum, daß Jemand meine, er wolle genug thun für seine Sünde,[4] so doch[5] Gott dieselben allezeit umsonst aus unschätzlicher Gnade verzeihet, nichts dafür begehrend, denn hinfürder wohl leben.[6] Die

[1] M a n  s a g t  w o h l. An inspection of the various examples found in most of these paragraphs will show that such adverbial phrases at the beginning of a sentence as z u m  z w ö l f-
t e n sometimes cause the principal verb to precede its nominative (invert the clause) and sometimes they do not. This circumstance suggests the limitation of the rule. Only when such adverbial phrases at the beginning of a sentence are closely connected with, and, as it were, incorporated into the clause does it cause an inversion. If the connection is very loose, which is ordinarily indicated by a comma, the natural order is observed. Whether the connection is to be regarded as close or not, will often depend on the mere feeling of the writer. Besides, the rule was less rigidly observed in Lnther's time than it is now. W o h l, is here used, as in paragraph 7th, in a concessive sense (*to be sure, indeed*) like z w a r or f r e i l i c h, as is indicated by the adversative (a b e r) in the second clause.

[2] D e r  ü b r i g e n  P e i n, that part of the penalty incurred, which is not actually inflicted must be referred either to purgatory, or to indulgences, i. e. must either be suffered in purgatory or commuted for the price of indulgences.

[3] M e h r  D i n g s. Indefinite adjectives, pronouns and numerals or adverbs of quantity govern the genitive. *More of thing, many a thing*. So harsh an expression would not be tolerated in modern German.

[4] E r  w o l l e  g e n u g  t h u n  f ü r  s e i n e  S ü n d e. See p. 11, Note 4.

[5] S o  d o c h, *whereas* (since yet).

[6] H i n f ü r d e r  w o h l  l e b e n. For h i n f ü r d e r, see p. 6, Note 5. The infinitive used substantively in German, corresponds very nearly to the present participle in English,—" desiring nothing in return (d a f ü r) but holy *living*." W o h l, here, is a pure adverb and a

Chriſtenheit fordert wohl etwas ;[1] alſo mag und ſoll ſie auch daſſelbe nachlaſſen und nichts ſchweres und unträgliches auflegen.

Zum vierzehnten, Ablaß wird zugelaſſen um der unvoll= kommnen und faulen Chriſten willen, die ſich nicht wollen kecklich[2] üben in guten Werken, oder unleidlich ſind.  Denn Ablaß fordert Niemand zum beſſern,[3] ſondern duldet oder zuläſſet ihre Unvollkommenheit.  Darum ſoll man nicht wi= der den Ablaß reden ; man ſoll aber auch Niemand dazu reden.[4]

Zum fünfzehnten, viel ſicherer und beſſer thäte der, der[5]

---

synonyme of g u t.  The latter refers to *that which is adapted to its end*, and may be said of inanimate things ; the former means *agreeably* and must always refer directly or indirectly to a sentient being.  W o h l   l e b e n  means living in a way that is agreeable *to God.*  In like manner, it is distinguished from  g e s u n d, *well.*  G e s u n d  means *healthy;*  w o h l  means *in an agreeable state*, either of health or of mind.

[1] D i e  C h r i s t e n h e i t  f o r d e r t  w o h l  e t w a s, "the (honor of) Christianity demands indeed something, (i. e. external discipline ; but it should not be severe).  Therefore it may, and even should, relax the same penalties, (whenever it is necessary), and impose nothing, etc."

[2] K e c k l i c h, *boldly, courageously*, obsolete in this sense.  It signifies the same as  g e h ö r i g, *properly.*  "Who are not willing to exercise themselves properly in good works."  O d e r  u n l e i d l i c h  s i n d, "or who are impatient under evil."

[3] Z n m  b e s s e r n, as to grammatical form, might be either an adjective in the comparative degree, or an infinitive used substantively.  Here it is probably the latter.  "Indulgences stimulate (require) no one to improvement, but rather bear with, and make allowance for one's (their, men's) imperfection."  Z n m  b e s s e r n, means literally, *to improve*, or *to be improved*, which would be expressed in Latin not by *emendare*, nor by *emendari*, but by *ad emendandum*.  Such is the force of the German infinitive when declined with the definite article, and governed by z u, as expressing *end* or *design.*

[4] N i e m a n d  d a z u  r e d e n, *persuade no one to it.*

[5] D e r,  d e r.  D e r,  w e r  means *any one who, whoever.*  D e r-

lauter um Gottes willen gäbe zu dem Gebäude St. Petri, oder was sonst genannt wird,[1] denn daß er Ablaß dafür nehme. Denn es fährlich[2] ist, daß er solche Gabe um Ablaß willen, und nicht um Gottes willen giebt.

Zum sechszehnten, viel besser ist das Werk einem Dürftigen erzeigt,[3] denn das[4] zum Gebäude gegeben wird, auch viel besser, denn der Ablaß dafür gegeben.[5] Denn (wie gesagt) es ist besser, ein gutes Werk gethan,[6] denn viel nachgelassen. Ablaß aber ist Nachlassung viel guter Werke, oder ist nichts nachgelassen.

Ja, daß ich[7] euch recht unterweise, so merkt auf: Du sollst vor allen Dingen (weder St. Petrus Gebäude noch Ablaß angesehen)[8] deinem armen Nächsten geben, willst du[9] etwas geben. Wenn es aber dahin kommt, daß Niemand in deiner Stadt mehr ist, der Hülfe bedarf (das, ob Gott will,

---

jenige, welcher (a modern form of expression) means *that particular person, who.* D e r, d e r is intermediate and may be used in either sense. It occurs more frequently in the early than in the later writers.

[1] O d e r  w a s  s o n s t  g e n a n n t  w i r d, etc., "or whatever other object is named, than that he contribute to it by purchasing indulgences." D a f ü r does not here mean *instead of that*, but *to that end.*

[2] F ä h r l i c h and F ä h r are obsolete forms for g e f ä h r l i c h and G e f ä h r.

[3] E r z e i g t is a participle agreeing with W e r k.

[4] D a s, was formerly employed in the sense of w a s, *what*, and so it is here.

[5] A b l a s s  d a f ü r  g e g e b e n, indulgence (money) given for that purpose.

[6] E i n  g u t e s  W e r k  g e t h a n, a good work performed is better than many relaxed (excused). This use of participles is still common.

[7] J a,  d a s s  i c h, etc. "Indeed, in order that I may instruct you properly, observe."

[8] A n g e s e h e n, *being regarded.*

[9] W i l l s t  d u, *if thou desirest.*

nimmer geschehen soll),[1] dann sollst du geben, so du willst, zu den Kirchen, Altären, Schmuck, Kelch, die in deiner Stadt sind. Und wenn das nun auch nicht mehr Noth ist, dann allererst,[2] so du willst, magst du geben zu dem Gebäude St. Peters, oder anders wo.

Auch sollst du dennoch das nicht[3] um Ablaß willen thun. Denn St. Paul sagt: Wer seinen Hausgenossen nicht wohl thut, ist kein Christ, und ärger denn ein Heide. Und halt's dafür frei,[4] wer dir anders sagt, der verführet dich, oder sucht je[5] deine Seele in deinem Beutel, und fünde er Pfennige darinne, das wäre ihm lieber, denn alle Seelen. So sprichst du, so[6] würde ich nimmermehr Ablaß lösen. Antworte ich,[7] das habe ich schon oben gesagt, das mein Wille, Begierde, Bitte und Rath ist, daß Niemand Ablaß löse. Laßt die faulen und schläfrigen Christen Ablaß lösen, gehe du für dich.[8]

Zum siebzehnten: Der Ablaß ist nicht geboten, auch nicht

---

[1] Das, ob Gott will, nimmer geschehen soll, "which (need of aid), if it be the pleasure of God, ought never to take place."

[2] Dann allererst, *then for the first time*, i. e. *then and not till then.*

[3] Auch sollst du dennoch. Auch, which cannot well be rendered in English, repeats and enforces what was said in paragraph 15th. Dennoch, *however*, refers to the concession just made.

[4] Und halt's dafür frei, "and hold the following opinion without hesitancy." Frei in the sense of unbedenklich. Dafür, *to this, for this*, referring to the following clause.

[5] Je and darinne, now provincial for ja and darin.

[6] So sprichst du, so. The first so, *thus*, is not to be translalated; the second means *then.* "Thou sayest, then I would never obtain indulgence."

[7] Antworte ich, a lively form of expression for, ich antworte.

[8] Gehe du für dich, "take your own course," i. e. follow your own convictions, do your own duty, and let others do as they please.

gerathen, sondern von der Dinge Zahl,[1] die zugelassen und erlaubt werden. Darum ist es nicht ein Werk des Gehorsams, auch nicht verdienstlich, sondern ein Auszug[2] des Gehorsams. Darum wiewohl man Niemand wehren soll[3] den zu lösen, so sollte man doch alle Christen davon ziehen, und zu den Werken und Peinen, die da nachgelassen, reitzen und stärken.

Zum achtzehnten: Ob die Seelen aus dem Fegfeuer gezogen werden durch den Ablaß, weiß ich nicht, und glaube das auch noch nicht;[4] wiewohl das etliche neue Doctores sagen, aber ist ihnen unmöglich zu bewähren,[5] auch hat es

---

[1] Von der Dinge Zahl, " of that class (number) of things." The article der belongs to Dinge, not to Zahl. In all such constructions, (once so common in German, but now occurring only in certain phrases) of a genitive coming between a substantive and its preposition, since two successive articles would be harsh, and since the omission of that belonging to the genitive would often occasion obscurity, while the other substantive is rendered sufficiently definite by the genitive, the article of the genitive is commonly inserted and that of the other substantive is always omitted. Compare zu der Christenheit Schmach, near the close of the 10th paragraph.

[2] Auszug, going beyond, an excess. No German would use such an expression at the present day.

[3] Man Niemand wehren soll, etc "Although one ought to prohibit no one from obtaining it (indulgence), we ought to dissuade (ziehen, draw, attract) all Christians from it, and stimulate and strengthen them to those works and sufferings, which are relaxed, i. e. from which one is dispensed by indulgences."—Nachgelassen (werden).

[4] Und glaube das auch noch nicht, " but I do not yet believe it."

[5] Aber (es) ist ihnen unmöglich (es) zu bewähren. Es is omitted, in the first instance, according to a very prevailing usage with Luther, but contrary to modern usage; in the second instance it is omitted to avoid repetition,(for it could not be used in the latter place and omitted in the former,) although it is inserted in the next clause. It might, indeed, stand thus: Aber (es) ist ihnen unmöglich (dies) zu bewähren.

die Kirche noch nicht beschlossen. Darum zu mehrer Sich=
erheit[1] viel besser ist es, daß du für sie[2] selbst bittest und
wirkest ; denn dieß ist bewährter und gewiß.

Zum neunzehnten : In diesen Punkten habe ich nicht
Zweifel, und sind genugsam[3] in der Schrift gegründet. Da=
rum sollt ihr auch keinen Zweifel haben, und laßt Doctores[4]
Scholasticos Scholasticos seyn ; sie sind allsammt nicht ge=
nug mit ihren Opinionen, daß sie eine Predigt befestigen
sollten.

Zum zwanzigsten : Ob etliche[5] mich nun wohl[6] einen Ket=
zer schelten, denen solche Wahrheit sehr schädlich ist im Ka=
sten,[7] so achte ich doch solch' Geplerre[8] nicht groß ; sintemal[9]

---

[1] M e h r e r  S i c h e r h e i t.  M e h r is sometimes declined, sometimes not.  M e h r e r is the dative singular feminine, for which the
irregular form  m e h r e r e r  is more commonly used.  See Gram.
p. 129.

[2] F ü r  s i e, *for them*, i. e. the souls in purgatory.  S e l b s t does
not belong to  s i e, but to  d u  and  b i t t e s t.  The sentiment here
expressed should not surprise us.  Luther had not yet written his
Theses.

[3] U n d  (s i e)  s i n d  g e n u g s a m.

[4] U n d  l ä s s t  D o c t o r e s, etc.  " And let the scholastic doctors be scholastic, they are, all taken together, not sufficient by their
opinions to confirm a discourse (are not enough with their opinions,
that they should, etc)."

[5] E t l i c h e. See p. 1, Note 3.  W o h l. See p. 12, Note 4.

[6] E i n e n  K e t z e r  s c h e l t e n, *scold me a heretic*, i. e. reproach
me as a heretic.  After the word  s c h e l t e n the accusative is always used without any such word as  a l s.

[7] D e n e n — i m  K a s t e n, " to whom in the coffer," i. e. to
whose coffers.

[8] S o l c h'  G e p l e r r e.  S o l c h e s  is written  s o l c h  sometimes (more commonly before an adjective), for the sake of euphony.
Before the article  e i n,  s o l c h'  is the only form in use.  G e p l ä r r
is now the settled orthography instead of  G e p l e r r e.

[9] S i n t e m a l, an obsolete word, for which  w e i l  is now employed.

das nicht thun denn[1] etliche finstere Gehirne, die die Biblien nie gerochen, die christliche Lehre nie gelesen, ihre eigenen Lehrer nie verstanden, sondern in ihren löcherichen und zerrissenen Opinien viel nahe verwesen.[2] Denn hätten sie die verstanden,[3] so wüßten sie, daß sie Niemand sollten lästern unverhört und unüberwunden. Doch Gott gebe ihnen und uns den rechten Sinn, Amen.

[1] Das nicht thun denn, *none do that except.* An abrupt expression. Denn, *than, except,* is frequently used after Nichts, but rarely after nicht. Nicht denn, may be rendered by *only.*

[2] Viel nahe verwesen (haben). Haben must be supplied to all the participles, gerochen, gelesen, and verstanden. Viel is used in the obsolete sense, *very,*—" have well nigh decayed (rotted) in their ragged and tattered opinions."

[3] Denn hätten sie die verstanden, "for had they understood *them* (those, i. e. the Bible, Christian doctrine and their teachers) they would have known that they ought to vilify no one, unheard and unvanquished."

# EXPOSITION OF THE THIRTY-SEVENTH PSALM.[1]

Der 37te Pſalm Davids, zu tröſten Diejenigen, ſo ungebul=
dig ſind,[2] daß die Gottloſen Uebels thun[3] und doch ſo

---

[1] This exposition was first published in 1521, and addressed to
D e m a r m e n H a ü f l e i n (the little flock) C h r i s t i z u W i t-
t e n b e r g, accompanied with an epistle of several pages. It was
revised in 1526, and addressed in a similar way, A n d i e K ö n i-
g i n M a r i a i n U n g a r n. A strict adherence to the chronological order, would require this to be the third piece of the Selections,
as the next succeeding one was published in 1520. But that the
more difficult pieces may not come first, except in the instance of
the short discourse on Indulgences, a slight variation from the chronological arrangement is here omitted, as being by far the least of the
two evils.

[2] Z u t r ö s t e n d i e j e n i g e n, s o u n g e d u l d i g s i n d.
A Psalm, written "to console those who are impatient because
(that) the wicked do evil, etc."

[3] U e b e l s t h u n. U e b e l s is not here the neuter of the adjective for U e b l e s, but is the substantive U e b e l used in the genitive in a partitive sense,—literally, *to do of evil*, like the old English expressions, "pour out *of* thy Spirit," "give us *of* your oil."
This word is etymologically the same as the English word *evil*, the *b*
and *v*, being cognate letters which are most frequently exchanged for
each other, as ; e b e n and *even;* o b e r and *over;* s i e b e n and *seven;*
l e b e n and *live;* s t r e b e n and *strive;* h e b e n and *heave;* g e b e n
and *give;* w e b e n and *weave;* S i e b and *sieve;* S i l b e r and *silver;*
S a l b e and *salve;* G r a b and *grave;* s c h a b e n and *shave;* N a b e l
and *navel.* In English, *f* often occurs instead of *v;* or like the latter
corresponds to the German *b*, as ; S t a b and *staff;* L e b e n and *life;*
W e i b and *wife;* D i e b and *thief;* s e l b and *self;* h a l b and *half;*
K a l b and *calf.* T h u n most commonly signifies *to do*; but it has
also a wider import, and is often to be rendered by *to make, to put;*
as, e i n e n S c h u s s, e i n e R e i s e, e i n e M a h l z e i t, e i n e n
T r u n k, *to make* (or take) *a shot, journey, meal, to drink.* V o n
m i r t h u n, *to put away from me;* d i e S c h u e a n d i e F ü s s e
t h u n, *to put on shoes.* The most common idioms formed with this

lauge ungeſtraft in großem Glücke[1] bleiben.

Erzürne[2] dich nicht über den Böſen, ſey nicht neidiſch über die Uebelthäter.

Wie gleich[3] greift zu und trifft der Prophet des Herzens

word, are, es thut mir weh, *it pains me*, or, I am sorry for it. Es thut nichts, *that is nothing*, or, it is of no consequence, or does no harm. Es thut Noth, *it is necessary.* Uebel thun (das Böse thun), *to do wrong* (different from Uebels thun). Einen in die Lehre thun, *to put one to a trade*, Es ist mir um etwas zu thun, *I feel an interest in something*, Es ist mir darum zu thun, *I am interested or concerned in that.* Er thut nur so, *he only feigns it so.* Es thut gelehrt, *he affects to be learned.* Er thut böse, *he makes a show of anger.* Zu wissen thun (do to wit), *to inform.* Jemandem zu viel thun, *to injure one.* Etwas zu Liebe thun, *to do a thing as a favor*, or, in order to gratify one. Einem wohl thun, or gut thun, *to gratify one* (sometimes also, *to benefit one*). Ihr habt gut thun, or gut sagen, *it is easy for you to do so*, or *to say so.* Though thun and machen correspond in general to the English words *do* and *make*, the former referring more to the action itself than to the result of it, and the latter more to the result, or the thing produced, still, machen is often to be rendered by *do*, and thun as often by *make.* This last use of thun, *to make*, is either idiomatic or antiquated; in the old language it was common. So Otfried, Thie Steina duan (thun) zi brote, i. e. die Steine zu Brot machen. Thuen, is duan (duen) in old German. Drop the ending en, and du, or *do* (Eng.) remains.

[1] Glück is a compound word, consisting of the prefix ge, and lück, which corresponds to the English word, *luck.* In the old German the prefix is fully written, Gelück.

[2] Erzürne. Zürnen signifies *to manifest anger, to be angry.* Erzürnen, *to put into a state of anger, to make angry.* Sich erzürnen, *to fall into a passion, to become angry.*

[3] Gleich, formed from the word leich, English *like*, and the prefix ge, means *like* or *equal* as an adjective. As an adverb of *time*, it means *instantly, directly*, that is, the two periods of time come so *near together*, or are so much *alike* as to leave little or no interval between them. Compare *continuo* in Latin.—"How directly does the prophet seize upon and hit the thoughts of the heart in this temptation, and remove entirely their cause!"

Gedanken in dieser Anfechtung[1] und hebt alle Ursache[2] derselben auf, und spricht zum Ersten : O Mensch, du bist zornig, hast auch Ursache, wie mich dünket.[3] Denn es sind
böse Menschen, thun Unrecht und viel Uebels und gehet
ihnen dennoch wohl ;[4] was die Natur achtet, redliche[5] Ursache des Zornes hier zu seyn. Aber nicht also, liebes Kind,

---

[1] A n f e c h t u n g, literally, *a hostile attempt against one ;* figuratively, *a temptation with a malicious design.* It is the common word
for *temptation* in a bad sense. V e r s u c h u n g may be either *temptation* or *trial.* A n f e c h t u n g e n never come from God ; V e r-
s u c h u n g e n sometimes come from him. As F e c h t means a
*skirmish,* rather than a *general assault,* A n f e c t u n g means an attempt against one that *may* be resisted.

[2] U r s a c h e, literally means *original* (u r) *thing* (S a c h e), and
hence admirably designates *a cause.*

[3] W i e  m i c h  d ü n k e t, *as it seems to me.* When the verb is
used impersonally, the accusative is, according to the grammarians,
properly used rather than the dative. But if it is a neuter verb and
not used impersonally, the dative only can be employed ; as, s i e
d ü n k e t  m i r  s c h ö n, *she appears to me beautiful.* As a reflective verb with the accusative of the person, it means, to think or imagine one's self something ; as, d u  d ü n k e s t  d i c h  k l u g, *you
think yourself wise.*

[4] T h u n  U n r e c h t—u n d  g e h e t  i h n e n  d e n n o c h  w o h l.
The omission of the nominatives s i e and e s, renders the representation more vivid. " They are bad men, they do wrong and much
harm, and yet it is well with them,—what nature [unsanctified] con-
siders to be a just cause of anger." E s  s i n d  b ö s e  M e n s c h e n
means more commonly, "*they* are bad men;" e s  g i e b t  b ö s e
M e n s c h e n always means, "*there* are bad men," corresponding
nearly to the French *ce sont* and *il y a.* U e b e l s is in the genitive
and governed by v i e l. See p. 13, Note 3.

[5] R e d l i c h e, is a somewhat difficult word to explain. Its ancient and etymological meaning is, *rational, reasonable, proper,* from
R e d e, account. Hence r e d l i c h, *that of which one can give a good
account.* So it was used in Luther's time. In modern German, it
means, *honorable, upright, honest.* Hence one is called a r e d l i c h e r
M a n n, *when he is without intrigue and is faithful in his duties to
others.*

laß Gnade[1] und nicht Natur hier regieren,[2] brich den Zorn und stille dich[3] eine kleine Zeit, laß sie übel thun,[4] laß ihnen wohl gehen,[5] höre[6] mich, es soll dir nicht schaden.[7] So[8]

---

[1] G n a d e, i. e. G e-n a d e, is from n a h (so in Latin, *propitius*, from *prope*, near). The termination d e is euphonic as in K u n d e from k e n n e n, B ü r d e from b ä h r e n and N i e m a n d for N i e-m a n. The word originally signified *approach by descending;* hence figuratively *condescension.* D i e  S o n n e  g e h t  z u  G n a d e n, in the old German, means "the sun was going down, or approaching the horizon." G n a d e, therefore comes to signify *favor shown to an inferior, grace.*

[2] R e g i e r e n. Verbs of all conjugations from the Latin, French and other languages, are adopted into German by changing the termination of the original into i r e n or i e r e n. The e after i in the last form simply shows that the latter is always long in this termination. The accent is always on the penult. The word r e g i e r e n comes directly from the French regir, or from some other similar modification of the Latin *regere.*

[3] S t i l l e  d i c h. The adjective s t i l l in German, as in English, is opposed, 1. to motion, 2. to noise. The verb, when applied to things, as the *sea*, the *wind*, means, *to stop their motion;* when applied to men, *to stop their commotion*, or *to quiet their passions*, as in this passage. It sometimes, though rarely, signifies *to silence a man.* Applied to an infant, it means, *to nurse, to put to the breast.*

[4] U e b e l  t h u n. This adjective form (ü b e l) denotes *wrong doing in general;* the substantive form (U e b e l s) implies injury done to any person or persons. U e b e l denotes properly whatever is *disagreeable to our feelings*, and is opposed to w o h l. B ö s e indicates something *bad in itself,* and is opposed to g u t.

[5] L a s s  i h n e n  w o h l  g e h e n, *allow it to be (go) well with them.* G e h e n is impersonal in all such constructions, with e s understood. Hence W i e  g e h t's  i h n e n, *how do you do? how do things go with you?*

[6] H ö r e n corresponds, in etymology, to *hear*, as s c h w ö r e n does to *swear.*

[7] S c h a d e n, *to injure*, is written *scathan* in Anglo-Saxon, from which comes the English word to *scathe*, in a restricted sense.

[8] S o  s p r i c h t  d e n n  d e r  M e n s c h. An objector is supposed here to say : " Yes, but when will this come to an end?"

ſpricht denn der Menſch: Ja, wenn wird es denn aufhö=
ren? Wer mag[1] die Länge halten? Er antwortet:

Denn[2] wie das Gras werden ſie bald abge=
hauen werden, und wie das grüne Kraut
werden ſie verwelken.[3]

Ein feines[4] Gleichniß iſt das, ſchrecklich[5] den Gleißnern[6]

---

[1] M a g corresponds to the English word *may*, as M a c h t does to
*might*, m ä c h t i g to *mighty*, and A l l m ä c h t i g to *almighty*.
M ö g e n is intermediate in signification between K ö n n e n and
w o l l e n, and expresses *power and will* in a weaker manner than
k ö n n e n does power, or w o l l e n will. It implies *ability with
some degree of inclination to do a thing.* That inclination may, or
may not, be predominant. Sometimes the idea of power, sometimes
that of inclination is the leading, if not the sole one, in the use of
the word. V e r m ö g e n expresses merely *ability.* The participle
g e m o c h t is not used with an infinitive dependent on it, but stands
itself in the form of the infinitive but with a participial meaning; as
i c h   h a b e   e s   n i c h t   t h u n   m o g e n (g e m o c h t).

[2] D e n n, *for*, is etymologically the same as *then*; d u the same as
*thou*; d e i n the same as *thine*; d i e s the same as *this*; d i e s e
the same as *these.* A b g e h a u e n, *cut off*; h a u e n, *to hew*, like
k a u e n, *to chew.*

[3] V e r w e l k e n, *to wither.* W e l k e n is preserved in the word
*welk*, in old English.

> " The sea nowe ebbeth, and now it floweth.
> The lond now *welketh*, and now it groweth."—*Gower.*

[4] F e i n in German differs from the English word *fine*, inasmuch
as it does not express mere *prettiness*, but expresses the higher qualities of *perfect accuracy, fitness and elegance* as the result of nice perception.

[5] S c h r e c k l i c h. S c h r e c k e n, in old German, signifies *to
spring, to leap.* Hence H e u s c h r e c k e means a *grasshopper*, as
if it were H e u s p r i n g e r. Then it means, to experience great
mental excitement, commonly of fear; *to frighten* one so as to make
him leap or *shriek.*

[6] G l e i s s n e r stands for g l e i c h s n e r (from g l e i c h s e n,
to imitate), *one who pretends to be like another.* Such was its etymology and use in the old German. In modern times, it has been
connected with the verb g l e i s s e n, *to shine*, and made to mean *one*

und tröftlich¹ den Leidenden. Wie fein hebt er uns aus
unferem Gefichte² und ſetzt uns vor Gottes Gefichte. Vor
unferem Gefichte grünet, blüht und mehrt ſich der Gleißner
Haufe und bedeckt alle Welt ganz, daß ſie allein etwas ſchei=
nen, wie das grüne Gras die Erde deckt³ und ſchmückt.

Aber vor Gottes Gefichte, was ſind ſie? Heu,⁴ das
man ſchier⁵ machen ſoll, und je höher das Gras wächst,⁶
defto näher ſind ihm die Senfen und Heugabeln: alfo
je höher, weiter die Böfen grünen und oben ſchweben,
defto näher ift ihr Unterliegen. Warum wollteft du denn
zürnen, ſo ihre Bosheit und Glück ſo ein⁷ kurzes We=

---

who assumes *shining qualities*. It means nearly the same as H e u c h-
l e r, *a hypocrite.* The difference is this; the H e u c h l e r seeks to
please, and to win *confidence* and respect, the G l e i s s n e r seeks
the *admiration* of others.

¹ T r ö s t l i c h, *consoling,* has a peculiar shade of meaning which
is best explained by its etymology. T r ö s t e n (from T r o s t, English *trust,* in etymology) means *to inspire confidence,* and thus to console in trouble.

² G e s i c h t, 1. *the power of vision ;* then *the view itself,* as in
this passage ; 2. *the countenance.* The plural, G e s i c h t e r, means
*faces ;* but the plural G e s i c h t e, means *visions, apparitions.*
" In our view, the multitude of hypocrites is verdant, flourishes and
spreads and covers the whole world entirely, so that they alone seem
to be anything, as the green grass covers and adorns the earth."

³ D e c k e n, *to cover ;* D a c h, *a covering of a house, a roof* (Saxon *thac,* English *thatch*). D e c k, *the covering* or *deck of a vessel.*
D e c k e l, *a lid* or *cover.* So in English, *to deck, to cover,* especially
with ornamented dress.

⁴ H e u, kindred with the English word *hay,* means *mown grass,*
from h a u e n, *to cut.*

⁵ S c h i e r, as an adverb, is nearly obsolete, and has two significations, 1. *soon,* 2. *nearly.* As an adjective, it means, *clear, pure, sheer.*
Luther employs it here as a modern writer would use s c h n e l l or
b a l d : " Hay, which one will soon make."

⁶ W ä c h s t. W a c h s e n is the same word as the English *to*
*wax.* O b e n s c h w e b e n, *wave on high.*

⁷ S o e i n, is now a colloquial expression for e i n s o l c h e r.

3

ſen[1] iſt?   So ſprichſt bu benn: Was ſoll ich bieweil[2] thun?
Woran ſoll ich mich halten, bis baß ſolches geſchehe?   Höre
zu ;[3] große Verheißung.

Hoffe[4] auf den Herrn und thue Gutes,
bleibe im Lande und nähre dich im Glauben.

Da nimmt[5] er alle ungebulbigen Gebanken ganz bahin

---

[1] W e s e n is often used nearly in the sense of D i n g (which, by
changing d into th, becomes thing).   The difference may be shown
thus : " Thou hast made all things (D i n g e) and by thy will have
they received their being (W e s e n)."   D a s s  W e s e n  e i n e s
D i n g e s is the *essence, qualities* or *charact*er of a thing.   W e s e n
is an old infinitive, (equivalent to s e y n,) used as a substantive.

[2] D i e w i e l, [in] *the* [mean] *while*, obsolete for w ä h r e n d  d e s-
s e n.

[3] H ö r e  z u is a compound verb.   If z u were a preposition, it
would require the dative case.   Z u h ö r e n, *to listen to*, also governs
the dative.   The expression appears to be elliptical, " give attention !
a great announcement !"   V e r h e i s s e n means, 1. *to make a declaration to an inferior;* 2. *to promise an inferior.*   V e r h e i s s u n g
seems to be used here with a latitude of meaning corresponding to
the first signification of the verb.   V e r s p r e c h u n g, *a promise,*
does not imply any difference of rank.   The reason of this distinction
lies in the nature of the word h e i s s e n, which is applied to a superior giving directions to an inferior.

[4] H o f f e n and *hope* are of the same etymology.   The letters *p*
and *f* correspond to each other, as is seen in the words, S c h i f f
(skiff) and *ship;* S t r e i f and *stripe;* K l i p p e and *cliff;* t i e f
and *deep;* r e i f and *ripe;* s c h a r f and *sharp,* and many others.

[5] N i m m t.   N e h m e n, *to take.*   The word *e* of the root was originally *i*, and of course, the letter *i* returns in what are termed the
irregular forms of the verb.   In Gothic it is *niman*, the ending *an*
being, as usual, changed to *en* in later German.   The old English has
preserved the original form of the word.

    " For looking in their plate
      He *nimmes* away their coyne."—*Corbet.*
" And hath our sermon of her *nomen*" (Ger. g e n o m m e n).-*Chaucer.*
N e h m e n signifies *to take,* in its widest and most general sense ;

und ſetzt das Herz zur Ruhe. Als ſollte er ſagen: Liebes
Kind, laß deine Ungeduld, und fluche oder wünſche ihnen
nichts Böſes, es ſind menſchliche und böſe Gedanken. Setze
deine Hoffnung auf Gott, warte was er daraus machen
will, gehe du für dich, unterlaſſe um Niemands willen,
Gutes zu thun, wie du angefangen haſt, wo und welchem du
magſt, und gieb nicht Böſes um Böſes, ſondern Gutes um
Böſes.

So du aber auch dächteſt, du wollteſt fliehen und an einen
andern Ort[2] ziehen, daß du ihrer los würdeſt und von ihnen

---

a n n e h m e n, *to take what is at hand,* or what is offered ; f a s s e n,
*to take, by embracing it on all sides* (as a vessel contains a fluid), or
on both sides (as we embrace a thing with both hands) ; g r i e f e n,
*to take by compressing* or *squeezing* (gripe). E i n n e h m e n means
*to take in, to receive;* a u s n e h m e n, *to take out, to except;* u n t e r-
n e h m e n, *to undertake;* a b n e h m e n, *to take away, to decrease;*
z u n e h m e n, *to add, to increase;* a u f n e h m e n, *to take up, to take
in charge,* or *accept.*

[1] S e t z t. S e t z e n, *to make to sit, to place,* is causative of s i t -
z e n, *to sit,* as s e n k e n, *to cause to sink,* is of s i n k e n, *to sink;*
and t r ä n k e n, *to cause to drink,* of t r i n k e n, *to drink ;* and f ä l l-
e n, *to fell,* of f a l l e n, *to fall.* The letters *z* and *t* are often exchanged for each other, as in s e t z e n and s i t z e n, English *set* and *sit;*
H e r z, English *heart,* (Dutch, *harrt* and *hert*) ; N e t z, *net;* H i t z e,
*heat;* s c h w i t z e n, *to sweat;* W i t z, *wit.*—L a s s  d e i n e  U n g e-
d u l d, *leave, give up your impatience,* neither curse them nor wish
them any ill. "*Those* are (see p. 22, Note 4) carnal and evil thoughts.
Put your hope in God ; wait (and see) what he will bring out of it ;
take your own proper course (do your duty). To do good, as you
have begun, when and to whom you can, omit on account of no one
(i. e. let no one hinder you)."

[2] O r t signifies *a place,* and generally *an inhabited place,* large or
small, and may comprehend under it S t a d t, S c h l o s s, B u r g,
F l e c k e n, and D o r f. P l a t z means *an open space,* or any unoc-
cupied place which may be used for any purpose. F l e c k is *any
small space.* But F l e c k e n (sometimes meaning a *spot* or *stain*) is
*a village with corporate rights,* and is thereby distinguished from
D o r f, *a hamlet, without such rights.* S t e l l e, means *a place where*

kämeſt: auch nicht alſo,[1] bleibe im Lande, wohne[2] wo du
biſt, wechśle oder wandle[3] um ihretwillen nicht deine Woh=

---

*a person or thing is placed*, and hence often implies a certain order,
as a particular office under the government, or particular passage in
an author.

[1] N i c h t  a l s o is elliptical, t h u e or some such word being understood. A l s o is never to be rendered by *also*, but by *thus*.
A u c h, *also*, refers to what had been said in the preceding paragraph.
A u c h  n i c h t is equivalent to *neither*, and the sentence may be
translated thus : " But if you should think you would flee, and go to
another place in order that you might be rid of them and get away
from them, do it not (not so either). Remain, etc."

[2] W o h n e, W o h n u n g. The original meaning of. w o h n e n
seems to be, *to remain*. Tatian, in the ninth century says, " the
branch will not bear fruit unless it w o h n e (remain) in the vine,"
and " the child Jesus w o h n e t e (remained) in Jerusalem." Hence
the secondary, but afterwards uniform meaning, *to dwell in a place as
one's home*, to reside permanently. W o h n u n g, the verbal noun,
signifies *the dwelling*, i. e. 1. the *act* of residence ; 2. the *place* of residence, which is more definitely expressed by W o h n s i t z. A u f e n t-
h a l t, on the contrary, means, not a permanent residence *at home*,
but *a temporary residence from home*. From w o h n e n, *to remain*, is
derived g e w ö h n e n, *to accustom ;* because one becomes *accustomed*
to a thing by remaining in *connection* with it ; G e w ö h n u n g, the
*act* of getting accustomed ; G e w o h n h e i t, *custom, usage ;* and g e-
w ö h n l i c h, *customarily, commonly*.

[3] W a n d l e. This word, as a *neuter* verb, signifies, *to walk about,
back and forth*, and is generally employed only in elevated style and
is then applied to a person in easy circumstances walking for pleasure. A gentleman walking in his garden to view the plants, is said
to w a n d e l n, but not the gardener who goes about to take care of
them. Then the word is applied to denote *any slow progressive motion*, mostly in poetry ; and when used of the course of life, it is like
the English word *walk* in its biblical use. So W a n d e l, *manner of
life*. H a n d e l  u n d  W a n d e l, is an idiomatic expression, the two
substantives conveying but one idea, meaning *barter, trade*.—As an
*active* verb, w a n d e l n meant, particularly in Luther's time, *to
change one place for another*, or *one thing for another*. To express
the idea of *changing one thing into another*, this word is now rarely
used, v e r w a n d e l n and u m w a n d e l n being, in modern lan-

nung oder Land, ſondern nähre dich im Glauben, treibe[1] deine Arbeit und Handel[2] wie vorhin. Hindern[3] oder be= ſchädigen ſie dich und geben dir Urſache zu fliehen, ſo laß fahren, bleibe im Glauben und zweifle nicht, Gott wird dich nicht laſſen, thue nur das Deine, arbeite und nähre dich, und laß ihn walten.[4]

Du ſollſt nicht aufhören, dich zu nähren, ob ſie dich an

---

guage, employed for that purpose. W e c h s e l means *to exchange* one thing for another; ä n d e r n and v e r ä n d e r n, to change a thing by altering, or *modifying* it, the latter implying the greater change.

[1] T r e i b e n (old German, d r i b a n) is the same word as the English *drive*, the *t* corresponding to *d*, and the *b* to *v*. T r e i b e n, when applied 'o business, does not mean *to drive*, or *press it*, but simply *to practise it*. T r i e b means, *the act of driving, natural impulse* (instinct); T r i f t (*drift*) is *the act of being driven*, or the course of action; also *a drove*, and the *pasture* to which cattle are driven.

[2] H a n d e l, formerly signified *action of any sort*. It now signifies 1. *transaction*, (e i n  s c h l i m e r  H a n d e l, *a bad affair*), especially *a quarrel*, or *a lawsuit* (H a n d e l  s u c h e n, *to pick a quarrel;* e i n e n  H a n d e l  v o r  G e r i c h t  b r i n g e n, *to bring a suit before the court*); 2. *a contract, bargain, barter, trade*. H a n d l u n g is now the common word for *action*, in general. When it relates to trade, it means *a large establishment*, or *mercantile house*. The verb h a n - d e l n, once signified, *to handle*, but now signifies *to act, to treat, to trade*. M i t  j e m a n d e m  ü b e r  e t w a s  h a n d e l n, is, *to treat* or *bargain with one respecting a thing*. M i t  e t w a s  h a n d e l n, means, *to trade in a certain* article: and h a n d e l n alone, means *to trade*. V o n  e t w a s  h a n d e l n, is *to treat of a subject*, in writing or speaking.—H a n d e l, in this passage is used in its original sense, of *activity, business*. "Carry on your labor and business as formerly."

[3] H i n d e r n, etc. "If they hinder or injure you, etc."—S o l a s s  f a h r e n, *then let it go* (disregard it).—T h u e  d a s  D e i n e, *do your duty*.

[4] W a l t e n, kindred with *wield*, signifies *to control, to manage*, and is used of one in authority. Hence v e r w a l t e n, *to administer*, or perform the functions of an office. S c h a l t e n signifies, to give direction to a motion, and then *to give direction, in general*, and is used of one who actually has power, whether lawful or unlawful

3*

einem Stücke[1] hindern; Gott, so du hoffest, giebt es dir am andern Ort, wie er Abraham, Isaak und Jacob that, die auch also versucht wurden.

Habe deine Lust[2] am Herrn, der wird dir geben, was dein Herz wünscht.

Das ist: Laß dich es nicht verdrießen,[3] daß Gott sie so läßt wohlfahren,[4] laß dir solchen seinen Willen wohlge-

---

**W a l t e n** is not limited to persons, but is said of things, as **V e r-n u n f t, F r i e d e**, etc.; but **s c h a l t e n** can be said only of persons, because they only can act *arbitrarily*.

[1] S t ü c k e, signifies *piece*, and means here, as it does often, *anything*. "Though they hinder you in some particular (anything), God, if you hope in him, will give it (gives it) to you in another place."

[2] L u s t, *pleasure, desire.* So the English word, *lust*, originally meant desire. In the singular number, the German word is generally used in a good sense (m i t L u s t h ö r e n, *to hear with pleasure;* i c h h a b e L u s t z u e s s e n, *I have a desire to eat*). It has a bad sense in the plural (L ü s t e d e s F l e i s c h e s, *lusts of the flesh*), and sometimes in composition (as W o l l u s t, *voluptuousness;* F l e i-s c h e s l u s t, *carnal lust;* L u s t d i r n e, *woman of pleasure*). In most instances in composition, it indicates pleasure or amusement. From L u s t is derived the verb l ü s t e n, *to desire;* and the same derivative form (i. e. the change of the vowel from *u* to *ü*) is preserved in the English verb *to list* (the *i* in English corresponding to the *ü* of the German). *Listless*, in English, means *without desire, without concern.* L ü s t e r n, the frequentative form of the verb in German, means *repeated or continued*, and consequently *strong desire.* G e-l ü s t e n means *a strong desire*, as a hankering for certain kinds of food, the prefix g e giving intensity to the simple word.

[3] V e r d r i e s s e n signifies literally *to render one unhappy by giving too much of a thing*, or by protracting it too long; then to occasion one chagrin by doing what is highly disagreeable to him, and this latter is the prevailing signification. So V e r d r u s s, a few lines below, means, *sorrow, chagrin*, occasioned by *another's* fault, or by an unpleasant occurrence, as opposed to L u s t and W o h l g e-f a l l e n.

[4] W o h l f a h r e n. F a h r e n, *to go*, or *to travel*, generally in a

fallen,¹ so vergeht dir die Unlust über der Gottlosen Glück,
ja erlüste dich drinnen, als in dem allerbesten und göttlichen
Willen, siehe, so hast du diese tröstliche Zusagung :² „Er

---

carriage or vessel, as opposed to g e h e n, *to go on foot*, and r e i t e n
*to ride on horseback.* F a h r e  w o h l, means literally, *journey
prosperously,* and was originally said to one who was on the eve of
taking a journey. F a h r e n was next applied to any proc?ss of business, as *to go on;* and w o h l f a h r e n, *to go on prosperously.* So in
English, *fare* signified originally *to go;* and *farewell*, go prosperously.
The substantive *fare* is what one has in travelling. *How fares
it with you;* means, how does it go with you. *Welfare,* German
W o h l f a r t, means a prosperous course of things.

⁶ W o h l g e f a l l e n. The root of this word is f a l l e n, *to fall,*
and, in those compound words formed from it, which signify some
effect produced upon the mind, or upon something else, it conveys
the incidental idea of *suddenness.* Something *falls* suddenly upon
the mind as an unforeseen occurrence. A u f f a l l e n, means *to surprise* by something strange falling upon one, (or, occurring to him);
b e i f a l l e n, *to fall in with one, to agree with him, or approve.* In
g e f a l l e n, the prefix ge, which corresponds to the Latin *con,* giving to substantives a collective sense (G e b i r g e, *a chain of moun-
tains*) and to verbs, sometimes the idea of coherence (g e f r i e r e n,
*to freeze together*), sometimes that of intensity resulting from union
(G e l ü s t e n as explained on p. 30, Note 2); and sometimes that of
coincidence or fitness, as in g e f a l l e n, *to fall together* so as to make
the object agree with the inclination and so, *to please.* The verb
w o h l g e f a l l e n, means accordingly, *to please highly,* but it is obsolete, though the substantive W o h l g e f a l l e n is still a common
word.

⁷ Z u s a g u n g, *a promise,* meant originally, *the giving of one's
word in respect to* (z u) *a thing,* an assurance in relation to something
without a formal compact or pledge as in V e r s p r e c h u n g. But
its more common signification is *the assenting to* (z u) *a request made,*
or compliance with a desire expressed or implied; and it is hereby
distinguished from V e r s p r e c h u n g and V e r h e i s s u n g. See
p. 26, Note 3. Instead of Z u s a g u n g, modern writers employ
Z u s a g e. "Let it not vex you that God allows them to prosper
so. Let this (such) his pleasure satisfy you, and then your sorrow
over the prosperity of the wicked will pass away; nay rejoice in it,
as in the perfect and divine will, (and) behold there you have this
consoling assurance."

wird dir geben Alles, was dein Herz begehrt."[1] Was
willst[2] du mehr haben? Siehe nur zu, daß du anstatt des
Verdrusses, so du von ihnen schöpfest,[3] diese Lust und Wohl-
gefallen in göttlichem Willen übest, so werden sie dir nicht
allein keinen Schaden thun, sondern dein Herz wird auch
voll Friedens seyn, und fröhlich[4] warten dieser Zusagung
Gottes.

Befiehl[5] dem Herrn deine Wege, und hoffe

---

[1] **Begehrt.** Begehren differs from wünschen, used a
few lines above, in the following manner. Wünschen, *to wish*,
does not imply effort to obtain the object of desire. Begehren is
stronger, and implies earnest and active desire. Gieren is the
same with the additional idea of *greediness*. Begierde and Gier
differ in the same way, the latter being more sensual, and violent.

[2] **Willst.** Wollen is not, in German, a mere auxiliary, but
a verb expressing *positive desire*. "What do you desire to have
more."

[3] **Schöpfest.** Schöpfen is kindred with *scoop* and signifies *to take away a fluid with any vessel*, a pitcher, spoon, *bucket*, etc.
Then it means figuratively, *to draw supplies or materials from any
source.* This must not be confounded with another word in the same
form, schöpfen, *to create*, mostly obsolete, schaffen having
taken its place in that sense. But Schöpfer, Schöpfung,
Geschöpf, *creator, creation, creature*, are in common use. "Only see to it, that you have (exercise) this joy and pleasure in the divine will, instead of the vexation which you derive from them, then
they will not only do you no harm, etc."

[4] **Fröhlich,** kindred with *frolic*, comes from froh, *joyful*, with
reference to the internal feeling; whereas fröhlich means *joyous*,
with reference to the external manifestations of joy. Freudig,
*joyful*, indicates a feeling of pleasure (Freude) arising from an
agreeable object, for the attainment of which, if need be, we cheerfully undergo labor and suffering. Lustig means *sportive*.

[5] **Befiehl.** Befehlen is here used in its original, but now
obsolete sense, *to surrender, to give up, to commend*. Tatian, in the
ninth century says, *Bifilihit* then uuingarten andern (befiehlt
den Weingarten andern), he gives over the vineyard to others; also, *biviluhu* minan geist in thino henti, which is given thus in

auf ihn, er wird es wohl machen.[1]

Nicht daß du müssig gehen solltest, sondern deine Wege, Werke, Worte und Wandel befiehl Gott, kehre dich an[2] sie nicht. Denn es muß nicht Gott also befohlen werden, daß wir nichts thun, sondern was wir thun, ob es von den Gleißnern versprochen,[3] verschmäht,[4] geläs-

---

Luther's translation, i c h  b e f e h l e  m e i n e n  G e i s t  i n  d e i n e H ä n d e.  B e f e h l e n  now signifies, *to command*.  G e b i e t e n expresses the same with a stronger idea of compulsion.  H e i s s e n and  v o r s c h r e i b e n, the one conveying *orally*, the other *in writing* an expression of one's will, rather *imply* than *assert* authority and compulsion.

[1] W o h l  m a c h e n, is here the same as  g u t  m a c h e n.  When g u t is an adverb,  g u t  m a c h e n means *to do a thing well*.  When it is an adjective, the phrase means *to render a thing good*, i. e. to restore or replace a *thing*, or to pacify a *person*.—W o h l signifies, 1. *agreeably*, 2. *well*, 3. *no doubt, indeed, nearly*. See p. 13, Notes 6 and 1 end, and p. 12, Note 4 mid.  In  w o h l  m a c h e n,  w o h l without the emphasis means *no doubt, surely*.  With the emphasis on it, as is probably the case here, it means, *he will manage it right* (do it well). W o h l t h u n signifies both *to do well*, and *to do good*, and  W o h l - t h a t is *an act of beneficence*.

[2] K e h r e  d i c h  a n.  K e h r e n, means *to turn*.  S i c h  z u  e t - w a s  k e h r e n signifies *to turn one's self to a thing*, to give one's self up to it.  S i c h  a n  e t w a s  k e h r e n, signifies *to have regard to a thing*, to hold it in special consideration.  " Not that you are to be indolent, but commit your ways, works, words and walk to God ; do not regard them," i. e. opposers.

[3] V e r s p r o c h e n.  In the middle ages the particle  v e r  in  v e r - s p r e c h e n, had its literal import, *away, out of the way* or *wrong*. The verb meant 1. *to refuse*, 2. *to speak against one*.  In this latter sense Luther often uses it.—W a s  w i r  t h u n,  o b  e s.  There is here a little irregularity in the construction, a license much more common in Luther's time than now, " what we do, whether it is spoken against, etc. one should not yield, etc.," for " whether what we do is spoken against, etc."

[4] V e r s c h m ä h t.  This word signifies *to despise a thing on account of its insignificance*, and thereby differs from  v e r a c h t e n, *to contemn a thing on account of its worthlessness or badness*, the opposite of  a c h t e n, *to respect*.

tert[1] oder verhindert wird soll man darum nicht weich wer=
den noch ablaſſen, ſondern immer fortfahren und ſie laſſen
ihren Muthwillen[2] haben, Gott die Sache befehlen, der wird
es wohl machen auf beiden Seiten, was recht iſt.

Und wird deine Gerechtigkeit hervor=
bringen wie das Licht, und dein Recht wie
den Mittag.

Dieß iſt die größte Sorge der Weichlinge,[3] daß ſie ver=
droſſen werden über die Gottloſen, daß ihre Bosheit ſo
ſcheint und wohl gehalten wird. Denn ſie ſorgen, ihre
Sache werde verdrückt[4] und verfinſtert, weil ſie ſehen der
Widerparte[5] Wüthen ſo hoch fahren und oben ſchweben.

---

[1] Gelästert. Lästern, signified in early times, *to reproach
one by exposing his faults.* It now means *to calumniate,* or to impute
what is false. So Laster, from which it is derived, once meant
*reproach, disgrace;* but it now signifies, *crime, scandalous vice.*

[2] Muthwillen, *will, arbitrary choice or way.* " Let them have
their own will, or way." At the present day, the word is used only
in a bad sense, *wilful wickedness, wantonness.*

[3] Weichling, here used of *one who is yielding,* i. e. *faint-hearted,* or *delicate* and *weak,* not, as is commonly the case, of a *voluptua-
ry.* Luther, in another passage speaks of the Weichlingen of
his flock as distinguished from die Starken, *the strong.* " This
is the greatest trouble of the faint-hearted, namely, that they are cha-
grined on account of the wicked whose iniquity (and that their iniquity) is so shining and so well sustained." Sorge, in the early
writers, means, *sorrow, distress;* in later authors, it means, *anxiety,
painful solicitude,* and refers solely to something future. With Lnther both seem to be united. The misery of the faint-hearted grows
out of the condition of the wicked,—out of the circumstances that
the wickedness of the latter triumphs, or that they triumph in their
wickedness.

[4] Verdrückt. Verdrücken, in Luther's time, signified *to
oppress,* as unterdrücken does now.

[5] Widerpart, *opponent,* is now little used; Gegner is more
common in that sense. The same remark is applicable to Gegen
part. Der Widerparte is in the gen. pl.

Darum tröſtet er und ſpricht: Laß ſeyn,[1] liebes Kind, daß ſie dich, deine Sache mit Wolken und Platzregen verdrücken und im Anſehen vor der Welt gar zu nichte[2] machen und in Finſterniß begraben, daß ihre Sache emporſchwebe und leuchte wie die Sonne. Befiehlſt du Gott deinen Handel, hoffeſt und warteſt auf ihn, ſo ſey gewiß, dein Recht und Gerechtigkeit wird nicht im Finſtern bleiben, ſie muß hervor[3] und Jedermann ſo öffentlich bekannt werden als der helle Mittag, daß alle die[4] zu Schanden werden, die dich ver= drückt und verdunkelt haben. Es iſt nur um das Warten zu thun,[5] daß du Gott in ſolchem Vornehmen durch dein Zürnen, Unmuth, Verdrießen nicht hinderſt. Darum ver= mahnt er aber[6] einmal:

Halte dem Herrn ſtille[7] und laß ihn mit

---

[1] Lass (es) seyn—dich (und) deine Sache. Such ellipses are very common in Luther.

[2] Zu nichte. Nicht, like our word *nought* was once a sub stantive, making Nichte in the dative. It is now an adverb; and Nichts, indeclinable, is used as a substantive.—Ihre Sache, *their cause.*

[3] Sie muss hervor (leuchten, or kommen), *it must shine or come forth.* So, er konnte nicht vorbei (gehen), *he could not pass by.* Ich muss weg (gehen), *I must leave.* Such omissions are very frequent in familiar discourse.

[4] Alle die—die, "all those who." See p. 14, Note 5. Zu Schanden werden, *to be put to shame.* Feminine nouns were anciently declined in the singular. Hence those phrases which have been handed down from early times, preserve the old forms of the cases.

[5] Es ist nur um das Warten zu thun, *there is nothing to do but wait.* Um, with zu thun, means *to do with, to be concerned with.*—" That you do not hinder God in such a design (undertaking) by your anger, vexation and chagrin."

[6] Aber, *again,* according to old usage, and the primary meaning of the word.

[7] Halte dem Herrn stille. Stille halten with the dative of a person, literally, *to hold still to one,* means *to be quiet in*

dir machen. Erzürne dich nicht über den
Mann, dem es wohl gehet und thut nach sei=
nem Muthwillen.

Als sollte er sagen: Es will dich verdrießen, daß du in
rechter Sache[1] Unglück empfindest und es Jenen in Bosheit
wohlgehet, und will nicht,[2] wie du gerne wolltest, von Stat=
ten geben, und siehest doch, daß dem Ungerechten Alles nach
seinem Muthwillen geht, daß ein Sprüchwort hieraus ge=
flossen ist: Je größer Schalk, je besser Glück. Aber sey
weise, liebes Kind, laß dich das nicht bewegen, halte auf
Gott, deines Herzens Begierde wird auch kommen gar reich=
lich.[3]

Es ist aber noch nicht Zeit, es muß des Schalks[4] Glück
vergehen und seine Zeit haben, bis es vorüber kommt. In=
deß[5] mußt du es Gott befehlen, in ihm dich erlüsten, seinen

---

the hands of one. Lass ihm mit dir machen, *let him do with
you*, i. e. *as he pleases*. Dem es wohl gehet und (der)
thut, etc., *with whom it is well*, and *who does*.

[1] In rechter Sache, *in a just cause*. Gerecht is more
commonly used in this sense, and recht in the sense of *right, proper*.

[2] Und (es) will nicht, " It will vex you that you, in a good
cause, feel misfortune, and that they prosper in iniquity (goes well
with them in iniquity) ; and things (it) will not go on, as you would
like, and yet you see that everything goes with the unjust man according to his will, so that a proverb, etc."

[3] Gar reichlich. Gar is nearly the same as ganz, and
they are often conjoined, ganz und gar, *wholly and in every part*.
But gar is a little weaker than ganz, and is therefore often to be
rendered by *very*.

[4] Des Schalks. Schalk signified originally *a servant*, as
in Gottschalk, *a servant of God*, Marshalk (from Marah
and Mähre, *horse*), *marshall*. In Luther's time it signified, *a dis-
sembler, a knave*. In modern German, it means, in its milder sense, *a
roguish, artful, cunning man*, and is even a gentler term than
Schelm. Both indicate men who practise arts of deception.

[5] Indess, 1. and literally, *interea, meanwhile*, in which sense in-

Willen dir gefallen lassen, auf daß[1] du seinen Willen in dir und in deinem Feinde nicht hinderst, wie die thun, die nicht aufhören zu wüthen, sie haben denn[2] ihr Ding[3] entweder mit dem Kopf hindurch oder zu Trümmern[4] gebracht.

---

d e s s e n is now more commonly used; out of this signification has grown that of *while* (which was formerly expressed by i n d e s s e n d a s s, *meanwhile that*); 2. *nevertheless*, synonymous with d o c h and j e d o c h.

[1] A u f d a s s, *in order that*, obsolete for *dass.*—H i n d e r s t. See Gram. p. 317, (2), on this use of the indicative.

[2] S i e h a b e n d e n n, is a peculiar idiom, like e s s e i d e n n, conveying the idea of an exception, *unless*. See Gram. p. 315. *They have then*, i. e. unless they have either carried their matter head-long through, or (brought it) to destruction.

[3] D i n g is the same word as *thing*. To show how the letters *d*, *th*, and *t* correspond to each other, we will present a few more similar examples. T h ü r, *door;* d ü n n, *thin;* D a u m, *thumb;* d e n-k e n, *think;* D i e b, *thief;* d i c k, *thick;* D i s t e l, *thistle;* D o r n, *thorn;* T o c h t e r, *daughter;* d r e i, *three;* d r e s c h e n, *thresh;* D u r s t, *thirst;* F e d e r, *feather;* L e d e r, *leather;* W o r t, *word;* G o t t, *God;* V a t e r, *father;* B r u d e r, *brother;* N o r d, *north.*

[4] T r ü m m e r n. T r ü m m e r is the plural of T r u m, now ob-solete. Still the singular is used in poetical and antique style. V o s s, speaks of a F e l s t r u m, *fragment of a rock* falling into the sea. Jean Paul, speaks of a broken watch-chain, and the T r u m, frag-ment. Compare the Greek ϑρύμμα. In old German, it meant the end of a thing, as, d e s m e r e s *drum*, (*trum*), *the end of the sea.* D a s s c h l a c h t e n n a m e i n d r u m, *the battle took an end*, i. e. ended. This same word is preserved in the English *thrum*, which retains the primitive signification, *ends of something cut off*, tangled threads cut off from cloth. The old German verb, d r u m o n (t r u-m e n) means *to cut off*. Hence the word T r ü m m e r has the wide signification of anything cut or broken off, as a piece of a broken vessel, thread, rock, ruins, wreck, etc., while R u i n e n (Latin, *rui-na* from *ruere*, to fall) is limited to a *fallen structure*, and things of that sort: S c h e i t e r, *scattered pieces of a wrecked vessel*, the plu-ral of S c h e i t, *a piece of wood*, (hence s c h e i t e r n, *to go to pieces, to wreck*); and W r a c k, what remains of a ship after the

4

Stehe ab vom Zorn und laß den Grimm,[1]
erzürne dich nicht, daß du auch übel thuest.

Siehe, wie fleißig warnt er, daß wir ja nicht Böses mit
Bösem vergelten, noch den Bösen folgen[2] um ihres Glückes
willen, wie die Natur zu treiben pflegt. Und was hilft
solcher Zorn? Er macht die Sache nicht besser, ja führt
sie nur tiefer in den Schlamm. Und ob es schon auf's Allerbeste geriethe,[3] daß du oben lägest und gewönnest,[4] was
hast du gewonnen? Gott hast du verhindert, damit[5] seine
Gnade und Gunst verloren, und den bösen Uebelthätern bist
du gleich geworden, und wirst gleich mit ihnen verderben,
wie folgt :

---

loose pieces are scattered away. Several late writers, as Voss,
Göthe, Seume and many others, have used T r ü m m e r as a mascu-
line singular, and formed from it a new and second plural, d i e
T r ü m m e r n.

[1] Z o r n, G r i m m. Z o r n means *anger*, a *fiery passion*.
G r i m m means *fury*. Hence one may say i n Z o r n e s G r i m m,
*in the fury of passion*. W u t h means *rage*, after the manner of the
ocean. So w ü t h e n in the preceding paragraph.—D a s s d u
a u c h ü b e l t h u e s t, *so as to do evil*.

[2] F o l g e n, is here used as it is sometimes in the old German,
in the sense of v e r f o l g e n, *to persecute*.

[3] G e r i e t h e. G e r a t h e n, means *to turn out*, as indicating an
unforeseen result, *to terminate in a certain way by chance*. But it is
more commonly used in the restricted sense, *to turn out well*, as
d a s G e t r e i d e i s t n i c h t g e r a t h e n, *the grain*, (crop) *has
not turned out well*. D i e A r b e i t i s t i h m g e r a t h e n, *the
work has turned out successfully to him*. U n g e r a t h e n e K i n-
d e r, *children that turn out poorly*.

[4] O b e n l ä g e s t u n d g e w ö n n e s t, "shouldst lie top and
win." G e w i n n e n which makes the imperfect in g e w a n n,
has the imperfect subjunctive g e w ä n n e, for which there is
another form g e w ö n n e. There is here an allusion to *wrestling*.
U n t e r l i e g e n is still used to express the opposite of o b e n l i e-
g e n which is obsolete. See both words in the first paragraph under
verse 24.

[5] D a m i t. "Thou hast hindered God [from delivering you, and]
*thereby* lost his grace and favor."

Denn die Bösen werden ausgerottet, die[1] aber des Herrn harren,[2] werden das Land erben.

Es hilft[3] dich nicht, daß du nicht angefangen[4] haft oder gereizt seyest. Denn es ist ein schlechtes[5] freies Urtheil: Wer Uebel thut, gereizt oder ungereizt, der wird ausgerot-

---

[1] (D i e) d i e, *those who.* The antecedent omitted.

[2] H a r r e n signified in old German, *to tarry.* It signifies *to wait in expectation of something* or *in great anxiety for it.* It is construed with a u f, or more poetically with the genitive, both forms having the same sense, viz. *to wait with anxiety for* a person or thing. It implies some present evil, and the confident expectation of some future good. W a r t e n signified originally, *to look, to look for.* Hence W a r t e means an elevated place from which one can look out, *a tower, an observatory.* W a r t t h u r m and W a r t b u r g, *a watch-tower.* W a r t e n, therefore, means, *to watch,* and hence, *to wait anxiously for.* This word also is sometimes followed by a u f, sometimes by the genitive. At present, h a r r e n is more elevated and is used in reference to God, and in written composition; while w a r t e n is more used in familiar style, and with reference to men.

[3] H e l f e n when used impersonally or with a neuter nominative, or when it governs the accusative, means, *to be of use* or *advantage.*

[4] A n g e f a n g e n, "that you did not begin (the strife) or that you were provoked." As f a n g e n, is equivalent to *capere,* to take, so a n f a n g e n is equivalent to *incipere* (in-capere), *to take hold of, to begin.* A n h e b e n, literally, *to take a thing up,* figuratively, *to begin,* is a more solemn and dignified word, perhaps from its implying greater effort or power (to raise, to lift up); as J e h o v a h o b d a s G e r i c h t a n, *Jehovah began the judgment.* B e g i n n e n, *to go about, to enter upon,* like the Latin, *in—ire* (if we may trust the etymology of g i n n e n as equivalent to g e h e n); *to begin.* A n-b r e c h e n, *to break upon,* has the same sense, (to begin) except that it implies *suddenness.* All of these may be used of precedence of *time* in beginning. Only a n f a n g e n can be applied to *space,* or that which is first, because nearest to us; as, D o r t f ä n g t m e i n e s R e i c h e s G r ä n z e a n, "there begin (in space) the boundaries of my kingdom."

[5] S c h l e c h t e s, *simple,* in a good sense, signified originally *even, level.* Luther renders Luke 3: 5, W a s u n e b e n i s t, s o l l s c h l e c h t e r W e g w e r d e n, "the uneven shall become a level

tet werden.   Das sieht man auch vor Augen in aller Welt,
in allen Geschichten.

Aber wer[1] auf Gott wartet, der bleibt, daß neben ihm

---

way." From this were derived the significations, *straight*, *true*, *simple*. But the form s c h l i c h t is, in modern German, employed
to designate those ideas, and s c h l e c h t has received another figurative signification. As what is *level* is lower than the eminences,
s c h l e c h t came to signify *low*, and then *worthless*. So the English verb *slight* signified originally, *to level*, *to cast down*; and then to
cast away and disregard. " They *slighted* and demolished all the
works of that garrison."—*Clarendon*. " The rogues *slighted* me into
the river."—*Shakespeare*. S c h l i m m differs from s c h l e c h t in
this, that it means something *positively bad* or *injurious*, while the
latter is *negatively bad*, or worthless. S c h l i m m signified anciently, *crooked*, and hence *out of form*, or *out of proper order*. E i n
s c h l i m m e r  H a l s, was *a crooked neck;* s c h l i m m  s c h r e i b-
e n, was *to write crookedly*. But in modern usage this meaning is
not common. E i n  s c h l i m m e r  F i n g e r, means *a bad* or *sore
finger;* e i n  s c h l i m m e r  H u n d, *a vicious dog*. In English,
the word *slim*, means *poor* and *bad*. Barrow says, " That was a
*slim* excuse." Webster seems to have inverted the proper order of
the significations of this word. In Dutch, the word *slim* and in the
Danish *slem* are used in the sense of s c h l i m m in German, so that
little doubt can remain of the origin of the English word.

[1] A b e r  w e r. " But he, who waits for God (looks to him for aid),
remains (waits) for the evil-doer to perish by his side, whoever can
but wait so long." W e r followed by d e r, like the Latin *qui* followed by *is*. " Wicked men are so very ripe, that, though no one
drives them on, they cannot restrain themselves ; they, of their own
accord, bring down calamity upon their own necks, so that they are
destroyed in one's sight." V e r t r e i b e n, to drive away, and consequently, to drive forward. A n r i c h t e n, *to prepare;* and then *to
bring*, or *to occasion something evil*, like a n s t i f t e n. Z u s e h e n s,
genitive of Z u s e h e n, *the act of seeing*, used adverbially and meaning, *at the time of seeing, while one is seeing, visibly*. In common life,
z u s e h e n d and z u s e h e n d s are so employed. " For ripe
grass must become hay, and it shall even dry in itself [standing] on
its stalk." N i e m a n d, on the next page, 7th line, is in the dative.
A n must always be used, when that is to be pointed out in which
anything takes place, " in murderers," etc.

untergehe der Uebelthäter, wer nur so lange harren könnte. Die bösen Menschen sind so gar reif, daß, ob sie Niemand vertreibt, so mögen sie sich selbst nicht enthalten, sie richten ein muthwillig Unglück an über ihren Hals, daß sie zusehens vertilgt werden. Denn das reife Gras muß Heu werden und sollte es an ihm selbst auf dem Stamme verdorren. Es ist ein böser Mensch Niemand so unerträglich und verderblich als sich selbst. Das sehen wir an den Mördern, Dieben, Tyrannen und dergleichen Exempeln.

Es ist noch um ein Kleines,[1] so ist der Gottlose nimmer,[2] so wirst du auf seine Stätte[3] achten, und er wird nicht da seyn.

---

[1] Um ein Kleines, *a short time*. U m, *about, not far from*, is often used where we should expect *exactness*; and, in such cases, is to be translated by *at*, when it refers to a *point of time*, and to be omitted altogether, when it refers to *measure*, either of time or of space; as, u m v i e r U h r, *at four o'clock*. U m d r e i J a h r e ä l t e r, *three years older*.

[2] N i m m e r. J e means *at any time*, distributively, and then *all times* collectively, *ever*. In the old Gothic form it was a i v, hence the English word *ever*), from which e w i g is derived. J e with a' negative particle prefixed, becomes n i e, and is just the opposite in signification. Compounded with m a l s (genitive of m a l) it forms j e m a l s, and is a stronger expression of the idea *at any time* (*ever of time, ever in the world*); which, in the negative form, is n i e- m a l s. J e with m e r (old German for m e h r) forms i m m e r, *evermore*, and negatively, n i m m e r, *never more*. These last differ from the preceding, by relating to the future, and being properly limited to it. N i m m e r m e h r, is a still stronger expression. But the word m e h r, in such cases, in denying something with reference to the future, does not imply its former existence, as the English expression, *no more*, does, and should not be rendered by these words, but simply by *never*, or *never in the world*.

[3] S t ä t t e, the place where anything *stands*, or *abides*. It is now used only in elevated style. S t a t t (English *stead*) was formerly used in this sense, of which we see traces in such compounds and phrases as, W e r k s t a t t, *work-place, work-shop;* B e t t - s t a t t,

Das erklärt, was droben[1] gesagt ist, daß sie sind wie das Gras, das schnell abgehauen wird, damit nur unsere Ungeduld gestillt werde, welches sich fürchtet, die Gottlosen bleiben zu lange. Möchtest aber sagen: Ja, ich sehe wohl, daß die Ungerechten gemeiniglich lange bleiben, auch mit Ehren zum Grabe kommen?

Antwort: Das geschieht gewißlich[2] darum, daß der andere Theil[3] sich nicht nach diesem Psalm gehalten[4] hat, sondern die Sache mit Zorn, Wüthen, Grimmen, Klagen und Schreien[5] verhindert und verdorbin hat. Darum weil Nie-

---

bedstead; an meiner Statt, *in my place;* statt meiner, *in my stead;* Statt haben, *to take place;* Statt geben (or obsolete Statt thun), *to grant a place;* i. e. *to yield, to permit;* von Statten (dat. pl.) gehen, *to prosper;* zu Statten kommen, *to be serviceable to one.*

[1] Droben, compounded of da (which becomes dar before a vowel) and oben. Dar, is frequently contracted into dr, as it easily forms a syllable with the following vowel.

[2] Gewisslich, is now nearly out of use, and gewiss is used adverbially in its stead. Inasmuch as all adjectives in German may, without change of termination, be used as adverbs, the adverbial ending lich is used less frequently than formerly.

[3] Theil, here used in the sense of *party,* properly signifies *a part,* that which goes to make up the whole. It is the same as the English word *deal* (Gothic *Dail,* Anglo-Saxon, *dæl*); which in old English signifies *a part.* So the verb *to deal,* originally signified, *to divide,* like the German theilen. Antheil, *a part,* signifies *that part* (Theil) *which falls to* (an) *one in distribution.*

[4] Sich nicht nach diesem Psalm gehalten, " has not held (or regulated) itself according to this Psalm."

[5] Wüthen, Grimmen, Klagen und Schreien, infinitives used as substantives and having the force of participial nouns in English, " raging, venting fury, complaining, and crying out," more forcible than " rage, fury, complaints and cries." While schreien, signifies *to utter loud cries,* whether in intelligible words or not, rufen means *to call by addressing one distinctly and intelligibly.* Hence Ruf, 1. *a call,* 2. *reputation,* literally, *what is spoken of one aloud, and what goes abroad.*

mand[1] da gewesen ist, der seine Sache Gott empfohlen hätte und seines Willens gewartet, so ist das Urtheil[2] des nächsten vorigen[3] Verses über beide Theile gegangen, und sind vertilgt allesammt,[4] die da Uebels gethan haben. Wäre aber ein Theil zu Gott bekehrt, so wäre doch das andre Theil gewißlich und eilend allein[5] untergegangen, wie dieser Vers sagt.

---

[1] Niemand, *nobody,* the opposite of jemand, *somebody,* is composed of *nie* and *man,* and in old German is written Nieman. D or de is often so appended to a word to give it strength of utterance. Niemand and jemand have no plural, and are commonly varied only in the genitive case (Niemands), though we often meet with Niemandem and Jemandem in the dative and Niemanden and Jemanden in the accusative. See p. 10, Note 5.

[2] Urtheil means originally *a judicial decision,* and in the old German and Saxon is found under the forms of *urdeli, oordel,* and or*dal,* whence or*dalium* in modern Latin, and or*deal, the judicial decision of God,* in English. *Die sele in urteile setzen,* in old German, means, *to submit one's life to the judgment of God, to submit to the ordeal.* Richardson, in his dictionary seems not to be aware of the early use of this word and its corresponding verb in the early German. The modern word for ordeal is Gottesurthiel, which is more definite. The derivative and common signification of the word Urtheil is *any judgment formed by the understanding.* An Urtheil in this sense may exist in the mind without being expressed; when it is expressed, it becomes a Satz, *a sentence,* or *declaration.*

[3] Vorigen, *preceding.* The adjective ending ig is frequently joined to particles, converting them into adjectives, as vorig, obig, hiesig, dortig, and even etwaig, from vor, oben, hier, dort, and etwa, meaning *the preceding, the above, belonging here, belonging there, that which may take place* (or incidental).

[4] Und sind vertilgt allesammt, die, etc., " and (those) who have done evil (evil-doers) are all destroyed together." This use of die for antecedent and relative, is not unlike the Biblical use of the word *that,* in such phrases, as " Other foundation can no man lay than *that* is laid." Da after this relative (die da) is regarded as an expletive.

[5] Allein, "certainly and speedily have perished *alone.*"

Darum sehen wir jetzt dieses Psalms Exempel[1] in der Welt nicht. Denn ein Jeglicher läßt Gott fahren durch Ungeduld und untersteht sich, mit Rechten oder Fechten[2] zu schützen. Damit wird Gott an solchem Werke verhindert, welches[3] dieser Psalm von ihm preist.

Aber die Elenden[4] werden das Land erben und Lust haben in großem Frieden.

Dieß bestätigt auch, was droben gesagt ist, wie die Gerechten bleiben nach dem Verderben der Uebelthäter. Nicht daß sie ewig auf Erden bleiben, sondern daß ihre Sache zum Ende und Frieden[5] mit Ehren kommt, auch auf Erden, welchen Frieden sie mit Leiden und Geduld und innerlichem Frieden verdient haben.

---

[1] Dieses Psalms Exempel, would be regarded as a harsh construction in modern German. "An exemplification of this Psalm."

[2] Mit Rechten oder Fechten, one of those alliterations in which the old German, particularly in legal phrases, abounds. "By contending at law, or by force." Infinitives used substantively. There is an old proverb, Rechten ist fechten; and another, Wer nicht kann fechten, gewinnt nichts im Rechten.

[3] Welches. This old interrogative, was not used in early times as a *relative*. It occurred less frequently in Luther's time than now. It has properly the nature and sense of an *adjective* (*which kind*, *qualis*), and must always be used after such words as solcher and others expressing quality. Solchem Werke, das, would be as much of a solecism, as *such a work*, *which*, in English. See a few lines below welchen Frieden, *which kind of peace.*

[4] Elend, in old German, elilenti and alilanti (*another land*) meant originally *an exile* (one in a foreign land). Hence, *wretched* and (as an exile is a criminal) *contemptible*. Arm, *poor*, *miserable* does not imply the same degree of wretchedness, nor does it include the idea of contempt.

[5] Zum Ende und Frieden, "their cause will come (comes) to its termination and to peace with honor."

Der Gottlose drohet den Gerechten, und beißet seine Zähne zusammen über ihn.

Das ist aber zu Trost den Weichlingen[1] und Schwach=gläubigen gesagt, die der Gottlosen Toben nicht leiden wol=len und verdrießt,[2] daß sie Gott nicht bald straft und so wohl dazu gehen läßt. Ich nenne Impium einen Gottlosen. Denn es heißt eigentlich[3] Den, der auf Gott nicht traut noch glaubt, der aus ihm selbst[4] und seinem freien Willen nach in der Natur lebt, als denn sonderlich sind die Gleißner, die Gelehrten und scheinenden Heiligen, als zu unseren Zeiten sind Pabst, Bischöfe, Pfaffen, Mönche,[5] Doctores und der=

---

[1] Zu Trost den Weichlingen, "as a consolation to the faint-hearted."

[2] Und verdriesst, "and (whom it) annoys that God does not immediately punish them, and, besides, (d a z u), allows it to go so well (with them)."

[3] Eigentlich, *in its proper and strict sense.* As applied to a word, it denotes *proper and literal signification* and is synonymous with ursprünglich. Uneigentlich, means *figuratively.*

[4] Der aus ihm selbst, etc., "who, in a state of nature, lives for himself (draws his motives *from himself*) and according to his own free will."

[5] Pabst, Bischöfe, Pfaffen, Mönche. Pabst, in old German Babst, but in the modern orthography Papst, literally means *father*, and comes not from *papa*, but from *papas*, or *pappas*, a Latin word, borrowed from the Greek, and much used in the middle ages. This form of the word for *father*, in a religious sense, was undoubtedly chosen, because the other form was appropri-ated to another use, as will be seen under the word Pfaff. Papst is applied exclusively to the bishop of Rome.—Bischof is a cor-ruption of the word *episcopus*, and corresponds in signification. So vescovo in Italian, and évêque (evesque) in French.—Pfaff, a *clergyman*, comes from *papa*, and was originally a title of honor giv-en to spiritual teachers. But the German word is not applied to the pope, nor even to bishops as such. It designates *the* or*dinary secu-lar clergy*, as distinguished from the regular clergy or monks on the one hand and from the laity (L a i e n) on the other. It was used in a good sense till about the time of the reformation, when it ceased

gleichen Volk, welche von Natur müssen, wüthen wider[1] das heilige Evangelium, wie wir sehen, daß sie auch weiblich thun. Aber was hilft sie ihr Wüthen und Toben ?[2] Höre, was da[3] folgt.

Aber der Herr lachet sein,[4] denn er sieht, daß sein Tag kömmt.

---

to be an honorable appellation; and since then P f a r r e r (P f a r r h e r r, from P f a r r e, *parish*, and H e r r) has been employed as a respectful term for an ordinary clergyman. G e i s t l i c h e r, is a general term, including bishops, secular clergy and monks. P r e d i g e r (from p r æ d i c a r e) means simply a *preacher*. That P f a f f comes from *papa* will be doubted by no one who is familiar with the frequent use of *pf* and *f* for *p* in German orthography. The following examples will sufficiently show this; P f a h l, Latin *palus;* P f a n n e, *pan;* P f a u, Latin *pavo;* P f e f f e r, *pepper;* P f e i f e, *pipe* and *fife;* P f e n n i g, *penny;* P f i r s i c h e contracted into P f i r s c h e, Latin *Persicum,* (Italian *persica* contracted into *pesca,* French *pêche* (pesche), and English *peach*); P f l a n z e, *plant;* P f l a s t e r, *plaster;* P f l a u m e, *plum;* P f l o c k, low German P l u g g e, English, *plug;* p f l ü c k e n, *to pluck;* P f o r t e, Latin *porta;* P f o s t e, *post;* P f u h l, *pool;* P f u n d, *pound;* P f a d, *path.* Most German words beginning with *pf,* are of foreign origin. —M ö n c h, and *monk*, come from *monachus* (μοναχὸς).

[1] W i d e r, *against;* g e g e n, *towards.* The former implies opposition or hostility, the latter may signify that, or may not; it depends on the connection, being itself indifferent.

[2] W ü t h e n u n d T o b e n. T o b e n means *the raving of one who, in a passion, has lost his self-possession.* It signifies *disorder* and *confusion* in passion rather than *violence,* which last is denoted by W ü t h e n, *raging,* a figure taken from the raging of the sea. See p. 38, Note 1.

[3] D a, is an expletive, like our word *there,* in such expressions as, " there is." So also after the relative d e r.

[4] L a c h e t s e i n. L a c h e t governs the genitive. In old German m e i n, d e i n, s e i n, were the genitives of i c h, d u and e r, the place of which m e i n e r, d e i n e r, s e i n e r, are now used to distinguish the genitive of the personal pronouns from the adjective pronouns, m e i n, m e i n e, m e i n; d e i n, d e i n e, d e i n; s e i n, s e i n e, s e i n. These old genitives are perserved in certain idio-

Wie möchte[1] uns ein stärkerer Trost gegeben werden, daß die wüthenden Feinde der Gerechten alle ihre Macht und Bosheit vorwenden, meinen[2] mit ganzem Ernste,[3] den Gerechten (das ist, den Gläubigen in Gott) mit Zähnen zu zerreißen, und Gott verachtet sie so gar, daß er ihrer lacht, darum daß er ansiehet, wie kurz sie wüthen werden, und ihr Tag nicht ferne ist.

Nicht daß Gott wie ein Mensch lache, sondern daß es lächerlich ist anzusehen in der Wahrheit, daß die tollen[4] Menschen so sehr wüthen und groß Ding vornehmen, dessen[5] sie nicht ein Haar breit ausrichten mögen. Gleich als ein

---

matic expressions, such as, g e d e n k e  m e i n  (m e i n e r), *remember me;* v e r g i s s  m e i n  (m e i n e r)  n i c h t, *forget me not.*

[1] W i e  m ö c h t e, etc. This sentence is a little irregular in its construction. " How could a stronger consolation be given us (than this ;—) that the furious enemies of the righteous should apply all their power and malice (and) suppose with all seriousness that they are about to rend in pieces the righteous (i. e. those who believe in God) with their teeth, and (that) God holds them in such utter contempt, that he laughs at them, because he sees how soon their rage will be over, and that their day is not far distant."

[2] M e i n e n, (low German  m e e n e n, English *mean*) signifies, *to hold an opinion without absolutely affirming its truth, to be of opinion.* W ä h n e n, (English *ween*) *to suppose,* or *to hold an opinion without good reason.* Hence commonly, *to imagine or suppose falsely.*

[3] E r n s t, as an adjective, was formerly written  e r n e s t and means the same as the English adjective *earnest.* As a substantive, it means, *earnestness, seriousness.*

[4] T o l l e n.  T o l l, *foolish, irrational, mad,* conveys very nearly the same idea as w ü t h e n d, *raging* (see w ü t h e n d e  F e i n d e, a few lines above), and hence the propriety of saying that d i e  t o l - l e n  M e n s c h e n  w ü t h e n; but it comes still nearer to t o - b e n d, *boisterous, ranting* (see p. 46, Note 2) as it represents one out of his senses as it were, like an insane person. Hence T o l l - h a u s, *mad-house,* e i n  t o l l e r  H u n d, *a mad dog.*  R a s e n d is r*aving,* opposed to *quiet,* as t o l l is to r*ational.*

[5] D e s s e n, is governed by H a a r, " of which they cannot bring a hair in breadth (a hair's breadth) to pass."

lächerlicher Mann wäre, der[1] einen langen Spieß und kur=
zen Degen nähme, und wollte die Sonne vom Himmel her=
abstechen, und jauchzte einmal[2] darauf, als hätte er einen
redlichen Stich gethan.

Die Gottlosen ziehen das Schwert aus
und spannen[3] ihren Bogen, daß sie fällen
den Elenden und Armen, und schlachten die,
so aufrichtig gehen im Wege.[4]

Schwert und Bogen heißen[5] hier die vergifteten bösen

---

[1] Gleich als ein lächerlicher Mann wäre (der)
der, " he who," etc.

[2] Einmal, like once in English, has two significations, the one
definite when the accent is on ein, the other indefinite when the
accent is on mal, thus, 1. *one single time*, as ich habe ihn nur
einmal gesehen, *I have seen him but once*; 2. *at some indefinite
time*, past, present, or future, as, es war einmal ein Mann,
*there was once a man*. In this last sense it is often used for emphasis merely and is not to be translated, or may be rendered by *even*,
as, denke dir einmal! *Only think!* (dir an expletive), ich
kenne ihn nicht einmal, *I do not even know him.*—" And
then (einmal) should shout over it, as if he had given (it) a real
thrust."

[3] Spannen, means, *to stretch*, (or bend) any elastic body; *to
stretch the fingers apart* and to form a Spanne, *span*, from the end
of the thumb to that of the little finger; (of animals) *to stretch or
prick up the ears; to fasten into any instrument* or machine as a lathe
by *straining it tight; to bind anything on with* ropes or *chains; to
harness a horse* (anspannen) by binding him close to the carriage (das Gespann, *a team so fastened;* der Gespann, *a
mate*, as if harnessed with another—used only in sport); also *to fetter a horse; to strain or pinch*, of a garment or shoe; and then figuratively *to strain and overstrain in any way.*

[4] So aufrichtig gehen im Wege, in the Hebrew sense,
" who walk uprightly in *their ways.*"

[5] Heissen, *to call*, (governing two accusatives, Adam hiess
sein Weib Eva); *to call for, to order a thing*, which is a milder
term than befehlen, gebieten (the accusative of the person
with an infinitive, as Er hiess mich kommen or the dative

Zungen,[1] damit sie lästern, schmähen, verkehren, verklagen und schänden die Sache des Gerechten, auf daß die Frommen[2] in Haß, Verfolgung und zum Tode dadurch kommen und vertilgt werden möchten.

Also spricht Ps. 57: „Der Menschenkinder Zungen sind Waffen[3] und Pfeile, und ihre Zunge ist ein scharfes Schwert," damit hauen sie[4] nach dem Gerechten, ob sie ihn fällen möchten und schlachten; das ist, nicht allein tödten, sondern nach ihrem Muthwillen in ihm wühlen und sudeln.

Er nennt auch die Gerechten den Geringen und Armen, darum daß sie vor der großen hochmüthigen Schwulst und

---

of the person and accusative of the thing; as Höre, was ich dir heisse). As a *neuter* verb (and so it is here used), it has a passive signification (*to be called*), or a mere explanatory sense, as, das heisst, *that is*, that *means*, or *is equivalent to*. Es heisst, means, *it is said*.

[1] Zungen. Zunge, *tongue.* Z often takes the place of *t* in English; as Zehe, *toe;* Zehn, *ten;* Zeichen, old Saxon *teken*, English *token;* Zinn, *tin;* Zipf, *tip;* Zoll, *toll;* Zwanzig, *twenty;* Zweig, *twig;* Zwei (old German zwo, fem. and zween, masc, *twain*), *two;* zwölf, *twelve.*

[2] Die Frommen. Fromm is a word of very wide signification, originally *that which forwards one's designs, useful, profitable.* This sense prevails in the verb frommen. Then, it meant *excellent, valuable, good;* applied to a man's moral character, *pious, religious;* applied to God, *benevolent, compassionate,* and so applied also to others; applied to animals, *innocent, harmless;* ein frommer Hund, *a dog that does not bite;* ein frommes Pferd, *a gentle horse,* and so sometimes when applied to persons, particularly to children.

[3] Waffen, old Saxon *wapan*, Anglo-Saxon *wæpen*, English *weapon*, any kind of armour whether offensive or defensive.

[4] Damit hauen sie, etc., " with which they strike at the righteous man that (if) they may strike him down and slay him, that is, not merely kill him, but roll the body (him) about and besmear it according to their pleasure."

**5**

Blasen[1] der Gottlosen verachtet und geringe sind. Aber was richten sie aus?[2] Höre:

Aber ihr Schwert wird in ihr Herz gehen und ihr Bogen wird zerbrechen.

---

[1] Schwulst und Blasen, *swelling and puffing*. The former is a substantive, and the latter an infinitive used substantively. Both, of course, are used here figuratively. Schwulst, literally, *a swelling tumor* for which the word Geschwulst is much more common. Figuratively, it is applied to a swollen style of speaking and writing, and means, *bombast, rant*. Blasen means *to blow*, in the widest sense of this term; in a restricted sense, it means *to blow with the mouth;* and figuratively, *to puff and swell*.

[2] Richten sie aus. Richten means, *to put straight, to put in order, to put right*, from which a variety of other significations are derived. Ausrichten, is *to carry a thing out properly to its end*, and hence to accomplish. Einrichten, *to bring a thing into its proper place* or order, *to arrange, to adjust*. Anrichten, *to arrange* or prepare a thing *for* something else, as food for the table, (mostly limited to such a use); *to occasion* (something evil). Aufrichten, *to erect, to build;* figuratively, *to raise up, and comfort*. Errichten, to build up, to complete that which is angelegt, or has a foundation already laid; figuratively, it is limited chiefly to *establishing universities* and *forming leagues*. Gardens, groves, nurseries for trees, ditches, pools, as also lower schools, factories, etc. are angelegt, (laid out) as they are on the surface of the ground or figuratively represented as low and inferior; buildings, trees and anything *raised up* in establishing it, are errichtet. Convents, hospitals, poor-houses, monuments and the like are gestiftet. Entrichten, is *to pay one's debts, taxes*, etc., i. e. to do what is right *towards* (ent) another in regard to payment. Hinrichten, *to direct a thing to its place*, to carry a criminal to execution, or to execute, to destroy. Verrichten, generally of mechanical labor, *to do* or *perform;* to carry a business forth (ver, away, to its end) to its completion. Zurichten, *to direct a thing or aim it towards* (zu) *its object; to fit* or *prepare*. This word is used in a much wider and looser sense and in more connections than anrichten. Abrichten, (in mechanical arts,) *to prepare work*, to fit it or make it ready by putting in order whatever is necessary; also, to teach any thing mechanically to men or animals, in a much lower sense than unterrichten.

Das ist: ihre bösen Worte müssen sie wieder freffen,[1] und ewiglich daran erwürgen, daß ihr Gewissen im Sterben damit durchstochen ewiglich wird gepeinigt. Dazu der Bogen[2] wird zerbrechen, daß Alles vergebens[3] ist und sie nichts ausrichten mit all ihrem Wüthen, denn daß sie ihnen selbst solches Unglück zurichten ewiglich, das arme elende Volk. Darum soll sich ihres Haffens und Schändens Niemand entfetzen,[4] es muß also feyn, daß sie ihnen selbst das Bad in der Hölle wohl bereiten, wiewohl die Natur solche schwere Läfterworte ungern leidet. Doch der Geist, nach diesem Psalm gerichtet, lachet ihrer mit Gott und sieht auf ihr Ende.

----

[1] F r e s s e n and e s s e n are thus distinguished by an old writer. E i n  W o l f  s o l l  f r e s s e n, e i n  M e n s c h  s o l l  e s s e n. Thus, f r e s s e n means *to eat greedily or devour;* e s s e n, *to eat.* So s a u f e n, *to drink like a beast,* t r i n k e n, *to drink like a man.* "Their malicious words shall devour them, and forever torment (strangle) them in this (d a r a n) that their conscience, filled with compunction (punctured) thereby, will be tormented forever. Besides (d a z u, *in addition to this*) the bow shall be broken, so that all is in vain, and they effect nothing by all their rage but (d e n n, like a l s; n i c h t s  d e n n, *nothing else than*) that they prepare for themselves forever such wretchedness—poor, miserable people ! Therefore should no one be terrified at their hate and abuse; so it must be in order that they may prepare for themselves a bed (bath) in hell, although (human) nature bears unwillingly such severe reproaches. Yet the spirit (as opposed to the flesh, or nature) regulated by this psalm laughs at them as God does (with God) and looks at their end."

[2] B o g e n, *a bow,* from b i e g e n, *to bend,* has a passive signification, *anything bent* (corresponding to g e b o g e n, *bent*), and therein differs from the active forms, B i e g u n g, *the act of bending,* and B i e g e, *the bend.* It means, *a bow, an arch, a crooked path,* or *a sheet of paper* (from its being doubled together).

[3] V e r g e b e n s, *in vain;* literally, *given away,* given to no purpose, or falsely.

[4] E n t s e t z e n, as an *active* verb, *to put one* (s e t z e n) *away* or out of his place (e n t); as a reflective verb, *to be put out of one's self.* i. e. *to be terrified* or *amazed in a very high degree.*

Es iſt beſſer[1] das Wenige des Gerechten, denn das große Gut[2] der Gottloſen.

Das iſt auch verdrießlich der Natur, daß die Gottloſen reich ſind und ihrer viel[3] und mächtig: aber der Gerechte iſt arm und allein, hat auch wenig, und ſie nehmen ihm dazu das Seine,[4] hindern ihn auch an der Nahrung. Darum tröſtet der heilige Geiſt ſein liebes Kind und ſpricht: Laß dich es nicht verdrießen, daß du wenig, ſie viel haben; laß ſie hier reich und ſatt ſeyn, es iſt dir beſſer, daß du ein wenig habeſt mit Gottes Gunſt,[5] denn ob[6] du große Haufen

---

[1] E s i s t b e s s e r, etc. When in a simple sentence a verb precedes its nominative, the expletive e s must come before the verb. "The little of the righteous is better than, etc."

[2] D a s G u t, ordinarily means as it does here, *an estate, property.* The plural, d i e G ü t e r, means generally, *goods, possessions;* but sometimes is applied to the possessions of the mind, or mental attainments. D a s G u t e, is the abstract form, *the good,* as we say, *the sublime, the beautiful.* G ü t e, means *goodness, kindness,* although the latter is more perfectly expressed by G ü t i g h e i t which is rarely used. So g u t, *good;* and g ü t i g, *kind.*

[3] R e i c h s i n d u n d i h r e r v i e l, etc. "are rich and many of them and powerful."

[4] U n d s i e n e h m e n i h m d a s S e i n e, "and besides they take from him what he has." I h m, *from him.* This idea (from) does not lie in the dative so much as it does in n e h m e n, *to take away;* and "to take away with reference to him," (the dative merely shows the indirect object of the action) is the same in sense, as "to take away from him." The Germans cannot use s e i n substantively for "his own," but must prefix the article and give it the form of the neuter adjective used as an abstract noun.

[5] G u n s t, *favor,* comes from g ö n n e n, *to favor, to grant.* St is a mere euphonic addition to the root. The vowel of the root is in such cases, ordinarily changed into *u.* This addition of *st* is limited to those verbs whose roots end with a liquid. So K u n s t from k e n n e n; B r u n s t, from b r e n n e n; R u n s t, from r i n n e n; S c h w u l s t from s c h w e l l e n.

[6] D e n n o b, etc. "than if you had great piles of goods, not only of one, but of many and of all the ungodly," etc.

Güter, nicht allein eines, sondern vieler und aller Gottlosen hättest mit Gottes Ungunst, wie sie haben. Auch höre, was für ein[1] Urtheil geht über deine Armuth und ihren Reich=thum.

Denn der Arm der Gottlosen wird zer=brechen, aber der Herr erhält die Gerech=ten.

Der Arm und Hand sind der Anhang[2] der Gottlosen, daß ihrer Viele zusammenhalten, und dadurch sind sie groß, mächtig und stark; gleichwie jetzt des Pabstes Arme sind die Könige,[3] Fürsten,[4] Bischöfe, Gelehrte, Pfaffen und

---

[1] **Was für ein,** *what kind of.* This phrase for describing the quality or character of a thing, is to be explained by a reference to the peculiar use of **für** in German. In English, we say, " he holds a thing to be good ;" the Germans say, " he holds it *for* good." Hence **Was für,** means " what it is held to be," and hence " of what kind it is."

[2] **Anhang.** Observe here the resemblance of several successive words to the English. **Arm, und, Hand, Anhang** (Eng. hang,) **Gottlos** (godless). **Hangen** signifies *to hang;* **Hang,** *declivity,* and (then as derived from this) *propensity.* **Abhang,** *precipice,* is a still stronger term for declivity, and is much more frequently used than **Hang. Anhang,** *appendix,* and (as applied to persons) *adherents, party.* **Vorhang,** something hung before, i. e. *a curtain* hung *before* a window, stage, etc. **Umhang,** a curtain hung *around* a bed, etc. **Aushang,** something hung out for show, as *show goods,* **Aushänge-schild,** *a sign-board.*

[3] **Könige.** The orthography of this word is various in the old German. Among other forms we find **Künic, Künc** and **King.** So, **Der edel king von franckenrieche** by one of the Meistersingers. The word comes from **Künne,** *race, genealogy,* i. e. noble race. This agrees well with what Tacitus says of the Germans, *Reges ex nobilitate sumunt.* Richardson on the word, *king,* is incorrect, or, at least, is at variance with the best German authorities.

[4] **Fürst,** is the superlative of **für** the old form of **vor,** *the foremost, the first,* and hence, *the leader,* like the Latin *princeps,* and the English *prince.*

5*

Mönche, auf welche er sich verläßt[1] und Gott nicht achtet.

Also hat ein jeglicher Gottlose den Haufen, die Gewalti=
gen auf seiner Seite.   Denn Reichthum und Gewalt[2] hat
noch nie oder gar wenig auf des Gerechten Seite gestanden.

Aber was hilft es?[3]   Traue nur Gott, es muß Alles
zerbrochen werden, darfst[4] dich darob nicht entsetzen noch
dich verdrießen lassen, Gott enthält[5] dich, du wirst nicht ver=
sinken, sein Arm und seine Hand ist über dir und hat dich
fest gefaßt.

Der Herr kennt[6] die Tage der Frommen,
und ihr Erbe wird ewiglich bleiben.

---

[1] **Verlässt. Verlassen** signifies, *to give up,* or abandon,
(**lassen,** *to leave,* **ver,** *away*).   **Sich verlassen auf,** means
*to give one's self up* (**auf**) *to something,* i. e. to rely on it, or trust
in it.

[2] **Gewalt,** from **walten,** *to control,* means *controling power*
which involves the idea of superiority, or ability to compel.   Neither **Macht,** *might, power,* nor **Stärke,** *strength,* conveys this
*relative* idea of power.   **Stärke** has reference to physical energy
as resulting from a vigorous body.   **Kraft** refers to efficiency, or
producing effect.   A medicine may have **Stärke,** or *be strong,* and
yet not have **Kraft,** or *be effective.*

[3] **Was hilft es?** "What does it avail them?"   So, **es hilft
nichts,** *it avails nothing, it is of no use.*   See p. 39, Note 3.

[4] **Dürfen** is rarely used in its original signification, *to dare.*
**Wagen** is used in its stead.   It commonly means *to have the power or liberty to do a thing* (may, can).   **Nicht dürfen,** implies
that one is prevented by a want of permission, reason, or propriety (i. e.
*may not, must not,* because it is not allowed, is not proper, or there is
no good reason).   Then it means furthermore, *to need,* though **bedürfen** and **brauchen** are much more common in this sense.

[5] **Enthält. Enthalten,** as a reflective verb signifies *to restrain one's self.*   As an *active* verb, it means, *to contain.*   In old German it also meant *to aid, to uphold.*   So Luther uses it here, and
in many passages in his version of the Scriptures.

[6] **Kennen** and **wissen** differ as *connoître* and *savoir* do in
French.   The former means *to know so as to distinguish or recognize,*
and approaches to **erkennen** in sense, *to recognize.*   Thus:

Gott erkennt ihre Tage, ihre Gelegenheit,[1] daß ist, die=
weil sie ihm frei glauben und nicht wissen wollen, wenn und
wie ihnen zu helfen sey, so nimmt Gott sich ihrer an,[2] und
ob es vor den Gottlosen scheint, als habe Gott ihrer verges=
sen, so ist es doch nicht also, Gott weiß wohl, wenn ihre
Zeit ist, ihnen zu helfen. Wie auch Psalm 9: „Gott ist
ein Helfer zu rechter Zeit," und Ps. 31: „Meine Zeit steht
in deinen Händen." Als wollte er sagen: Sie sind arm
und wenig,[3] Jene sind reich und mächtig; aber laß gehen,
sie werden dennoch genug haben und keine Noth leiden.
Gott weiß wohl, wenn es Zeit ist, ihnen zu helfen und zu

---

Ich kenne ihn dem Namen nach—von Gesicht, *I
know him* (can distinguish him) *by name—by sight.* Wissen can
never be so used. Hence it is applied more to things than to persons.
In fact so broad is the distinction that the Germans never treat them
as synonyms. Observe the use of these three words in this and the
following lines.

[1] Gelegenheit means, literally, *situation.* From the local
idea is derived that of *situation in respect to circumstances,* i. e. *condition,* and finally, *occasion.*

[2] So nimmt Gott sich ihrer an. "Since they voluntarily trust in him, and do not desire to know when and how they
are to be helped (it is to help them), *he takes care of them.*" Annehmen means *to accept,* to take what is offered, or is at hand. Einen Rath, eine Meinung annehmen, *to accept,* or
*adopt, advice, an opinion.* Angennommen is sometimes equi-
volent to verstellt, *affected, pretended, assumed;* and sometimes
to gesetzt, *taken for granted.* Sich annehmen with the
genitive, *to take an interest in, to feel a concern for,* literally *to put
one's self,* or *engage* (sich nehmen) *in* (an) *something.* For this
wide use of the genitive, corresponding to all the relations expressed by von, vor and an, see Gram. p. 326.

[3] Wenig, in the old German often written weinig, comes
from weinen, to lament, and signifies in the oldest writers, *la-
mentable, deplorable;* then it came to signify *weak and small,* for
which gering and klein are now used; and finally *a small portion either of a mass or number,* i. e. *little, few.* The connection here
shows that wenig is used in its ancient sense; for it is opposed to
mächtig as arm is to reich.

rathen, welchem sie auch trauen, ohne eigene Hülfe und Rath zu suchen.

Dazu wird ihr Erbe seyn ewig, nicht allein in jener Welt, sondern auch in dieser Welt. Denn sie werden müssen immer genug haben. Ob sie wohl nicht überflüssigen Vorrath[1] haben wie die Gottlosen; Gott ist ihr Vorrath und Kornboden, Weinkeller und all ihre Gut.[2] Darum auch folgt:

Sie werden nicht zu Schanden[3] in der bösen Zeit, und in der Theurung werden sie genug haben.

Wenn Krieg oder theure Zeit kommt, so werden die Alle zu Schanden, die ihren Trost auf ihren Kornboden und

---

[1] **Ueberflüssigen Vorrath.** Compare the etymology of these words with that of *superfluous* and *provisions.*

[2] **All ihre Gut,** "and all their property." We should here expect **alles** instead of **all,** for the termination **es** in modern German is properly omitted only when no particular stress is to be laid on the word. But **all** seems to be emphatic here. The old writers indulged in much greater freedom in such matters than those of later times. That license has descended to us in many forms of expression in which the word **all** occurs, for it is frequently undeclined before a substantive, and declined when it comes after; as **bei all dem** and **bei dem allen,** *in all this;* **der Wein ist shon alle** (i. e. *all gone*); and a few lines below **die Alle,** those all, or "all those, who have put their trust, etc."

[3] **Sie werden nicht zu Schanden,** *they are not disgraced.* **Schande** means literally *shame* arising from improper exposure of the person, also from the *marring* or *disfiguring of the body.* This will best account for the use of the plural (which occurs only in the expressions **zu Schanden, mit Schanden,** both occurring in this and the following paragraph), each mutilation being regarded as a disgrace. The plural is often, as in the passage before us, used in the derivative and more common signification of *disgrace.* **Werden zu Schenden** *to come to disgrace.* **Schimpf,** originally *sport,* now signifies *derision, reproach;* **Schmach,** *contumely, contemptuous treatment.*

Weinkeller oder Gut gestellt haben; denn es ist bald ver=
schlungen und umgebracht.[1] So stehen sie denn übel und
mit Schanden, die zuvor so muthig und stolz gewesen sind.
Aber die Gerechten, weil Gott ihr Trost und Vorrath ist,
mögen nicht Mangel haben, es müßten eher[2] alle Engel vom
Himmel kommen und sie speisen. Denn der Vorrath läßt
sie mangeln, dem sie trauen, weder zeitlich noch ewiglich.
Wie aber die Gottlosen? Höre zu:

Denn die Gottlosen werden umkommen[3]
und die Feinde des Herrn, wenn sie gleich
sind wie eine köstliche Aue,[4] werden sie doch
alle[5] werden, wie der Rauch alle wird.

---

[1] Umgebracht. Umbringen, in the sense of *destroying a
thing*, is now used only in common life, although, to *spoil and destroy in war*, appears to have been its original signification. So it
seems to be employed by Luther. It now generally means, *to put
one violently to death*, always, however, *illegally*, and in this it differs
from hinrichten, *to execute.*—Es refers to Gut.

[2] Eher, *sooner*, is undoubtedly the same word as the English
*ere*, and the superlative erst, *first*, the same as the obsolete English
word *erst*.

[3] Umkommen, more fully um das Leben kommen, *to
come to one's end.* *Um* in many cases means, *around* a thing as taking
the measure of it, and when one has come round to the point where
he began, he has reached the *end* of the measure. Hence um,
means often, *to the end.* In the word umbringen, i. e. um das
Leben bringen, in the sense of *to kill*, probably is to be explained in the same way, *to bring one to his end;* but in the sense of
*plundering* and *destroying* it may, perhaps, find an easier explanation in the *marauding movements* of an army.

[4] Aue or Au. Gothic ahwa, kindred with *aqua*, signifies originally, *a stream of water;* then *the rich vale lying along a stream*,
and now its most common meaning is, *a rich meadow as a pasturage*,
whereas Wiese means *a rich meadow* (literally a meadow *clothed
with* grass) *from which the grass is to be cut.*

[5] Alle, as an adverb, signifies *all gone*, and is now used only in
common life, as, das Geld ist alle, *the money is exhausted;*
es ist alle, *it is all gone;* er hat sein väterliches Ver-

Das ist je nahe[1] geredet und verächtlich geurtheilt die großen mächtigen reichen Junker. Er spricht: „Ob sie gleich[2] wären die allerreichste und köstlichste Aue," darinnen übrig genug wüchse, wie sie denn auch sind, denn sie haben genug. Sie sind die goldene reiche Aue in der Welt; dennoch müssen sie untergehen, ja vergehen, und Alle werden wie der Rauch. Wo sind sie, die zuvor gewesen und großes Gut gehabt? Es ist ihrer Keiner im Gedächtniß: aber die Gerechten sind in gutem Gedächtnisse und in allen Ehren.

Darum, liebes Kind, laß sie reich seyn wie sie wollen, siehe auf's Ende, so wirst du finden, wie alles ihr Ding[3] ein

---

mögen alle gemacht, *he has wasted his paternal estate;* Wein alle machen, *to consume all the wine;* est ist alle mit mir, *it is all over with me* (actum est de me), I am ruined; alle werden, *to be consumed,*—" will be consumed or pass away as the smoke is consumed, or passes away."

[1] Nahe, *near,* is often employed in an idiomatic way. Thus einen etwas nahe legen, means, *to bring a thing so closely home upon one that he will feel it.* Nahe reden, means, *to speak home upon one,* to thrust him through with sharp words. Zu nahe treten, *to infringe upon one's rights,* to offend him by some impropriety. Ihm ist zu nahe geschehen, *injustice is done him.* Es geht mir nahe, *it goes near my heart,* it troubles or pains me. Zu nahe, in such idioms, is very similar in meaning to our phrase, *too far,* to carry a thing beyond what is proper. What is *too far towards one,* or too near to him, is of course, *too sensitively felt,* and becomes offensive.—The sentence has the irregularity of a colloquial, pointed saying. "That is, indeed (je for ja) speaking to the quick, and deciding with contempt,—the great, the mighty, the rich nabobs!" That is, they are summarily disposed of. Junker stands for junger Herr, *a young nobleman,* or *a gentleman of rank,* as Jungfer stands for junge Frau.

[2] Ob sie gleich, etc. "Even though they were the richest and finest meadows, in which there should be a superabundant growth (as they really are, for they have abundance. They are the golden rich meadows in the world) *still* they must perish, nay vanish and pass away as the smoke."

[3] Ding, designates *whatever is,* or *exists,* and is often equivalent

Rauch ist, darum daß sie Gottes Feinde sind und ihm die Seinen[1] hassen und verfolgen. Dazu laß dich das auch trösten, daß er sie nennt Gottes Feinde, so doch[2] bisher sie nur deine Feinde genannt sind, auf daß du wissest,[3] wie sich Gott seiner also annimmt, daß deine Feinde[4] seine Feinde sind.

---

to etwas. Sache, is a species included under the genus Ding, excluding persons, whereas Ding includes them. Sache must always be some object of human pursuit, occupation or interest. Ding, is subject to no such limitation. Es ist nicht meine Sache (*business*—not Ding, *thing*) dass ich Complimente mache, *it is not my business to make compliments.* Eure Sache (*cause, interest*, not Ding) nicht allein, ich habe meine eigne auszufechten, *I have to fight out not only your cause, but my own.*—Personen und Sachen, not Personen und Dinge, which would make no contrast. Meine Sachen, *my baggage*, *things pertaining to me*, not meine Dinge, in this sense. Occurrences and a course of events are Sachen but not Dinge. On the contrary Gott ist der Schöpfer aller Dinge (not Sachen). Dinge, not Sachen may be imaginary; er geht mit grossen Dingen (not Sachen) um, *he has wonderful projects in his head.* Guter Dinge (not Sache) seyn, *to be cheerful.* When a definite object or person is called a *thing* by way of indefiniteness, Ding only is used. This is most frequent in speaking of young girls, as das Madchen ist ein albernes Ding, *the girl is a silly thing.* In old German, Ding was also used in the sense of *property*, and so here by Luther. Gegenstand like our word *object*, always implies a *subject* or person, to perceive or contemplate it.

[1] Ihm die Seinen. Ihm, as in many other instances, the dative is not to be rendered. It is so remotely connected as the indirect object of the verb as to be regarded as an expletive, although it is not strictly so. See Gram. p. 347.

[2] So doch, *whereas.*

[3] Auf dass du wissest, "in order that you may know that (how) God so interests himself in his own (seiner for der Seinigen?) that, etc." Ordinarily the subjunctive is employed in such dependent clauses as express design; but when the clause is to be rendered particularly forcible, the indicative is used.

[4] Feind (old German fiant and feient) was originally a

Der Gottlose borgt[1] und zahlt nicht;
der Gerechte aber ist barmherzig und
milde.[2]

Das ist aber ein tröstlicher Unterschied der Gemüther,[3]
daß der Gottlosen Güter nicht allein vergänglich sind und
ein Ende haben, sondern auch böse Güter sind und ver-

---

present participle from f i a n, *to hate,* as H e i l a n d (H e i l a n t),
*Savior,* was a participle from h e i l e n (h e i l a n, old German);
F r e u n d (old German, F r i u n t), *a friend,* from f r i j o n, *to love·*
F e i n d, means *a bitter, malignant enemy;* and hence the word is
often applied to *Satan,* which is the prevailing use of the same word,
*fiend* in English. W i d e r s a c h e r, (originally, an adversary at
law), now generally signifies *one who seeks to harm another.* As
g e g e n implies less opposition than w i d e r, so G e g n e r means
*an opponent,* who yet may be a friend.

[1] B o r g t. B o r g e n, l e i h e n, and l e h n e n all have this
remarkable peculiarity, that they signify *both to lend and to borrow.*
This always perplexes a student till he observes.that e i n e m e t-
w a s b o r g e n, l e i h e n or l e h n e n, always means *to lend something to another,* while e t w a s v o n j e m a n d b o r g e n, l e i-
h e n, or l e h n e n always means *to borrow something of some one.*
Observe, then, whether the dative of the person is used *with* or *without* the preposition v o n, and that will decide the meaning. B o r-
g e n is used of moveable property, but not of landed estates. L e i-
h e n and l e h n e n are used of both, and often means to *rent* or
*hire.* These last two have the same signification, but l e i h e n is
the more dignified word and l e h n e n the more vulgar. This last
sometimes means in good usage, *to enfeoff.* B o r g e n frequently
means *to buy* (v o n e i n e m) or *sell* (e i n e m) *goods on* credit.

[2] M i l d e, means the same as the English word *mild,* but has a
secondary sense which the English word has not, viz., *benevolent, beneficent.* E i n m i l d e r G e b e r, e i n e m i l d e G a b e, *a benevolent giver, a benevolent gift.* S e i n e m i l d e h a n d a u f-
t h u n, *to open his liberal hand.* M i l d e S t i f t u n g e n, *benevolent institutions.* M i l d t h ä t i g k e i t, *liberality, benevolence.*

[3] G e m ü t h e r. G e m u t h means *animus, sensus, feelings, dispositions,* as distinguished from G e i s t, V e r n u n f t, *mens, ratio.*
G e m ü t h e r, here stands for *characters, different dispositions* of the
righteous and the wicked.

dammlich,¹ darum daß sie nur auf Haufen gesammelt und nicht den Dürftigen mitgetheilt werden, welches wider die Natur der Gemüther ist.

Aber der Gerechten Gut² hat nicht allein kein Ende, darum daß er Gott traut und sein Gut von ihm wartet, sondern ist auch ein recht nützlich Gut, das Andern mitgetheilt und nicht auf einen Haufen gesammelt.³ Also hat er genug ohne allen zeitlichen Vorrath, und giebt auch Andern genug. Das heißt⁴ ein recht Gut. Hast du nicht viel, so ist es doch göttlich und nützlich.⁵ Die Gottlosen haben viel, aber unchristlich und unnützlich.

Daß er aber sagt: „Der Gottlose borget,‟ ist nicht zu verstehen, daß die Reichen von den Menschen Gut entlehnen, sondern es ist gesagt in einem Gleichniß und Sprüchwort: Gleich als der da viel borgt⁶ und nicht bezahlt, darnach

---

¹ Böse Güter sind und verdammlich, "are evil possessions and damnable." Observe that the adjective böse is declined because it precedes its substantive, whereas verdammlich is undeclined on account of its coming after its substantive, and being regarded as a mere predicate (die Güter sind verdammlich).—Natur der Gemüther, which (i. e. to be hoarded up niggardly) is contrary to the nature of mind, or spiritual possessions.

² Der Gerechten Gut, "the property of the righteous."

³ Mitgetheilt und nicht auf einen Haufen gesammelt (wird).

⁴ Heisst, is. See p. 48, Note 5.

⁵ So ist es doch göttlich und nützlich, yet it (what you have) is godly and useful.

⁶ Gleich als (der) der da viel borgt. "As he who borrows much and does not repay, strives (unconsciously) for this, (namely) that he shall not long remain in his possessions (i. e. endangers his property), just so all the rich and ungodly (i. e. all who are rich and ungodly) receive much from God, accumulate and borrow from him, and yet do not repay him by giving (in that they give) to the poor, for which end it was given them. Therefore [this is the completion of the comparison] their estate will have a bad end and pass away as the smoke. That this is the meaning is proved (by the

ſtrebt, daß er nicht lange im Gute ſitzen will; alſo alle Rei=
chen und Gottloſen empfangen viel von Gott, ſammeln und
borgen von ihm, und zahlen ihn doch nicht, daß ſie den Dürf=
tigen austheilen, wozu es ihnen gegeben wird. Deßwegen
wird ihr Gut ein böſes Ende nehmen und wie der Rauch
vergehen. Daß dieß die Meinung ſey, beweist, daß er ſie
gegen einander hält, den Gottloſen und den Gerechten; der
Eine giebt, der Andre nicht, und empfangen doch Beide von
Gott.

Darum iſt des Gottloſen Empfangen verglichen dem Bor=
gen und nicht Bezahlen. Aber des Gerechten Gut iſt nicht
Borgen noch Schuld, ſondern frei von Gott empfangen und
nützlich gebraucht ihm und ſeinem Nächſten.

Denn ſeine Geſegneten[1] erben das Land,
aber ſeine Verfluchten werden ausgerot=
tet.

Siehe da, er nennt die gottloſen Reichen Gottes Verma=
ledeite[2] und die Gläubigen Gottes Gebenedeite, auf daß dich

---

circumstance, or proves the circumstance) that he (the sacred writer)
holds them side by side (by way of comparison), the wicked and the
righteous; the one gives, the other does not, and yet both receive
from God."

" Therefore the act of receiving on the part of the wicked, is compared to borrowing and not paying. But the property of the righteous is neither borrowing nor debt, but (something) freely received
from God and used advantageously for him (God) and one's (his)
neighbor."

[1] Seine Gesegneten. " His blessed," i. e. those blessed of
him. Segen is a corruption of *signum, a sign*, and segnen a
corruption of *signare, to make a sign*. When Christianity was introduced into Germany, these words, as designating the sign of the
cross, were introduced with it. As the sign of the cross was made
in benedictions, the sign itself came to stand for benediction. In the
old German, the word is found in its original meaning, *signum* and
*vexillum*.

[2] Vermaledeien and maledeien from the Latin *male-*

ja nichts[1] verdrieße, noch deinen Glauben hindere ihr großes Gut und deine Armuth. Was willst du mehr? Ist das nicht Trostes genug[2] zur Geduld? Hast du nicht überflüssig,[3] wie sie haben, so wirst du dennoch genug haben und das Land besitzen.

Nicht daß du ein Herr der Welt seyest,[4] sondern du wirst Gutes genug haben auf Erden, und im Lande wohnen mit gutem Frieden. Denn Gott benedeiet dich zeitlich und ewiglich, darum daß du ihm trauest, ob du wohl von den Gottlosen vermaledeit und beschädigt wirst. Wiederum, die gottlosen Reichen, ob sie jetzt eine Zeitlang überflüssig haben, so werden sie doch verderben und nicht im Lande und Gute sitzen bleiben,[5] sie werden gewißlich ausgeschöpft und ein

---

*dicere*, and b e n e d e i e n from *benedicere*, are antiquated words, for which v e r f l u c h e n and s e g n e n are now commonly used.

[1] N i c h t s, here used adverbially, *in nothing*, as a stronger expression than n i c h t. I h r g r o s s e s G u t u n d d e i n e A r m u t h, all put together as making out one condition of inequality, forms the nominative to v e r d r i e s s e and h i n d e r e. " That their great riches and your poverty may not vex you nor hinder your faith."

[2] T r o s t e s g e n u g, *enough of encouragement.*

[3] H a s t d u n i c h t ü b e r f l ü s s i g, "aboundest thou not," i. e. if thou dost not abound. The substantive for property or riches is understood.

[4] S e y e s t. The conjunctive is used particularly in all those dependent clauses, which, instead of positively asserting a thing, state it problematically, or as a mere supposition or conception of the mind. T r a u e s t and b e s c h ä d i g t w i r s t, a few lines below, by being in the indicative, represent the subject, as a matter of fact, and not as a supposition. The conjunctive might have been used, but with a different shade of meaning.

[5] S i t z e n b l e i b e n, *to continue to sit*, or *to remain sitting.* B l e i b e n and several other verbs take an infinitive where in English a participle would be used. L i e g e n, s i t z e n, or s t e h e n b l e i b e n, means *to continue lying, sitting or standing*, i. e. not to move, or not to rise. W o s i n d w i r s t e h e n g e b l i e b e n,

Anderer drein gesetzt, darum daß sie Gott vermaledeit und ihnen entzieht seine Gnade zeitlich und ewiglich. Denn sie glauben nicht an ihn, ob sie wohl von Menschen gebenedeit und begabt werden.

Darum wo die Gerechten sind, da haben sie genug auf Erden, und bleiben im Gute sitzen. Wiederum, die Gottlosen werden ausgewurzelt, wo sie sitzen in Gütern. Das beweisen alle Fürstenthümer, Reiche[1] und große Güter, die wir sehen,[2] wie sie hin und her fahren von einem Geschlechte zum andern.

Siehe, so hast du[3] das Urtheil über die zeitlichen Güter, das kürzlich beschlossen ist. Der Gerechte muß genug haben und der Ungerechte verderben, darum daß der Gerechte Gott trauet und der Güter wohl braucht; der Gottlose trauet nicht und brauchet ihrer nicht wohl.

Also lesen wir, daß Abraham und Loth reich waren und

---

*where did we stop?* (where have we remained stopping?). S i t z e n, *to sit,* means here, *to be in possession of,* (to sit in the enjoyment of).

[1] R e i c h e, *kingdoms.* This word, and the adjective r e i c h, *rich,* come from the verb r e i c h e n, *to extend.* They refer to *extent* of territory and of power. R e i c h was formerly applied to smaller governments as well as large, but is now limited to kingdoms, empires, etc. F r a n k r e i c h means *the kingdom of the Franks,* or France; O e s t e r r e i c h, *the Eastern part of the empire;* K ö n i g r e i c h, *kingdom;* K a i s e r r e i c h, *empire;* E r d r e i c h, *the whole earth* (the extent of the earth). Smaller territories are designated by other words, as H e r z o g t h u m, F ü r s t e n t h u m, though H e r z o g r e i c h was once in use.

[2] A l l e — d i e w i r s e h e n. This must not be translated " all *the* principalities, kingdoms, and great estates, which we see," etc. The sense would be complete, were the sentence to close with the word G ü t e r. The irregularity, if it may be called such, consists in saying, " which we see how they pass back and forth" instead of " which we see pass," etc.

[3] S i e h e, s o h a s t d u, etc. " Look now, and you have the decision in regard to temporal goods, which is included in few words (k ü r z l i c h), viz." etc.

gerne beherbergten[1] die Pilger.  Darum ob sie wohl[2] kein
eigen Land noch Vorrath hatten, dennoch blieben sie im
Lande sitzen und hatten genug.

**Von Gott werden des Mannes Gänge ge-
fördert, und hat Lust an seinem Werke.[3]**

Siehe da abermal Trost.  Nicht allein wirst du zeitlich
Gut genug haben, sondern Alles, was du thust,[4] dein ganzes Leben und Wandel, auch gegen die Gottlosen, wird
schleunig seyn und fortgehen, darum daß du Gott trauest
und ihm dich und deine Sache ergiebst, in deinem Leben ihm
gelassen stehest.[5]  Damit machst du,[6] daß  er Gefallen, Lust
und gleich eine Begierde hat, deinen Weg und Wandel zu
fördern.

Aber dagegen ficht[7] nun, daß solcher gottgefälliger Weg
nicht gefördert, ja verhindert und verworfen wird von den
Gottlosen.  Das verdrießt denn die Natur: darum muß

---

[1] **B e h e r b e r g t e n.  H e r b e r g e** is a place where a person
travelling stops for a time, whether at the house of a friend, or at a
monastery, or tavern or any other place.  Hence the person may be
received gratuitously as a guest, or he may pay his bills as at an inn.
**W i r t h s h a u s** is a general term, and  very often means a small
country tavern ; **G a s t h a u s,** a more respectable inn ; **G a s t h o f,**
a spacious and  more splendid hotel, especially  for persons of rank.
**B e h e r b e r g e n,** means *to receive a guest into* one's house.

[2] **D a r u m,  o b  s i e  w o h l.**  " Therefore  (because  they  were
rich), though," etc.

[3] **U n d  (e r,  G o t t)  h a t  L u s t  a n  s e i n e m**  (his own)
**W e r k e,** (work, creature).

[4] **A l l e s  w a s  d u  t h u s t,** etc. " whatever you do, your whole
course of life, even towards (in respect to) the wicked, will  prosper
and move on."

[5] **U n d  i n  d e i n e m  L e b e n  i h m  g e l a s s e n  s t e h e s t,**
" and in thy life yieldest passively (remainest passive) to him."

[6] **D a m i t  m a c h s t  d u,**  " thereby thou causest, that he have
gratification, pleasure, and as it were a desire," etc.

[7] **A b e r  d a g e g e n  f i c h t,** " but with that conflicts (the circumstance) that," etc.

man ſich hier tröſten, daß unſer Weſen[1] Gott gefällt und
von ihm gefördert wird, nicht anſehen die Hinderniß und
Wegwerfung der Gottloſen.

Fällt er, ſo wird er nicht weggeworfen,
denn der Herr erhält ihn bei ſeiner Hand.

Das Fallen[2] möchte verſtanden werden, daß der Gerechte
zuweilen ſündigt, aber wieder aufſteht, wie Salomon ſagt
Sprüchw. 24.   Aber das laſſen wir jetzt fahren und bleiben
auf der Bahn, das Fallen hier heiße ſo viel, als ob er ein=
mal unterliege und die Gottloſen obliegen, als David, da
er von Saul und Abſalom gejagt wird, und Chriſtus, da er
gekreuzigt ward.   Denn ſolches Fallen währt nicht lange ;
Gott läßt ihn nicht liegen und weggeworfen ſeyn, ſondern
ergreift ſeine Hand, richtet ihn wieder auf, daß er beſtehen[3]
muß.

Damit tröſtet der Geiſt und antwortet den heimlichen[4]
Gedanken, die Jemand haben möchte und bei ihm ſelbſt ſa=
gen : Ja, ich habe dennoch[5] etwa geſehen, daß der Gerechte

---

[1] Unser Wesen, *ourselves and every thing belonging to us,*
(conduct).   Trösten—(und) nicht ansehen, "one must
be encouraged—and not regard the obstacles and rejection," etc.

[2] Das Fallen, etc.   "Falling might mean that, etc."—"But
we let that pass, and go upon the ground"—"as if he may once (one
day) be overcome, and the wicked conquer."   See p. 38, Note 4.

[3] Bestehen, *to stand firm and unmoved.*

[4] Heimlichen.   This word, derived from heim, *home,* was
once used as heimish now is, to indicate *what was at home* or
what pertained to home.   But its common meaning is *secret,* or concealed designedly, whereas geheim means *private,* i. e. not public, in which the idea of secresy is not intended.   Ein gehiemer
Rath is *a privy counseller,* who may be known to the public; but
ein heimlicher Rath, would mean, *a concealed counsellor.*
Science has its mysteries, Geheimnisse; but jugglers have
their secrets, Heimlichkeiten.

[5] Dennoch, from denn (in the old sense of dann, *then*)
and noch, *still,* means, *still then, even then, still,* and generally fol-

hat müssen[1] unterliegen, und ist seine Sache gar in die Ab=
scheu gefallen vor den Gottlosen? Ja, spricht er, liebes
Kind, laß das auch seyn, er falle; aber er wird dennoch
nicht so liegen bleiben und verworfen seyn: er muß wieder
auf,[2] obschon alle Welt daran verzweifelt habe. Denn Gott
erwischt[3] ihn bei der Hand und hebt ihn wieder auf.

Ich bin junge gewesen und alt geworden,
und habe noch nie gesehen den Gerechten
verlassen oder seinen Samen nach Brode
gehen.

Siehe, da setzt er zu mehrerer[4] Sicherung seine eigene

---

lows some *concession* and introduces something *apparently*, but not
*really opposed* to what preceded. D o c h, is a stronger adversative,
and introduces an *unexpected modification of a previous concession*,
i. e. where a thing would naturally be *inferred*, from the concessive
statement, d o c h intimates that the *fact* is at variance with the
*inference*. I c h  h a b e  d e n n o c h  e t w a  g e s e h e n, "(though
all this may possibly be true) *still* (d e n n o c h, apparently irrecon-
cilable with that) I have seen," etc. And a little below, "be it so,
(that) he fall; but *still* (d e n n o c h) he will not continue," etc.
D o c h would be much stronger here, and would imply that the two
things were not so easily reconcilable. W i e  s t e h t  e s  u m  D i -
d i e r ?—d o c h  e r  s c h l ä f t  w o h l  l a n g e  s c h o n, "how is it
with Didier?—(withdrawing that supposition or concession, the
writer says) *but* he is probably long since dead."

[1] H a t  m ü s s e n, for h a t  g e m u s s t, which would be harsh.

[2] E r  m u s s  w i e d e r  a u f (s t e h e n).

[3] E r w i s c h t. W i s c h e n, signifies, *to move or slip away
hastily*. E n t w i s c h e n, *to escape quickly*. E r w i s c h e n, now
but little used except in common life, means *to seize quickly*, and is
synonymous with e r t a p p e n, *to catch one or to fall upon him* (a
thief) *as if by accident;* e r h a s c h e n, *to catch one who is running
away, or escaping;* e r g r e i f e n, *to seize*, or to get a secure hold of
one; and f a n g e n, means simply *to catch*.

[4] M e h r e r e r. M e h r, *more*, is commonly used adverbially
without the form either of comparison or declension. In the comparative *form* as an adjective it is either m e h r e r, m e h r e, m e h r e s,
or m e h r e r e r, m e h r e r e, m e h r e r e s. Here it is in the lat-

Erfahrung. Und ist auch wahr, die tägliche Erfahrung giebt es, und müssen bekennen alle Menschen, daß es also sey. Wird aber Jemand verlassen, daß er das Brod suchen muß, so ist es gewiß, daß es ihm am Glauben gebrochen[1] hat; darum er auch recht und billig verlassen ist.

Aber dieß Brod suchen[2] oder nach Brod gehen muß man so verstehen, daß er nicht Hunger leide oder Hungers sterbe,[3] ob er wohl arm ist und wenig zuvor hat. Er wird gewißlich ernähret, ob er gleich nichts Uebriges hat bis auf den andern Tag; giebt ihm Einer nicht, so giebt ihm der Andere, es muß seine Nahrung gewißlich kommen. Wiewohl die sündigen, die ihm nicht geben und helfen.

Denn der arme Lazarus, Lucä 16, ob ihm der reiche Mann nichts gab, ist er dennoch ernährt worden, obwohl es mit Armuth zugieng.[4] Armuth nimmt Gott nicht von seinen Heiligen; aber er läßt sie nicht untergehen noch verderben.

---

ter form, dative feminine. Used substantively, it signifies *more than one*, i. e. *several* and loses its comparative force. See p. 18 Note 1.

[1] G e b r o c h e n. E s g e b r i c h t with a dative is nearly equivalent to e s m a n g e l t, *there is wanting to him, he fails in.*

[2] D i e s s B r o d s u c h e n. Observe the substantive use of B r o d s u c h e n and n a c h B r o d g e h e n.

[3] H u n g e r s s t e r b e. Several neuter verbs are accompanied by a genitive expressing the *manner* of the action; as g e h e n s e i n e r W e g e, *to go* (how?) *his own ways;* l e b e n d e r H o f f n u n g, *to live in the hope,* to entertain the hope; l e b e n d e s G l a u b e n s, *to be filled with,* or *to have the belief;* e i n e s n a t ü r l i c h e n T o d e s s t e r b e n, *to die a natural death;* v e r b l e i c h e n e i n e s T o d e s, *to turn pale with death,* i. e. to die. So H u n g e r s s t e r b e n, *to die of hunger.*

[4] Z u g i e n g. Z u g e h e n, is used impersonally in the sense of, *to take place, to happen,* with some adverbial phrase, expressing the manner. " Although it was with poverty." U n t e r g e h e n n o c h v e r d e r b e n, *perish nor* (even) *be ruined.* V e r d e r b e n, *to render unfit for use* (either by being marred or destroyed).

Täglich ist er barmherzig und leihet, und sein Saame wird gesegnet seyn.

Das ist von dem habenden[1] Gerechten gesagt, ob er also sey,[2] daß er Kinder habe; so derselbe schon austheilt, giebt und leihet täglich, dennoch wird er und sein Kind genug haben. Denn die Benedeiung ist, daß sie werden genug haben hier und dort,[3] gar keinen Mangel leiden an Leibes Nahrung und der Seelen Heil, ob es wohl zuweilen nicht übrig ist.

Also haben wir,[4] wie Gott die Gläubigen handelt in zeitlicher Nahrung und ihren Sachen, daß wir ja sicher seyen in beiden Stücken, er werde uns nicht verlassen und werden dazu genug haben an der Nahrung. Und also geht es auch gewißlich, so wir glauben und uns der Gottlosen Glück nicht verdrießen noch bewegen lassen. Darum wiederholt und schließt er abermal und spricht:

Laß vom Bösen und thue Gutes, und bleibe immerdar.[5]

Als sollte er sagen: Laß Gott sorgen, thue nur du, was gut ist, und laß dich nicht bewegen, Böses zu thun, bleibe nur immerdar, wie du bist, und laß gehen, was da gehet. Wie auch St. Petrus sagt: „Werfet auf ihn alle eure

[1] Habenden, *possessing property.* Wohlhabend is generally used in such cases.

[2] Ob er also sey, "though he be such," that, i. e. though one who has children. "Though he distributes, gives and lends daily, still," etc.

[3] Hier und dort, "in this world and in the other," to which the words, Leibes Nahrung and der Seelen Heil, refer. "Although at times nothing will be on hand," (übrig)

[4] Also haben wir—dass wir ja sicher seyen. "Thus, as God treats the righteous, etc., we have security (we have that we are secure)." Und [wir] werden.

[5] Immerdar, obsolete and poetic for immer.

Sorge. Denn er trägt Sorge über uns.‟[1] Und Psalm 55: „Wirf alle dein Anliegen[2] auf Gott, und er wird dich wohl beschicken[3] oder besorgen und nicht lassen ewiglich[4] bewegen.

Denn der Herr hat das Recht lieb, und verläßt seine Heiligen nicht, ewiglich werden sie bewahret: aber der Gottlosen Samen wird ausgerottet.

Darfst nicht sorgen,[5] daß dein Recht untergehe, es ist nicht möglich. Denn Gott hat das Recht lieb, darum muß er es erhalten, und die Gerechten werden nicht verlassen. Wenn er ein Abgott[6] wäre, der Unrecht lieb hätte oder dem Rechten feind wäre, wie die gottlosen Menschen, so hättest du Ursache zu sorgen und dich zu fürchten. Aber nun[7] du weißst, daß er das Recht lieb hat, was sorgest du? Was fürchtest du? Was zweifelst du? Ewiglich, nicht allein zeitlich, werden seine Heiligen erhalten und die Gottlosen mit Kind und all dem Ihren[8] ausgerottet.

---

[1] **Er trägt Sorge über uns.** "He takes care of us." Für commonly follows Sorge, *care for;* Sorge über, *care respecting* or *of*, is a little more general, but means nearly the same thing.

[2] **Anliegen**, signifies, *what lies upon the heart, anxiety, care, wish.* The verb **anliegen** means, *to lie hard upon anything, to lie close upon the heart, to be solicitous.* **Angelegen**, the participle, *careful, anxious.* **Angelegentlich**, *earnestly, zealously.*

[3] **Beschicken** signifies 1. *to send to,* 2. *to arrange,* 3. *to take care of.* It is here used in the last sense, of course.

[4] **Ewiglich**, belongs to **nicht**, *never.* Connected with **bewegen**, it would give a ludicrous sense.

[5] **(Du) darfst nicht sorgen.** The ellipsis makes the expression more pointed.

[6] **Abgott**, *a false god*, viewed as a living being. **Götze**, *an image to be worshipped.* **Götzenbild**, a *likeness* of an **Abgott** or of a **Götze**, but not an object of worship, as they are. Hence, figuratively an idolized *person* is called an **Abgott**; an idolized *thing*, a **Götze.**

[7] **Nun**, *now since, now that.*

[8] **Dem Ihren.** Das Ihre is used as das Ihrige is,

Die Heiligen allhier[1] heißen nicht die im Himmel sind, von welchen die Schrift selten redet, sondern gemeiniglich[2] von denen, die auf Erden leben, die da glauben in Gott, und durch denselben Glauben Gottes Gnade und Geist haben, davon[3] sie heilig genannt werden, wie wir Alle sind, so wir glauben wahrhaftig.

Die Gerechten erben das Land, und bleiben ewiglich drinnen.[4]

Das ist, wie droben gesagt ist, sie haben genug auf Erden, dürfen es nirgends denn[5] bei Gott gewarten, wo sie wohnen

---

and signifies, *what belongs to them, their property.* Die Ihrigen means *their relatives or friends.* On all undeclined, see p. 56, Note 2.

[1] Allhier. In general, all prefixed to a word makes no other alteration in the signification than to give intensity to the word, and even that force is frequently no longer perceptible.

[2] Gemeiniglich is generally employed in the sense of gewöhnlich, *commonly, usually,* though of much less frequent occurrence than the latter. Gemeinhin is a more vulgar word of the same import. Gemeiniglich is sometimes used nearly as insgemein is, meaning *in general,* or *collectively* as opposed to *in particular.* There is an apparent absurdity in the use of the word in the case before us, as if the writer would say, "the word (die Heiligen) commonly means in this passage (allhier)." But the sentence takes a new turn after the words, von welchen die Schrift, and gemeiniglich, instead of referring to the main clause (allhier heissen nicht) refers to the word selten in the relative clause. Thus: "The saints in this passage does not mean those which are in heaven, of whom the Scriptures seldom speak; but they commonly speak (and so here) of those, etc."

[3] Davon stands for von diesem, *from this, whence.* It being *always a neuter singular,* it refers to several preceding words collectively, and these are all thrown together and viewed as one thing, or circumstance. Davon is therefore limited in its use to such cases.

[4] Drinnen, droben. See p. 42, Note 1.

[5] Nirgends denn, *nowhere except.* Nirgends refers indefinitely either to time or to place, *nowhere, never.*

in der Welt.   Denn Gott läßt sie nicht: läßt er sie aber[1]
so sind sie gewißlich ungerecht und gottlos, ohne Glauben
und Trauen in Gott.   Und also ist das beschlossen, daß wir
nur gut thun und bleiben auf der Bahn und im Lande, las=
sen ihn sorgen und machen.   Nun folgt, was die Sache[2]
sey des Gerechten, darob solches Wesen sich erhebt zwischen
ihm und den Gottlosen.

Der Mund des Gerechten gehet mit Weis=
heit um, und seine Zunge redet vom Ge=
richt.[3]

Darüber erhebt sich der Hader, die Gottlosen wollen die
göttliche Weisheit und Recht nicht hören, verfolgen verdam=
men und lästern es für Thorheit und Unrecht, und geht den=
selben[4] Schälken eine Weile wohl darob.   Das verdrießt

---

[1] Lässt er sie aber, conditional, " Forsakes he them," i. e.
if he forsakes them.

[2] Was die Sache, etc.  " Now follows, what the part (duty)
of the righteous is, respecting which (daroh) such a difference (or
difficulty) arises (such a thing or affair raises itself) between him and
the wicked." The word Wesen often means *difficulty, disturbance.*
Viel Wesens machen, *to make much trouble.* Ein grosses
Wesen in der Welt machen, *to make a great stir in the world.*
It frequently gives a mere collective sense, meaning *whatever pertains
to a thing*, its nature, character, arrangement, and the like.  Das
gemeine Wesen, *the Commonwealth.* Das Staats-we-
sen, *the state.* Das Kirchen-wesen, *the church*, or the ecclesiastical government.  Das Stadt-wesen, *the city government.* Das Haus-wesen, *household matters.* Das Kriegs-
wesen, *military affairs*, the war department.  Das Schul-we-
sen, *the public schools*, the department of education.

[3] Gericht, though commonly meaning *judgment, court of justice*, and theologically, *divine punishment*, appears to be used here as
the English word judgment often is in the Bible, to signify, *equity,
righteousness.* The word Recht is substituted for it below.

[4] Und geht denselben, etc., "and for a while it goes well
with these wrong-doers, in the matter."

denn und bewegt natürlich[1] die Gerechten, und werden dadurch gereizt zum Bösen und Wiedervergelten oder Ungeduld.

Darum lehrt sie dieser Psalm stille halten und immer fortfahren, immer lehren, dichten und reden[2] solche Weisheit und Recht, Gott die Sache befehlen, Jene lassen beißen, wüthen, Zähne knirschen, lästern, schlagen, Schwert blößen,[3] Bogen spannen, sich häufen und stärken ꝛc., wie gesagt ist. Denn Gott wird es wohl machen, so wir sein nur gewarten[4] und immer auf der Bahn bleiben, und um ihretwillen nicht aufhören oder nachlassen, Gutes zu thun. Es muß doch zuletzt das Urtheil dieses Verses bleiben und kund werden wie der helle Mittag, daß der Gerechte habe recht und weislich geredet, die Gottlosen sind Narren und Unrecht gewesen.

**Das Gesetz seines Gottes ist in seinem Herzen, seine Tritte gleiten nicht.**

Darum redet er recht und dichtet Weisheit, daß Gottes Gesetz nicht in dem Buche, nicht in den Ohren, nicht auf der Zunge, sondern in seinem Herzen ist. Gottes Gesetze mag Niemand recht verstehen, es sey ihm denn im Herzen,[5] daß er es lieb habe und lebe darnach, welches thut der Glaube an Gott. Darum ob die Gottlosen wohl viel Worte machen von Gott und seinem Gesetze, rühmen sich der Schrift Lehrer und Erfahrne,[6] so reden sie doch nimmer recht noch weislich. Denn sie haben es nicht im

---

[1] Natürlich, *of course*, according to the general course of things.  So this word should generally be translated.

[2] Dichten und reden, *think and speak*.  See p. 4, Note 1.

[3] Blössen, *to make naked or bare*, and applied to a sword, *to draw it from its scabbard*.

[4] Sein nur gewarten.  Sein an old genitive and governed by gewarten.  See p. 46, Note 4.

[5] Es sey ihm denn in Herzen, *unless it is in his heart*.

[6] Erfahrne for Erfahrene, *experienced, skilled*, and as a substantive, *adepts*,—"teachers of, and adepts in the Scriptures."

Herzen; darum verstehen sie sein nicht,[1] es betrügt sie der Schein, daß sie die Worte der Schrift führen, und darob wüthen und verfolgen die Gerechten.

Item, des Gerechten Tritte schlüpfern[2] nicht, sondern gehen gewiß frei einher im guten Gewissen,[3] darum daß er der Sache gewiß ist, und mag nicht verführt werden durch Menschengesetz und Beilehren.[4] Aber die Gottlosen fallen und schlüpfern allezeit hin und her, haben keinen gewissen Tritt, darum daß sie Gottes Gesetz außer dem Glauben[5] nicht recht verstehen. Und also fahren sie hin und her, wie sie ihr Dünkel[6] führt oder Menschengesetz lehrt, jetzt dieß, jetzt jenes Werk, jetzt lehrt man sie sonst, jetzt so,[7] und schlüpfern hin, wo man sie hinführt mit der Nase, ein Blinder den Andern. Darum wie sie nicht recht verstehen, so

---

[1] Verstehen sie sein nicht. Verstehen does not commonly take a genitive after it (sein for seiner), and scarcely ever except when it is a reflective verb. " They do not understand it (the law). The show (of knowledge, from the circumstance) that they quote the words of Scripture, deceives them, and on that account they rage and persecute the just."

[2] Schlüpfern, now properly means to be slippery. In the sense of schlüpfen, to slide, it is at present not used.

[3] Gewissen, conscience, is here used in its original and etymological sense, of consciousness, or certain knowledge. This whole passage illustrates well the way in which the word Gewissen (certain knowledge) came to signify conscience.

[4] Beilehren, collateral teaching, what is taught aside from the Scriptures.

[5] Ausser dem Glauben, not in faith, i. e. in faith, or a state of faith, men can understand the law of God; out of that state of faith, they cannot understand the law.

[6] Dünkel, from dünken, notion, whim, different from Dunkel, darkness, obscurity.

[7] Jetzt lehrt man sie sonst, jetzt so, etc. " One teaches them (they are taught) now otherwise, now so (now this way, now that), and they slide away wherever one leads them by the nose, a blind man (leading) the other (blind men).

wandeln sie auch nicht recht; noch[1] wüthen sie um solche ihre schlüpfrige Lehre und Leben, wider die gewisse Lehre und Leben der Gerechten, wollen je ihr Ding allein bestätigen.

Der Gottlose sieht an[*] den Gerechten und gedenkt ihn zu tödten.

Es verdrießt ihn und kann es nicht leiden, daß man seine Lehre und Leben straft, als ein unrechtes und unweisliches[2] Wesen. Darum denkt er nicht mehr, denn wie[3] er seine Sache befestige. Nun kann er[4] vor dem Gerechten nicht, welcher sein Unrecht nicht ungestraft läßt; darum treibt ihn sein falsches Wesen dahin, daß er des Gerechten los werde, ihn umbringe, damit sein Wesen recht und ungestraft bleibe. Wie der Pabst und die Seinen allezeit und noch thun,[5] wie wir wohl sehen, daß sie Gottes Gesetze auch schier nicht in den Büchern haben, geschweige denn im Herzen: noch wollen sie die seyn, die da Weisheit dichten und recht lehren, wüthen und rasen darüber, wie die tollen Hunde ohne Aufhören.

Aber der Herr läßt ihn nicht in seinen

---

[1] N o c h does not refer to n i c h t, (*not, nor*); but begins a distinct clause and, of course, means, *still*.

[2] U n w e i s l i c h e s, *unwise;* an unusual word. W e i s l i c h, *wisely,* is common.

[3] N i c h t  m e h r  d e n n  w i e, "of nothing but how he may establish his cause" (no more than how).

[4] N u n  k a n n  e r, etc. "Now he cannot (establish his cause) in the presence of the righteous, who does not suffer his iniquity to go unrebuked. Therefore his false (and corrupt) character impels him to rid himself of the righteous man, etc."

[5] (G e t h a n  h a b e n)  u n d  n o c h  t h u n. "As the pope and his adherents have always done, and still do; as we see, (that) they have not the law of God even in their books, not to say in their hearts; neither do they desire to be those who meditate and rightly teach wisdom; they rage and rave about it, etc."

Händen, und verdammt ihn nicht, wenn er verurtheilt wird.

Gott läßt[1] den Gerechten wohl in ihre Hand kommen; er läßt ihn aber nicht drinnen: sie mögen ihn nicht dämpfen, wenn sie ihn gleich tödten. Dazu hilft ihr Urtheil nicht, ob sie gleich rühmen, sie thun es an Gottes Statt und in Gottes Namen; denn Gott richtet das Gegenurtheil.[2] Das sehen wir auch zu unsern Zeiten.

Der Pabst[3] mit den Seinen haben Johannes Huß verdammt; noch hilft sie kein Verdammen, kein Schreien, kein Plärren, kein Wüthen, kein Toben, keine Bulle, kein Blei, kein Siegel, kein Bann, er ist hervorgeblieben allezeit, da kein Bischof, keine Universität, kein König, kein Fürst etwas dawider vermocht, welches noch nie von einem Ketzer gehört ist. Der einzige todte Mann, der unschuldige Abel, machet den lebendigen Kain, den Pabst, mit allem seinem Anhang zu Ketzern, Abtrünnigen, Mördern, Gotteslästerern, sollten sie sich darob zerreißen und bersten.

Harre auf den Herrn und bewahre seinen Weg, so wird er dich erhöhen, daß du

---

[1] Gott lässt, etc. "God does indeed suffer the righteous to come into their hands, but he does not leave (lässt) him there. They cannot extinguish him even though they kill him."

[2] Gegenurtheil, an opposite decision, a reversal of the decision.

[3] Der Pabst, etc. "The pope and his party condemned John Huss; but no condemning sentence, no outcry, no howling, no raging, no blustering, no bull, no lead, no seal, no excommunication avails them anything; he still (always) exists (is extant), because no bishop, no university, no king, no prince could prevail (effect anything) against him—which was never known (heard of) in respect to a heretic. This simple man (though) dead, this innocent Abel makes the living Cain, the pope and all his followers, heretics, apostates, murderers, blasphemers, though they lacerate themselves and burst over it."

das Land erbeſt, wenn die Gottloſen ausge=
rottet werden, wirſt du ſehen.

Abermal ermahnt er, auf Gott zu trauen und Gutes zu
thun, darum daß[1] die ungebrochene, ungelaſſene, blöde Natur
ſich ſchwerlich ergiebt, und anſ Gott erwägt, daß ſie gewarte
Deſſen, das ſie nirgends ſieht noch empfindet, und ſich Deſ=
ſen äußere, was ſie ſichtlich empfindet.

Nun iſt auch genugſam geſagt, wie die Beſitzung des
Landes zu verſtehen ſey, nämlich daß ein Gerechter bleibt
und genug hat auf Erden. Dazu wo er zu wenig hat zeit=
lich, hat er deſto mehr geiſtlich; wie Chriſtus lehrt und
ſpricht: Wer einerlei[2] verläßt, der ſoll es hundertfältig wie=
der haben auf dieſer Welt und dazu das ewige Leben.

Wiewohl[3] ich nicht widerfechte, daß ſolches Erdenbeſitzen
möchte verſtanden werden nicht von einem jeglichen Gerech=
ten inſonderheit, ſondern von dem Haufen und der Ge=
meine: obwohl vielleicht Etliche zeitlich vertilgt werden,
bleibt dennoch zuletzt ihr Samen und Lehre oben;[4] wie die
Chriſten in der Welt geblieben ſind und die Heiden vergan=
gen, ob ihrer wohl Viele von den Heiden zeitlich gemartert
und getilgt worden, wie Pſalm 112. auch ſagt: „Selig iſt

---

[1] D a r u m   d a s s, etc. " Because (that) unsubdued, insubmis-
sive weak nature reluctantly surrenders, and reflects upon God, that
it may wait for that which it nowhere sees or feels, and abstain from
that which it sensitively (visibly) feels," i. e. live in view of future
spiritual blessings and disregard present evils.

[2] E i n e r l e i generally means, *one and the same.* Here it is used
in its original, etymological sense as the antithesis of h u n d e r t f ä l-
t i g, " He who forsakes *one* thing shall receive it back a hundred
fold."

[3] W i e w o h l—o b w o h l,—d e n n o c h; *although—although* (repeated in a slightly different form) is the protasis or first member of
the sentence, and d e n n o c h corresponding to both, introduces the
apodosis or second member.

[4] B l e i b t   o b e n is the opposite of u n t e r l i e g e n or u n-
t e r g e h e n. See p. 38, Note 4.

der Mann, der Gott fürchtet und an seinen Geboten Lust hat, sein Samen wird regieren auf Erden, und das Geschlecht der Gerechten wird vermehrt werden" rc.

Doch wie gesagt, über das Alles[1] hat ein Jeglicher auch für sich selbst genug, und Gott giebt ihm auch, was er darf und bittet: und wo er es nicht giebt, da ist gewißlich der Gerechte so willig, daß er es nicht haben will von Gott, und wehret Gott,[2] daß er es ihm nicht gebe ; so gar Eins ist er mit Gott, daß er hat und nicht hat, wie er nur will vor Gott, wie Psalm 145. sagt : „Gott thut den Willen derer, die ihn fürchten, und erhört ihr Bitten, und hilft ihnen."

Daß er hier sagt : Du wirst es sehen, wenn die Gottlosen ausgerottet werden, ist nicht von einem schlechten Sehen[3] gesagt, sondern nach dem Gebrauche der Schrift heißt es Sehen nach seinem Willen oder daß er längst gerne gesehen hätte, wie wir anf Deutsch sagen : das wollte ich gerne sehen.

Ich sehe einen Gottlosen mächtig und eingewurzelt, wie einen grünenden Lorbeerbaum.

Hier setzt er die andre Erfahrung zu[4] einem Exempel und Zeichen vom Gottlosen. Droben hat er eine Erfahrung

---

[1] Ueber das Alles, *beyond or notwithstanding all that.*

[2] Wehret Gott, *hinders God, so that he may not give it,* i. e. prays him to withhold it. So perfectly is he one with God, that he has, or fails to have, whatever he will from (before) God. (God gives or withholds whatever the worshipper in his presence, asks him to give or withhold).

[3] Schlechten Sehen, *simple,* i. e. *mere seeing,* (See p. 39, Note 5), " but — seeing according to one's desire," that is, be gratified with what you desire. Heisst es (it, the word Sehen means or is equivalent to) Sehen nach seinem Willen.

[4] Die andere Erfahrung zu, etc. " Here he presents the opposite (other) experience as (zu) an example," etc. Zu is used to point out that to which a thing is destined, or what it is to be.

gesagt von dem Gerechten, daß er noch nie Keinen[1] verlassen gesehen habe.

Hier sagt er eine Erfahrung vom Widertheil,[2] von dem Gottlosen, wie der vergangen sey, und spricht: Er war reich, mächtig, groß, daß sich Jedermann vor Ihm fürchtete und was er sagte, that ließ, das war gesagt, gethan, gelassen.[3] Denn einen solchen bedeutet das hebräische Wörtlein „Ariz,"[4] das habe ich zuvor verdeutscht „mächtig." Das bedeutet auch, was er dazu thut: „Er brüstete sich und ward fürbrächtig, that sich hervor, war etwas sonderlich vor Allen, machte sich breit und hoch, gleichwie ein Lorbeerbaum vor andern Bäumen allezeit grünet und etwas sonderlich prangt vor Allen, sonderlich vor den zahmen Bäumen und Gartenbäumen, ist auch nicht ein schlechter Busch oder niedriger Baum, deß man auch warten und pflegen muß, welches man den wilden Bäumen und Zedern nicht thut." Also muß man auf diesen gottlosen Junker auch sehen und sprechen: Gnädiger Herr, lieber Junker.

---

[1] N i e K e i n e n. Such double negatives are not uncommon in the older German.

[2] W i d e r t h e i l, *opposite party.* See p. 34, Note 5, W i d e r p a r t in a similar sense.

[3] " What he said, did (or) omitted, that was said, done (or) omitted." No one contradicted or opposed him.

[4] A r i z, " which (Hebrew word) I have above (z u v o r, i. e. in the text) translated, m ä c h t i g." It also signifies how he acts, viz. " He tossed up his head, was impetuous, rushed onward, signalized himself before others, branched out and grew up as a laurel-tree, is always verdant more than (v o r) other trees, and decks itself preëminently above (v o r) all, particularly above the cultivated trees, and trees of the garden,"—is not a mere shrub or low tree, which one must attend and cultivate,—(a labor) which one does not perform for the wild trees and cedars.—S i c h  b r ü s t e n, means literally, *to raise one's breast,* and hence *to make a show of energy,* and is used now only in this figurative sense of making a boastful display. F ü r b r ä c h t i g is a word entirely out of use, so far as we know, and probably means, *breaking* or pushing forward, f ü r standing as it often does with Luther, for v o r.

Da man vorübergieng,[1] siehe da war er dahin, ich fragte nach ihm, da ward er nirgend gefunden.

Solch Exempel[2] hat David an dem Saul,[3] Ahitophel, Absalon und dergleichen wohl gesehen, welche mächtig waren in ihrem gottlosen Wesen, und ehe man sich umsah, waren sie dahin, daß man fragen und sagen mochte: Wo sind sie hin? Ist es nicht wahr? Zu unsern Zeiten ist der Pabst Julius auch ein solcher Mann gewesen, welch ein[4] Ariz und gräulicher Herr war das? Ist er aber nicht verschwunden, ehe man sich's versah? Wo ist er nun? Wo ist sein Trotzen und Prachten? Also sollen wir nur stille halten, sie werden Alle also[5] verschwinden, die jetzt wüthen, und wollen den Himmel zerstören und Felsen umstoßen. Lasset uns nur ein wenig[6] schweigen und vorüber gehen, wir werden uns schier umsehen und ihrer Keinen sehen, so wir nur Gott recht trauen.

---

[1] Da man vorübergieng, "as one passed by." A mistranslation; it should have been Er ging vorüber, "he passed away; behold he was gone (dahin)."

[2] Soleh Exempel. Neuter substantives with Luther often take adjectives without the termination es (solches).

[3] An dem Saul. Where we use the English word, in, literally and strictly, implying the idea of within or interior, or keeping before the mind the image of locality within something, the Germans also use the word in. But where we use the word to signify where a thing takes effect, or takes place, pointing out specimens, materials or external marks in which (but not within which) a thing is done or realized, the Germans employ an. See Gram. p. 359.

[4] Welch ein. Welch and solch are used instead of welcher and solcher, etc., when they take ein immediately after them. See p. 18, Note 8. Ariz, see p. 79, Note 4.

[5] Also — also. The first is a conjunction (therefore), the second an adverb (so).

[6] Ein wenig, a little while. "Let us, for a little time, be silent and pass along."

Bewahre die Frömmigkeit[1] und schaue, was aufrichtig ist. Denn zuletzt wird derselbige Frieden haben.

Das ist so viel gesagt, als Paulus Tit. 2. Sey nur rechtschaffen im einfältigen Glauben zu Gott, und wandle aufrichtig und redlich, darauf siehe allein[2] und richte dich darein, laß Gottlose Gottlose seyn, siehe, so wirst du zuletzt Friede haben, und wird dir wohl gehen. Die hebräische Sprache hat die Art, daß, wo wir auf deutsch sagen: Es geht ihm wohl, er gehabt sich wohl, es steht wohl um ihn, und auf Lateinisch: Valere, bene habere, etc. das heißt sie :[3] Friede haben.

Also Genes. 37. sprach Jacob zu seinem Sohne Joseph: „Gehe hin in Sichem zu deinen Brüdern, und siehe, ob ihnen Friede und dem Viehe Friede sey, und sage mir wieder," das ist: ob es ihnen auch wohl gehe.' Daher kömmt der Gruß[4] im Evangelio, ansi hebräische Weise : Pax vobis, Friede sey euch, welches wir auf Deutsch sagen : Gott gebe euch einen guten Tag, guten Morgen, guten Abend ! Item, im Abscheiden sagen wir : Gehabt euch wohl, habt gute Nacht, laßt es euch wohl gehen ! Das heißt Pax vobis.

---

[1] Bewahre die Frömmigkeit, etc., "preserve piety and regard what is upright." An error in translation. It should be, " Observe the righteous man and behold the upright."

[2] Darauf siehe allein, etc., "regard only that and regulate (exercise) yourself in it ; let the wicked be wicked," etc.

[3] Das heisst sie. " The Hebrew language hast his peculiarity, that where we say in German, es geht ihm wohl, etc. and in Latin valere, etc., that it (the Heb. language) calls, ' having peace.' " Notice the use of the colon before examples, quotations, etc.

[4] Daher kömmt der Gruss, etc. Hence the salutation in the Gospel comes after the Hebrew manner, pax vobis, peace be with you, which we express in German by, " God grant you a good day, good morning, good evening." Also we say in parting, " fare you well, (may you) have a good night," " let it be well with you," that is, pax vobis.

Also wenn der Gottlose dahin ist, so geht es dem Gerechten und Gläubigen wohl, und ist hernach eitel[1] Friede.

Die Uebertreter aber werden vertilgt mit einander, und die Gottlosen werden zuletzt ausgerottet.

Das ist das Widerspiel: die Gerechten bleiben, und geht ihnen wohl; die Abtrünnigen gehen unter, und gehet ihnen übel hernach und zuletzt.

Es möchten diese zwei Verse auch wohl verstanden werden von beider Theile[2] nachgelassenen Lehren, Erben und Gütern, daß die Meinung sey: Die Gerechten, was sie hinter sich lassen, das besteht und geht ihnen wohl, wie droben im 26. Vers gesagt ist, daß des Gerechten Kind auch genug haben werden; aber Alles, was die Gottlosen hinter sich lassen, verschwindet und kömmt zusehends unter, wie Psalm 109. sagt: „Sein Gedächtniß soll in einem Gliede des Geschlechts vertilgt werden.‟ Das sieht man auch täglich in der Erfahrung.

Das Heil der Gerechten aber ist von dem Herrn, der ist ihre Stärke[3] in der Zeit der Noth.

Die Ursache der vorigen[4] zwei Verse ist: denn das Heil der Gottlosen ist von ihnen selbst, und ihre Stärke ist ihre

---

[1] Eitel, *empty;* mere, *pure.* In the latter sense, it is not declined, " pure peace," " nothing but peace." So eitel Brod essen, " eat nothing but bread." It is now superseded in this sense by lauter. See p. 10, Note 4.

[2] Von beider Theile, etc., " of the doctrines, inheritance and property of both parties, left behind" (at their death).

[3] Der ist ihre Stärke, *he is their strength.* Der cannot be a relative here, for it would invert the clause and throw the verb (ist) to the end.

[4] Die Ursache der vorigen, etc. (this verse) is the ground of the two preceding verses; for, etc.

eigene Macht, sie sind groß, viel,[1] reich und mächtig, dürfen Gottes Stärke und Heil nicht. Aber die Gerechten, die ihr Gesicht müssen abkehren von Allem, was man sieht und fühlt und allein Gott trauen, die haben kein Heil noch Stärke, denn von Gott, welcher sie auch nicht läßt, und thut, wie sie ihm glauben und trauen, als dieser folgende letzte Vers beschließt und sagt:

Und der Herr wird ihnen beistehen und wird sie erretten, und wird sie von den Gottlosen erretten und ihnen helfen; denn sie trauen auf ihn.

Siehe, siehe, welche eine reiche Zusage, großer Trost und überflüssige Ermahnung ist das, so wir nur trauen und glauben. Zum Ersten, Gott hilft ihnen, nämlich mitten in dem Uebel, läßt sie nicht allein drinnen stecken, ist bei ihnen, stärkt sie und enthält sie.[2] Ueberdieß, nicht allein hilft er ihnen, sondern errettet[3] sie auch, daß sie kommen.[4] Denn dieses hebräische Wörtlein[5] heißt eigentlich dem Unglück entlaufen und davon kommen. Und daß es die Gottlosen verdrießen möchte,[6] so drückt er sie mit Namen aus und spricht: „Er wird sie erretten von den Gottlosen," ob es ihnen wohl

---

[1] Viel, *many.* This adjective, being a predicate here, cannot be declined, and of course could not be put in the plural number.

[2] Enthält sie. In old German enthalten signified, *to sustain, to protect.* See p. 54, Note 5.

[3] Errettet. Retten is *to rescue one from danger or evil by a quick action*, by seizing one and snatching him away. Erretten is the same, except that e r adds the idea of successful or complete deliverance. Erlösen, literally means *to make one loose* or *free* from something that holds him firmly, to free one by the exertion of power, or with effort; *to redeem.* Befreien, is *to set one at liberty.*

[4] Kommen, for wegkommen.

[5] " For this Hebrew word (i. e. the Hebrew word translated by erretten) signifies, properly, etc."

[6] Und das es — mochte, "and in order that it might."

leid ſey, und ſoll ihr Wüthen[1] ſie nichts helfen, wiewohl ſie meinen, der Gerechte ſolle ihnen nicht entlaufen, er müſſe vertilgt[2] werden.

Zum Dritten, nicht allein errettet er ſie, ſondern er hilft ihnen auch fürder immerdar,[3] daß ſie hinfort in keinem Unglücke bleiben, es komme, wenn es will : und das Alles darum,[4] daß ſie ihm vertraut haben. Alſo ſpricht er auch Pſ. 91 : „Darum daß er mir vertraut, ſo will ich ihn erretten und beſchirmen.[5] Denn er erkennt meinen Namen, er hat mich angerufen, darum will ich ihn erhören. Ich will bei ihm ſeyn in ſeinem Uebel, und will ihn herausreißen und will ihn zu Ehren ſetzen, und ihn füllen mit Länge der Tage und ihm offenbaren mein Heil.‟

O der ſchändelichen Untreue, Mißtreue[6] und verdammten Unglaubens, daß wir ſolchen reichen, mächtigen, tröſtlichen Zuſagungen Gottes nicht glauben, und zappeln ſo gar leicht-

---

[1] S o l l  i h r  W ü t h e n. These words are not connected to the foregoing clause, o b  e s  i h n e n  w o h l  l e i d  s e y ; neither the position, nor the meaning of s o l l would admit that. S o l l, when it represents what is said or thought by another, as it does here, means, *must according to what is said or thought.* Hence it is often rendered *is said to be.* " And (according to these words) their rage will not help them." The clause is connected by u n d to the words quoted, and is a paraphrase or explanation of those words.

[2] V e r t i l g t. The word t i l g e n corresponds to the Latin word *delere;* and v e r t i l g e n means *to blot completely out,* to destroy utterly. V e r n i c h t e n, *to annihilate,* is often used differently, especially in figurative language, as, e s  s t e h t  j e m a n d  v e r n i c h t e t  d a, *one stands there annihilated,* i. e. exposed in his nothingness, or made to feel his nothingness.

[3] F ü r d e r, *further, afterwards;* i m m e r d a r, the same as i m m e r. See p. 69, Note 5.

[4] U n d  d a s  A l l e s  d a r u m, "and all this because."

[5] B e s c h i r m e n, *to cover with a shield, to defend.* S c h i r m, *a defence, a shield, a screen.* S o n n e n s c h i r m, *a parasol.* R e g e n s c h i r m, *an umbrella.*

[6] M i s s t r e u e, for M i s s t r a u e n, *mistrust, distrust.*

lich in geringen Anstößen, so wir nur böse Worte von den Gottlosen hören. Hilf Gott, daß wir einmal rechten Glauben überkommen,[1] den wir sehen, daß er in aller Schrift gefordert werde, Amen.

---

## ADDRESS TO THE GERMAN NOBILITY.*

Schrift an den christlichen Adel deutscher Nation; Von des christlichen Standes Besserung.

---

*Introductory Notice by Pfizer.*

[Unter diesem Titel schrieb Luther in der Mitte des Jahrs 1520 eine, dem christlichen Adel deutscher Nation gewidmete Schrift, in mancher Beziehung eine der wichtigsten und merkwürdigsten, sofern er darin einen Vorschlag macht zur umfassenden Reformation der Kirche, und mehr als in andern Schriften ein zusammenhängendes, lebendiges Bild von den Mißbräuchen in der Kirchenverfassung und Regierung entwirft, während die von ihm sonst bekämpften Lehren hier mehr zurücktreten, wie es angemessen war in Betracht des Publikums, für welches er hier

---

[1] Ueberkommen in the sense of bekommen. "God grant that we may one day obtain true faith which we see (that it is) required in all the Scriptures."

* Of this eloquent production of Luther we can here present only a part, though the connection will be generally maintained. In order that the general plan and peculiar character of it may be better comprehended, we prefix, by way of analysis, a very interesting notice of it by Gustav Pfizer, omitting most of his quotations. The article from the pen of this elegant scholar, is taken from his life of Luther, written in 1836.

schrieb. Aber Lehre und Kirchen-Einrichtung hiengen so eng und unzertrennlich zusammen, daß mit Abstellung der Mißbräuche in letzterer, auch jene gereinigt und ihrer Fesseln entledigt werden mußte.

Schon die Zuschrift an Nikolaus von Amsdorf, seinen Freund und Collegen, ist bezeichnend und anziehend. Sie beginnt mit den Wortem: „Die Zeit des Schweigens ist vergangen, und die Zeit des Redens ist kommen! Ich habe zusammengetragen etliche Stücke, christlichen Standes Besserung belangend, dem christlichen Adel deutscher Nation vorzulegen, ob Gott wollte doch durch den Laienstand seiner Kirchen helfen; sintemal der geistliche Stand, dem es billiger gebührt, ist ganz unachtsam worden. Ich bedenke wohl, daß mir's nicht wird unverwiesen bleiben, als vermesse ich mich zu hoch, daß ich verachteter begebner Mensch solche hohe und große Stände darf anreden, in so trefflichen und großen Sachen, als wäre sonst Niemand in der Welt, denn Doktor Luther, der sich des christlichen Standes annehmen und so hoch verständigen Leuten Rath gebe. Ich lasse meine Entschuldigung anstehen, verweise mir's, wer da will; ich bin vielleicht meinem Gott und der Welt noch eine Thorheit schuldig; die habe ich mir jetzt fürgenommen, so mir's gelingen mag, endlich zu bezahlen und auch einmal Hoffnarr zu werden." So mußte die herrliche, reiche Natur dieses Mannes auch die ihm ernstesten Angelegenheiten mit einer heiteren Laune zu behandeln, aber selbst unter diesem Scherzen leuchtet die fromme Demuth hervor. Denn so heißt es weiter: „Auch dieweil ich nicht allein ein Narr, sondern auch ein geschworner Doktor der heiligen Schrift, bin ich froh, daß sich mir die Gelegenheit giebt, meinem Eid eben in derselben Narren-Weise genug zu thun. Ich bitte, wollet mich entschuldigen bei den mäßig Verständigen, denn der über hoch Verständigen Gunst und Gnade weiß ich nicht zu verdienen. —Gott helfe uns, daß wir nicht unsre, sondern allein seine Ehre suchen. Amen."

In manchen Fällen haben Narren, welche die Fürsten ehemals an ihren Höfen zur Kurzweil zu halten beliebten und die wohl oft keinem der Höflinge an Verstand wichen, ihre Gebieter mit freimüthigen Wahrheiten bedient, welche kein Höfling auszusprechen sich getraut hätte; das mochte Luthern' vorschweben bei dieser Zuschrift, daß er sich selbst mit einem Hofnarren verglich. Aber in der Schrift selbst hat er seine Sache nicht mit verdeckten Scherzen und belustigenden Spässen geführt, sondern mit einem Ernst und einer Würde, mit einer schonungslosen Aufrichtigkeit und mit einem unverstellten Gefühl, dergestalt, daß Deutschland einen beredteren und edleren Vertreter und Dolmetscher seiner Noth und Schmach, seiner Bedürfnisse und Wünsche nicht hätte finden mögen, als diesen für seine Person so demüthigen, aber im Vertrauen auf Gott so starken und getrosten Mönch. Aber vor Allem ermahnet er, die Sache nicht mit Vertrauen auf eigne Macht, sondern mit Gott anzugreifen. „Aus dem Grunde, sorge ich, sey es vor Zeiten kommen, daß die theuren Fürsten, Kaiser Friedrich der erste und der andere, und viel mehr deutscher Kaiser so jämmerlich sind von den Päbsten mit Füßen getreten und verdruckt, vor welchen sich doch die Welt fürchtete. Sie haben sich vielleicht verlassen auf ihre Macht, mehr denn auf Gott, darum haben sie müssen fallen."—„Drei Mauern haben die Romanisten um sich gezogen." Diese drei papierenen Mauern reißt Luther mit siegreicher Beredsamkeit, auf das Zeugniß der Schrift und der Geschichte sich stützend, zusammen. Er zeigt, in Beziehung auf das erste: wie alle Christen geistlichen Standes und Priester seyen, und kein Unterschied zwischen Geistlichen und Weltlichen sey, denn des Amts halber allein; darum kommt dem Geistlichen kein besonderer Vorzug zu; nicht größere Heiligkeit, nicht eigne Jurisdiktion, nicht Straflosigkeit der weltlichen Obrigkeit gegenüber, noch härtere Bestrafung des gegen Geistliche begangenen Unrechts. Ebenso wird die zweite Behauptung klärlich widerlegt, die dem Pabst die Auslegung der h. Schrift vorbehält, da der Pabst nicht höheren Stands ist in geistlichen Dingen, denn jeder Christ, und er eben so gut irren kann, weßhalb ein Concilium über ihm stehen muß, das zu berufen nicht ihm, sondern Jedem, der es vermag, am schicklichsten dem Kaiser gebühre. Mit kräftigen Zügen zeichnete Luther einem zu haltenden Concilium die Hauptgegenstände seiner Thätigkeit vor, als da sind: Einschränkung der weltlichen, ärgerlichen Pracht und Hoffart des Pabsts, Herabsetzung der Kardinäle, die eine Plage für Deutschland, weil ihre Dotationen alle Kirchengüter in Deutschland aussaugen. Ermäßigung des päbstlichen Hofhalts, Abschaffung der ursprünglich zum Türkenkrieg erhobnen, nachher schändlich vergeudeten und verschleuderten Annaten, des Mißbrauchs, daß der Pabst die Pfründen vergebe, wie der Palliumgelder, der Bischofseide wodurch ein Bischof sich in sklavische Abhängigkeit von Rom versetze. Der erblichen Pfründen, der Simonie, der unwürdigen Kunstgriffe von pectoralis reservatio, des proprius motus, der Unio et incorporatio, des Pfründenhandels und Verkaufs von Dispensationen jeder Art; (solcher Handel sey sogar an Fugger in Augsburg übertragen,) so wie noch andere schändliche und schädliche Mißbräuche und Praktiken, welche die geitzigen Römer gegen die von ihnen verachteten, v o l l e n  t o l l e n  Deutschen ausüben. Nun aber räth Luther, all dem Unwesen mit folgenden Anordnungen ein Ende zu setzen:

Die Annaten, die mißbraucht werden, sollen von allen Fürsten, Adeligen, Städten dem Pabst verweigert werden, weil die weltliche Gewalt schuldig, die Unschuldigen zu schützen; in allen jenen römischen Praktiken, wodurch der Pabst Lehen und Pfründen an sich reißt, den Deutschen entzieht und Fremden, „groben ungelehrten Eseln und Buben

zu Rom," zuwendet, soll der christliche Adel sich ihm wider-
setzen; es solle verboten werden Einholung des Palliums
und der Bestätigung der Bischöfe von Rom, damit der Pabst
sich nicht eine unbillige Gewalt über dieselben anmaße und
in alle Sachen eingreife, da ihm doch nur gebühre, schwie-
ge, streitige Fälle zwischen Primaten und Erzbischöfen zu
schlichten und auszurichten; verboten solle werden, weltliche
Sachen nach Rom zu ziehen und die „Schinderei" der Of-
fizialen; alle Priester sollen ermächtigt seyn, für alle Sünden die Absolution zu ertheilen; die unverschämten An-
sprüche des Pabsts auf Huldigung von Seiten des Kaisers
sollen, als frevelhaft, aufhören; ebenso die weltliche Herrschaft des Pabsts, die zu seinem geistlichen Amt und Beruf
nicht stimme; die Wallfahrten, die Jubeljahre, die Bettelklöster, die Theilungen Eines und desselben Ordens abgethan, Klöster und Stifte reformirt, die Gelübde für unver-
bindlich erklärt, den Priestern der schriftwidrige und verder-
bliche Cölibat erlassen, die Jahrtage, Begängnisse, Seelmes-
sen wenigstens vermindert, das sinnlose Interdikt nicht mehr
verhängt, die Strafen des geistlichen Rechts 10 Ellen tief
in die Erde begraben werden; man solle allein die Feier
des Sonntags und weniger Festtage behalten, weil die vielen Feiertage nur dem Leib und der Seele schaden, die Fasten und Speiseverbote aufgeben, die wilden Kapellen und
Feldkirchen, d. h. die neuen Wallfahrtsorte zerstören vom
Pabst nicht mehr Dispensationen und Indulgenzen kaufen, die
Bettelorden, die auf Kosten der fleißigen Leute faul und üp-
pig lebten, einschränken oder aufheben, die gestifteten Messen eingehen lassen, nicht gestatten, daß Einer mehr als
Eine Pfründe habe, die päbstlichen Nuntien verjagen, da
man von ihnen nichts als Böses lerne. Man sollte etliche
fromme und verständige Bischöfe und Gelehrte, bei Leibe
keinen Kardinal oder Ketzermeister nach Böhmen schicken,
um die Gemeinschaft wieder herzustellen; der Pabst solle

sich, um der Seelen willen, eine Zeit lang seiner Oberkeit äußern und einen Erzbischof aus den Böhmen selbst wählen lassen; man sollte sie nicht zwingen, dem Genuß des Sacraments in beiderlei Gestalt zu entsagen, weil es nicht unchristlich noch ketzerisch. Auch die Universitäten bedürfen einer starken Reformation; Aristoteles sollte man nicht mehr so abgöttisch wie bisher treiben, das geistliche Recht vom ersten Buchstaben bis zum letzten von Grund aus vertilgen und das weltliche Recht, das auch eine Wildniß geworden, doch in Vergleich mit dem geistlichen noch gut und redlich sey, weil es zu weitläuftig geworden, beschränken, das Studium der heiligen Schrift aber vor Allem treiben und hegen. Die Klöster sollen ihrer ursprünglichen Bestimmung des Unterrichts und der Erziehung zurückgegeben und Pflanzschulen der Zucht und Sittlichkeit werden. Auch auf das römische Kaiserthum kommt Luther zu sprechen. Eine unheilvolle Gabe sey den Deutschen damit zu Theil geworden; „es hat nun der römische Stuhl Rom eingenommen, den deutschen Kaiser herausgetrieben und mit Eiden verpflichtet, nicht immer zu Rom zu wohnen. Soll Römischer Kaiser seyn und dennoch Rom nicht innen haben; dazu allzeit in's Pabsts und der Seinen Muthwillen hangen und weben, daß wer den Namen haben und sie das Land und die Städte.

Hiemit schließt Luther seine Anzeige geistlicher Gebrechen, aber auch die weltlichen will er nicht ungerügt lassen. Hochnoth wäre, schreibt er, ein gemein Gebot und Bewilligung Deutscher Nation wider den überschwenglichen Ueberfluß und Kost der Kleidung, dadurch so viel Adel und reiches Volk verarme. Er warnt vor Sammt und Seide und Specerei und wucherischem Zinsnehmen und vor dem Handel. — Auch Fressen und Saufen sey eingerissen unter den Deutschen, woraus die andern Laster folgen; diesem allem zu steuern, ermahnet er die Obrigkeit und entschuldigt zum Schluß seine Freimüthigkeit mit dem Drang seines

Gewissens, da ihm lieber sey, die Welt zürne mit ihm als
Gott.

So schrieb Luther zu der Zeit, wo er den völligen Bruch
mit dem Pabst und der alten Kirche noch nicht für nothwen=
dig erachtete, wo er noch Vertrauen oder Hoffnung hatte auf
die Möglichkeit einer durchgreifenden Reformation. Er
mochte es selbst wohl ahnen, daß diejenigen, welche er auf=
forderte, sich zu diesem Werke zu vereinigen, nicht Alle be=
reitwillig seyn würden; er konnte es sich selbst schwerlich
verbergen, daß der Pabst in eine solche Beschränkung seiner
Macht und Gewalt nimmermehr willigen würde: aber er
hatte das Seinige gethan, er hatte Vorschläge gemacht, nicht
nur die Kirche in ihrer Einheit zu erhalten, sondern auch die
von ihr getrennten Böhmen wieder mit ihr auszusöhnen und
zu vereinigen, er hat damit gezeigt, daß er nicht zerreißen
wollte, sondern heilen. Religiosität und sittlicher Ernst,
Vaterlandsliebe und tiefes Nationalgefühl vereinigten sich,
solche Worte auf seine Zunge zu legen; sein Auge, auf das
Höchste gerichtet, ließ auch das Kleine, Unbedeutendere sei=
ner Aufmerksamkeit nicht entgehen; die Ehre Gottes, die
ihn beseelte und entflammte, machte ihn nicht gleichgültig
gegen die Ehre seines Volks, die schamlosen Erpressungen,
unter welchen die Nation verarmte, giengen dem Mönche,
der keine Habe besaß, an's Herz; die Mißhandlungen und
der Hohn, welche große Kaiser von den Päbsten erduldet,
empörten das Gefühl eines Mannes, der, seiner Bescheiden=
heit ungeachtet, soviel Hochsinn besaß, daß er im Namen
und aus der Seele der deutschen Nation zuversichtlich redete,
und so redete, daß diese seiner Worte sich nicht zu schämen
hatte. Gewiß, man kann ihm nicht vorwerfen, er habe
ganz Deutschland in seine persönliche Angelegenheit hinein=
ziehen und durch Ausstreuung der Saat der Feindschaft sich
Schutz und Sicherheit verschaffen wollen! Das sind nicht
die Worte eines Mannes, der sich zu verstecken und zu ver=

gen trachtet in feiger Angſt; es ſind die beſchwörenden, ge=
waltigen Sprüche eines mächtig ergriffenen, über perſön=
liche Rückſichten und Wünſche erhabenen Mannes, der den
Blinden die Augen öffnen, die Lahmen aufrütteln, die Matt=
herzigen befeuern möchte, und der nur in dem klaren Be=
wußtſeyn, daß das Höchſte auf dem Spiele ſtand, an die
Ehre und das Pflichtgefühl einer großen edeln Nation ap=
pellirte. Mit dieſer Schrift hat Luther ſich ein Denkmal
geſtiftet, das ihn billig ſchützen ſollte vor allen Anklagen, die
ihm Schuld geben: Deutſchland zerriſſen und zertheilt zu
haben; wenn Einer, ſo hatte e r Sinn dafür, daß es einig,
groß, mächtig und frei ſey von ſchändlichem Joche; daß
ſeine Vorſchläge und Räthe zeitgemäß und klug waren, ha=
ben auch diejenigen, welche ſich ihm nicht anſchloßen, früher
oder ſpäter durch die That, durch theilweiſe Aufhebung der
von ihm gerügten Mißbräuche, anerkannt; daß die deutſch=
en Fürſten, daß der Kaiſer ſelbſt nicht ſein Werk unterſtütz=
ten und gemeinſam handelten, war ſeine Schuld nicht.]

---

Gnade und Stärke[1] von Gott zuvor.[2] Allerdurchlauch=
tigſte,[3] gnädigſte liebe Herren! Es iſt nicht aus lauter Vor=

---

[1] S t ä r k e. A blessing appropriate to be invoked upon princes and
nobles, especially in a military age. This word is undoubtedly taken
from the Scriptures, in which God is often called *the strength* of his
servants.

[2] Z u v o r, *first*, a common form of official salutation, because it
stands *at the beginning* of the address, and is designed to conciliate
favor; as, M e i n e n  f r e u n d l i c h e n  G r u s s  u n d  D i e n s t e
z u v o r! *first of all, I present my friendly salutation and offer my
service.*

[3] A l l e r d u r c h l a u c h t i g s t e, *most illustrious*, a title given
now to emperors and kings only. D u r c h l a u c h t i g, is a literal,
but awkward translation of the Latin title *perillustris*. A l l e r, prefixed to superlatives to give them intensity, was originally a genitive
plural governed by the superlative, *the most illustrious of all.*

witz[1] noch Frevel geschehen, daß ich einiger[2] armer Mens
mich unterstanden,[3] vor euern hohen Würden zu reden
Die Noth und Beschwerung,[4] die alle Stände der Christen
heit, zuvor Deutschland drückt, nicht allein mich, sonderr
Jedermann beweget hat vielmal zu schreien und Hülfe zu
begehren, hat mich auch jetzt gezwungen zu schreien und ru
fen, ob[5] Gott Jemand den Geist geben wollte, seine Han
zu reichen der elenden Nation. Es ist oft durch Concilien
etwas vorgewandt, aber durch etlicher Menschen List behen
diglich[7] verhindert und immer ärger geworden; welche
Tücke und Bosheit ich jetzt, Gott helfe mir, zu durchleuchten

[1] V o r w i t z. In the old writers F ü r w i t z often occurs, th
particles v o r and f ü r being used indiscriminately. It means *im
pertinent forwardness and rashness.*

[2] E i n i g, which now expresses unity; as, G o t t i s t e i n i g
*God is one and indivisible,* was formerly used in the sense of e i n
z i g, *one alone.* So here, and elsewhere, as in Mark 10: 18; N i e
m a n d i s t g u t, d e n n d e r e i n i g e Gott, *No one is good bu
God alone.*

[3] U n t e r s t a n d e n, with, the auxiliary h a b e omitted, as it of
ten is.

[4] D i e N o t h u n d B e s c h w e r u n g. As these two word
designate *one and the same thing,* the verbs agreeing with them ar
put in the singular. Z u v o r D e u t s c h l a n d, *especially Ger
many.* B e w e g t h a t is connected with d r ü c k t by u n d un
derstood. This copulative conjunction is frequently omitted betwee
verbs in German where it would be indispensable in English.

[5] O b. Before this word, the English reader would expect som
such expression as u m z u s e h e n; but it is not necessary in Ger
man.

[6] C o n c i l i e n, especially those of the 15th century, held at Pisa
Constance and Bâle.

[7] B e h e n d i g l i c h, *dexterously.* B e h e n d e stands for b e
d e r H a n d. So v o r h a n d e n means *at hand.* B e h e n d i g
k e i t, *dexterity,* occurs below.

[8] D u r c h l e u c h t e n, *to clear up,* governs T ü c k e u n d B o s
h e i t, and these govern w e l c h e r in the genitive plural. " Whos
intrigues and wickedness I now intend, with God's help, to expose.'

gebenfe, auf daß ſie erkannt,[1] hinfort nicht mehr ſo hinder=
lich und ſchädlich ſeyn möchten.   Gott hat uns ein junges
edles Blut zum Haupt[2] gegeben, damit viel Herzen zu großer
guter Hoffnung erwecket ;[3] daneben[4] will ſich's ziemen, das
Unſere dazu zu thun, und der Zeit und Gnade nützlich
brauchen.[5]

Die Romaniſten haben drei Mauern mit großer Behen=
digfeit um ſich gezogen, damit ſie ſich bisher beſchützet,[6] daß
ſie Niemand hat mögen reformiren, dadurch die ganze
Chriſtenheit greulich gefallen iſt.

Zum erſten, wenn man hat auf ſie gedrungen mit welt=
licher Gewalt, haben ſie geſetzt und geſagt :[7] Weltliche Ge=

---

[1] Erkannt, a participle used adjectively with sie.  Auf dass
for dass or damit, *to the end that.*

[2] Ein junges Blut zum Haupt.  Charles V. who had been
recently elected zum Haupt, *for a head*, or emperor.  Zu is the
proper word for expressing destination, or that which anything is designed or appointed to become.

[3] [Und] damit viel Herzen—erwecket, "and thereby ex-
cited many hearts to high and pleasing hopes."  The predominant
meaning of damit in Luther's writings is *therewith, thereby*, whereas, in modern German *in order that*, is as common a signification.
This last idea Luther generally expressed by auf dass.

[4] Daneben, etc.  "In connection with that, it will be proper
[for us] to contribute our part."  Dazu thun, as an active verb,
means *to add;* as a neuter verb, it signifies, *to be attentive* or *careful.*

[5] Brauchen, sometimes governs the genitive, and sometimes the
accusative.  With the former, it has a more elevated and antique air.
"And to make a good use of the occasion and favor."

[6] Damit sie sich bisher beschutzet [haben], "with
which they have hitherto defended themselves, so that no one has
been able to reform them ; and by this means (dadurch) all Christendom has sadly fallen."

[7] Gesetzt und gesagt, "established (as a law) and proclaim-
ed, that the civil power has no authority over them."  And a few
lines below, setzen sie dagegen, "they, on the contrary, lay
it down as a law, that it belongs to none but the pope to interpret the
Scriptures."  See p. 11, Note 5.

walt habe nicht Recht über sie, sondern wiederum, geiftliche sey über die weltliche.

Zum andern, hat man sie mit der heiligen Schrift wollen strafen, setzen sie dagegen : Es gebühre die Schrift Niemand auszulegen, denn dem Pabst.

Zum dritten, dräuet[1] man ihnen mit einem Concilio, so erdichten sie, es möge Niemand ein Concilium berufen denn der Pabst.

Also haben sie drei Ruthen uns heimlich geftohlen, daß sie mögen ungeftraft feyn, und fich in fichere Befeftigung diefer drei Mauern gefetzet,[2] alle Büberei und Bosheit zu treiben, wie wir denn jetzt fehen. Und ob fie fchon ein Concilium müßten machen, haben fie doch daffelbe zuvor matt gemacht damit, daß[3] fie die Fürften zuvor mit Eiden verpflichten, fie bleiben zu laffen wie fie find ; dazu dem Pabst volle Gewalt geben über alle Ordnung des Conciliums ; also, daß gleich gilt, es feyen viel Concilien, oder keine Concilien, ohne daß fie uns nur mit Larven und Spielgefechten betrügen. So gar greulich fürchten fie der Haut[4] vor einem

---

[1] Dräuet, from dräuen, which is obsolete for drohen.

[2] Sich — gesetzt, *placed themselves*, connected with gestohlen by und. Zu treiben is used in the sense of um zu treiben. "Thus have they secretly stolen from us three cudgels, that they might go unpunished, and put themselves under the sure defence of these three walls, in order to practise all kinds of mischief and iniquity, as we now behold."

[3] Damit, dass, "*by this means* (viz.) that they first bound the princes with an oath, to let them (the Romanists) remain as they are ; and besides (dazu), to give to the pope full power over the entire arrangement of the council, so that (also dass) it was indifferent whether there be (es seyen, *there be*, subjunctive) many councils or no councils, except that they deceive us with mere masks and mockfights." Ohne dass, in modern German, does not mean *except*, but *without*, and ohne dass sie uns betrügen, would, at the present day, mean the same as ohne uns zu betrügen, *without deceiving us.*

[4] Der Haut, *for their skin.* Such an adverbial use of the genitive, limiting or qualifying the verb, is very common.

rechten freien Concilio, und haben damit[1] Könige und Für=
sten schüchtern gemacht, daß sie glauben, es wäre wider
Gott, so man ihnen nicht gehorchte in allen solchen schalk=
haftigen listigen Spügnißen.

Nun helfe uns Gott, und gebe uns der Posaunen eine,[2]
damit die Mauern Jericho wurden umgeworfen, daß wir
diese strohernen und papiernen Mauern auch umblasen, und
die christlichen Ruthen, Sünden zu strafen,[3] los machen,[4]
des Teufels List und Trug an den Tag zu bringen, auf daß
wir durch Strafe uns bessern, und seine Huld wieder erlan=
gen. Wollen[5] die erste Mauer am ersten angreifen.*

---

Zuerst zeiget er also,[6] daß alle Christen an dem geistlichen

---

[1] D a m i t, *with that*, more commonly indicates *instrumentality ;*
but it may also express mere *concomitancy*, as it does here. " Thus
terribly are they frightened for their lives (skin) by (v o r, *before, in
view of*) a really free council, and with this (fear in their hearts), they
have intimidated kings and princes, so that the latter believe, that it
would be an offence against God, if one should not obey them (the
Papists) in all such mischievous hobgoblin tricks (trickish hobgob-
lins)." S p ü g n i s s e n, is now a Thuringian provincialism, for which
Luther sometimes uses G e s p ü g n i s s, which is found in the glos-
saries of the old German. It is derived from S p u k, by the addition
of the termination n i s s, and a dialectical change of the *k* into *g*.

[2] D e r  P a u s a u n e n  e i n e, " *one of the trumpets*, with which the
walls of Jericho were overthrown." U m b l a s e n, *to blow over*, or
*down.*

[3] Z u  s t r a f e n, depends on R u t h e n, *rods to punish sin.*

[4] L o s  m a c h e n, *to pull away from*, the hands of the Romanists
who held them fast, to prevent their being used.

[5] [W i r]  w o l l e n.

[6] A l s o, here in its secondary, or illative sense, *there, therefore.*

* Instead of the theological discussions respecting " the three walls
of the Romanists," which here ensue, we have preferred merely to
preserve the connection by substituting an abridgement from Mar-
heinecke, mostly in the words of Luther.

Wesen[1] Theil haben und hier kein Unterschied sey, denn des Amtes[2] halben allein, daß wir allesamt[3] sind zu Priestern[4] geweihet durch die Taufe, obwohl nicht Jedem geziemet, das Amt zu verwalten. Darum,[5] sagt er, sollte ein Priesterstand[6] nichts anderes seyn in der Christenheit, denn als ein Amtsmann; weil er am Amt ist, gehet er vor, wo[7] er aber abge-

---

[1] Geistlichen Wesen, spiritual or ministerial character. For the peculiar use of the word Wesen, see p. 26, Note 1.

[2] Denn des Amtes, "no other difference than that of the office alone." So denn and als are often used after kein, "no other than."

[3] Allesamt, etymologically the same as *altogether*, meaning, however, *all collectively*.

[4] Zu Priestern. See p. 94, Note 2, and Nöhden's Gram. p. 338. This clause, in simple modern German, would be arranged thus: dass wir allesamt durch die Taufe zu Priestern geweihet (worden) sind, obwohl (es) nicht, etc.

[5] Darum causes sollte to precede its nominative. Sagt precedes er when any words of a quotation precede. So in English the phrase, "says he."

[6] Priesterstand. The modern taste for minute accuracy in expression would be offended with the incongruity, not felt at all in Luther's time, of representing "the *priesthood* to be nothing else in Christianity than an *officer*." "Because he is in office, he takes the precedence (gehet er vor); but if he be deposed, he is a peasant and (or) citizen, as the other (the individual supposed, i. e. any other, who is not a priest)."

[7] Wo, now nearly obsolete in the sense of wenn, and which was originally an adverb of place (*where*); afterwards it was a conditional conjunction (*if*). It expressed, at first, a *local* condition, *in what place*, or *wherever a certain thing shall occur*, equivalent to, *if anywhere it occur*. Hence it expresses a condition more emphatically than wenn, *if*, which barely indicates a condition without any intensity of expression. So (if) is sometimes used in the same sense as wo (a condition emphatically expressed); but this use is less frequent and has more of an antique air. Wofern, sofern, and dafern (if), limit the condition to a certain measure or degree, *to the extent that, so far as*. They differ from wo in intensity as wo differs from wenn. Falls (if), expresses more uncertainty as to the

feßt, ift er ein Bauer und Bürger,[1] wie der andere. Und
so hat auch weltliche Obrigkeit, von Gott eingesetzet, ihr
Amt,[2] die Bösen zu strafen, die Frommen zu schützen; so
soll man ihr Amt lassen frei gehen und unverhindert[3] durch
den ganzen Karper der Christenheit, niemand angesehen,[4]
sie treffe Pabst, Bischöfe, Pfaffen, Mönche, Nonnen oder
was er ist.[5]   Denn so das genug wäre,[6] weltliche Gewalt
zu hindern, weil sie geringer ist unter den christlichen Aem=
tern, denn der Prediger und Beichtiger Amt oder der geist=
liche Stand, so sollte man auch hindern den Schneidern,[7]
Schustern, Steinmetzen, Zimmerleuten, Koch, Kellnern,
Bauern und allen zeitlichen Handwerkern, daß sie dem Papst

---

event, and differs from wenn, as *in case that,* in English, differs
from *if.*

[1] Bauer, Bürger.  The termination e r, indicates one who cul-
tivates (b a u e n) the soil, or who lives in a castle (B u r g) or town.
See Gram. p. 70.

[2] I h r  A m t, explained by the following words in apposition.
" So also the civil government, appointed by God, has its office (viz.)
to punish, etc."

[3] U n v e r h i n d e r t is used adjectively and connected by u n d
to f r e i.

[4] N i e m a n d  a n g e s e h e n, (an obsolete expression) nominative
absolute, " no one regarded," i. e. without respect of persons, " be it
(fall it upon,) pope, bishops," etc.  See p. 15, Note 8.

[5] W a s  e r  i s t differs from w e r  e r  i s t, just as " whatever he
be," differs from " whoever he be."  W a s refers not to one's individual character, but to his standing, or rank.

[6] S o  d a s  g e n u g  w ä r e, " if that were (reason) sufficient for
hindering the civil power, because among the Christian offices it is
lower than the office of preachers and confessors, or than the priesthood," etc. See p. 97, Note 7, on s o.  D a s refers to the clause, w e i l
s i e  g e r i n g e r  i s t, etc.  Z u  h i n d e r n is dependent on g e n u g.

[7] H i n d e r n  d e n  S c h n e i d e r n — d a s s  s i e  d e m  P a p s t
k e i n e  K l e i d e r  m a c h t e n, hinder tailors, etc. from making (hinder them, so that they make no shoes, etc.).   H i n d e r n, which
commonly governs the accusative, here governs the dative.  W e h-
r e n is now used for h i n d e r n, which is obsolete in this sense.

Bischöfen, Priestern, Mönchen keine Schuh, Kleider, Häuser, Essen und Trinken machten, noch Zins gäben. Also mein ich, diese erste Papiermauer liege darnieder, sintemal[1] weltliche Herrschaft ist ein Mitglied worden des christlichen Körpers.

Ebenso widerleget er auch den andern Irrthum, daß die Schrift allein in den Händen des Papstes sey, daß er nicht irren könne[2] in Auslegung derselben. Wo das wäre,[3] wozu wäre die heilige Schrift noth oder nütze? Lasset sie uns verbrennen[4] und uns begnügen an[5] den ungelehrten Herren zu Rom, die der heilige Geist inne hat;[6] wenn ich's nicht gelesen hätte, wäre mir's[7] unglaublich gewesen, daß der Teu-

---

[1] S i n t e m a l, see p. 18, Note 9. The construction is antiquated for s i n t e m a l  w e l t l i c h e  H e r r s c h a f t  e i n  M i t g l i e d  d e s  c h r i s t l i c h e n  K ö r p e r s  (ge)  w o r d e n  i s t.

[2] S e i — i r r e n  k ö n n e. These verbs, s e i  and  k ö n n e, are put in the subjunctive because they relate not to a reality, but to a conceit or imagination, indicated by the word I r r t h u m, which they are employed to explain.

[3] W o  d a s  w ä r e,  w o z u, *if that were* (so), *for what*, etc.? for W e n n  d a s  s o  w ä r e.  See p. 97, Note 7.

[4] L a s s e t  s i e  u n s  v e r b r e n n e n, *let us burn it.*  S i e  refers to S c h r i f t.

[5] U n s  b e g n ü g e n  a n, *content ourselves with.*  For the use of a n with the dative, as pointing out an agreeable object, see p. 80, Note 3.

[6] I n n e  h a t, "whom the Holy Ghost has in charge."  Literally, *to have within one's self*, i. e. *to have in one's power* or *at one's disposal.*  It differs from b e s i t z e n, *to possess*, i. e. *to have the ownership of*, because one may have in his power, or at his control, (i n n e h a b e n), a *hired* house, and yet not possess it (b e s i t z e n).  A commander-in-chief is the I n h a b e r (disposer) but not the B e s i t z e r (owner) of his army.

[7] W ä r e  m i r' s, for w ä r e  e s  m i r.  "Had I not read it, it would have been incredible to me that Satan should, at Rome, have made such absurd pretences (have pretended such absurd things) and have found adherents, or a party."  V o r w e n d e n, almost precisely similar to *pretend* (*prae* and *tendo*) both in etymology and in signifi-

fel follte zu Rom folche ungeschickte Dinge vorwenden und Anhang finden. Luther eignet hier einem jeden Christen das Recht zu,[1] die heilige Schrift zu lefen und die Macht, zu schmecken[2] und zu urtheilen, was da recht oder unrecht im Glauben sey.

Die dritte Mauer fällt von selbst um, so die ersten zwo[3] fallen, nämlich, daß der Pabst allein das Recht habe, Concilien zu versammeln. Denn wäre das nicht, sagt er, ein unnatürlich Vornehmen, so ein Feuer in einer Stadt aufs ginge und jedermann sollte stille stehn, lassen für und für[4]

---

cation, always, when used in this secondary sense, conveys the idea of making a *false* pretence, while v o r g e b e n has the same general meaning, except that there may be some truth in the pretence. E. g. To avoid an engagement, one may v o r g e b e n a pressure of business (which may be the truth) or he may v o r w e n d e n a feigned illness. — A n h a n g, *appendix*, i. e. something appended to a book or chapter of the *same character* with it, (and therein differing from Z u s a t z, which may be *similar* or *dissimilar*) but designedly separated from it (and therein differing from N a c h t r a g, which is the addition of something omitted before, either from forgetfulness, or from ignorance). Applied to persons, A n h a n g means, a clique which a man gathers around him of persons of the *same sentiments and feelings* with himself. See p. 53, Note 2.

[1] E i g n e t — z u. Z u e i g n e n, means literally *to give* or *to accord to one something as his own. To dedicate* (a book), *to ascribe* (an act) to one, are derived significations.

[2] S c h m e c k e n, (like the Latin *sapere*), *to taste ;* then *to feel, to experience, to perceive.* This is particularly the biblical use of the word, as also of the English word *taste,* as " come taste and see," etc. " Luther concedes to every Christian the right to read the Scriptures and the power to perceive and to decide what (d a is an expletive) is right and wrong in (matters of) faith."

[3] S o d i e e r s t e n z w o, *if the first two.* For s o, see p. 97, Note 7; for z w o as the intermediate form between z w e i and the English *two,* see p. 49, Note 1. N ä m l i c h refers not to z w o, but to d i e d r i t t e M a u e r. M a u e r, is derived from the Latin *murus,* though with a change of the gender, for the ground of which see Gram. p. 91.

[4] F ü r u n d f ü r. This is an old form of expression which orig

brennen, was da brennen mag, allein darum, daß sie nicht die Macht des Burgermeisters hätten oder das Feuer vielleicht nicht an des Burgermeisters Haus anhübe?[1] Ist hier nicht ein jeglicher Bürger schuldig, die andern zu bewegen und zu berufen? Wieviel mehr soll das in der geistlichen Stadt Christi geschehen, so ein Feuer des Aegernisses sich erhebet, es sey an des Papstes Regiment oder wo es wolle. Daß sie aber ihre Gewalt rühmen, der sich nicht zieme[2] zu widerfechten, ist gar nichts geredt. Es ist keine Gewalt in der Kirche, denn nur zur Besserung: darum wo sich der Pabst[3] wollte der Gewalt brauchen, zu wehren, ein frei Concilium zu machen, damit verhindert würde die Besserung der Kirche, so sollen wir ihn und seine Gewalt nicht ansehen

---

inated when f ü r was equivalent to v o r, and means literally *forwards and forwards*, i. e. *ever onward*, 1. in regard to space, 2. and more commonly, in regard to time, *incessantly*. " Stand still (and) let it burn on continually as far as it will (whatever may burn).

[1] A n h ü b e, obsolete for a n h ö b e imperfect subjunctive from a n h e b e n. See h e b e n in Gram. p. 420. For the signification of the word, see p. 39, Note 4.

[2] D e r s i c h [e s] n i c h t z i e m e. " That they boast of a (their) power, which it is not becoming (s i c h n i c h t z i e m e) to resist, is saying (or amounts to) nothing at all;"—literally " is nothing said." See p. 9, Note 5.

[3] D a r u m w o s i c h d e r P a p s t " Therefore if the pope should be disposed (w o l l t e) to make use of (s i c h [g e] b r a u - c h e n) power to prevent holding (z u m a c h e n) a free council, in order that the reformation of the church may (might) be hindered, we ought to disregard (both) him and his power; and if he should come and thunder (in his bulls), we should look down upon it as upon the work (undertaking) of a mad man, in reliance upon God (i n G o t t e s ʼ Z u v e r s i c h t) put him, in turn, under the ban, and drive him away as well as we can (as one can)." According to good modern usage, b r a u c h e n signifies *to need*, and g e b r a u c h e n is employed in the sense of *to use*. S i c h g e b r a u c h e n, *to make use of*, with the genitive, is now provincial. Such is the change which the language has undergone since Luther's time.

wo er kommen und donnern würde, sollte man das verach=
ten, als eines tollen Menschen Vornehmen, und ihn in Got=
tes Zuversicht wiederum bannen und treiben, wie man mag.
Denn solch eine vermessene Gewalt ist nichts;[1] er hat sie
auch nicht und wird bald mit einem Spruche der Schrift
niedergeleget; denn Paulus sagt 2 Cor. 10, 8.  Gott hat
uns Gewalt gegeben, nicht zu verderben, sondern zu bessern
die Christenheit.   Wer will über diesen Spruch hüpfen?

## Wovon in den Concilien zu handeln.

Nun wollen wir sehen die Stücke,[2] die man billig[3] in den
Concilien sollte handeln, und damit Päbste, Cardinäle, Bi=
schöfe und alle Gelehrten sollten billig Tag und Nacht umge=
hen,[4] so sie Christum und seine Kirche lieb hätten.  Wo sie
aber das nicht thun, daß der Haufe und das weltliche
Schwert dazu thue, unangesehen ihr Bannen oder Donnern.
Denn ein unrechter Bann ist besser denn zehen rechte Abso=
lutionen; und eine unrechte Absolution ärger denn zehn
rechte Bänne.  Darum lasset uns aufwachen, liebe Deutsche,
und Gott mehr denn die Menschen fürchten, daß wir nicht
theilhaftig werden aller armen Seelen, die so kläglich durch)

---

[1] N i c h t s, *a nonentity.*  "Nor has he it;" u n d  (s i e)  w i r d
b a l d, etc.

[2] S t ü c k e, *the particulars.*  See p. 30, Note 1.

[3] B i l l i g, *reasonably,* is not to be connected with h a n d e l n,
*to act reasonably,* which would give a false sense ; but it must be
connected with s o l l t e, *ought reasonably,* i. e. ought in justice.
To neglect to do these things would be unreasonable.  So also a few
words below b i l l i g indicates the reasonableness of the obligation
expressed by s o l l t e n.

[4] D a m i t — u m g e h e n, " with which popes, etc. ought in reason to concern themselves night and day, if they had any regard for
Christ and his church."  The subjunctive, h ä t t e n, implies that
they had no regard for Christ.

das schändliche, teufelische Regiment der Römer verloren
werden.

Zum ersten ist's greulich und erschrecklich anzusehen,[1] daß
der Oberste in der Christenheit, der sich Christi Vicarium,
und St. Peters Nachfolger rühmet,[2] so weltlich und präch=
tig fähret, daß ihn darinnen kein König, kein Kaiser mag
erlangen und gleich werden, und indem der Allerheiligste[3]
und Geistlichste sich läßt nennen, weltlicher Wesen ist, denn
die Welt selber ist. Er trägt eine dreifältige Krone, wo die
höchsten Könige nur Eine Krone tragen; gleicht sich das[4]
mit dem armen Christo und St. Peter, so ist's ein neu
gleichen. Man plärret, es sey ketzerisch, wo man dawider

---

[1] A n z u s e h e n, is not here used in an active sense, governing
the following clause, but that clause is in apposition with e s (in
i s t's) and consequently in the nominative; and e r s c h r e c k l i c h
a n z u s e h e n corresponds to the Latin *horribile visu.*

[2] S i c h — r ü h m e t, ordinarily signifies to *praise one's self,* or *to
boast of,* with the genitive of the thing of which he boasts. But
originally the word meant *to call one's self something,* and so it is used
here. V i e l e  M e n s c h e n  w e r d e n  f r o m m  g e r ü h m t, "many men *are called* pious." Prov. 20: 6. Comp. Prov. 16: 21. in Luther's version.

[3] D e r  a l l e r h e i l i g s t e, etc., "and while he allows (causes)
himself to be called the most holy and most spiritual, he is a more
worldly creature (being) than the world itself." Observe the use of
the nominative (d e r  a l l e r h e i l i g s t e) after n e n n e n with s i c h
which is in the accusative. So in closing a letter one says, I c h
e m p f e h l e  m i c h  a l s  I h r  g e h o r s a m s t e r (not I h r e n  g e-
h o r s a m s t e n) D i e n e r. Titles as well as proper names are often
used without the ordinary variations of declension. See analogous
instances in Gram. p. 323, infra. In all other cases the accusative is
used when in apposition with s i c h in reflective verbs. — W e l t l i-
c h e r for w e l t l i c h e r e s. For an explanation of the omission of
the ending e s, which is so common in the writings of Luther, see
p. 4, Note 3. S e l b e r an indeclinable pronoun is nearly obsolete
for s e l b s t.

[4] G l e i c h t  s i c h  d a s, "if that resembles, etc:, it is a new (kind
of) resemblance."

rebet ; man will aber auch nicht hören, wie unchriſtlich und ungöttlich ſolch' Weſen ſey. Ich halte aber, wenn er mit Thränen beten ſollte vor Gott, er müßte je ſolche ⸱Krönen ablegen ; dieweil[1] unſer Gott keine Hoffahrt mag leiden. Nun ſollte ſein Amt nichts anderes ſeyn, denn täglich wei=nen und beten für die Chriſtenheit, und ein Erempel⸱aller Demuth vortragen.

Zum andern, wozn iſt das Volk nütze[2] in der Chriſtenheit, das da heißet die Cardinäle? Das will ich dir ſagen. Welſch=[3] und Deutſchland haben viel reicher Klöſter,[4] Stifte, Lehen und Pfarreien ; die bat man nicht gewußt beſſer gen Rom zu bringen, denn daß man Cardinäle mache,[5] und den=ſelbigen die Biſthümer, Klöſter, Prälaturen zu eigen gäbe,[6] und Gottesdienſt alſo zu Boden ſtieße. Darum ſiehet man jetzt, daß Welſchland faſt wüſte iſt, Klöſter verſtöret, Bis=

---

[1] D i e w e i l originally meant *while, during.* See p. 26, Note 2. Afterwards, it came to signify as it does here, *since, because,* which is now provincial, and w e i l is now the common word for *since, be-cause.*

[2] W o z u  i s t  d a s  V o l k  n ü t z e — d a s, " for what is that [class of ] people useful (i. e. of what use are they) which are called car-dinals ?"

[3] W e l s c h [l a n d].  W e l s c h signifies what is *foreign,* particu-larly what is of Roman origin ; and hence more commonly it means *Italian,* but sometimes it means *French.*

[4] K l ö s t e r in the genitive plural, governed by v i e l.  K l o s t e r comes from the Latin *claustrum,* a closed, or secluded place.  S t i f-te r, L e h e n  u n d  P f a r r e n, *religious foundations, ecclesiastical fiefs,* and *parishes.* The two former are indefinite terms for which B i s t h u m e r and P r ä l a t u r e n seem to be used a little below.

[5] D e n n  d a s s  m a n — m a c h t e, " than that one should make," i. e. than to make.

[6] Z u  e i g e n  g ä b e, *to give for their own.* Z u, expressing *des-tination,* is to be variously translated by *to, for,* and *as.* All the grammatical relations are here fully and clearly expressed ;—" that one should give⸱to the same (the cardinals) the sees, etc., to be their own."

thümer verzehret,[1] Prälaturen und aller Kirchen Zinse gen
Rom gezogen, Städte verfallen, Land und Leute verdorben,
da kein Gottesdienst noch Predigt mehr gehet. Warum?
Die Kardinäle müssen die Güter haben. Kein Türke hätte
Welschland so mögen verderben, und Gottesdienst niederle=
gen.

Nun[2] Welschland ausgesogen ist, kommen sie in's Deutsch=
land, heben sein säuberlich[3] an : aber sehen wir zu, Deutsch=
land soll bald dem Welschen gleich werden. Wir haben
schon etliche Cardinäle. Was darinnen[4] die Römer suchen,
sollen die trunknen Deutschen[5] nicht verstehen, bis sie kein
Bisthum, Kloster, Pfarrei, Lehen, Heller oder Pfennig[6]

---

[1] Verstöret — verzehret, participles for verstört and
verzehrt and construed like wüste; "Therefore we see that Italy is almost desolate, cloisters broken up, episcopal sees consumed,
prebends and the revenues of all the churches carried to Rome, cities
decayed, the country and people ruined, in which (d a in the sense
of w o) there is no longer religious service nor preaching."

[2] N u n. See p. 12, Note 4.

[3] S ä u b e r l i c h means, *neatly, nicely, with finesse.* "Now that
Italy is drained, they come to Germany, and go to work with admi-
rable finesse. But behold! Germany, in their view, (s o l l) is soon
to become like Italy." H e b e n—a n, see p. 39, Note 4. S e h e n
w i r z u, *lo!* as an imperative is unusual. See Gram. p. 169, note.
The common form would be, s e h e t n u r z u. S o l l, *is said,* or
*is thought,* see Gram. p. 180, 3. So s o l l e n a little below, expresses
merely the *view* or *intention* of the Romans.

[4] D a r i n n e n, *therein,* refers not to D e u t s c h l a n d, but to
C a r d i n ä l e. "What the Romans seek therein (in the appoint-
ment of cardinals), the sottish Germans must not understand."

[5] D i e t r u n k n e n D e u t s c h e n. Here used in the sense of
the Italians, as a term of reproach, and we are sorry to add that the
reproach was but too well merited. Hence the Italians despised the
Germans as a sottish people. Luther often alludes to this sottishness
and stupidity, and calls on his countrymen to wipe off the reproach.

[6] P f e n n i g, often in old German and Upper German P f e n-
n i n g formerly meant *money, coin* in general, and hence had various adjectives prefixed to it, which have at length come to be used

mehr haben.   Der Antichrift muß die Schäße der Erde he=
ben,[1] wie es verkündiget ift.   Es gehet daher,[2] man fchäu=
met oben ab[3] von den Bisthümern, Klöftern und Lehen;
und weil fie noch nicht Alles dürfen gar verfchwenden, wie
fie den Welfchen gethan haben, brauchen fie dieweil[4] folche
heilige Behendigkeit, daß fie zehn oder zwanzig Prälaturen
zufammen koppeln, und von einer jeglichen ein jährliches
Stück reißen, daß doch eine Summa daraus werde.   Die
Probftei zu Würzburg giebt taufend Gulden, die zu Bam=
berg auch etwas, Mainz, Trier und der mehr;[5] fo möchte

---

alone as nouns; thus g u l d e n  P f e n n i g, a gold Pfennig or Gulden; g r o s s  P f e n n i g, a large Pfennig or  Groschen;  H a l l e r,
or  H e l l e r  P f e n n i g, a Pfennig made at  H a l l  in Suabia, or
a  H e l l e r  (or  H a l l e r);  K r e u z e r  P f e n n i g, a Pfennig with
the  stamp  of  the cross  upon it (originally), or a  K r e u z e r  equal
now to four Pfennigs.   A  P f e n n i g  is about 1-4 of a cent, and a
H e l l e r  about 1-8 of a cent.

[1] D i e  S c h ä t z e  d e r  E r d e  h e b e n.   H e b e n, *to elevate,*
forms with various words peculiar idioms, most of which spring from
the signification *to take up, to take away;* as, e i n e n  S c h a t z  h e -
b e n, *to dig up and carry away a treasure;* e i n  K i n d  a u s  d e r
T a u f e  h e b e n, *to be godfather or godmother at baptism;* e i n e n
a u s  d e m  S a t t e l  h e b e n, *to supplant one;* G e l d—S t e u e r n
h e b e n, *to raise or receive money—taxes;* e i n e  K r a n k h e i t—e i n
H i n d e r n i s s—e i n e n  Z w e i f e l  h e b e n, *to remove a disease
—an obstacle —a doubt;* e i n e n  S t r e i t  h e b e n, *to terminate a
quarrel.*

[2] E s  g e h e t  d a h e r, *hence it comes that.*   D a h e r  often expresses the *ground* or *cause* from which anything proceeds or results.
D a h e r  k o m m t  e s,  d a s s  is the common phrase, for, *hence it
comes that.*

[3] M a n  s e h ä u m e t  o b e n  a b, " they skim off the cream."
A b s c h ä u m e n, means *to take off the scum,* or *skim off the cream.*

[4] B r a u c h e n  s i e  d i e w e i l, " meanwhile they exercise such
holy skill that they unite ten or twenty benefices together [for one
cardinal], and seize on an annual amount from each, so that a [good
round] sum is raised [without exciting alarm].

[5] U n d  d e r  m e h r, *and many others,* literally, *and of these more,*

man ein taufend Gulben ober zehn[1] zufammenbringen, da= mit ein Carbinal ſich einem reichen Könige gleich halte zu Rom.

Wenn wir nun das gewonnen,[2] ſo wollen wir dreißig ober vierzig Carbinäle[3] auf einen Tag machen, und einem geben den Münchberg[4] zu Bamberg, und das Bisthum zu Würzburg dazu, daran gehängt[5] etliche reiche Pfarreien, bis

---

d e r being a demonstrative pronoun in the genitive plural, governed by m e h r. "The provostship of Wurceburg will furnish (furnishes) a thousand guldens ; that at Bamberg also something, (and so) May- ence, Triers and many others."

[1] Z e h n, i. e. z e h n t a u s e n d. "One thousand guldens or ten," is a very peculiar idiom, found also in Dutch, for "about ten thousands guldens." D a m i t, *with which sum.*

[2] W e n n w i r n u n d a s g e w o n n e n (h a b e n). So Lu- ther represents the Romans as saying to themselves.

[3] D r e i s s i g o d e r v i e r z i g C a r d i n ä l e. This number of cardinals for Germany will not appear so extravagant and void of verisimilitude, if we recollect that in Italy, which Luther holds up as a specimen of what is to be expected in Germany, there were fourteen cardinal deacons, and fifty cardinal presbyters, connected with the different churches in the city of Rome, and seven cardinal bishops from adjacent Italian cities. The number of cardinals was variable till Sixtus V. in 1586, fixed them at seventy, corresponding to the number of the elders among the Israelites. Luther undoubt- edly had in mind the recent instance of arbitrary power by which Leo X. created thirty-one new cardinals in a single day. Hurter's Innocenz III. vol 3, p. 156.

[4] M ü n c h b e r g. "In it (Bamberg) is the cathedral of St. Ste- phen and St. James, *together with the grand and rich Benedictine clois- ter of Münchberg,* and the nunnery of St. Theodore." Büsching's Geography.

[5] G e h ä n g t, a participle used absolutely with P f a r r e i e n. "And give to one (of the cardinals) Münchburg in Bamberg, and the bishopric of Wurceburg besides, several rich parishes being at- tached to it, till churches and cities are desolate" (their revenues go- ing to cardinals); and then say, we are the vicars of Christ, the shepherds of Christ's flock ; — the senseless, sottish Germans must bear it." These last words represent the feelings, not of the Ro-

daß Kirchen und Städte wüste sind, und darnach sagen, wir sind Christi Vicarien, und Hirten der Schafe Christi ; die tollen vollen Deutschen müssen es wohl leiden.

Ich rathe aber, daß man der Cardinäle weniger mache,[1] oder lasse sie[2] den Pabst von seinem Gute nähren. Ihrer wäre übrig genug an zwölf,[3] und ein Jeder hätte[4] des Jahres tausend Gulden einzukommen. Wie kommen wir Deutschen dazu, daß wir solche Räuberei, Schwinderei[5] unsrer Güter, von dem Pabst leiden müssen ? Hat das Königreich Frankreich sich's erwehret,[6] warum lassen wir Deutsche uns also narren und äffen ?[7] Es wäre Alles erträglicher, wenn sie das Gut allein uns also abstöhlen ; die Kirchen verwüsten sie damit, und berauben die Schafe Christi ihrer frommen Hirten, und legen den Dienst und Wort Gottes nieder. Und wenn schon kein Cardinal wäre,

---

mans, whom Luther had just introduced as speaking, but of Luther himself.

[1] D e r   C a r d i n ä l e   w e n i g e r   m a c h e n, *make fewer cardinals.*  W e n i g e r, as an adverb of quantity, governs the genitive, d e r   C a r d i n ä l e.

[2] S i e, is governed by n ä h r e n, and d e n   P a p s t by l a s s e.

[3] I h r e r   w ä r e   ü b r i g   g e n u g   a n   z w ö l f, "quite enough of them would be left with about twelve," i. e. about twelve of them would be amply sufficient.  U e b r i g is used in the sense of ü b e r - f l ü s s i g when it qualifies g e n u g, *plenty enough.*  A n, when it relates to number, is indefinite and signifies *about.*

[4] U n d   e i n   j e d e r   h ä t t e, etc., "and each one might have a thousand guldens to come in yearly," i. e. annual income.

[5] S c h i n d e r e i is a coarse word which would not now be used. It is connected to R ä u b e r e i by u n d understood.

[6] S i c h's   e r w e h r e t, the use of the accusative (e s in s i c h's) with this verb is provincial.  S i c h   e r w e h r e n is a reflective verb governing the genitive of the object.  "If the kingdom of France has kept it off," etc.

[7] N a r r e n   u n d   ä f f e n means, *to be treated as fools and apes.* "All this would be more tolerable, if they plundered only property thus ; [but] they," etc.

die Kirche würde dennoch nicht verſinken; ſo thun ſie
Nichts,[1] das zur Chriſtenheit dienet, nur Geld und Haber-
ſachen um die Biſthümer und Prälaturen treiben ſie;[2] das
auch wohl ein jeglicher Räuber thun kann.

---

[1] So thun sie nichts, "but now they do nothing;" — a
peculiar use of the word s o. It may be regarded here as nearly
equivalent to j e t z t.

[2] Nur Geld und Hadersachen — treiben sie, "they
only seek to get money and to excite litigation respecting benefices
and fiefs." Treiben, in such connections, simply means *to follow* or *practice*. See p. 29, Note 1. — All that Luther has here af-
firmed might be proved by the testimony of Catholic writers, if
this were the place for such demonstrations. To prevent the suspi-
cion that the Reformer misrepresents the case (which would be very
silly in an address to those who certainly could not be misled by him)
we will give a few brief specimens of the language held by the Cath-
olics themselves on the subject. In 1359, the chancellor of the Palatinate said in a diet, " The Romans have always regarded Germany
as their gold mine ; and what does the pope give in return but letters,
bulls and words?" Clemangis, in the same century, said, " Scarcely can a bishop be found, who, though he could give a demonstra-
tion of his right clearer than the sun, has been able to obtain his benefice without a lawsuit." An account of the city of Salzburg, published in 1784, states that, " in 1388, the pope gave the archbishop
permission to levy taxes on all the benefices of his province for re-
building his cathedral and for redeeming his pawned palace and estates, *provided half the sum collected should go to the apostolic treasu-
ry.*" Clemangis says again, " Churches that were formerly rich
and affluent bore for a long time the rapacity of Rome, but now that
they are exhausted they cannot bear it longer." In 1367, says Wes-
senberg, " single dignitaries of the church were found, who by special permission of the pope held more than twenty benefices." Ber-
nard said, " A whole year passes away, in which those who have the
care of souls, do not utter a word of religious instruction." Gerson
said in the Council of Pisa, " Scarcely a benefice below the high pre-
lacies is conferred, but that the pope confers it on one, a legate on
another, and the ordinary on a third." He insisted on " the residence
of the higher clergy, and the suppression of the *commendams* and of
all the system of plunder practised by the Apostolic See." At the
Council of Constance John Zachariah said, " that Socrates, who

Zum dritten, wenn man des Pabstes Hof[1] ließ das hunderte Theil bleiben, und thät ab ne$_{un}$ und neunzig Theile, er wäre dennoch groß genug, Antwort zu geben in des Glaubens Sachen. Nun aber ist ein solches Gewürm und Geschwürm[2] in dem Rom, und alles sich päbstisch rühmet,[3] daß zu Babylonien nicht ein solches Wesen gewesen ist. Es sind mehr denn 3000 Pabst-Schreiber allein; wer will die andern Amtleute zählen, da der Aemter so viel sind,[4] daß man sie kaum zählen kann, welche alle auf die Stifte und Lehne deutsches Landes warten,[5] wie ein Wolf auf die Schafe.

---

laughed when he saw great robbers hanging little thieves, would laugh still more, if he were here to see great thieves suspending the little ones from office."

[1] Des Papstes Hof liess, etc. Hof is perhaps in the accusative, and das hunderte Theil, in apposition with it; unless, Hof stands for Hofes, for the sake of euphony. "Were one to let the pope's court remain the hundreth part [of it] and to do away ninety-nine parts, that (er, referring to Hof) would be large enough still to give responses (decisions) in matters of faith."

[2] Gewürm und Geschwürm, collectives from Wurm and Schwarm, "such a nest of reptiles and such a swarming hive." For the formation of collectives from their primitives, see Gram. p. 73. 1. In the word Geschwürm, the letter ü is employed instead of ä for the sake of the alliteration. Indeed, there is no necessity for forming a collective from Schwarm, as it is already a collective; and this may be the reason why Luther elsewhere says Gewürm und Schwürm, preserving the alliteration, but dropping the collective prefix ge. As the Grammars contain the rules for forming collectives, it is not to be expected that these forms should all be found in the lexicons.

[3] Und Alles sich päpstlich rühmet is to be regarded as parenthetical, and dass to be connected with solch in the preceding clause. In referring indefinitely either to persons or things before mentioned, the German employs the neuter singular. Thus Alles is to be translated as though it were alle, *all men, every body.* Sich rühmen, *call themselves* or *boast of being.* See p. 103, Note 2.

[4] Da der Aemter so viel sind, "since there are so many offices." See p. 13, Note 3.

[5] For the force of the word warten, see p. 39, Note 2. Instead

Ich achte, daß Deutschland jetzt weit mehr nach Rom giebt dem Pabst, denn vor Zeiten den Kaisern. Ja es meinen Etliche, daß jährlich mehr denn 300,000 Gulden[1] aus Deutschland nach Rom kommen, lauter vergebens und umsonst, dafür[2] wir nichts denn Spott und Schmach erlangen. Und wir verwundern uns noch, daß Fürsten, Adel, Städte, Stifte, Land und Leute arm werden ; wir sollten uns verwundern, daß wir noch zu essen haben.[3]

---

of deutsches Landes, modern usage would admit, but perhaps not require deutschen Landes. That is, in the genitive singular of the masculine and neuter genders, the adjective termination e n is now much used instead of e s. See Gram. p. 116. med.

[1] G u l d e n, standing alone, without the word G o l d (as G o l d-g u l d e n) generally means a silver coin, or the common g u l d e n, worth from about two-thirds to three-fourths of a T h a l e r, according to the places where they were coined. A G o l d-g u l d e n was valued at about $2\frac{1}{2}$ T h a l e r.

[2] D a f ü r, *for which.* As d a is often used by the old writers for w o, so is d a f ü r, for w o f ü r. Present usage, however, does not allow such a license. They ought never to be employed in referring to *persons*, and not commonly, to things of an individual or definite character. So also we must say, E s w a r m e i n V a t e r m i t w e l c h e m (not w o m i t) i c h g i n g. T h u e n i c h t s, w o m i t (not m i t w e l c h e m) D u D i r s c h a d e n k ö n n t e s t.—The passage in the text is highly tautological—" purely thrown away, and for nothing, for which we receive nothing but ridicule and reproach." We have endeavored to indicate in the translation, though at the sacrifice of good English, the etymological difference between the words v e r g e b e n s, and u m s o n s t.

[3] D a s s w i r n o c h z u e s s e n h a b e n, "that we still have [anything] to eat." The idioms of the English and of the German, in this use of *have* and h a b e n with the infinitive, are very different. In English, the word *have* with a mere infinitive, expresses necessity like *must.* But if an accusative intervene, as the word *anything* in the example above, the verb *to have,* has, for the most part, its ordinary signification. In German, the rule is reversed in regard to the former, while, in regard to the latter, it is much as in English. I c h h a b e z u e s s e n, means, " I have something to eat;" and I c h h a b e e t w a s z u e s s e n, means, "I have a little of something to

Dieweil wir denn hier in das rechte Spiel[1] kommen, wollen wir ein wenig[2] still halten, und uns sehen lassen,[3] wie die Deutschen nicht so ganz grobe Narren sind, daß sie die römischen Praktiken[4] gar nicht wissen noch verstehen. Ich klage hier nicht, daß zu Rom Gottes Gebot und christliches Recht verachtet ist ;[5] denn so wohl stehet es jetzt nicht in der Christenheit, sonderlich zu Rom, daß wir von solchen hohen Dingen klagen möchten. Ich klage auch nicht, daß das natürliche oder weltliche Recht und Vernunft nichts gilt ; es liegt noch Alles tiefer im Grunde. Ich klage, daß sie ihr eigen erdichtetes geistliches Recht nicht halten, das doch an ihm selbst eine lautere Tyrannei, Geizerei und zeit-

---

eat;" but, I c h  h a b e  e t w a s  z u  t h u n, means, "I must do something."

[1] S p i e l is often used figuratively for any *business, action or affair of hazard.* "Since we here come into the very action," i. e. have come to the main point. R e c h t, *proper, real.*

[2] W e n i g does not qualify s t i l l ("a little still") but e i n  w e-n i g, here means, *a little while.*

[3] U n s  s e h e n  l a s s e n, *cause ourselves to see,* i. e. take occasion to see.

[4] P r a k t i k e n. P r a k t i k, from the modern Latin word, *practica,* means, in the singular, *practice ;* but in the plural (P r a k t i k e n), it means *low tricks,* or *mean arts.* Most of the smaller lexicons in use among us, are inaccurate on this word.

[5] G o t t e s  G e b o t  u n d  c h r i s t l i c h e s  R e c h t  v e r a c h t e t  i s t. A verb in the singlar with two connected nominatives, explained p. 93, Note 4. So a few lines below R e c h t  u n d  V e r n u n f t  g i l t, and p. 110, line 2, i s t  e i n  s o l c h  G e w ü r m  u n d  G e-s c h w ü r m. See also p. 46, line 3.—" I do not here complain that at Rome, the command of God and the Christian law is contemned, for things are not in so favorable a state in Christendom, especially at Rome, that we may complain in respect to things so elevated. Nor do I complain that natural or civil law and reason are of no account; everything is depressed to still lower depths (Rome is sunken below that too). I complain that they do not even observe their own pretended canonical law, which, however, is in itself, pure tyranny, avarice and luxury, rather than law" (right).

liche Pracht iſt, mehr denn ein Recht. Das wollen wir
ſehen.

Es haben vor Zeiten[1] deutſche Kaiſer und Fürſten ver-
williget dem Pabſte die Annaten auf alle Lehen deutſcher
Nation einzunehmen, das iſt die Hälfte des Zinſes des erſten
Jahres, auf einem jeglichen Lehen. Die Verwilligung aber
iſt alſo geſch·hen, daß der Pabſt durch ſolch großes Geld ſollte
ſammeln einen Schatz, zu ſtreiten wider die Türken und
Ungläubigen, die Chriſtenheit zu ſchützen, auf daß dem Adel
nicht zu ſchwer würde, allein zu ſtreiten, ſondern die Prie-
ſterſchaft auch etwas dazu thäte. Solcher guten einfältigen[2]

---

[1] Vor Zeiten. Vordem, vor diesem and vormals,
all agree in expressing indefinitely *time prior to the present*, without
intimating whether it is near or remote. Vor Zeiten refers
to a former period that is somewhat remote; and vor Alters. to
one very remote, *anciently*. " In a former age, German emperors
and princes allowed the pope to receive annats from all the fiefs [i. e.
the larger benefices] of the German nation, that is, half the income
of the first year from each fief [after passing into new hands]. But
this permission (the permission so) was granted, that the pope might,
by so ample a contribution, raise a fund for carrying on war against
the Turks and infidels [and] defend Christendom, in order that it
might not be too burdensome to the nobility to carry on the war
alone, but that the priesthood might come to their aid." This last circumstance requires that the word, Lehen, *fief*, as so often elsewhere,
should be restricted to *ecclesiastical* fiefs. Furthermore, the word
Annaten relates only to ecclesiastical estates. The *annats* were
ordinarily the entire income of a benefice. In this instance there
was a special *concordat* between the pope and the Empire, restricting
the contribution to half the income, if Luther's statement is correct.
But we find no such concordat; and as the annats varied according
to the arbitrary rates of the pope and sometimes fell below the income of the year, Luther probably put them at the very lowest estimate, not aiming at strict accuracy in a matter so common and yet
so variable.

[2] Einfältigen Andacht. An appeal to the pride of the
German nobility. Their very piety and simplicity had been abused
by the intriguing court of Rome.

Andacht der deutschen Nation haben die Päbste dazu gebraucht, daß sie bisher mehr denn hundert Jahre[1] solch Geld
eingenommen, und nun einen schuldigen und verpflichteten
Zins und Aufsatz daraus gemacht, und nicht allein nichts
gesammelt,[2] sondern darauf gestiftet viel Stände und Aemter zu Rom, die damit jährlich, als aus einem Erbzins, zu
besolden.

Wenn man nun wider die Türken zu streiten vorgiebt, so
senden sie[3] heraus Botschaft, Geld zu sammeln, haben vielmal auch Ablaß heraus geschickt, eben mit derselben Farbe

---

[1] **Mehr denn hundert Jahre.** " In the year 1318, pope
John XXII. published a *constitution* in which he reserved for himself
one year's income of all the non-elective benefices, (of all those who
are inferior to the bishops) *pro necessitatibus ecclesiae Romanae.*"—
Planck. Long before that, each bishop, consecrated at Rome, paid
for the ceremony his first year's income. At the time of the Council of Constance in 1417, these contributions had become so established by usage as to be claimed as regular taxes, which Planck af-
firms had become necessary " to support the thousands of officials,
reporters, assistants, commissaries, secretaries and copyists of the
Roman court." The abuse continued, notwithstanding all the efforts
of the councils of Constance and of Basle to the contrary. Planck's
Gesellschafts-Verfassung, V. 572—793.

[2] **Nicht allein nichts gesammelt,** etc., " not only
have collected no fund [for the war against the Turks] but have used
the money to found departments and offices at Rome, which are to be
paid with it annually, as if from a *perpetual tax.*" **Haben** is to be
supplied after **gestiftet** and referred to the preceding participles,
**eingenommen, gemacht** and **gesammelt;** and **sind**
is to be supplied after **zu besolden.** Such omissions of the auxiliary verb are mostly limited to subordinate clauses, and are rarely
to be found in the principal sentence or clause.

[3] **So senden sie,** etc. " They despatch messengers to col-
lect money, and have often sent out indulgences, with just the same
pretext of carrying on (to carry on) war against the Turks."
**Schicken,** means merely *to send away persons or things.* **Senden** means to send *persons* for accomplishing some *special object,*
and is therefore a word of more elevated character, and implies a more
honorable office in the person sent.

wider die Türken zu streiten, meinend, die tollen Deutschen
sollen unendlich todte Stocknarren bleiben,[1] nur immer Geld
geben, ihrem unaussprechlichen Geiz genug thun, ob wir
gleich öffentlich sehen, daß weder Annaten noch Ablaß, Geld,
noch alles Andere, ein Heller wider die Türken, sondern all=
zumal in den Sack, dem der Boden aus ist, kömmt ; lügen,
trügen, setzen und machen mit uns Bünde, der sie nicht ein
Haar breit zu halten gedenken ; das muß darnach der heil=
ige Name Christi und St. Petri Alles gethan haben.

Item, darnach ist getheilt worden das Jahr[2] zwischen dem

---

[1] Unendlich todte Stocknarren bleiben, "forever
remain senseless (lifeless), arrant fools, and always (n u r gives intensity to i m m e r) give money, and satisfy their inexpressible avarice, although we clearly see, that neither annats, nor indulgence-
money, nor collections [taken up by the B o t s c h a f t], nor anything else, a farthing of it, goes against the Turks, but it goes all of
it together into that sack,which has no bottom ;—[they] lie, deceive,
make laws and treaties, not a hair of which do they intend to observe.
All that, consequently, the sacred name of Christ and St. Peter must
have done." S t o c k gives intensity to the word to which it is prefixed, like our word *stone*, in *stone-blind*, etc. O e f f e n t l i c h is used
in its original signification, *openly, before the eyes of all*. The omission of s i e before l ü g e n is abrupt, and would not now be considered as allowable. For an explanation of this use of s e t z e n see
p. 11, Note 5 and p. 94, Note 7. D e r is in the genitive plural, for
which d e r e r is now used, and is governed by H a a r b r e i t. See
p. 47, Note 5. A l l e s near the end, agrees with d a s at the beginning of the clause.

[2] D a r n a c h i s t g e t h e i l t w o r d e n d a s J a h r, etc.
In the V i e n n a Concordat of 1448, it was agreed that besides all those
benefices, which were reserved for the disposal of the pope, to be
conferred according to his pleasure, he should have one half of the
remainder, the other half to belong to the ordinary authorities. Those
which became vacant in the even months of the year, namely, Jann-
ary, March, etc., were to fall to the latter ; and those which became
vacant in the odd months, February, April, etc., to fall to the pope.
These were called the P a p s t-M o n a t e, or *menses papales*. The
pope sold these places to the highest bidder at public auction !—Eichhorn's Staats-und Rechtsgeschichte, Vol. III. p. 543.

Pabſt und regierenden Biſchöfen und Stiften, daß der Pabſt
ſechs Monate hat im Jahr, einen um den andern,[1] zu ver=
leihen die Lehen, die in ſeinem Monat verfallen, damit faſt
alle Lehen hinein nach Rom werden gezogen, ſonderlich die
allerbeſten Pfründen und Dignitäten.  Und welche[2] einmal
ſo nach Rom fallen, die kommen darnach nimmer wieder he=
raus, ob ſie hinfort nimmer in des Pabſts Monat verfallen,
damit den Stiften viel zu kurz geſchieht,[3] und iſt eine rechte
Räuberei,[4] die ihr vorgenommen hat, nichts heraus zu laſ=
ſen.  Darum iſt ſie faſt reif, und iſt hohe Zeit, daß man die
Pabſt=Monate gar abthue, und Alles, was dadurch nach
Rom gekommen iſt, wieder herausreiße.

Denn Fürſten und Adel ſollen darauf ſeyn,[5] daß das ge=

---

[1] Einen um den andern, "every other, or second one."—
Damit, *whereby.*

[2] Und welche, etc.  "And such as once fall to Rome, these
never come back (out) again, though they never afterwards become
vacant in the pope's months."

[3] Damit den Stiften viel zu kurz geschieht, "by
which these institutions come short of their rights," i. e. are deprived
of their rights.  Literally "it comes far too short to the institutions,
or religious establishments."  The word kurz is often used in a
peculiar way; as, kurz halten, "to hold one by a short rope,"
or to allow him little freedom.  Den kürzeren ziehen, "to
draw the shorter lot," or to be excelled or overcome.  Zu kurz
kommen, "to come short of what is due," or to suffer injury or
loss.  Einen zu kurz geschehen, "to turn out to the injury of one."

[4] Und [es] ist eine rechte Räuberei, etc., "and it is
downright robbery, which has proposed to itself to let nothing escape.
Therefore it has nearly reached its acme, and it is high time," etc.
Ihr is here used instead of sich, the personal pronoun feminine
in the dative for the reflective pronoun.  Heraus, *out of its hands.*
Und [es] ist hohe zeit.

[5] Darauf seyn, "be [intent] upon this," a form of expression
not now in common use, and similar to darauf sehen, except
that it is much stronger.  Und die [die], "and those who abuse
their privilege, be deprived of it."

ſtohlne Gut werde wieder gegeben, die Diebe geſtraft, und die ihres Urlaubs mißbrauchen, Urlaubs beraubt werden. Hält und gilt es, ſo[1] der Pabſt des andern Tages ſeiner Erwählung Regel und Geſetze macht in ſeiner Kanzlei,[2] dadurch unſre Stifte[3] und Pfründen geraubt werden, da er kein Recht dazu hat; ſo ſoll es vielmehr gelten, ſo[4] der Kaiſer Carl des andern Tages ſeiner Krönung Regel und Geſetze gäbe, durch ganz Deutſchland kein Lehen und Pfründe mehr nach Rom

---

[1] **Hält und gilt es, so**, etc. " If it holds [good] and passes, that the pope on the second day after his election," etc. **Hält** is here explained by **gilt**, as a synonyme. **Tages seiner Erwahlung.** These words illustrate the wide use of the old genitive, for which prepositions with their cases are now more commonly used. **Tages** is a noun in the genitive used adverbially, which is very common with those words which designate *time* and *manner.* " The second day of his election" is a very loose expression for " the second day after (n a c h) his election."

[2] **In seiner Kanzelei.** The **Kanzelei** or *Cancellaria* is one of the four departments or bureaus of the Roman court. The others are the *Rota Romana*, or court of appeal, the *Dataria* for the distribution of favors, particularly offices, and the *Poenitentiaria* for absolutions. The *Cancellaria* was both a court of judicature and a kind of office of registry, where all official documents were prepared. The rules which the pope gave to this bureau for adjusting disputed claims were called **Kanzeleiregeln.** As they were special and temporary (being limited to the lifetime of the pope) they were not a part of the canonical law, and therefore were not of any binding authority, except with the pope's secretaries or registrators. Eichhorn III. 510. A good historical view of the subject will be found in Planck, V. 587, Note 14.

[3] **Dadurch unsre Stifte**, etc., " whereby our religious foundations and benefices are plundered, as he has no right to do so (to it)," etc. This imposition was extensively practised by the popes after the time of John XXII.

[4] **So soll es vielmehr gelten, so**, " so should it much rather pass (be valid) that the Emperor Charles V," etc. If the pope's authority be pleaded, on the one hand, for the abuse, let the emperor's be brought forward to confront it.

laſſen¹ kommen durch des Pabſts Monat, und was hinein ge=
kommen iſt, wieder frei werde, und von dem römiſchen Räu=
ber erlöſet, dazu er Recht hat von Amts wegen ſeines
Schwerts.

Nun hat der römiſche Geiz= und Raubſtuhl² nicht mögen
die Zeit erwarten, daß durch Pabſt=Monate alle Lehen hin=
ein kämen, eines nach dem andern, ſondern eilet nach ſeinem
unſättigen Wanſt, daß er ſie alle auf's Kürzeſte hinein
reiße, und über die Annaten und Monate einen ſolchen Fund
erdacht,³ daß die Lehen und Pfründe noch dreierlei Weiſe zu
Rom behaftet werden:

---

¹ Lassen, for zu lassen, (Gesetze, kein Lehen
nach Rom kommen zu lassen) is in the infinitive and dependent on Gesetze.  The form of the imperative is, by a change
in the construction (anacoluthon), used in the second member (w e r-
d e) which is connected to l a s s e n by u n d, "gave rules and laws
in all Germany to let no fief or benefice go any longer to Rome, on
account of the pope's month, and let, what is already gone thither,
become free again, and be recovered from the Roman plunderer.  To
this he (the emperor) is entitled by virtue of his sovereignty (sword)."

² N u n  h a t  d e r  r ö m i s c h e  G e i z–u n d  R a u b s t u h l,
etc.  "Now the seat of avarice and plunder at Rome could not wait
for the time that all the fiefs might come in one after another, through
the pope's months, but, in compliance with his insatiable appetite
(belly), he hurries on that he may in the shortest time bring them
within his clutches," etc.  H a t  m ö g e n  for  h a t  g e m o c h t,
*has been able.*  See p. 24, Note 1, and Gram. p. 260, med.  E r w a r-
t e n means, *to wait to the end,* or till the time arrives.  W a r t e n is
*to wait* simply.  N a c h  must not be translated as if it were followed
by an accusative, which would give a ludicrous meaning here.

³ E i n e n  s o l c h e n  F u n d  e r d a c h t [h a t], "has invented
such a device."  Are the charges, made in this paragraph, false or
malignant?  Let us hear the judgment of one of the most candid of
historians.  "In every misapplication which the popes now (13th,
century) made of their power, money was the object.  Every new
operation which they performed was one of extortion, and every new
act of oppression, was, on their part, a financial speculation.—These
oppressions were so intolerable, and the evils which grew out of

Zum erſten, ſo, der ſo eine Pfründe hat, zu Rom oder auf dem Wege ſtirbt,[1] dieſelbe muß ewig eigen bleiben des rö= miſchen (räuberiſchen) Stuhls, ſollt' ich ſagen,[2] und wollen dennoch nicht Räuber heißen ; ſo ſolche Räuberei Niemand je gehöret noch geleſen hat.

Zum Andern, ſo, der ein Lehen hat[3] oder überkommt, der des Pabſtes oder Cardinäle Geſinde iſt, oder, ſo er zuvor ein Lehen hat, und darnach Pabſts oder Cardinals Geſinde wird. Nun wer mag des Pabſts und der Cardinäle Geſinde zählen,[4] ſo der Pabſt, wenn er nur ſpatzieren rei t, bei drei=

---

them so crying, that no one could excuse them on the ground of the necessities of the court of Avignon."—Planck, V. 574.

[1] Z u  R o m  o d e r  a u f  d e m  W e g e  s t i r b t.  "In 1266, Clement IV. issued a decree in which he reserved for the chair of St Peter provisionem omnium beneficiorum apud Curiam vacantium, i. e. the right of presentation to all those places whose incumbents died at the court of Rome, or within two days' journey of it.  This reservation was made at a time when multitudes were resorting to Rome on pilgrimages, and most frequently fell upon the richest bene- fices, for the holders of these most frequently visited Rome."—Planck, V. 580.  Eichhorn, II. 508.

[2] R ö m i s c h e n  (r ä u b e r i s c h e n)  S t u h l s,  s o l l t' i c h s a g e n.  A play upon the word,—" the  r o m i s c h e n  (or as I should say, r ä u b e r i s c h e n)  S t u h l s."  The genitive  S t u h l s  is here governed by  e i g e n,  — "always continue to be the pope's own (pe- culiar to the pope)."  See p. 3, Note 5.  U n d  [s i e]  w o l l e n, etc., " and still they refuse to be called robbers, though no one ever heard or read of such robbers."

[3] S o  d e r,  e i n e n  L e h e n  h a t, etc.  [" It also belongs to the pope] if he has a fief, who belongs to the retinue of the pope or of his cardinals, or  if  he  before  held (holds) a fief, and afterwards becomes  attached  to  the court of the pope or of his cardinals."  In this paragraph, the first  d e r  is a demonstrative and the second a rel- ative pronoun.  At the beginning of the preceding paragraph, the demonstrative which is nominative to  s t i r b t,  is omitted.

[4] G e s i n d e  z ä h l e n.  In the bull of Benedict XII. to which Luther here alludes, the pope himself kindly furnished a list of those who are to be regarded as  G e s i n d e.  He names the officiales, camerarios, vicecancellarios, notarios, auditores literarum contradicta-

ober vier taufend Maulreuter um fich hat, troß[1] allen Kai=
fern und Königen.   Denn Chriftus und St. Peter giengen
zu Fuß, auf daß ihre Statthalter deftomehr zu prachten und
zu prangen[2] hätten.   Nun hat der Geiz weiter fich erflü=
get,[3] und fchaffet, daß auch draußen Viele den Namen haben,[4]
päbftlichen Gefindes, wie zu Rom, daß nur in allen Orten
das bloße fchalfhaftige Wörtlein, Pabfts Gefinde, alle Le=
hen an den römifchen Stuhl bringen und ewiglich heften
foll.   Sind das[5] nicht verdrießliche, teuflifche Fünde ?   Se=

---

rum, auditores causarum palatii apostolici, correctores et scriptores
literarum apostolicarum, poenitentiarios, abbreviatores, commensales,
capellanos, et quoscunque alios legatos, nuntios, rectores in terris ecclesiae Romanae, sive thesaurios et collectores hactenus missos et in
posterum mittendos!   Planck, V. 586 adds :  " The number of the
courtiers was countless, and most of them had several benefices a piece ;
but to increase the number, the title of *officiales* and *curiales* was
conferred upon hundreds, who had no real connection with the court."

[1] T r o t z, generally signifies *in spite of, notwithstanding*.  But it
also means, *assuming an equality with*, or even *superiority over*, and
so here. — B e i   d r e i - o d e r   v i e r   t a u s e n d, a little above,
means, " not far from three or four thousand."   B e i   used with reference to numbers, is indefinite, and is nearly the same as a n, or
g e g e n   in the same connections.

[2] A u f   d a s s   i h r e   S t a t t h a l t e r   d e s t o m e h r   z u   p r a c h t e n
u n d   z u   p r a n g e n, " in order that their vicars might, so much the
more, have the means of making, or be able to make, a parade and
show." ' The irony is skilfully applied.

[3] E r k l ü g e t.  The word e r k l ü g e n, which is not found in the
dictionaries, must not be confounded with the frequentative e r k l ü-
g e l n, which means *to invent by subtlety*, and *to refine in speculation*.
E r, prefixed to an adjective with the addition of the verbal termination e n, forms a derivative verb which means *to come into that state
expressed by the adjective*.  Thus k l u g, *wise ;* e r k l u g e n, *to become wise*, which by a change of the vowel becomes a causative verb,
e r k l ü g e n, *to make wise*.  S i c h   e r k l ü g e n, *to render one's self
wise*, i. e. to become wise.  See Gram. p. 249. 4. for the first change,
and p. 49. 1. for the second.

[4] D e n   N a m e n   h a b e n.  See p. 119, Note 4, end.

[5] D a s, when used indefinitely, is indeclinable.  See Gram. p. 303.

ḧen wir zu,[1] so soll Mainz, Magdeburg, Halberstadt, gar sein nach Rom kommen, und das Cardinalat theuer genug bezahlt werden. Darnach wollen wir alle deutsche Bischöfe, Cardinäle machen, daß nichts draußen bleibe.

Zum dritten,[2] wo um ein Lehen ein Hader sich zu Rom angefangen, welches[3] ich achte, fast die gemeinste und größeste Strafe[4] ist, die Pfründe nach Rom zu bringen. Denn

---

[1] S e h e n  w i r  z u, etc. "*Let us see*, or behold ! [the Romans are supposed to say] ; then Mayence, Magdeburg, and Halberstadt shall be a good hall for Rome [the funds of these large sees being appropriated to make a cardinal] and the cardinalate shall be paid for dearly enough. After that, we will make all the German bishops cardinals, so that nothing shall be left out of our hands."

[2] Z u m  d r i t t e n, etc. "Thirdly [this takes place] if a controversy respecting an ecclesiastical fief has originated at Rome (which, I think, is well nigh the most common as well as the greatest calamity), in order to bring the livings to Rome." The first sentences of these three paragraphs, beginning with, z u m  e r s t e n, z u m  a n-d e r n and z u m  d r i t t e n, all taken together, are in apposition with the words d r e i e r l e i  W e i s e, at the close of the preceding paragraph, and are an explanation of that expression. This will be rendered obvious by the following arrangement. D a s s  d i e  L e h e n u n d  P f r ü n d e  n a c h  d r e i e r l e i  W e i s e  z u  R o m  b e h a f t e t s i n d ; — z u m  e r s t e n, s o, d e r  s o  e i n e  P f r ü n d e  h a t, etc.; z u m  a n d e r n, s o  d e r  e i n  L e h e n  h a t, etc.; z u m  d r i t t e n, w o  u m  e i n  L e h e n, etc., "that fiefs and prebends are attached to Rome in three ways; viz. 1. If he who has such a prebend dies at Rome, or on the way, it must always belong to the Roman see. 2. If he who possesses or obtains a fief, belongs to the retinue of the pope or of the cardinals, or if he had one before, and afterwards becomes attached to the retinue of the pope or of the cardinals, [that also becomes the property of the Roman see]. 3. [The same is true], if a litigation respecting a fief commences at Rome," etc.

[3] A n g e f a n g e n [h a t], w e l c h e s, etc. W e l c h e s, referring to the preceding clause as an antecedent, introduces a parenthetical remark..

[4] G r ö s s e s t e  S t r a f e. We cannot give a better comment upon these words than an abstract from Planck, V. 651, on the subject. "So far did the unnatural extension of the judicial functions of Rome

wo hier[1] fein Haber ist, findet man unzählige Buben zu
Rom, die Haber aus der Erde graben,[2] und Pfründen an=
greifen, wo sie nur wollen, da mancher fromme Priester seine
Pfründe muß verlieren, oder mit einer Summe Geldes den
Haber abkaufen, eine Zeitlang solches Lehen[3] mit Haber=
recht oder Unrecht[4] verhaftet, muß auch des römischen
Stuhls ewig eigen seyn.  Es wäre nicht Wunder, daß Gott

---

go, that all other  courts of judicature in the church were almost annihilated.   Cases were  taken  in  the first instance from the inferior
courts, without any regard to the nature of the trial, even when one
of the parties protested against it.   Sometimes they were taken from
the  lowest  courts  during  trial, no regard being had to the intervening court of the metropolitan.   And finally, instead of the proper and
legal way of appointing judges from Rome, who should attend to tri-
als  on  the spot where they originated, the pope removed the trial to
Rome, where, to  say nothing  of the bribes which were necessary to
any degree  of success, the expenses of travel and  court-fees were
enormously augmented."   Hence the council of Basle found  it necessary to decree, that no litigation originating at a distance exceed-
ing a four day's journey from Rome, should, in the first  instance, be
tried there, but in  the  appropriate  courts where the parties reside ;
that all  appeals should  ascend in regular gradation from the lowest
court to the highest; and  that in appeals to the highest court, the
pope should  not  remove  the  trial to Rome, but appoint a judge to
hold a court in the place where the parties reside.   This Council gave
a melancholy description of the evils resulting from the abuses com-
plained of, which is quoted by Eichhorn, III. 522, Note a.

[1] H i e r, in Germany.

[2] D i e  H a d e r  a u s  d e r  E r d e  g r a b e n, " who dig quarrels out
of the earth, (i. e. who hatch up law-suits) and lay their greedy hands
on prebends wherever (w o  n u r) they wish, in which (d a  in the
sense of w o) many a pious priest must either lose  his living or with
a large  sum of money purchase a respite from lawsuits for a time."
See the words of Clamangis, p. 109, Note 2.

[3] S o l c h e s  L e h e n, with which the participle v e r h a f t e t
agrees, is nominative to m u s s.

[4] H a d e r r e c h t  o d e r  U n r e c h t.   The word U n r e c h t is a
play upon the latter part of the compound H a d e r r e c h t ; — " a
court of justice, or rather of injustice."

vom Himmel Schwefel und höllisches Fener regnete, und
Rom in den Abgrund versenkte,[1] wie er vor Zeiten Sodom
und Gomorra that. Was soll[2] ein Pabst in der Christenheit, wenn man seiner Gewalt nicht anders braucht, denn
zu solcher Haupt-Bosheit, und er dieselben schützet und hand-
habet? O edle Fürsten und Herren, wie lange wollt ihr
ener Land und Leute solchen reißenden Wölfen öffnen und
frei lassen?

Da nun[3] solche Praktiken nicht genug war, und dem Geiz
die Zeit zu lange ward, alle Bisthümer hinzureißen, hat
mein lieber Geiz doch so viel erfunden, daß die Bisthümer
mit Namen außen, und mit dem Grund und Boden zu Rom
sind. Und daß also kein Bischof mag bestätiget werden, er
kaufe denn mit großer Summe Geldes das Pallium, und
verpflichte sich mit greulichen Eiden zu einem eigenen Knecht
dem Pabst. Daher kommt es, daß kein Bischof wider den

---

[1] R e g n e t e — v e r s e n k t e, imperfect subjunctive, " should rain,
should sink.''

[2] S o l l, is often, as here, used in the sense of h e l f e n  n ü t z e n,
" What is the utility of a pope, if men make no other use of his power than for such arch-iniquity, and he (himself) defends and practises it?''

[3] D a  n u n, etc. " Now as these tricks were not sufficient, and
as time became too long to avarice for seizing all the bishoprics, the
dear creature (my dear avarice) found out all this (so much) namely,
that the bishoprics were nominally foreign, but in truth and reality
(in ground and soil) were at Rome! and that thus no bishop could be
confirmed, unless he purchase with a great sum the pallium and obligate himself with horrible oaths to (be) an own servant to the pope.''
Luther does not introduce these usages in a chronological, but in a
rhetorical order. This last practice is older than that of annats.
W a r, after a plural nominative, is a little irregular, unless a noun
in the singular be understood as a predicate. H i n z u r e i s s e n is
dependent on l a n g e. G r u n d  u n d  B o d e n, being capable of a
double sense can be but imperfectly rendered into English. For the
idiom, e r  k a u f e  d e n n, see Gram. pp. 315, 362. For the peculiar
use of z u, see Gram. p. 338. l. and note.

Pabſt darf handeln. Das haben[1] die Römer auch geſucht mit dem Eide, und ſind alſo die allerreichſten Bisthümer in Schuld und Verderben gekommen. Mainz, höre ich, giebt 20,000 Gulden; das ſind mir je Römer,[2] als mich dünkt.[3] Sie haben es wohl vor Zeiten geſetzt im geiſtlichen Recht,[4] das Pallium umſonſt zu geben, des Pabſts Geſinde weni= gern, Hader mindern, den Stiften und Biſchöfen ihre Frei= heit laſſen. Aber das wollte nicht Geld tragen;[5] darum iſt daß Blatt umgekehrt,[6] und iſt den Biſchöfen und Stiften alle Gewalt genommen,[7] ſitzen wie die Ziefern, haben weder

---

[1] Das haben. Das seems to refer to the preceding sentence on-ly, to the obligation of the bishop never to oppose the pope. Also, *thus*, refers not to the same, but more particularly to purchasing the pallium at great cost, so that the richest sees were ruined and ren-dered bankrupt.

[2] Das sind mir je Römer, "that is a genuine specimen of the Romans," or "that is the way the Romans manage." On the use of das, as nominative to sind, see Gram. p. 303. On mir as an expletive, see Gram. p. 348. Je was often employed by Luther for ja, which is now a provincialism.

[3] Mich dünkt. See p. 22, Note 3.

[4] Gesetzt im geistlichen Recht, etc. See p. 11, Note 5. "They (the Romans, or rather the church) have indeed decided in the canonical law to give the pallium without charge, to reduce the number of the pope's dependents, to diminish litigation (at Rome by transferring it to the bishops and) to leave," etc. If this refers, as it probably does, to the concordat between the pope and the Council of Constance, the statement is a little exaggerated. To the decisions of the Council of Basle, which went much farther than those of the Council of Constance, the pope never gave his assent.

[5] Geld tragen, ' to bear, bring forth or yield money,' a figurative expression, for which eintragen is now used, as applied to money.

[6] Ist das Blatt umgekehrt, *the leaf is turned over*, i. e. the tables are changed. Blatt in such idioms means, *the case, fortune, things*. "To turn over a new leaf" conveys a different idea. Das Blatt hat sich gewendet, fortune has changed.

[7] Den Bischöfen—genomen, "taken *from* the bishops." See p. 52, Note 4.—Sitzen, i. e. the bishops.

Amt, Macht noch Werke, sondern regieren alle[1] Dinge die
Hauptbuben zu Rom, auch schier des Küsters und Glöckners
Amt[2] in allen Kirchen ; alle Haber werden nach Rom gezo=
gen, thut Jedermann durch Pabsts Gewalt, was er will.

Bisher haben wir verstanden, wie sie mit den Pfründen
handeln, die verfallen und los werden.[3] Nun erfällt[4] dem
zarten Geiz zu wenig los, darum hat er seine Vorsichtigkeit
erzeigt auch in den Lehen, die noch besessen sind durch ihrer
Verweser, daß dieselben auch[5] loß seyn müssen, ob sie schon
nicht loß sind, und das mancherlei Weise.

Zum ersten lauert er, wo fette Präbenden sind oder Bis=

---

[1] R e g i e r e n  a l l e, etc., " the great ones (H a u p t b u b e n) at
Rome control all things." In modern style it would be E s  r e g i-
r e n  a l l e, etc. So a few lines above, u n d (e s)  s i n d  a l s o  d i e
a l l e r r e i c h e s t e n  B i s t h ü m e r.

[2] D e s  K ü s t e r s — A m t, " even the sacristan's and sexton's office." T h u t  J e d e r m a n n, " every one [at Rome] by the aid, or
through the power of the pope, does what he pleases."

[3] D i e  v e r f a l l e n  u n d  l o s  w e r d e n. P f r ü n d e n, or L e-
h e n  v e r f a l l e n, when the occupant by any neglect or violation
of his trust, loses his title to them ; they w e r d e n  l o s, when in
any way they become vacant, e. g. by the death of the occupant.
The latter expression is more generic than the former.

[4] N u n  e r f ä l l t, etc , " now too few (too little, z u  w e n i g) become vacant for gentle avarice (personified)." E r f a l l e n as an active verb, means *to cut down, to slay*, and s i c h  e r f a l l e n, *to be cut
down*, or *to fall*. But here it is a neuter verb and refers not to a person, but to a thing, for which the lexicons give no explanation. Its
etymology will sufficiently explain its peculiar use here. E r as a
prefix shows that the action expressed by the verb is *for some one,
for his benefit*, (d e m  G e i t z, in this instance). See Gram. p. 248.
The prebends, or ecclesiastical fiefs *fall to* avarice, (i. e. the pope).

[5] D a s s  d i e s e l b e n  a u c h, etc. D a s s depends on V o r s i e h-
t i g k e i t. " Therefore has he exercised (shown) his foresight in respect to (ecclesiastical) fiefs, which are still held by their incumbents,
that they also should become vacant (though they are not so) and
that in various ways." (A u f)  m a n c h e r l e i  W e i s e, *in many
a way.*

**11\***

thümer, durch einen Alten[1] oder Kranken, oder auch mit einer erdichteten Untüchtigkeit beseſſen ; demselben giebt der heilige Stuhl einen Coadjutor, d. i. : einen Mithelfer ohne seinen Willen und Dank, zu Gute dem Coadjutor, darum, daß er des Pabſts Gesinde iſt, oder Geld darum giebt, oder ſonſt mit einem römiſchen Frohndienſt verdienet hat. Da muß denn abgehen[2] freie Erwählung des Capitels, oder Recht deß, der die Pfründen hat zu verleihen, und Alles nur nach Rom.

Zum andern, heißt ein Wörtlein Commenden,[3] d. i. :

---

[1] Durch einen Alten. " He lies in wait where there are fat prebends or bishoprics, possessed by (bessessen durch, a rare use of durch) an old incumbent, or an invalid, or even one of a pretended incompetency. A man who belongs to the retinue of the pope, or who has given him money, or done him some other service, is appointed coadjutor (colleague) where he is not needed, but is appointed merely *for his own benefit*" (zu gute dem Coadjutor, *for good to the coadjutor*, literally). For a similar use of zu gute, see Gram. p. 334.

[2] Da muss denn abgehen, etc. " These then must vanish, a free election (of the bishop) by the chapter, or the right of him (dess for dessen) who has the prebend to bestow (i. e. the patron) ; and everything (goes) towards Rome."

[3] Heisst ein Wörtlein, etc. " There is a little word called *commendam*." The canonical law often stood in the way of the most advantageous sale of benefices. A rich person, not ordained and therefore not competent to hold a benefice, would often offer for a place, which he particularly desired, much more than others would give. So sometimes one of the secular clergy would particularly desire one which could lawfully be held only by one of the regular clergy and vice versa. To make sure of such advantageous bargains, the places were sold under the title of *commendams*, respecting which the canonical law said nothing by way of prohibition. By resorting to such evasions the pope could gratify a prince who wished a place for one of his young sons, (he might be but eight years of age), or a canon who wished to enjoy four or five incompatible incomes. What it was unlawful for one to hold as an actual incumbent, he could hold as a protector under the title of a *commendam*. The duties of the

wenn der Pabst einem Cardinal oder sonst seiner Einem,[1] ein
reiches, fettes Kloster oder Kirche befiehlt zu behalten, gleich
als wenn ich dir hundert Gulden zu behalten thäte.[2]   Dieß
heißt[3] das Kloster nicht geben noch verleihen, auch nicht ver=
stören, noch Gottesdienst abthun, sondern allein zu behalten
thun ; nicht daß er es bewahren oder banen soll, sondern
die Personen austreiben,[4] die Güter und Zinsen einnehmen,
und irgend einen Apostaten, verlaufenen Mönch hineinsetzen,
der fünf oder sechs Gulden des Jahrs nimmt, und sitzt des
Tages in der Kirche, verkauft den Pilgern Zeichen und Bild=
lein, daß weder Singen noch Lesen daselbst mehr geschieht.
Denn wo das hieß Klöster verstören und Gottesdienst ab=
thun, so müßte man den Pabst nennen einen Verstörer der
Christenheit und Abthäter Gottesdiensts.   Denn er treibet
es fürwahr mächtig.   Das wäre eine harte Sprache zu
Rom ; darum muß man es nennen ein Commenden oder
Befehlung, das Kloster zu behalten.   Dieser Klöster kann
der Pabst vier oder mehr[5] in einem Jahre zu Commenden

station would, in such cases, be scandalously performed, if performed at all, by a cheap vicar.  Thus everything sacred was made to
yield to avarice.—Planck, V. 621.

[1] O d e r   s o n s t   s e i n e r   E i n e m, "or to some other one of
his dependents," literally, "or otherwise to one of his," a construction that has ceased to be very common.

[2] Z u   b e h a l t e n   t h ä t e.   T h u n is here used in the sense of
*put, commit.*  "As if I should commit to you a hundred guldens."
A preposition as, a u f or i n generally follows instead of a dative
when the word is used in this sense.  See p. 20, Note 3.

[3] D i e s s   h e i s s t, etc., "this is not *called* giving, etc. (although
it *is* so)."

[4] P e r s o n e n   a u s t r e i b e n, monks, if it be a cloister, the persons belonging to a chapter, if it be a cathedral institute.   G ü t e r
u n d   Z i n s e n, the property and income appropriated to the support of such persons.

[5] D e i s e r   K l ö s t e r — v i e r   o d e r   m e h r, "four or more of
these cloisters can the pope make into *commendams* in one year,
in which (d a)," etc.

machen, da eines mehr denn 6000 Gulden Einkommen hat. Also mehren[1] sie zu Rom Gottesdienst, und erhalten die Klöster; das lernet sich in deutschen Landen auch.

Zum dritten, sind etliche[2] Lehen, die sie heißen Incompatibilia, die nach Ordnung geistlichen Rechts nicht mögen mit einander behalten werden. Als da sind zwei Pfarren, zwei Bisthümer und dergleichen. Hier drehet sich der heilige römische Stuhl und Geiz also aus dem geistlichen Recht, daß[3] er ihm Glossen macht, die heißen unio et incorporatio,

---

[1] Also mehren, etc. " This is the way (thus, also) they promote religious worship, etc. at Rome." Das lernet sich, "one learns that, or that is learned in Germany also." This reflective form for the passive, with a *neuter* nominative, is peculiar and limited chiefly to colloquial style.

[2] (Es) sind etliche, etc., " there are some ecclesiastical fiefs which they call," etc. Als da sind, *such as.* Da sind, cannot easily be translated without disturbing the sense in English.

[3] Also aus dem — dass, " winds its way (drehet sich) *in this manner* (also) out of the canonical law (viz.), it (that it) makes glosses to the law, which glosses are (called) *unio et incorporatio,* i. e. (that) it incorporates many *incompatabilia* into one body so that one shall be member with another and thus (all) be regarded as one prebend. Thus they are never more (no longer) *incompatabilia*, and the difficulty with the canonical law is overcome (and help is brought to the canonical law), so that it is no longer binding except (denn) with those only, who do not purchase those glosses (i. e. buy the places under those names) of the pope and of his *datarium* (a sort of office or court). Of this sort (der Art) is the *unio,* i. e. union, that it (der römische Stuhl und Geiz) couples many (of) such fiefs together, like a bundle of sticks, on account of which coupling they are all regarded as one fief. Thus one may find one courtier at Rome, who holds for himself twenty-two parishes, seven provostships and forty-four prebends besides, all which such a masterly gloss helps on, and maintains that it is not contrary to law. Now, what the cardinals and other prelates have, let each one consider for himself. Thus must men drain the purses of (to) the Germans, and drive out their pruriency (sinful desires)."—A device of the same character with the commendam is the *unio* or *incorporatio,* to evade the illegality of holding a plurality of benefices, or such as were in-

d. i. : daß er viel incompatibilia in einander leibet, das eines
des andern Glied sey, und also gleich als Eine Pfründe
geachtet werden ; so sind sie nimmer incompatibilia, und ist
dem heiligen geistlichen Recht geholfen, daß es nicht mehr
bindet, denn allein bei denen, die solche Glossen dem Pabst
und seinem Datario nicht abkaufen.  Der Art ist auch die
Unio, d. i. : Vereinigung, daß er solcher Lehen viel zusam=
men koppelt, als ein Bund Holz, um welches Koppels wil=
len sie alle für ein Lehen gehalten werden.  Also findet man
wohl einen Courtisanen zu Rom, der für sich allein 22 Pfar=
ren, 7 Probsteien und 44 Pfründen dazu hat ; welches alles
hilft solche meisterliche Glosse, und hält, daß nicht wider
Recht sey.  Was nun Cardinäle und andere Prälaten ha=
ben, bedenke ein Jeder selbst.  So soll mann den Deutschen
den Beutel räumen und Kitzel vertreiben.

Aber alles, was bisher gesaget,[1] ist fast alt und gewöhn=

compatible with each other.  As in the time of wars weak dioceses
were united together to form one strong and prosperous one, so several might be united, and one of them be called the *principal* and that
be conferred without any mention of the others in the document, the
latter being enjoyed as a matter of course.  Thus different and incompatible kinds of benefices could be conferred upon a favorite in
this way.  They could be incorporated and that one could be called
*principal* which it was lawful for the individual of a particular character to hold ; and the others need not be mentioned by name ; their
funds would find an easy passage to the place of destination.  Children, and any person, no matter what his character, could be accom-
modated in this way, by giving them nominally a *beneficium simplex*,
with trifling duties such as the observance of the canonical hours, or
repeating the breviary, while the *beneficium curatum*, which required
ordinary clerical duties, might be incorporated, and enjoyed without
service in the name of the former.—Planck, V. 627.

[1] W a s  b i s h e r  g e s a g e t  (i s t), "but all that has been said
thus far, is well nigh old and has become common at Rome.  One
trick (thing) more has (Roman) avarice invented, which I hope (so
that I hope it) will be the last, of which (I hope) it will die."  D a -
r a n  e r  e r w ü r g e, "of which it will choke to death."  The evil
is represented as a disease which produces strangulation.

lich geworden zu Rom. Noch Eines hat der Geiz erdacht, daß ich hoffe, soll das Letzte seyn, daran er erwürge. Der Pabst hat ein edles Fündlein,[1] das heißt pectoralis reservatio, d. i.: seines Gemüths Vorbehalt, et proprius motus, und eigener Muthwille der Gewalt. Das gehet also zu :[2] Wenn Einer zu Rom[3] ein Lehen erlangt, das ihm wird signirt und redlicher Weise zugeschrieben, wie da der Brauch ist, so kommt denn Einer, der Geld bringet, oder sonst verdienet hat, da nicht von zu sagen ist, und begehret dasselbige Lehen von dem Pabst, so giebt er es ihm und nimmt es dem Andern. Spricht man denn, es sey unrecht, so muß der allerheiligste Vater sich entschuldigen, daß er nicht so öffentlich mit Gewalt wider Recht zu handeln, gestraft werde,[4] und spricht: Er habe in seinem Herzen[5] und Gemüth das-

[1] Fündlein, diminutive of Fund, "a precious invention," (a noble little invention). Eigener Muthwille der Gewalt, his own arbitrary power, (arbitrariness of power).

[2] Das geht also zu, this takes place thus. Zugehen, signifies first, and in common life, to go quick, as geh zu, hasten (or in the vulgar New-England dialect, "be spry"). 2. To close, to shut (and sometimes to end, to terminate). 3. To proceed, to take place, (but only with reference to manner and generally impersonally), as, Wie geht es zu? How does it happen that; how is it that? Qui fit? in Latin. Es geht natürlich zu, it takes place naturally. Est geht bunt zu, everything is topsy turvy. See p. 68, Note 4.

[3] Wenn Einer zu Rom, etc. "When one obtains a fief (or prebend) at Rome, which is promised to him in writing (which is signed and written to him) in good faith (auf redlicher Weise) according to custom, there comes another person (Einer) who brings money, or otherwise has done some service that is not to be named (da nicht von, for davon nicht, "of which nothing is to be said") and desires the same prebend of the pope, and the latter gives it to him and takes it from the other."

[4] Zu handeln, gestraft werde, "that he be not censured for acting (to act, or to have acted) so openly," etc.

[5] Er habe in seinem Hertzen, etc., "he had, in his heart and mind, reserved that prebend for himself (ihm selbst — vor-

ſelbe Lehen ihm ſelbſt und ſeiner vollen Gewalt vorbehalten, ſo er doch ſein Lebtag zuvor nie daran gedacht noch gehöret hat. Und hat nun alſo ein Glößlein[1] gefunden, daß er in eigener Perſon lügen, trügen, und Jedermann äffen und narren mag; und das alles unverſchämt und öffentlich; und will dennoch das Haupt der Chriſtenheit ſeyn, läſſet ſich mit[2] öffentlichen Lügen den böſen Geiſt regieren.

Dieſer Muthwille[3] und lügenhafte Vorbehalt des Pabſts macht nun zu Rom ein ſolches Weſen, daß Niemand davon reden kann. Da iſt ein Kaufen,[4] Verkaufen, Wechſeln, Tauſchen, Ranſchen, Lügen, Trügen, Rauben, Stehlen, Pracht, Hurerei, Büberei auf allerlei Weiſe, Gottes Verach= tung, daß nicht möglich iſt dem Antichriſt läſterlicher zu regieren. Es iſt nichts mit Venedig, Altorf, Alkair,[5] ge=

---

behalten) and for his plenary power, although (so — doch) he never before, in all his life, thought of it, nor heard of it."

[1] Glösslein, diminutive of Glosse. "And he has now so invented a fine little gloss, that he can," etc. The diminutive is both ironical and contemptuous.

[2] Lässet sich mit, etc. "(and) allows the Evil Spirit with open falsehood to rule him."

[3] Dieser Muthwille, etc. "Now (nun, differing widely from jetzt) this arbitrary will and pretended reservation of the pope [viewed as a nominative singular, because they are but two names of the same thing] creates such a disorder (Wesen) at Rome that no one can describe it." Davon reden, *to speak of it,* has a general sense; but here the connection gives it a special meaning.

[4] Da ist ein Kaufen, etc. "There is buying, selling, money-changing, bartering, carousing (making a tumult), lying, deceiving, robbing, stealing, extravagant parading, dissoluteness, knavery of every sort [and], irreverence for God, so that it is not possible for antichrist himself to reign more iniquitously."

[5] Venedig, Altorf, Alkair, *Venice, Altorf* and *Algiers,* celebrated places of trade, where the love of gain is supposed to be stronger than moral principle. Altorf, a small town in the canton of Uri on the Reuss in Switzerland, was, on account of the transportation of goods through it from Germany to Italy, a place of much trade. The orthography Alkair for Algier is no longer in use. That place was once a great slave market.

gen[1] diesen Jahrmarkt und Kaufhandel zu Rom, ohne daß dort doch Vernunft und Recht gehalten wird ; hier gehet es, wie der Teufel selbst will. Und aus dem Meere fließt nun in alle Welt gleiche Tugend. Sollten sich solche Leute nicht billig[2] fürchten vor der Reformation und einem freien Concilio, und ehe alle Könige und Fürsten in einander hängen,[3] daß je nicht durch ihre Einigkeit ein Concilium werde ? Wer mag leiden, daß solche seine Büberei[4] an den Tag komme ?

Zuletzt hat der Pabst[5] zu diesen allen edeln Händeln ein

---

[1] G e g e n, *in comparison with.* "There is nothing with Venice, Altorf and Algiers, (i. e. Venice, Altorf and Algiers, are nothing) in comparison with this market and trade, except, however, that there (o h n e  d a s s  d o r t  d o c h), reason and justice are regarded, (while) here everything goes as Satan will have it." J a h r m a r k t, literally means an annual fair, but by usage it is also employed to designate the greater fairs which occur only in a few times in a year to distinguish them from the weekly markets. Hence figuratively it signifies, not an *annual* sale, but a *great* sale at Rome.

[2] S o l l t e n  s i c h  s o l c h e  L e u t e  n i c h t  b i l l i g, etc. " Is it not natural that such men should stand in fear of a reformation and a free council ?" Literally, " Should not such men reasonably fear," etc.? See p. 102, Note 3, on the word b i l l i g.

[3] I n  e i n a n d e r  h ä n g e n, *embroil,* make kings and princes seize and hold upon each other like tigers. The expression corresponds in character to the English, " to set by the ears." H ä n-g e n as an active verb is causative of h a n g e n, a neuter verb. I n  e i n a n d e r  h a n g e n would, applied to persons, mean *to be at variance,* while a n  e i n a n d e r  h a n g e n, would be, *to be attached to each other, to love each other.*

[4] S o l c h e  s e i n e  B ü b e r e i, "such knavery of his." The use of these two adjectives together is unusual. The word s e i n e is not necessary after s o l c h e.

[5] Z u l e t z t  h a t  d e r  P a b s t, etc. " Finally the pope has erected for all these honorable transactions, a proper market house." H ä n d e l n is, as the change of the vowel would indicate, the plural of H a n d e l n, an infinitive used substantively. E i g e n e s does not refer to P a b s t (" his own"), but to H ä n d e l n. D i e-

eigenes Kaufhaus aufgerichtet, d. i. : des Datarii Haus zu
Rom. Dahin müssen alle die kommen, die dieser Weise
nach um[1] Lehen und Pfründen handeln, demselben muß[2]
man[2] solche Glossen und Handthierung abkaufen, und Macht
erlangen, solche Haupt-Büberei zu treiben. Es war vor
Zeiten noch gnädig zu Rom, da man das Recht mußte kau=
fen, oder mit Geld niederdrücken ; aber jetzt ist sie so köstlich
geworden, daß sie Niemand lässet Büberei treiben, es muß
mit Summen zuvor erkauft werden.

Hast du nun Geld in diesem Hause, so kannst du zu allen
den gesagten Stücken[3] kommen, und nicht allein zu densel=
ben, sondern allerlei Wucher[4] wird hier um Geld redlich,

---

s e n would according to present usage, be placed after a l l e n, and
n a c h a little below would more commonly be placed before d i e-
s e r  W e i s e.

[1] U m, in trading, means *for*, either the money for the article purchased or the article for the money. "To trade for fiefs and prebends."

[2] D e n s e l b e n  m u s s  m a n, etc. "Of this *datarium* one must
(first) purchase such glosses (i. e. such as the *commendam, unio*, etc.)
and obtain the authority (power) to practise such superlative kna
very. Formerly they were (it was, i. e. comparatively) gracious at
Rome, when one had (merely) to purchase justice, or to oppress by
bribes ; but now it has come to such a fine pitch, that it (Rome) allows no one to practise iniquity, unless it (the right) first be purchased with a large sum of money." Here we see the natural explanation of the idiom, e s  s e i  d e n n, e s  m u s s  d e n n, etc. "It
allows no one to practise iniquity [freely, gratuitously] ; the right
must first be purchased," i. e. it allows no one to practise *except* it
purchase. A *negation* is followed by a hypothetical *statement* which
has the nature of a condition or exception.

[3] S t ü c k e, *things*, or priviliges.

[4] S o n d e r n  a l l e r l e i  W u c h e r, etc., "but all kinds of unlawful gain are here made (become) honorable for money, as, e. g.
stolen and plundered property is justified." [W i r d]  g e r e c h t-
f e r t i g t. There is no convenient English word for rendering
W u c h e r. *Usury* is too specific. The word *shaving*, as vulgarly

**12**

als geſtohlenes, geraubtes Gut gerechtfertiget. Hier wer=
den die Gelübde aufgehoben, hier wird den Mönchen Frei=
heit gegeben, aus dem Orden zu gehen, hier iſt frei der ehe=
liche Stand den Geiſtlichen, hier mögen Hurenkinder ehelich
werden, alle Unehre und Schande hier zu Würden kommen,
aller böſer Tadel und Mal[1] hier Ritter geſchlagen und edel
wird. Hier muß ſich der eheliche Stand leiden, der in ver=
botenem Grad[2] oder ſonſt einen Mangel hat. O welch eine
Schäßerei[3] und Schinderei regieret da, daß einen Schein
hat, daß alle geiſtlichen Geſeße darum geſeßt, daß nur viel
Geldſtricke würden, daraus ſich müßte löſen, wer ein Chriſt
ſeyn ſoll. Ja hier wird der Teufel ein Heiliger und ein
Gott dazn. Was Himmel und Erde nicht vermag,[4] das

---

used, often comes nearer to it. They are both comprehended under
the German word.

[1] Aller böser Tadel und Mal, etc., "every vicious defect and stain is here knighted and ennobled." The two senses of
Tadel, 1. fault, censurableness, 2. the imputation of fault, censure,
correspond to the two in which the English word *blame* is used.
Mal, or Maal, in the sense of *spot, stain* (formerly Mahl) is so
written for the sake of distinction. It is of the same etymology as
Mahl.

[2] Der in verbotenem Grad [ist], etc., "here the con-
jugal state which exists within the prohibited degree of relationship,
or is defective for any other reason, must endure it. Sich leiden, *to endure one's self*, i. e. *to put up with one's condition*, is an obsolete expression.

[3] O welch eine Schätzerei. "Oh, what a tax-levying
and fleecing (flaying) is there [two nominatives regarded as one], so
that it has the appearance that all canonical laws are established for
this end, that there might only be many pecuniary bonds, out of
which he, who would be a Christian, must deliver himself!" Gesetzt [sind].

[4] Was Himmel und Erde nicht vermag, etc.,
"What heaven and earth cannot do, that can this house do. It is
called *compositiones ;—compositiones*, to be sure, or rather *confusiones !*
How poor a treasure is the toll on the Rhine compared to this sacred
house !"

vermag dieß hans. Es heißen compositiones, freilich compositiones, ja confusiones. O welch ein schlechter Schaß ist der Zoll am Rhein gegen dieses heilige Haus.

Niemand soll achten,[1] daß ich zu viel sage; es ist Alles öffentlich, daß sie selbst zu Rom müssen bekennen, es sey greulicher und mehr, denn Jemand sagen könnte. Ich habe noch nicht, will auch noch nicht, rühren die rechte helle Grundsuppe von den persönlichen Lastern; ich rede nur von gemeinen läufigen Sachen, und kann sie dennoch mit Worten nicht erlangen. Es sollten Bischöfe, Priesterschaft, und zuvor die Doctoren der Universitäten, die darum besoldet sind, ihrer Pflicht nach, hiewieder einträchtiglich geschrieben und geschrieen haben. Ja wende das Blatt um,[2] so findest du es.

Es ist auch das Valete dahinten,[3] das muß ich auch geben. Da nun der unausmeßliche Geiz[4] noch nicht genug hätte an allen diesen Schäßen, da billig sich drei mächtige

---

[1] Niemand soll achten, etc., "No one should suppose that I am saying too much. It is all notorious (public) so that they themselves at Rome must confess that it is worse in character and degree (more abominable and more extensive) than can be told. I have not yet touched, nor will I, the genuine (real, clear) sediment of personal corruptions; I speak only of common, current matters, and yet I cannot find words to express them (reach them with words). Bishops, the priesthood, and especially the teachers in the universities, who are paid for this purpose, should, in obedience to their duty, have cried and written against this with one consent."

[2] Ja wende das Blatt um. "Turn the tables, (i. e. look for the opposite) and you find it." These men have concealed or defended what they ought to have exposed.

[3] Valete dahinten, "the farewell is still behind," or is still to come. The Germans often call the last thing or the end of a thing, a Lebewohl. The Latin word *valete* explains itself. The sense is, "There is still one thing remaining; I must bring that forward also."

[4] Da nun der unausmessliche Geiz, etc. "Since, now, the immeasurable avarice would not have enough with all these

Könige ließen daran begnügen, hebt er nun an, solche seine Händel zu versetzen und zu verkaufen dem Fugger zu Augsburg, daß nun Bisthum und Lehen zu verleihen, tauschen, kaufen, und die liebe Handthierung geistlicher Güter treiben, eben auf den rechten Ort ist gekommen, und nun aus geistlichen und weltlichen Gütern, eine Handthierung geworden. Nun möchte ich gerne eine so hohe Vernunft hören, die erdenken möchte, was nun hinfort geschehen könne durch den römischen Geiz, das nicht geschehen sey; es wäre denn, daß der Fugger seine beide, und nun einigen Handel auch Jemand versetzt oder verkauft. Ich meine, es sey an's Ende gekommen.

Wir sind hier schuldig allen Fleiß vorzuwenden,[1] solchem

---

treasures, with which (d a for w o) three powerful kings would have good reason to be satisfied (would reasonably let themselves be satisfied with it), it began now (n u n, *in these circumstances*, or *therefore*), to transfer this (such) its trade and to sell [the privilege] to the house of Fugger in Augsburg, so that now conferring, bartering and purchasing sees and fiefs, and following the (darling) business of [dealing in] ecclesiastical property, have come to exactly the right place ; and now from ecclesiastical and secular property a regular business has arisen. Now I should like to hear of (so high) an ingennity which can invent what further can be effected by Roman avarice, which has not been effected ; unless it be (e s  w ä r e  d e n n) that Fugger should transfer and sell to some one (to some third person) both of his (branches of business, the pope's and his own). I think, the matter has gone to its height, (is come to its end, i. e. can be carried no farther). U n a u s m e s s l i c h e is not a common word, but it is easy to learn its import from its derivation. A u s m e s s e n, means *to measure out*. A u s m e s s l i c h (not used), *that which can be measured out ;* n n a u s m e s s l i c h, *that which is immeasurable.* *Fugger* was a great banker, the *Rothschild* of that age. H a n d t h i - e r u n g means, *mechanical employment, business, trade.* A u f  d e n r e c h t e n  O r t, as the conferring of benefices had become a regular matter of trade, it is just in character to let it out to a great banker. The only conceivable way in which the matter could be carried farther, was that Fugger should let out the business to others, who should sustain the relation of retailers to him as a wholesale dealer.

[1] V o r z u w e n d e n. The word v o r w e n d e n literally means, *to turn* or *to bring forward,* and hence to exhibit, to manifest. So it

Jammer und Zerstörung der Christenheit zu wehren. Wollen wir[1] wider die Türken streiten, so lasset uns hier anheben, da sie am allerärgsten[2] sind. Hängen wir die Diebe, und köpfen die Räuber, warum sollten wir frei lassen den römischen Geiz, der der größte Dieb und Räuber ist, der auf Erden gekommen ist oder kommen mag; und das Alles in Christi und St. Peters heiligen Namen. Wer kann's doch zuletzt leiden oder schweigen? Es ist ja gestohlen und geraubet fast Alles was er hat, das ist je nicht anders,[3] welches aus allen Historien bewähret wird. Es hat ja der Pabst[4] solche große Güter nicht gekauft, daß er von seinen Officien mag aufheben bei zehn hundert tausend Dukaten, ohne die oben genannten Schatzgruben und sein Land. So hat es ihm Christus und St. Peter auch nicht aufgeerbet,[5] so hat es ihm auch Niemand gegeben noch geliehen; so ist es auch

---

is used here and on p. 93, line 4.   But, at present, it is employed only in the figurative sense, *to pretend*.   W e n d e n, old English, *to wend*.

[1] W o l l e n  w i r, *if we wish*.   So a little below, h ä n g e n  w i r, *if we hang*.

[2] A m  a l l e r ä r g e s t e n, *the worst of all*.   For this form of the superlative, see Gram. p. 126.   A l l e r, once a genitive governed by the superlative, has come to coalesce with it into one word.   Compare p. 3, Note 4, and p. 92, Note 3.   The Papists are here called the worst of Turks.

[3] D a s  i s t  j e  n i c h t  a n d e r s, *it is not otherwise*, or *it is indeed so*, is tautological.   W e l c h e s, refers not simply to this expression, but to the preceding words.   " Nearly all that he has is stolen and plundered,—it is exactly so—which is proved by all history."

[4] E s  h a t  j a  d e r  P a b s t, etc.   " The pope has not *purchased* such great wealth that he can raise a million ducats from his officers [of business and trade at Rome] in addition to the above-mentioned treasures and his lands."   The meaning is, the pope can raise a million ducats, etc. but this ability or wealth has not come to him by purchase, but by stealth and plunder.   G e k a u f t  is emphatic.

[5] A u f g e e r b t, *left by inheritance*.   A u f e r b e n  is out of use at present, except as a provincial word.

nicht erseffen[1] noch erjähret. Sage du mir, woher mag er
es haben? Daraus merke, was sie suchen und meinen,
wenn sie Legaten heraus senden, Geld zu sammeln wider
die Türken.

---

### Rath von Besserung christlichen Standes.

Wiewohl ich nun zu gering bin, Stücke[2] vorzulegen, zu
solchen greulichen Wesens Besserung[3] dienstlich, will ich doch

---

[1] **Ersessen** participle from **ersitzen**, "to obtain a right to
a thing by long occupancy," which is the same in sense as **erjahr-
en**, to "*acquire by prescription.*"

[2] **Stücke.** The extensive use of the word **Stück**, and the
many idioms formed with it, render it necessary to explain its nature.
It means 1. literally, *what sticks together, or adheres, or one solid mass ;*
as, **etwas aus einem Stücke, machen**, *to make a thing
out of one unbroken piece* (of timber, etc.) **In einem Stücke
fort arbeiten** (figuratively), *to labor on without interruption*, (in
one piece). *A piece*, i. e a coherent mass, broken off from something else. In this signification it corresponds exactly to the English
word *piece*. 3. A solid mass, or a whole *with respect to a settled or
customary measure* ; as a **Stück Tuch**, a piece of cloth containing a certain number of yards ; **ein Stück Garn**, a certain
number, (four or six) of skeins of yarn or thread ; **ein Stück
Wein**, a pipe of wine ; **ein Stück Salz**, a certain measure
of salt, varying in different places from three bushels to three fourths
of a bushel. 4. *An individual viewed as a part* (piece) *of a class or
species*, as a piece of money, of artillery. **Zehn Stück Bücher**, ten books ; **Zehn Stück Vieh**, ten head of cattle ; **ein
Stück von einem Mensch**, a blustering or contemptible man,
(applied to a human being, **Stück** is a word of contempt, as "a
miserable thing of a man"). 5. *A piece, as a work of art*, especially
of painting, poetry, music, etc., 6. *A bad act, trick*, especially in
biblical usage. *i. A thing, a circumstance, a particular, a point*, as
**in diesem Stücke**, in this matter ; **von freien Stücken**,
voluntarily, of his own accord ; **grosse Stücke auf ihn
halten**, to make much (great things) of him.

[3] **Zu solchen greulichen Wesens Besserung.**

das Narrenspiel hinaus singen, und sagen, so viel mein Ver=
stand vermag, was wohl geschehen möchte und sollte, von
weltlicher Gewalt oder gemeinem Concilio.

Zum ersten, daß ein jeglicher Fürst,[1] Adel, Städte, in
ihren Unterthanen frisch an verbieten die Annaten nach
Rom zu geben, und sie gar abthun. Denn der Pabst hat
den Pact gebrochen, und eine Räuberei gemacht aus den
Annaten, zu Schaden und Schanden gemeiner deutscher[2]
Nation, giebt sie seinen Freunden, verkauft sie für großes
Geld, und stiftet Officien darauf; darum hat er das Recht
dazu verloren und Strafe verdient. So ist die weltliche
Gewalt schuldig zu schützen die Unschuldigen, und zu wehren
das Unrecht, wie St. Paulus Röm. 13. lehret.

Zum andern, dieweil der Pabst mit seinem römischen
Praktiken,[3] Commenden, Adjutorien, Reservation, Gratiis
expectativis, Pabst=Monat, Incorporation, Union, Pension,

---

This last word is governed by z u, and governs s o l c h e n  g r e u-
l i c h e n  W e s e n s. Although I am too insignificant to set forth
particulars, (which would be) subservient (d i e n s t l i c h) to the
reformation of such an abominable state of things (affair, or concern),
yet I will carry out (or sing out my merry Andrew song) my part as
court fool, (alluding to his presumption in offering advice to the
emperor, and to princes and nobles), and say what might and should,
perhaps (w o h l), be done (take place) by the civil government or by
a general council."

[1] D a s s  e i n  j e g l i c h e r  F ü r s t, etc., "that every prince, the
nobility and (the free) cities prohibit promptly (f r i s c h  a n, *briskly
on*, *spiritedly*) their subjects (among or in their subjects) from giving
(to give) annats to Rome, and abolish them altogether" (g a r).

[2] G e m e i n e r  d e u t s c h e r, for a l l g e m e i n. (E r) g i e b t
s i e.

[3] R ö m i s c h e n  P r a k t i k e n, etc, "Roman tricks (viz)., *commendams*, *adjutoria*, (right to appoint coadjutors to bishops), reserva-
tions (mental), expectancies (promise of a benefice, when it shall
become vacant), papal months, pensions, palliums (purchased by
archbishops), rules of the court or office (where such business was
transacted, the *datarium*), and the like knavery."

Palliis, Canzelei-Regeln und dergleichen Büberei, alle
deutschen Stifte ohne Gewalt[1] und Recht zu sich reißt, und
dieselben zu Rom Fremden, die nichts in deutschen Landen
dafür thun, giebt und verkauft, damit er[2] die Ordinarien
beraubt ihres Rechtes, macht aus den Bischöfen nur Ziffern
und Oelgötzen, und also wider sein eigen geistliches Recht,
Natur und Vernunft handelt, daß zuletzt dahin kommen,
daß die Pfründen und Lehen nur groben ungelehrten Eseln
und Buben zu Rom, durch lauter Geiz verkauft werden,
fromme und gelehrte Leute ihrer Verdienste und Kunst nichts
genießen, dadurch das arme Volk deutscher Nation guter gelehrter Prälaten muß mangeln und verderben; so soll hier
der chhristliche Adel sich gegen ihn setzen, als wider einen
gemeinen Feind und Zerstörer der Christenheit, um der
armen Seelen Heil[3] willen, die durch solche Tyrannei verderben müssen; setzen, gebieten und verordnen, daß hinfort
kein Lehen mehr nach Rom gezogen, keines mehr darin erlangt werde auf keinerlei Weise, sondern wieder von der
tyrannischen Gewalt herausrückt, draußen behalten,[4] und

---

[1] Ohne Gewalt, without lawful power.

[2] Damit er, etc., " whereby he robs the ordinary or regular
bishop of his right, makes the bishops mere ciphers and drones (Oel-
götze, a lazy fellow, now a low word), and thus violates his own
canonical law, (as well as) nature and reason, so that at last it has
(they have) come to this, that prebends and fiefs are, out of mere avarice, sold to coarse, ignorant asses and knaves at Rome, (and) pious
and learned men derive no benefit from their merit and talents,
whereby the unhappy people of Germany must do without learned
prelates, and suffer (be ruined), therefore," etc. (so refers to dieweil der Papst, etc.).

[3] Heil instead of Heils in the genitive for the sake of euphony.   Luther often uses such a license.

[4] Heraus(ge)rückt, draussen behalten (werde),
" be wrested again from its tyrannical power, and kept from it (out
of Rome) and the rights and office of the ordinary bishops, to dis-
pose, to the best of their power, of such benefices among the Germans, be restored to them."

den Ordinarien ihr Recht und Amt wiederstatten, solch Le=
hen zu verordnen, auf's Beste sie mögen, in deutscher Na=
tion.

Und wo ein Courtisan heraus käme,[1] daß demselben ein
ernster Befehl geschehe abzustehen, oder in den Rhein und
das nächste Wasser zu springen, und den römischen Bann
mit Siegel und Briefen zum kalten Bade führen, so würden
sie zu Rom merken, daß die Deutschen nicht alle Zeit toll
und voll[2] seyen, sondern auch einmal Christen geworden
wären, als die[3] den Spott und Schmach des heiligen Na=
mens Christi, unter welchen solche Büberei und Seelverder=
ben geschieht, nicht mehr zu leiden gedenken, Gott und Got=
tes Ehre mehr achten denn der Menschen Gewalt.

Zum dritten, daß ein kaiserliches Gesetz ausgehe, keinen
Bischofsmantel, auch keine Bestätigung irgend einer Digni=
täten[4] fortan aus Rom zu holen; sondern daß man die
Ordnung des allerheiligsten und berühmtesten Concilii Ni=
cäni wieder aufrichtete, darinnen gesetzt ist,[5] daß ein Bischof

---

[1] Heraus käme, etc. "And if a courtier should come out
here (from Rome), that (dass, here as in the second paragraph,
dependent on sagen in the first paragraph) a strict command be
given to him to keep at a distance, or to leap into the Rhine or (and)
the nearest river, and take the Roman bull of excommunication with
seal and letters to a cold bath. Thus would they at Rome perceive."

[2] Toll und voll. Voll, has reference to feasting and drinking, which tends to make one toll Compare *Vollerei.* This fond-
ness for alliteration is apparent in numerous phrases, transmitted
from the earliest times.

[3] Als die, *as who,* i. e. *as those who.*

[4] Irgend einer Dignitäten. Dignitäten, is either
genitive singular after the old form, according to which feminine
nouns were declined in the singular, or genitive plural, governed by
einer, "any one of the dignities."

[5] Aufrichtete, darinnen (darin) gesetzt ist, "should
be restored, or one should restore (imperfect subjunctive) in which
it is established," etc.

foll beſtätiget werden von den andern zwei nächſten, oder von dem Erzbiſchof.

Zum vierten, daß verordnet werde, daß keine weltliche Sache gen Rom gezogen werde, ſondern dieſelben alle[1] der weltlichen Gewalt laſſen ; wie ſie ſelbſt ſetzen in ihren geiſt= lichen Rechten, und doch nicht halten. Denn des Pabſts Amt ſoll ſeyn, daß er der Allergelehrteſte in der Schrift, und wahrhaftig,[2] nicht mit Namen, der Allerheiligſte, regiere die Sachen, die den Glauben und heiliges Leben der Chriſten betreffen, die Primaten und Erzbiſchöfe dazu halten,[3] und mit ihnen drinnen handeln und Sorge tragen, wie St. Paulus 1. Cor. 6. lehret, und härtiglich ſtrafet,[4] daß ſie mit weltlichen Sachen umgiengen. Denn es bringet unerträg= lichen Schaden allen Landen, daß zu Rom ſolche Sachen werden gehandelt, da große Koſten aufgehen, dazu[5] dieſelbi=

---

[1] Sondern (man solle) dieselben (Sache) alle, etc., "but one should leave all these to the civil power, as they them-selves (the Romanists) lay it down in their canonical law, and yet do not observe it."

[2] Und wahrhaftig, etc., "and in reality and not (merely) in name, the most holy (of all)." Allerheiligste (sei).

[3] Dazu halten, and obligate them to do the same (hold them to it)."

[4] Härtiglich strafet, etc., "as Paul teaches and severely censures (them) that they," etc. Härtiglich, is obsolete, as used here for hart. In the sense of a little hard, the form härtlich, is now used instead of härtiglich. Strafen is no longer used in the sense of censuring, but tadeln is now the common word to express that idea.

[5] Aufgehen, dazu, etc., " much money is consumed, and be-sides (dazu) these judges (at Rome) are ignorant of the customs, laws and usages of (other) countries, so that they often force matters (causes) and bring them to (conform to) their laws and opinions, by which injustice must be done to the parties." Aufgehen, to ascend, comes to signify, as here, to consume, probably from the figure drawn from fire, in which the thing consumed, is said to ascend, or go up in flames or smoke. The other derivative significations of the word are easily traced out.

gen Richter nicht wiſſen die Sitten, Recht und Gewohnheit
der Länder, daß mehrmal die Sachen zwingen und ziehen
nach ihren Rechten und Opinionen, damit den Parteien
muß unrecht geſchehen.

Dabei[1] müßte man auch verbieten in allen Stiften die
greuliche Schinderei der Officiale, daß ſie nicht mehr denn[2]
des Glaubens Sache und guter Sitten ſich annehmen; was
Geld, Gut und Leib oder Ehre anbetrifft, den weltlichen
Richtern laſſen. Darum ſoll die weltliche Gewalt das Ban=
nen und Treiben[3] nicht geſtatten, wo es nicht Glauben oder
gutes Leben anbetrifft. Geiſtliche Gewalt ſoll geiſtliches
Gut regieren, wie das die Vernunft lehret; geiſtlich Gut
aber iſt nicht Geld noch leiblich Ding,[4] ſondern Glauben und
gute Werke.

Zum fünften, daß keine Reſervation mehr gelte, und kein
Lehen mehr behaftet werde zu Rom, es ſterbe der Beſitzer,[5]
es ſey Hader darob, oder ſey eines Cardinals oder Pabſts
Geſinde. Und daß man ſtrenge verbiete und wehre, daß
kein Courtiſan auf irgend ein Lehen Hader anfange, die
frommen Prieſter zu citiren, tribuliren[6] und auf's Conten=

---

[1] D a b e i, *with this*, or in connection with this. D e r O fficiale.
An O fficial, is generally a substitute or vicar of the bishop in judicial matters.

[2] D a s s i e n i c h t m e h r d e n n, etc., "that they meddle with
(interest themselves in) nothing but matters of faith, and good
morals." S a c h e, is the genitive without the article. It governs
d e s G l a u b e n s, and is itself like S i t t e n governed by s i c h
a n n e h m e n, for an explanation of which, see p. 55, Note 2, end.

[3] B a n n e n u n d T r e i b e n, *excommunicating and banishing.*

[4] G e i s t l i c h (e s) G u t, and l e i b l i c h (e s) D i n g. See
p. 4, Note 3.

[5] E s s t e r b e d e r B e s i t z e r, etc., " whether the incumbent
die (at Rome, or on the way), or a law-suit be commenced respecting
it (the benefice, d a r o b) or (the incumbent) be attached to the retinue of a cardinal or of the pope."

[6] T r i b u l i r e n, from the corrupt Latin, *tribulare.* Any foreign

tiren treiben.  Und wo darum[1] aus Rom ein Bann oder
geiftlicher Zwang käme, daß man[2] den verachte, als wenn
ein Dieb Jemand in Bann thäte, darum, daß man ihn nicht
wollte stehlen laffen.

Zum sechsten, daß auch abgethan werden die Casus re
servati, die behaltenen Fäile, damit nicht allein viel Geld
von den Leuten geschunden wird, sondern viel armer Gewif=
fen von den wütherichen Tyrannen verstrickt und verwirret,
zu unträglichem Schaden ihres Glaubens zu Gott.

Zum siebenten, daß der römische Stuhl die Officia abthue,
das Gewürm und Schwürm[3] zu Rom wenigere, auf daß des
Pabsts Gesinde möge von des Pabsts eigen Gut[4] ernähret
werden, und laffe seinen Hof nicht aller Königen Hof mit
Prangen und Kosten übertreten :[5] angesehen,[6] daß solch
Wesen nicht allein nie gedienet hat zur Sache des christlichen
Glaubens, sondern sie auch dadurch verhindert[7] am Studi=

---

verb may be adopted into German by adding the ending i r e n to
the root.  See p. 23, Note 2.  C o n t e n t i r e n, is formed in the
same way from the French verb *contenter*, and is used as a substantive, as all infinitives may be.  A u f s  c o n t e n t i r e n  means,
*to their satisfaction*, i. e. till they are satisfied.

[1] U n d  w o  d a r u m, *and if on that account.*

[2] D a s s  m a n, here, as so often elsewhere in this connection, referring to what Luther says or advises, as implied in the first paragraph.  See p. 141, Note 1.

[3] G e w u r m  u n d  S c h w ü r m, see p. 110, Note 2.  " Abolish
the offices (and) diminish the swarm (of dependents) at Rome."
A u f  d a s s, see p. 37, Note 1.

[4] E i g e n  G u t, is in the dative.  When the *e* in the genitive
termination of such substantives is omitted (G u t s, for G u t e s),
it is omitted also in the dative (G u t for G u t e).  Luther generally adopts this form.  The adjective being prefixed to a *neuter* substantive, is here, undeclined, (e i g e n for e i g e n e m).

[5] U e b e r t r e t e n obsolete, for ü b e r t r e f f e n.

[6] A n g e s e h e n, *considering*, like a n g e n o m e n, *supposing*

[7] S i e  d a d u r c h  v e h i n d e r t (h a t), " but has thereby hindered them (s i e, the persons concerned) from study and prayer so
that."

ren und Gebet, daß sie selbst fast nichts mehr wissen vom
Glauben zu sagen, welches sie gar gröblich bewiesen haben
in diesem letzten römischen Concilio.

Zum achten, daß die schweren greulichen Eide aufgehoben
würden, so die Bischöfe dem Pabst zu thun gezwungen, ohne
alles Recht, damit[1] sie gleich wie die Knechte gefangen werden; wie das untüchtige, ungelehrte Kapitel, Significasti,[2]
von eigener Gewalt[3] und großem Unverstand setzet. Ist's
nicht genug,[4] daß sie uns Gut, Leib und Seele beschweren
mit vielen ihren tollen Gesetzen,[5] dadurch den Glauben ge-
schwächt, die Christenheit verderbet, sie nehmen denn auch[6]
gefangen die Person, ihr Amt und Werk: dazu auch die

---

[1] Gezwungen (werden) ohne alles Recht, damit,
etc., "which the bishops are compelled to swear (take) to the pope
without any right (or law requiring it) by which they are bound like
servants."

[2] Untüchtige, ungelehrte Kapitel, *Significasti*. *Significasti* means the chapter in the canonical law beginning with this
word. Tüchtig, meant originally, *strong, able*. Thence it signified, *that which has force and excellence*. It often means *useful*, or
*fit*, but only in those cases in which *strong and high qualities* constitute the usefulness or fitness. Herein does it differ from tauglich,
which means *that which can be put to some particular use, which one
can use*. Bequem is *convenient*, and is used of *things* which can
be easily and readily used. Geschickt, with reference to persons, means, *skilful, an adept;* with reference to things, it means,
*adapted*.

[3] Eigener Gewalt, grammatically referring to Kapitel,
must of course relate to the *author* of the chapter. Such freedoms
of construction are of perpetual occurrence.

[4] Ist's nicht genug, is not a conditional clause, but interrogative; or possibly an emphatic assertion.

[5] Vielen ihren tollen Gesetzen instead of ihren
vielen. It is a harsh construction, but it gives great emphasis to
the word vielen.

[6] Sie nehmen denn auch, etc., "unless they take cap-
tive." See Gram. pp. 362, 315.

13

Inveſtitur, die vor Zeiten der deutſchen Kaiſer geweſen, und
in Frankreich und etlichen Königreichen noch der Könige
ſind.[1]   Darüber ſie mit den Kaiſern[2] großen Krieg und Ha=
ber gehabt, ſo lange, bis daß ſie mit frecher Gewalt genom=
men und behalten haben bisher ; gerade als müßten die
Deutſchen vor allen Chriſten auf Erden des Pabſts und rö=
miſchen Stuhls Göckelnarren[3] ſeyn, thun und leiden, was
ſonſt Niemand leiden noch thun will.   Dieweil denn dieß
Stück eitel Gewalt[4] und Räuberei iſt, zu Hinderniſſen bi=
ſchöflicher ordentlicher Gewalt, und zu Schaden der armen

---

[1] Die — der Kaiser gewesen (ist) und — noch der
Könige sind, *which was the emperors', and are now the kings'*,
i. e. which belonged to the emperors, etc.   The subject is here changed from the singular to the plural.   The genitive is sometimes used
as a predicate, and approaches the nature of an adjective or adjective pronoun (which was his or theirs).

[2] Darüber sie mit den Kaisern, etc.   There is a little
irregularity in the construction of this sentence, near the close.
There is an incongruity in saying, " On account of that (the right of
investitures) they have had severe wars and contests with the emper
ors until (so lange bis dass) they seized them with shameless violence, *and retained them up to this time.*  (And they have retained them, etc.)."

[3] Göckelnarren.   Göckel is written in old German go-
gel, and sometimes gigel (the root of our word *giggle*, respecting which Richardson has some strange fancies).   As an adjective it
means, *jesting, wanton.*   Hence Göckelnarr, is a merry Andrew.

[4] Dieweil denn diess Stück eitel Gewalt, etc.,
" since then, this thing is sheer violence and plundering," etc.   On
the force of eitel, see p. 10, Note 4.—Tyrannei zu wehren,
*to restrain such tyranny.*   The verb wehren in the early writers
sometimes governs the accusative as the direct object of the action.
So it is found several times in Luther's version of the Scriptures.
But according to modern usage, the dative is required by this verb.
With this dative, however, there may be an accusative of the thing,
as, einem etwas wehren, *to hinder one in respect to anything*,
i. e. to restrain, hinder or prevent him from doing it.

Seelen, ift der Kaiſer mit ſeinem Adel ſchuldig, ſolche Ty=
rannei zu wehren und zu ſtrafen.

Zum neunten, daß der Pabſt über den Kaiſer keine Ge=
walt habe, ohne daß[1] er ihn auf dem Altar ſalbe und kröne,
wie ein Biſchof einen König krönet; und je nicht die teufe=
liſche Hoffahrt hinfort zugelaſſen werde, daß der Kaiſer des
Pabſts Füße küſſe, oder zu ſeinen Füßen ſitze, oder wie man
ſagt, ihm den Stegreif halte, und den Zaum ſeines Maul=
pferds,[2] wenn er aufſitzt zu reiten; noch vielweniger dem
Pabſt Huld und treue Unterthänigkeit ſchwöre, wie die Pä=
bſte unverſchämt vornehmen zu fordern, als hätten ſie Recht
dazu. Es iſt das Kapitel Solite, darinnen päbſtliche Ge=
walt über kaiſerliche Gewalt erhoben wird, nicht eines Hel=
lers werth,[3] und Alle, die ſich darauf gründen oder davor
fürchten; dieweil es nicht anders thut, denn die heiligen
Gottes=Worte zwinget und bringet von ihrem rechten Ver=
ſtand, auf ihre eigene Träume: wie ich das angezeiget habe
im Latein.

Es iſt auch lächerlich und kindiſch, daß der Pabſt aus ſol=
chem verblendeten, verkehrten Grund ſich rühmet in ſeinem
Decretal Pastoralis, er ſey des Kaiſerthums[4] ein ordentlicher
Erbe, ſo es ledig ſtünde. Wer hat es ihm gegeben? Hat's
Chriſtus gethan, da er ſagt, Luc. 22. „Die Fürſten der

---

[1] Ohne dass, in the sense of ausgenommen, or ausser,
obsolete. See p 95, Note 3.

[2] Maulpferd, obsolete for Maulthier or Maulesel.

[3] Nicht eines Hellers werth, *is not worth a Heller.*
Werth governs the genitive; but in modern style, the accusative
often follows it, especially when a *definite number* of anything is giv-
en, as in this case.—Und alle, die sich, etc., " and all (i. e.
nor any of) those who act on its authority, or stand in fear of it; inasmuch as it does nothing but (not otherwise than that it) force God's
holy words and press them away from their proper meaning to their
own dreams."

[4] Er sei des Kaiserthums, etc., " that he is the (a) proper
heir of the Empire, should it become (stand) vacant."

Heiden ſind Herren ; ihr aber ſollt nicht ſo ſeyn ?" Hat's ihm St. Peter aufgeerbet ?[1] Mich verdrießt, daß wir ſolche unverſchämte, grobe, tolle Lügen müſſen im geiſtlichen Recht leſen und lehren, dazu für chriſtliche Lehre halten, ſo es doch teufeliſche Lügen ſind. Welcher Art[2] auch iſt die unerhörte Lüge, de donatione Constantini. Es muß eine beſondere Plage von Gott geweſen ſeyn, daß ſo viele verſtändige Leute ſich haben laſſen bereden,[3] ſolche Lügen aufzunehmen, ſo ſie doch ſo gar grob und unbehend ſind, daß mich dünkt, es ſollte ein trunkener Bauer behender und geſchickter lügen können. Wie ſollte beſtehen bei einem Kaiſerthum zu regieren, pre=digen,[4] beten, ſtudiren und der Armen warten ? Welches Amt[5] auf's allereigentlichſte dem Pabſt zuſtehet, und von Chriſto mit ſo großem Ernſt aufgelegt, daß er auch verbot, ſie ſollten nicht[6] Röcke, nicht Geld mit ſich tragen ; ſintemal

---

[1] **Aufgeerbet**, *bequeathed.* See p. 137, Note 5. **Mich ver-driesst**, for **es verdriesst mich.** See Gram. p. 304. 2.

[2] **Weleher Art**, *of which sort*, genitive as a predicate. See p. 146, Note 1. The fiction of the donation of the empire to the pope by Constantine, was exposed by Laurentius Valla.

[3] **Haben lassen bereden**, would according to present usage ordinarily stand thus, **haben bereden lassen. Sollte — kön-nen.** If defective English verbs be employed in the translation of such words as **können**, (can) there is a difficulty in expressing the force of **sollte.** It will be perfectly easy, however, if, in all such cases, a regular English verb, or a circumlocution be substituted (for *can*) ; as " should be able."

[4] **Zu regieren, predigen,** etc. "How would ruling, preach-ing, praying, studying and attending to the poor, consist with an em-pire ?" i. e. how could he who had an empire under his care do all these things ? **Zu regieren** and the following infinitives are used substantively, and are nominative to **sollte.** All those infinitives refer to the episcopal office. **Regieren** is perhaps to be under-stood of *ecclesiastical* rule. This seems to be required by the next sentence.

[5] **Welches Amt**, viz. that of " ruling, preaching," etc.

[6] **Verbot, sie sollten nicht.** This form of expression, like

der kaum solcher Amt warten kann, der einiges[1] Haus regieren muß; und der Pabst will Kaiserthum regieren, dazu Pabst bleiben. Es haben die Buben erdacht,[2] die unter des Pabsts Namen gerne Herren wären über die Welt, und das verstörete römische Reich durch den Pabst und Namen Christi wieder aufrichten, wie es vorher gewesen ist.

Zum zehnten, daß sich[3] der Pabst enthalte, die Hand aus der Suppe ziehe, sich keines Titels unterwinde des Königreichs zu Neapel und Sicilian. Er hat eben so viel Recht

---

all double negatives, is nearly out of use, and is now regarded as inelegant.

[1] E i n i g e s, in the sense of e i n z i g e s. See p. 93, Note 2.

[2] B u b e n e r d a c h t, *devised, invented.* " This has been invented by the knaves (the knaves have invented it) who would gladly (g e r n e, familiar form for g e r n), under the name of the popes, be masters of the world, and, by the pope and the name of Christ, restore the fallen Roman empire, as it was before."

[3] Z u m z e h n t e n d a s s s i c h, etc. The genitive K ö n i g- r e i c h s is equally dependent on e n t h a l t e, S u p p e and u n- t e r w i n d e  " Tenthly [in my view, it is necessary] that the pope relinquish (e n t h a l t e) the kingdom of Naples and Sicily, that he keep his finger out of that pie (the pie of it), and that he assume (or venture to claim) no title to it. He has just as much right to it as I have [and no more], and yet he wishes to be its feudal lord. It is a robbery and violence as nearly all his other possessions are. Therefore the emperor should not allow him such a fief, and, in case it had been done, he should not permit it any longer; but direct him to the Scriptures and prayer-books to this end (viz.) that he let civil rulers govern territory and people especially those which (d i e) no one has given to him, and that he preach and pray." D i e  H a n d  a u s d e r  S u p p e  z i e h e, " to take his hand out of the porridge." G e- w a l t is here employed with great license, for a *possession seized by power.* W ä r e, in the subjunctive, implies that the concession had never been made, thus: " and even if it had been done" (which is not the case). B i b e l n, is plural, after the analogy of the Greek and Latin, *biblia,* books. D a f ü r. The following clause is in apposition with d a, *for this,* viz. for what he is going on to state. D i e [d i e], *those which.*

13*

daran als ich, will dennoch Lehensherr darüber seyn. Es
ist ein Raub und Gewalt, wie fast alle andere seine Güter
sind; darum sollte ihm der Kaiser solches Lehen nicht ge=
statten, und wo es geschehen wäre, nicht mehr verwilligen;
sondern ihm die Bibeln und Gebetbücher dafür anzeigen,
daß er weltliche Herren lasse Land und Leute regieren, son=
derlich die ihm Niemand gegeben hat; und er prebige und
bete.

Solche Meinung[1] sollte auch gehalten werden über Bono=
nien, Imola, Vincenz, Raven, und Alles was der Pabst in
der Anconitaner[2] Mark, Romandiol, und mehr Länder
Welschlandes[3] mit Gewalt eingenommen, und mit Unrecht
besitzt, dazu wider alle Gebote Christi und St. Pauli sich
drein menget. Denn also sagt St. Paulus: „Niemand
wickelt sich in die weltlichen Geschäfte, der göttlicher Ritter=

---

[1] Solche Meinung sollte, etc. "The same opinion should
be entertained respecting Bologna, Imola, Vicenza, Ravenna, and
everything in the Mark of Ancona, in Romandiola and other countries of Italy, which the pope has seized with violence, and holds with
injustice, and moreover meddles with, contrary to all the commands
of Christ and of St. Paul."

[2] Anconitaner is an adjective. The proper adjective termination for names of places is isch, as spanisch, preussisch.
But frequently the substantive termination er, indeclinable, is used
adjectively for the sake of euphony, as die Berliner Jahrbü-
cher, the Berlin Annals; die Leipziger Zeitung, the Leip-
sic Times, or Gazette; der Magdeburger Dom, the Magdeburg Cathedral. The cases, which are comparatively few, in which
the termination er is used adjectively, must be learned by usage.
For example we must say Cölnisches Wasser, Cologne water,
and die Cölner Domkirche, the Cologne Cathedral. To all this
there is some analogy in English in such terminations as ian and er
in the words, the Bostonians, and the Vermonters; the Philadelphi-
ans and the New Yorkers. Romandiola was an Italian province on
the Adriatic extending from the Mark of Ancona to the Po.

[3] Und mehr Länder Welschlands. Mehr is used
substantively and governs the genitive Länder, and is itself, like
the two preceding substances, governed by in.

ſchaft warten ſoll." Nun ſoll der Pabſt das Haupt und der Erſte ſeyn in dieſer Ritterſchaft; und menget ſich mehr[1] in weltliche Geſchäfte, denn kein Kaiſer noch König: je ſo müßte[2] man ihm heraus helfen, und ſeiner Ritterſchaft war= ten laſſen. Chriſtus auch, deß Statthalter er ſich rühmet, wollte noch nie mit weltlichem Regiment zu ſchaffen haben,[3] ſo gar, daß er zu einem, der ein Urtheil von ihm über ſeinen Bruder begehrte, ſprach: „Wer hat mich dir zu einem Rich= ter gemacht?" Aber der Pabſt fähret einher[4] unberufen, unterwindet ſich aller Dinge, wie ein Gott, bis daß er ſelbſt nicht mehr weiß, was Chriſtus ſey, zu deß Statthalter er ſich aufwirft.[5]

Zum eilften, daß das Füße küſſen des Pabſts auch nicht mehr geſchehe. Es iſt ein unchriſtliches, ja antichriſtiſches Erempel, daß ein armer ſündiger Menſch ihm läſſet ſeine Füße küſſen[6] von dem, der hundertmal beſſer iſt denn er. Geſchieht es der Gewalt[7] zu Ehren, warum thut es der

---

[1] Und (doch) menget sich mehr, etc, "and yet he in-termeddles in worldly business more than any emperor or king (no emperor nor king)." See p. 148, Note 6.

[2] Je so müsste, for ja, " now then one ought to help him out and let him attend to his (spiritual) warfare."

[3] Zu schaffen haben mit, " to have (anything) to do with." Viel zu schaffen haben, "to have much to do." It does not mean *to be obliged to do.* See p. 111, Note 3.

[4] Färet einher, "*plunges in,* uncalled," etc.

[5] Aufwirft. This word means literally *to throw up,* both in the sense of *raising* (a mound, a billow, scum, a wrinkle in cloth) and of *turning up, out* or *open* (a nose, lip, door with violence, a question, or doubt, by proposing it). With sich followed by zu or für, it means, *to volunteer to be, to give one's self out for ;* but when followed by wider, it means *to revolt.*

[6] Ihm lässet seine Füsse küssen. Ihm, as a dative, merely points out the person to whom the action is performed, and stands, as it often does in Luther, for sich.

[7] Geschieht es der Gewalt, "if it is done out of honor to the (imperial) power, why does not the pope do it to others out of

Pabſt auch nicht den andern, der Heiligkeit zu Ehren? Halt
ſie gegen einander[1] Chriſtum und den Pabſt. Chriſtus
wuſch ſeinen Jüngern die Füße und trocknete ſie; und die
Jünger wuſchen ſie ihm noch nie. Der Pabſt, als höher
denn Chriſtus, kehret das um, und läſſet es eine große
Gnade ſeyn, ihm ſeine Füße zu küſſen; der doch das billig,[2]
ſo es Jemand von ihm begehret, mit allem Vermögen weh=
ren ſollte, wie St. Paulus und Barnabas, die ſich nicht
wollten laſſen ehren als Gott, von denen zu Liſtra, ſondern
ſprachen: „Wir ſind gleich Menſchen als[3] ihr." Aber un=
ſerer Schmeichler haben's ſo hoch gebracht, und[4] uns einen
Abgott gemacht, daß Niemand ſich ſo fürchtet vor Gott, Nie=
mand ihn mit ſolchen Geberden ehret, als den Pabſt. Das
-können ſie wohl leiden, aber gar nicht,[5] ſo des Pabſts Prach=

honor to the holiness (of the pope)." This is obscure. Probably,
the Papists gave such an explanation, referring to the example of
Christ in washing the disciples' feet.

[1] H a l t (h a l t e t) s i e  g e g e n  e i n a n d e r, etc., " hold them,
Christ and the pope, side by side (i. e. compare them). See p. 132,
Note 1.

[2] D e r  d o c h  d a s  b i l l i g, etc., " who ought rather (yet) by
good rights (b i l l i g), should any desire it of him, to resist it with all
his might."

[3] G l e i c h  M e n s c h e n  a l s.  G l e i c h — a l s, literally, *like
as.*

[4] S o  h o c h  g e b r a c h t  u n d, " have brought it so high (have
carried it so far) as to make, etc." S o does not correspond to d a s s
in the next line, but by a peculiar idiom, to u n d. Thus in the colloquial phrase, S e i e n  S i e  s o  g u t  u n d  s a g e n  s i e  m i r,
" be so good *as to* tell me." D a s s of itself, often means *so that,*
and does so here.

[5] A b e r  g a r  n i c h t,  s o, etc., " but (they could not endure it) at
all, if the splendor of the pope should be abridged a hair's breadth. If
now they were Christians, and held the honor of God dearer than
their own, the pope would never be happy; but should he perceive
that the honor of God was trampled on, and his own exalted, he
would allow no one to honor him until," etc. N i e m a n d is here
in the accusative, as the connection shows.

ten ein Haarbreit würde abgebrochen. Wenn sie nun Christen wären, und Gottes Ehre lieber hätten, denn ihre eigene, würde der Pabst nimmer fröhlich werden; wo er aber gewahr würde, daß Gottes Ehre verachtet, und seine eigene erhaben wäre, würde auch Niemand lassen ihn ehren, bis er vermerkte, daß Gottes Ehre wieder erhaben, und größer denn seine Ehre wäre.

Derselben großen ärgerlichen Hoffahrt[1] ist auch das ein häßliches Stück, daß der Pabst ihm nicht läßt begnügen, daß er reiten oder fahren möge, sondern ob er wohl stark und gesund ist, sich von Menschen, als ein Abgott, mit unerhörter Pracht tragen lässet. Lieber, wie reimet sich[2] doch solche luciferische Hoffahrt mit Christo, der zu Fuße gegangen ist und alle seine Apostel? Wo ist ein weltlicher König gewesen, der so weltlich und prächtig je gefahren hat, als der fähret, der ein Haupt seyn will Aller derer, die weltliche Pracht verschmähen und fliehen sollen, d. i.: der Christen?[3] Nicht daß uns[4] das fast soll bewegen an ihm selbst; sondern daß wir billig Gottes Zorn fürchten sollen, so wir solcher

---

[1] Derselben grossen ärgerlichen Hoffarht, etc. " Of the same (great) wicked arrogance is this a hateful piece, that he is not content (i h m for s i c h) with riding (that he can ride) on horseback or in a carriage, but though he is strong and healthy, he causes himself to be carried by (v o n) men," etc. R e i t e n is used only of riding on *horses, mules, camels;* f a h r e n, only of being conveyed in vehicles, ships, etc. G e h e n includes both these modes of conveyance, and also walking. Hence figuratively f a h r e n means to move with *velocity* or *violence.*

[2] L i e b e r, w i e r e i m e t, etc. "Dear sir, how does such satanic pride comport with," etc.? U n d a l l e s e i n e A p o s t e l, "and (i. e. as well as) all his apostles," is irregular in its construction.

[3] d. i. d e r C h r i s t e n, in apposition with the genitive d e r e r.

[4] N i c h t d a s s u n s, etc. "Not that this (d a s) should, in itself, very much (f a s t) affect us." F a s t in the sense of s e h r is obsolete; it is used now almost exclusively in the sense of b e i n a h e. U n d u n s e r n V e r d r u s s n i c h t m e r k e n l a s s e n, " and do not manifest (cause to be observed) our displeasure."

Hoffahrt schmeicheln, und unsern Verdruß nicht merken las=
sen. Es ist genug, daß der Pabst also tobet und narret ; es
ist aber zu viel, so wir das billigen und vergönnen.

Denn welches Christen=Herz mag oder soll[1] das mit Lust
sehen, daß der Pabst, wenn er sich will lassen communiciren,
stille sitzt, als ein Gnaden Jungherr, und lässet ihm das
Sacrament von einem knieenden gebeugten Cardinal mit
einem goldenen Rohr reichen ; gerade als wäre das heilige
Sacrament nicht würdig, daß ein Pabst, ein armer stinken=
der Sünder aufstünde, seinem Gott eine Ehre thäte ; so
doch alle andere Christen, die viel heiliger sind, denn der al=
lerheiligste Vater, der Pabst, mit aller Ehrerbietung dasselbe

---

[1] M a g  o d e r  s o l l, etc., "may (can) or ought to view it with
pleasure, that the pope, when he communes (causes himself to com-
mune), sits still, like a gracious young lord, and causes the sacrament to be reached to him with a golden reed, by a kneeling, bow-
ing cardinal, just (g e r a d e) as if the holy sacrament were not worthy that a pope, a poor, filthy sinner should rise up (and) do his God
honor, whereas (s o  d o c h) all other Christians, who are much ho-
lier than the most holy father, the pope, receive it (kneeling) with
all respect? What wonder would it be that (i. e. if) God should send
judgment upon us all indiscriminately (a l l e s a m m t), that (i. e.
because) we suffer, etc." Notice the various uses of the word d a s s.
See p. 144, Note 2.—R o h r. J. Vogt has written an essay entitled,
Historia fistulae eucharisticae, *cujus ope sugi solet e calice vinum bene-
dictum*, " by the aid of which the consecrated wine was sucked from
the cup." This explains the word, R o h r, or *fistula*. See also
Coleman's Ch. Antiquities, p. 329. The object of the instrument was
to prevent the loss of a single drop of the sacred element. After the
communion under only one form, which arose from the same superstitious veneration, was introduced, there was no further use for the
*fistula*, or tube. It was retained, however, in the mass in which the
pope participated, and was of gold, as we here learn. — E h r e r-
b i e t u n g, *act of reverence by kneeling*. Nunc solus sacerdos cele-
brans communicat *stans, reliqui omnes genibus flexis* de manu sacer-
dotis communionem accipiunt Summus Pontifex, cum solemniter
celebrat, *sedens* communicat. *Bona, Rer, Liturg*. quoted by Augus-
ti, Archaeol. II. 768.

empfangen? Was wäre es Wunder, daß uns Gott alle=
sammt plagete, daß wir solche Unehre Gottes leiden und
loben in unsern Prälaten, und solcher seiner verdammten
Hoffahrt uns theilhaftig machen, durch unser Schweigen
oder Schmeicheln?

Also gehet es auch, wenn er das Sacrament in der Pro=
cession umträgt: ihn muß man tragen; aber das Sacra=
ment stehet vor ihm wie ein Kandel[1] Weins auf dem Tisch.
Kürzlich, Christus gilt nichts[2] zu Rom; der Pabst gilt's
alles sammt: und wollen uns dennoch dringen und bedräu=
en, wir sollen solche antichristische Tadel billigen, preisen
und ehren wider Gott und alle christliche Lehre. Helfe nun
Gott einem freien Concilio, daß es den Pabst lehre, wie er
auch ein Mensch sey, und nicht mehr, denn Gott, wie er sich
unterstehet zu seyn.[3]

---

[1] K a n d e l, *cup*, provincial for K a n n e.

[2] K ü r z l i c h, C h r i s t u s   g i l t   n i c h t s, etc. "In short,
Christ passes for nothing, at Rome; the pope passes for everything
(taken together a l l e s   s a m m t, different from a l l e s a m m t a
few lines above); and yet (they, the Papists) wish to force us and
threaten us (d r a ü e n for d r o h e n), that we should approve (i. e.
to force and drive us to approve) commend and honor such an unchristian abuse in opposition to God and all Christian doctrine."

[3] E r   s i c h   u n t e r s t e h e t   z u   s e y n, *as he undertakes or assumes to be.* S i c h   u n t e r s t e h e n, *to take upon one's self unnecessarily*, generally construed with the infinitive, is nearly the same as
the expression, s i c h   u n t e r w i n d e n. They both mean *putting
one's self voluntarily under a burden or difficult work.* S i c h   u n-
t e r w i n d e n, implies that the undertaking is too arduous for one's
strength. S i c h   u n t e r f a n g e n, means the same, except that it
expresses mere difficulty, without implying that the undertaking
is either *unnecessary*, or *too great.* S i c h   g e t r a u e n, or s i c h
t r a u e n, expresses the same general idea of *undertaking a difficult
work*, with a shade of difference conveying the signification of *personal confidence*, which, when carried to a *dangerous* extent, is expressed by s i c h   e r k ü h n e n; and when carried to an *immodest*
extent, is expressed by s i c h   e r d r e i s t e n.

Zum zwölften, daß man die Wallfahrten gen Rom ab=
thäte, oder Niemand von eigenem Vorwitz oder Andacht
wallen ließe,[1] er würde denn zuvor von seinem Pfarrherrn,
Stadt oder Oberherrn erkannt, genugsame und redliche Ur=
sache haben.  Das sage ich nicht darum, daß Wallfahrten
böse seyen ; sondern daß sie zu dieser Zeit übel gerathen :[2]
denn sie zu Rom kein gutes Exempel, sondern eitel Aerger=
niß sehen, und wie sie selbst ein Sprüchwort gemacht haben:
Je näher Rom, je ärger Christen ; bringen sie mit sich Ver=
achtung Gottes und Gottes Geboten.  Man sagt, wer das
erstemal gen Rom gehet, der suchet einen Schalk ; zum an=
dernmal findet er ihn ; zum drittenmal bringt er ihn mit
heraus.  Aber sie sind nun so geschickt worden, daß sie die
drei Reisen auf einmal ausrichten, und haben fürwahr uns
solche Stücklein[3] aus Rom gebracht.  Es wäre besser, Rom
nie gesehen noch erkannt.

Und ob schon diese Sache nicht wäre, so ist doch noch da

---

[1]  W a l l e n   l i e s s e, etc., " allow no one, from his own indis-
crete curiosity or devotional feeling to perform a pilgrimage, unless he
be first known, on the part of (v o n) his pastor, city or ruler, to have
(h a b e n  for  z u  h a b e n) a satisfactory and good reason."  On the
word  r e d l i c h  see p. 22, Note 5.  W a l l e n, is the same as  w a n -
d e r n, except that it has an elevated character, arising from the dig-
nity of the object of pursuit, or the serious nature of the termination
of the journey, or career.  It seems also to have borrowed a shade of
meaning from its application to the *rolling* waters of the ocean and
the *waving* fields of grain, especially when multitudes are represented as thronging to a place of special sanctity.  It is hardly necessary to add, that it relates to a journey made *on foot.*

[2]  U e b e l   g e r a t h e n, *turn out badly*, lead to evil consequences.
See p. 38, Note 3.  " For they see no good example at Rome, but
mere scandal, and as they (the pilgrims) have it in their own proverb, ' the nearer Rome, the poorer Christians ;' they bring back
with them contempt of God and of his word." — " But they have
become such adepts that they make all three journeys at once."

[3]  S t ü c k l e i n, diminutive of  S t ü c k, " such a fine thing" (viz.
as a  S c h a l k) or " such ware."  It is an expression of contempt.

eine vortrefflichere,[1] nemlich die, daß die einfältigen Men=
schen dadurch verführet werden in einem falschen Wahn und
Unverstand göttlicher Gebote. Denn sie meinem, daß sol=
ches Wallen sey ein köstlich[2] gutes Werk; das doch nicht
wahr ist. Es ist ein geringes gutes Werk, zu mehrmalen ein
böses verführerisches Werk; denn Gott hat es nicht gebo=
ten. Er hat aber geboten, daß ein Mann seines Weibes
und Kinder warte, und was[3] dem ehelichen Stand zuge=
bührt, dabei seinem Nächsten dienen und helfen. Nun ge=
schieht es, daß einer gen Rom wallet, verzehret fünfzig,
hundert, mehr oder weniger Gulden, das ihm Niemand be=

[1] Vortrefflichere, nemlich die. Vortrefflich, and
trefflich, like our word *precious*, are often used ironically, or in a
bad sense. Lessing says of Salmasius: "He brings together, respecting this passage, einen trefflichen Wirrwarr, *a precious jumble.*" " And although this evil (this thing) did not exist,
there is still another (noch ein, *yet one* or *one more*) of more moment, namely, that simple-hearted men are thereby led away to a
false notion and a perverse view of the divine commandments."

[2] Köstlich gutes Werk. Köstlich is capable of being
construed in three ways, in conjunction with the two following
words. It might be an adverb qualifying gutes, "a particularly
good work." But both the nature and the connection of the word
geringes, in the corresponding part of the antithesis, show that it
cannot be so used here. Again, it might be coördinate with gutes,
and like this agree with Werk alone, as "a precious (and) good
work." But then it ought properly to have the full form of declension (köstliches) and be separated from gutes by a comma,
though these rules are not always observed by German writers. See
höses verführisches Werk, below, where only one of the
rules is observed. Thirdly, it is here used as an adjective qualifying
gutes Werk taken together. The question here is, what kind of
good work it is, or rather what its rank is among good works. It is
not an *exalted* good work, but ein geringes gutes Werk,
an inferior good work, and often an evil, seductive work.

[3] Seines Weibes und Kinder warte, und [thue]
was, etc. "that a man take care of his wife and children, and do
whatever belongs to a husband, and also (dabei, *with that*) serve
and aid his neighbor."

fohlen hat, und läſſet ſein Weib und Kind, oder je ſeinen
Nächſten daheime Noth leiden ; und meinet doch, der thö=
richte Menſch,[1] er wolle ſolchen Ungehorſam und Verachtung
göttlicher Gebote mit ſeinem eigenwilligen Wallen ſchmücken,
ſo es doch ein lauterer Vorwitz oder Teufels Verführung iſt.

Da haben nun dazu geholfen die Päbſte mit ihren falſchen,
erdichteten, närriſchen goldenen Jahren, damit das Volk er=
regt,[2] von Gottes Geboten geriſſen, und zu ihrem eigenen
verführeriſchen Vornehmen gezogen, und eben daſſelbe an=
gerichtet, das ſie ſollten verboten haben.  Aber es hat Geld
getragen, und falſche Gewalt geſtärkt, darum hat's müſſen[3]
fortgehen, es ſey wider Gott oder der Seelen Heil.

Solchen falſchen verführeriſchen Glauben der einfältigen
Chriſten auszurotten,[4] und wiederum einen rechten Verſtand

---

[1] Der thörichte Mensch.  These words are rendered emphatic by coming after the verb.  " And yet he thinks, foolish man,
that he will garnish over such disobedience and contempt of God's
commands with his self-willed pilgrimage ; whereas it (the latter) is
nothing but foolish presumption, or a temptation of the devil."

[2] Damit das Volk erregte  "[and] thereby stirred up the
people, and drawn them away from the commands of God, and attached them to their own seductive scheme, and set up just what
they ought to have prohibited."  In respect to angerichtet, see
p. 50, Note 2, and p. 40, Note 1.

[3] Hat's müssen fortgehen.  See p. 67, Note 1.  " Therefore was it necessary that it should go on, though it be contrary to
God and to the interests of the soul."

[4] Solchen—Glauben—auszurotten would be a little
more perspicuous, if um were prefixed, thus ; Um solchen, etc.
"In order to root out this false, enticing faith of simple-hearted
Christians, and to implant in its stead a just perception of good
works, all pilgrimages should be put down ; for there is nothing good
in them ; [there is] no command, no obedience ; but innumerable
causes of sin and for contempt of God's command."  The construction at the close of the sentence is changed from the genitive
(der Sünden) to the dative with zu (zur Verachtung) to
avoid the concurrence of three genitives differently governed, all
coming after und (" and of the contempt of the command of God").

guter Werke aufzurichten, sollten alle Wallfahrten nieder=
gelegt werden; denn es ist kein Gutes nicht darinnen, kein
Gebot, kein Gehorsam, sondern unzähliche Ursachen der
Sünden, und Gottes Gebot zur Verachtung. Daher kom=
men so viel Bettler, die durch solches Wallen unzählige Bü=
bereien treiben, die betteln ohne Noth lernen[1] und gewohnen.

Da kömmt her[2] freies Leben und mehr Jammer, die ich
jetzt nicht zählen will. Wer nun wollte wallen oder wallen
geloben, sollte vorhin seinem Pfarrherrn oder Oberherrn die
Ursache anzeigen; fände sich's,[3] daß er's thäte um guten
Werks willen, daß dasselbe Gelübde und Werk durch den
Pfarrherrn oder Oberherrn nur frisch mit Füßen getreten

---

[1] Die betteln ohne Noth lernen. The construction,
though somewhat harsh, is demanded by the sense. Die ohne
Noth betteln lernen, which would be smoother and more
flowing, would mean, " who unnecessarily *learn* to beg;" whereas
the meaning of the author is, " who learn to *beg* unnecessarily." The
rule is simple, where the governing infinitive (lernen) follows the
one which it governs (betteln), or more briefly, when two connected infinitives close a sentence, no word should intervene. Betteln ohne Noth, therefore, is to be regarded as one word, and
therein consists the abruptness of the expression.

[2] Da kömmt her freies Leben, for daher kömmt,
etc. Freies Leben does not mean *a free living*, which would
be expressed by ein freier Tisch, freie Kost, but it is
equivalent to eine freie Betragung, *a licentious life or de-
portment*. The difference between jetzt and nun, is clearly
perceptible as they appear at the close of this sentence and at the
beginning of the next.

[3] Fände sich's, das er's thäte, etc. " if it is found that he
does it for the sake of a good work (i. e. as a meritorious work), then
[I advise] that this vow and work be trampled instantly under foot
by the pastor or ruler, as a Satanic emissary, and [that the same
individual] should teach him to apply (anzulegen) the money and
labor, which would be required for the pilgrimage, to what God has
commanded (God's command), and to a work a thousand times better,
that is, either to his own family, or to his poor neighbors." On the ex
pression den Seinen, compare p. 70, Note 8. Nächsten Ar-
men, literally means *nearest poor*, or *the poor nearest to one's doors*.

würde, als ein teuflisches Gespenst, und ihm anzeigete, das
Geld und die Arbeit, so zur Wallfahrt gehört, an Gottes
Gebot und tausendmal besser Werk anzulegen, d. i. : an den
Seinen oder seinen nächsten Armen. Wo er's aber aus Ver=
witz thäte, Land und Städte zu besehen, mag man ihm sei=
nen Willen lassen.[1]　Hat er's aber in der Krankheit gelo=
bet, daß man dieselben Gelübde verbiete,[2] verspreche, und
die Gottes Gebote dagegen empor hebe, daß er hinfort ihm
begnügen lasse an dem Gelübde in der Taufe geschehen,
Gottes Gebot zu halten.　Doch mag man[3] ihn auf das
mal, sein Gewissen zu stillen, sein närrisch Gelübde lassen
ausrichten.　Niemand will die richtige gemeine Straße gött=
licher Gebote wandeln ;[4] jedermann macht ihm selbst neue

---

[1] Ihm seinen Willen lassen, "leave his will to him ;"
whereas, in English, we say, " leave him to his will."　Luther did
not wish to abridge the personal freedom of the people, but to deliver
them from superstition.

[2] Dass man dieselben Gelübde verbiete, etc.　Here,
as in so many other places, there is an ellipsis before dass. " [I ad-
vise] that one forbid and prohibit these vows, and bring up the commands in opposition to them ; that he (the person who made the vow)
henceforth be satisfied with his baptismal vow to keep the command
of God."　Er cannot refer to man ; for this latter, not being a substantive, can never be referred to by a pronoun, but must always be
itself repeated.　Ihm begnügen lassen is explained p. 135,
Note 4.　Ihm is frequently used for sich.　See p. 151, Note 6.
Geschehen is a participle agreeing with Gelübde, although
such a construction would not now be used. " The vow which
took place, or was made in baptism."

[3] Doch mag man, etc. " Still one may, for this time, allow
him, in order to quiet his conscience, to perform his foolish vow."
Ausrichten, see p. 50, Note 2.

[4] Wandeln, as a neuter verb, generally takes a preposition after it to govern a substantive.　But it may take an accusative of a
similar signification.　So in English, " to walk the street," etc.
" No one will walk in the right, the common path of the divine commands ; every one makes to himself new ways and vows [beyond
the one required in baptism] as though he had fulfilled all God's
commands."

Wege und Gelübde, als hätte er Gottes Gebote alle voll=
bracht.

Darnach kommen wir auf den großen Haufen,[1] die da viel
geloben und doch wenig halten. Zürnet nicht, lieben Her=
ren, ich meine es wahrlich gut, es ist die bittere und süße
Wahrheit,[2] und ist, daß man ja nicht mehr Bettelklöster bau=
en lasse; hilf Gott, ihrer sind schon zu viel; ja wollte
Gott, sie wären, alle ab, oder je auf zwei oder drei Orte
gehäufet! Es hat nichts Gutes gethan, es thut auch nim=
mermehr gut, irre laufen auf dem Lande. Darum ist mein
Rath, man schlage zehn, oder wie viel ihrer[3] Noth ist, auf

---

[1] Den. grossen Haufen. The reader must not infer from
the plural pronoun (die), that Haufen is in the plural. Den
Haufen might, indeed, be the dative plural; but auf after a
verb of *motion*, requires the accusative, and therefore den Haufen must be in the accusative singular, and as it is a noun of multitude, the relative die can be used in the plural. " Next we come
to the great multitude, who," etc.

[2] Es ist die bittere und süsse Wahrheit, equivalent
in sense to, "unwelcome, but wholesome truth." The words bitter und süss, or more frequently, bittersüss, is used to describe a thing which is pleasant in one respect and unpleasant in another. In other instances, opposite qualities are, in a similar way,
attributed to the same thing. Wahrlich, before gut, does not
qualify that, but the verb. " Truly good," would not be expressed
by these two words, but by wirklich gut. "My intention is
certainly good; it is unwelcome, but wholesome truth [that I am
about to communicate; and] it is this, that no more convents of mendicant friars be built. God deliver us; there are already by far too
many of them (ihr Gen. for ihrer). Would to God, that they
were all abolished, or collected together in two or three places. Wandering about the country, has never done any good, and never will."
[Irre laufen, etc. is the nominative.] Ab might possibly be
used here for abgethan; but more probably it is used without
any ellipsis, in the sense of *away, out of the way*.

[3] Ihrer is in the genitive, and governed by viel, as it is by zu
viel a few lines above. " Put ten, or as many of them as is necessary, into one great one (lump), and of them make one, which, being

einen Haufen, und mache Eines daraus, das genugsam ver=
sorget, nicht betteln dürfe. O es ist hier vielmehr anzuse=
hen, was gemeinem Haufen zur Seligkeit noth ist,[1] denn
was St. Franciscus, Dominicus, Augustin oder je ein
Mensch gesetzt hat,[2] besonders weil es nicht gerathen ist
ihrer Meinung nach. Und daß man sie überhebe[3] Predi=
gens und Beichtens, es wäre denn, daß[4] sie von Bischöfen,

---

·sufficiently provided for, will not need to beg." Versorget is a
participle used adjectively.

[1] Was gemeinem Haufen zur Seligkeit noth ist.
Noth, *necessary*, is construed directly, not with a preposition, but
with the dative ; consequently it is here immediately connected, not
with zur ¡Seligkeit, but with Haufen. The sense is always given in English by making the noun in the dative, nominative, and by rendering noth est by *needs*. "What the common mass needs for its salvation, rather than (vielmehr denn)."
See p. 10, Note 3.

[2] Gesetzt hat, see p. 11, Note 5, and Gerathen ist, see p.
38, Note 3.

[3] Ueberhebe. When the accent is on the preposition, or first
part of the compound, this word, as an active verb, signifies *to raise
a thing and put it over something else*, e. g. to put a basket over, or
on the other side of a wall. But when the accent is on the verb, or
second part of the compound, the word means, *to raise one above a
thing* (in the genitive), *so as to deliver or release him from it;* and
that is the sense here. As a reflective verb (sich überheben)
it signifies, *to exalt one's self* in the sense of being *proud, insolent* or
*arrogant*, with the genitive of that of which one is proud. Sometimes it is used of too great physical effort, and means *to strain one's
self*, or injure one's self by lifting too hard. The following may serve
as examples of the two uses of the reflective verb. Dass ich
mich nicht der hohen Offenbarung überhebe, ist
mir gegeben ein Pfahl ins Fleisch, "that I might not be
elated for, or proud of, the high revelation, a thorn in the flesh was
given me." Es war mir zu schwer, ich habe mich
damit überhoben, "it was too heavy for me, I have strained
myself with it."

[4] Es wäre denn, dass, *except that, unless*. Dass near the
beginning of this sentence, depends on darum ist mein Rath
several lines above.

Pfarrern, Gemeine oder Obrigkeit dazu berufen und begehret würden. Ist doch[1] aus solchem Predigen und Beichten nichts mehr denn eitel Haß und Neid zwischen Pfaffen und Mönchen, großes Aergerniß und Hinderniß des gemeinen Volks erwachsen, damit es würdig würde, und wohl verdienet aufzuhören, dieweil sein mag[2] wohl gerathen werden. Es hat nicht ein ungleiches Ansehen,[3] daß der heilige römische Stuhl solches Heer nicht umsonst gemehret hat, auf daß nicht die Priesterschaft und Bisthum seiner Tyrannei unleidig, einmal ihm zu stark würden, und eine Reformation anfiengen, die nicht träglich seiner Heiligkeit wäre

Zum vierzehnten, wir sehen auch, wie die Priesterschaft gefallen, und mancher arme Pfaffe, mit Weib und Kindern überladen, sein Gewissen beschwert,[4] da doch Niemand zuthut, wo ihnen zu helfen wäre.[5] Läßt's Pabst und Bi-

---

[1] [Es] ist doch. See p. 17, Note 5, and p. 22, Note 4.

[2] Dieweil sein mag, etc. " because one can get along well without it." Gerathen is the participial form from rathen, which in old German is used, as it is here, in the sense of entbehren, *to do without*. It governs the genitive (sein for seiner, p. 46, Note 4). Mag gerathen werden, being impersonal and in the passive, cannot be translated literally into English. " It may well be deprived of it," would be the form of the expression, the first word being impersonal like *there may be*, and the last word (it) referring to the subject of discourse, viz. solchem predigen, etc.

[3] Es hat nicht ein ungleiches Ansehen. Ungleich here means corresponding to the person or character spoken of. " It is quite in character that," or " it has no unbecoming appearance that."

[4] Wie die Priesterschaft gefallen [ist], und [wie] mancher arme Pfaffe, mit Weib und Kindern überladen, (participle), sein Gewissen (accusative) beschwert, " how the priesthood is fallen, and how many a poor priest, burdened (morally) with wife and children, brings upon himself remorse of conscience (burdens his conscience)."

[5] Da doch Niemand zuthut wo ihnen zu helfen wäre, " whereas no one puts his hand to the work, where it is pos-

ſchöfe[1] hie gehen, was da gehet, verderben, was verdirbt, ſo
will ich erretten mein Gewiſſen und das Maul frei aufthun,[2]
es verdrieße[3] Pabſt, Biſchöfe oder wen es will, und ſage
alſo:

Daß nach Chriſti und der Apoſtel Einſetzen[4] eine jegliche
Stadt einen Pfarrherrn oder Biſchof ſoll haben, wie klärlich
Paulus ſchreibet Tit. 1.; und derſelbe Pfarrherr nicht gedrungen[5] ohne ein eheliches Weib zu leben, ſondern möge
eines haben, wie St. Paulus ſchreibt 1. Timoth. 3. und
ſpricht: „Es ſoll ein Biſchof ſeyn[6] ein Mann, der unſträ-

---

sible to aid them." Z u t h u n, as a verb, is, at present, but little
used in the sense of *to take a part in a work, to assist, to help.* But
it is still in good use as a verbal noun, or infinitive used substantively, *assistance, aid,* i. e. the act of assisting, or aiding. Compare d a-
z u t h u n, p. 94, Note 4. Z u h e l f e n after the verb s e i n, embraces the idea of *possibility.* See p. 12, Note 3.

[1] L ä s s t's (d e r) P a b s t u n d (d i e) B i s c h ö f e, etc. "If
the pope and bishops, in this matter (h i e for h i e r), let things (e s,
*it*) go as they now go (let *it* go *which* goes) and (let) that be ruined
which now goes to ruin (i. e. the priests and their households), *still I
will keep my conscience,* and speak freely, though it annoy pope, bishops, or whomsoever it may."

[2] A u f t h u n, differs from a u f m a c h e n, as t h u n does from
m a c h e n. See p. 20, Note 3, near the end. The former expresses
merely the *act* of opening without any regard to the circumstance
whether the thing *remains* open or not, while the latter has reference
chiefly to the *result,* i. e. that a thing not only be opened, but kept
open. A u f t h u n is especially appropriate where a thing is closed
very fast, and where great effort is requisite to open it. O e f n e n,
is the most general and indefinite word, and conveys neither of the
specific ideas which are conveyed by the other two words.

[3] V e r d r i e s s e. See p. 30, Note 3.

[4] E i n s e t z e n corresponds both in etymology and signification
with *institution,* i. e. the act of instituting. It is an infinitive used
substantively, and corresponding to our participial noun, *the instituti-
ing.* See p. 13, Note 6.

[5] G e d r u n g e n (w e r d e).

[6] E s s o l l e i n B i s c h o f s e i n, for E i n B i s c h o f s o l l s e y n.
See p. 52, Note 1.

flich[1] sey und nur eines ehelichen Weibs Gemahl, welches[2] Kinder gehorsam und züchtig sind" ꝛc.   Denn ein Bischof und Pfarrherr ist Ein Ding[3] bei St. Paulus, wie das auch St. Hieronymus[4] bewähret.   Aber von den Bischöfen, die jetzt sind, weiß die Schrift nichts, sondern sind von christ= licher gemeiner Ordnung gesetzt,[5] daß einer über viel Pfarr= herren regiere.

Da sind nun hernachmals,[6] da so viel Verfolgung und Streites war wider die Ketzer, viel heiliger Väter gewesen, die sich freiwillig des ehelichen Standes verziehen haben,[7] auf daß sie desto besser studirten,[8] und bereit wären auf alle

---

[1] Unsträflich.   For the signification of its primitive, see p. 130, Note 4.

[2] Welches, *whose*, obsolete.   See p. 52, Note 1.

[3] Ein Bischof und Pfarrherr ist Ein Ding.  Pfarr- herr, is used in the sense of presbyter or elder.   When the word ein, as an adjective, is emphatic, it is written with a capital letter, which is equivalent to writing the word in Italics in English; as Ein, *one*.

[4] Hieronymus.   The words of Jerome are : *Idem est ergo pres- byter qui episcopus.*  Com. on Tit. 1.

[5] Sondern sind von christlicher gemeiner Ord- nung gesetzt, "but they are created (established) by mere (ge- meiner, *common*) ecclesiastical authority (arrangement)."

[6] Hernachmals, obsolete for hernach, which means *imme- diately after*, whereas nachmals means *afterwards*, without the idea of immediate succession.   Luther uses the word hernach- mals here in a general sense, when nachmals might be used. " Now, afterwards, when there was so much (of) persecution, and controversy with the heretics [in which the vanquished party were often banished], there were many holy fathers," etc.

[7] Verziehen haben.  Sich verzeihen, with the genitive, which is now nearly obsolete, means *to surrender something valuable*, and thereby differs from entsagen, *to renounce* anything whether it be good or evil.  Sich verzeihen, like verzichten (auf), means also, to make a *formal* surrender of anything, and thereby differs from sich begeben, *to give a thing up* in fact, without saying anything about it.

[8] Studirten, subjunctive, *might study.*

Stunden zum Tode und zum Streit. Da ist nun der römische Stuhl aus eigenem Frevel drein gefallen,[1] und ein gemein Gebot daraus gemacht, verboten dem Priesterstand ehelich zu seyn; das hat ihnen der Teufel geheißen,[2] wie St. Paulus 1. Tim. 4. verkündigt: „Es werden kommen Lehrer, die Teufels-Lehre bringen, und verbieten, ehelich zu werden" ꝛc. Dadurch leider so viel Jammers entstanden,[3] daß nicht zu erzählen ist, und hat dadurch Ursach gegen[4] der griechischen Kirche, sich abzusondern, und unendliche Zwietracht, Sünde, Schande und Aergerniß gemehrt: wie denn thut alles, was der Teufel anfähet und treibet. Was wollen wir nun hie thun?

Ich rathe, man mach's[5] wieder frei und lasse einem Jeglichen seine freie Willführ, ehelich oder nicht ehelich zu werden. Aber da muß gar viel ein ander Regiment[6] und Ord-

---

[1] Drein gefallen, *has intermeddled*, or *fallen in upon recklessly*. Drein, or darein, properly differs from darin, as *thereinto* differs from *therein*. It implies *motion into*. Hence with many verbs, it conveys the idea of *interruption, disturbance, intermeddling without regard to consequences;* as, darein reden, *to interrupt*, drein schlagen, *to strike on, hit where it may*.

[2] Das hat ihnen der Teufel geheissen, "Satan commanded them that, instigated them to that." Heissen, see p. 32, Note 5.

[3] Entstanden (ist). "Thereby, alas! has so much (of) trouble arisen, that it cannot be told." Zu erzählen ist, see p. 12, Note 3.

[4] Geben for gegeben, "and has thereby given to the Greek church cause to separate and occasioned (multiplied) infinite dissension, sin, scandal and offence, as does everything which Satan begins and prosecutes." Anfähen, obsolete for anfangen.

[5] Mach's, present subjunctive for mache es. See p. 5, Note 4.

[6] Aber da muss gar viel ein ander Regiment, etc. "But then there must be (take place) a very widely different control and disposal of the property, and the entire canonical law must sink, and not many fiefs go to Rome. I fear that avarice has been a cause of the miserable unchaste chastity; whence it has come

nung der Güter geschehen, und das ganze geistliche Recht zu
Boden gehen und nicht viel Lehen gen Rom kommen. Ich
besorge, der Geiz sey eine Ursache gewesen der elenden, un=
keuschen Keuschheit; daraus denn gefolget, daß Jedermann
habe wollen Pfaff werden und sein Kind darauf studiren
lassen: nicht der Meinung, keusch zu leben, das wohl ohne
Pfaffenstand geschehen könnte; sondern sich mit zeitlicher
Nahrung ohne Arbeit und Mühe zu ernähren wider das
Gebot Gottes, Gen. 3. „Du sollst dein Brod essen im
Schweiß deines Angesichts," haben ihm[1] eine Farbe ange=
strichen, als sollte ihr Arbeiten seyn Beten und Messe halten.

Ich lasse hier anstehen Pabst, Bischöfe, Stifte, Pfaffen
und Mönche, die Gott nicht eingesetzt hat. Haben sie ihnen
selbst Bürden aufgelegt, so tragen sie sie auch. Ich will
reden von dem Pfarrstand, den Gott eingesetzt hat, der eine
Gemeinde mit Predigen und Sacramenten regieren muß,
bei ihnen wohnen und zeitlich haushalten; denselben sollte
durch ein christliches Concilium nachgelassen[2] werden Frei=
heit, ehelich zu werden, zu vermeiden Gefährlichkeit und'

---

(g e f o l g e t [i s t], *has followed*) that every body would become
priest, and every body would put his son to study for it (the priesthood), not with (of) the purpose of living chastely (which might
take place without entering the priesthood)," etc.

[1] H a b e n  i h m, etc , " they have given it (i h m, i. e. d a s  G e-
b o t a gloss (color) as if their labor were to be praying and holding
mass. I leave to themselves (I here let remain, or stand) bishops,
convents, priests and monks, which God did not institute. If they
have imposed upon themselves burdens, let them bear them. I will
speak only of the ministry which God ordained, which is to guide a
church with preaching and ordinances, live with them (the church),
and maintain a household relation (i. e. live otherwise than in a con-
vent)."

[2] N a c h g e l a s s e n, *yielded back, restored, conceded.* Liberty in
this respect had been taken from the ministry by the papacy; it
should now be formally conceded or restored by a council. Z u  w e r-
d e n is dependent on F r e i h e i t. Z u  v e r m e i d e n, is equiva-
to u m  z u  v e r m e i d e n, *in order to avoid.*

Sünde. Denn dieweil sie Gott selbst nicht verbunden hat, so soll und mag sie Niemand verbinden, ob es gleich ein Engel von Himmel wäre, schweige denn[1] Pabst; und was dagegen im geistlichen Recht gesetzt, sind lauter Fabeln und Geschwätze.

Zum sechszehnten, es wäre auch Noth,[2] daß die Jahrtage, Begängnisse, Seelenmessen gar abgethan, oder je gar geringert würden; darum, daß[3] wir öffentlich sehen vor Augen, daß nicht mehr denn ein Spott daraus geworden ist, damit Gott höchlich erzürnet wird, und nur auf Geld, Fressen und Saufen gerichtet sind. Was sollte Gott für einem Gefallen darin haben, wenn die elenden Vigilien und Messen so jämmerlich geschlappert werden, noch gelesen, noch gebetet; und

---

[1] S c h w e i g e  d e n n, *not to say.* S c h w e i g e for g e s c h w e i - ge. G o t t, and N i e m a n d are in the nominative.

[2] E s  w ä r e  a u c h  n o t h, etc. " It would also be needful, that the holy-days, processions, and mass for the dead, be abolished, or at least, (their number) greatly diminished." Instead of J a h r t a g, the word J a h r s t a g is now used. It means any yearly festival, as Christmas, New-years, saints' days, etc. B e g ä n g n i s s, is now limited to *funeral* processions; it was formerly used of processions in general.

[3] D a r u m  d a s s, etc. " Because we openly see (right before our eyes) that only (n i c h t  m e h r  d e n n) contempt comes from it (it is all turned into ridicule) with which God is highly displeased, and that (they) are appropriated only for gain, feasting and drinking. What kind of pleasure can God have in it, when vigils and mass, are neither read nor prayed, but slabbered out; and even though offered in prayers, they are not performed on God's account, out of love to him, but for the sake of money, and on account of obligations entered into? V o r  A u g e n is tautological after ö f f e n t l i c h. G e r i c h t e t  a u f, *directed to.* F r e s s e n differs widely from e s s e n. See p. 51, Note 1. So does s a u f e n differ in the same way from t r i n k e n. S c h l a p p e r n, and the more common word s c h l a p p e n (*to lap,* as a dog), of a kindred meaning, are also written s c h l a b b e r n, and s c h l a b b e n, in the former of which (s c h l a b b e r n) we see the original of the English word *slabber,* with which it agrees precisely in signification.

ob fie fchon gebetet würden, doch nicht um Gottes willen aus freier Liebe, fondern um des Geldes willen und verpflichte= ter Schuld vollbracht werden.

Nun ift es doch nicht möglich, daß Gott[1] ein Werk gefalle, oder etwas bei ihm erlange, das nicht in freier Liebe ge= fchieht. So ift es je chriftlich, daß wir Alles abthun, oder je weniger machen, was[2] wir fehen in einen Mißbrauch kom= men, und Gott mehr erzürnt denn verföhnt. Es wäre mir lieber, ja Gott angenehmer und viel beffer, daß ein Stift, Kirche oder Klofter alle ihre jährlichen Meffen[3] und Vigilien auf einen Haufen nähmen, und hielten einen Tag, eine rechte Vigilien und Meffe mit herzlichem Ernft, Andacht und Glauben für alle ihre Wohlthäter, denn daß fie ihr taufend und taufend alle Jahre einem Jeden eine befondere hielten, ohne folche Andacht und Glauben. O lieben Chriften, es liegt Gott nicht an viel, fondern an wohl heten,[4] ja er verdammt

---

[1] G o t t  is in the dative.

[2] A l l e s — w a s, " abolish, or at least diminish everything which we see come to abuse, and (which) offends God," etc.

[3] A l l e  i h r e  j ä h r l i c h e  M e s s e n, etc. " put all their an-nual masses together (into one heap), and should hold, during one day, a genuine vigil and mass, etc.—than that they should every year hold their thousands upon thousands (of masses and vigils), a sepa-rate one for each benefactor."  E i n e n  T a g, *during one day;* e i n e s  T a g s, *on a certain day.*  E i n e  r e c h t e  V i g i l i e n. V i g i l i e n, is not here plural, but singular.  The Thuringians still say e i n e  f a m i l i e n, e i n e  S c h u l e n, e i n e  M ü h l e n, e i n e  K i r c h e n, *a family, a school, a mill, a church.* The addi-tion of the letter *n* is peculiar, and now provincial.

[4] E s  l i e g t  G o t t  n i c h t  a n  v i e l, s o n d e r n  a n  w o h l b e t e n, " God attaches importance not to praying *much*, but to pray-ing *well*.  L i e g t  is here an impersonal verb; G o t t  is the dative of the person, which is the logical subject, and v i e l  b e t e n, as a substantive, is the dative of the thing, governed by the preposition a n.  The compound verb a n l i e g e n, in which the preposition is separable, has a similar signification and construction; but the differ-ence in construction is this, that with the former (l i e g e n) a sec-ond dative follows the preposition a n  and is governed by it; in the

15

die langen und vielen Gebete, Matth. 6. und sagt, sie werden
nur mehr Pein damit verdienen.   Aber der Geiz, der Gott
nicht kann trauen, richtet solch Wesen an,[1] hat Sorge, er
müsse Hungers sterben.

Zum siebenzehnten, man müßte auch abthun etliche Pöne
oder Strafen des geistlichen Rechts, sonderlich das Inter=
dikt,[2] welches ohne allen Zweifel der böse Geist erdacht hat.

---

latter (a n l i e g e n), this is not the case.   L i e g e n, in its literal
sense, followed by  a n, is very simple, as  C ö l n  l i e g t  a m
R h e i n,  "Cologne lies on the Rhine."   A n, after this verb, very
often indicates a *cause* of something ;  a s,  e r  l i e g t  a n  e i n e m
F i e b e r,  "he lies sick of a fever," i. e. the fever is the cause of his
lying sick.   D i e  Z ö g e r u n g  l i e g t  a n  i h m,  "the delay
lies in him," i. e. he is the cause of the delay.   E s  l i e g t  d a r a n,
d a s s,  "this is the reason that" (the reason lies in this).   E s  l i e g t
v i e l  (or  w e n i g,  or  n i c h t s)  d a r a n,  "it is of great (or *little*,
or *no*) consequence, or importance ;"  and  e s  l i e g t  i h m  v i e l
a n  d i e s e r  S a c h e  (which is the construction to be illustrated),
"this thing is very important to him," or "he attaches great importance to this thing."   I s t  g e l e g e n  is much used in the same
way as  l i e g t.   See the lexicons on  g e l e g e n.   A n l i e g e n
is construed thus : " D i e  S a c h e  l i e g t  m i r  a n,  "the thing
affects my heart, or is important to me."   See p. 70, Note 2.

[1]  R i c h t e t  s o l c h  W e s e n  a n, etc.   "makes such work
(produces such disorder) and fears, it will starve "   A n r i c h t e n,
see p. 40, Note 1, and p. 50, Note 2.   S o l c h, p. 18, Note 8.   W e -
s e n, p. 72, Note 2.   H u n g e r s  s t e r b e n, p. 68, Note 3.

[2]  S o n d e r l i c h  d a s  I n t e r d i k t,  "especially the interdict."
" The interdict is the  ban of excommunication extended to whole
kingdoms or provinces.   If it be pronounced against a country and
its inhabitants, no church bell is to be rung, no religious service held,
no child baptized, no penitent to receive absolution, no person to receive  Christian burial, — in short, the curse of God, as it were, was
made to rest upon them."   Neudecker, Lexikon der Kirchenge-
schichte, 1. 198.   Hence the indignant language of Luther, " Is that
not a Satanic work, to correct one sin by means of many and greater
sins ?   It is a greater sin to close and  lay  down (neglect) the  word
of God and his service, than to murder twenty popes, at once, not to
say than to detain a  priest, or ecclesiastical property."   S c h w e i-

Iſt das nicht ein teufliſches Werk, daß man eine Sünde beſ=
ſern will mit vielen und größeren Sünden? Es iſt ja grö=
ßere Sünde, daß man Gottes Wort und Dienſt ſchweiget
oder niederlegt, denn ob einer zwanzig Päbſte hätte erwür=
get auf einmal, geſchweige denn einen Prieſter, oder geiſtlich
Gut behalten. Es iſt der zarten Tugenden eine,[1] die im
geiſtlichen Rechte gelernet werden ; denn das geiſtliche
Recht heißt auch darum geiſtlich, daß es kommt von dem
Geiſt, nicht von dem heiligen Geiſt, ſondern von dem böſen
Geiſt.

Den Bann[2] müßte man nicht eher brauchen, denn wo die
Schrift weiſet zu brauchen, d. i. : wider die, ſo nicht recht
glauben, oder in öffentlichen Sunden leben, nicht um das
zeitliche Gut. Aber nun iſt es umgekehrt,[3] glaubt, lebt Je=

---

g e n as an active verb, is now an archaism, v e r s c h w e i g e n
having taken its place in that sense. S c h w e i g e is frequently
used by Luther in the sense of g e s c h w e i g e, *not to say*. N i e -
d e r l e g e n, is here used in its literal sense, *to lay or put down.* It
is more commonly used figuratively, *to resign.* E i n e n P r i e s t‗
e r, o d e r g e i s t l i c h G u t b e h a l t e n, refers to foreign
princes, such as the kings of France and England, who often seized
prelates, and ecclesiastical property in order to maintain their sovereignty in their own dominions.

[1] E s i s t d e r z a r t e n T u g e n d e n e i n e, " It (putting
under the interdict) is one of the amiable virtues, which are learned
in the canonical law ; for it is called spiritual law because (d a r u m,
d a s s) it comes from the spirit, not from the Holy Spirit, but from
the evil spirit." For the construction of the genitive T u g e n -
d e n with e i n e, see p. 96, Note 2.

[2] D e n B a n n. Luther here condemns what is called the *greater ban,* or civil proscription, and pleads for a return to the primitive
practice of excommunication from an individual church by the proper authorities, or the *lesser ban.*

[3] A b e r n u n i s t e s u m g e k e h r t, etc. " But now the rule
is reversed. Every man believes and lives as he chooses. Precisely
these fleece and disgrace other people most with their bans ; and all
bans are now resorted to only for the sake of spoil (temporal goods),
for which we have to thank no one but the holy code of *in*justice (ca-

dermann, wie er will; eben die am meisten die andern Leute
schinden und schänden mit Bannen, und alle Banne jetzt
nur um's zeitliche Gut ganghaftig sind, welches wir auch
Niemand denn dem heiligen geistlichen Unrecht zu danken
haben, davon ich vorhin im Sermon weiter gesagt habe.

Die andern Strafen[1] und Pönen, Suspension, Irregu-
larität,[2] Aggravation,[3] Reaggravation, Desposition, Blitzen,
Donnern, Vermaledeien, Verdammen, und was der Fünd-
lein mehr sind,[4] sollte man zehn Ellen tief begraben in der
Erde, daß auch ihr Name und Gedächtniß nicht mehr auf
Erden wäre. Der böse Geist,[5] der durch das geistliche Recht

---

nonical law), of which I have spoken more at large in my Sermon
(on the subject)." E b e n  d i e is very emphatic, and must be so
read. A m  m e i s t e n, *the most*. This form of the superlative is
strictly relative, or makes a definite comparison. The other form,
m e i s t e n s, is absolute and indefinite, *mostly, for the most part*.
The same rule obtains with all the superlatives of these two forms.
The other forms of the superlative, as m e i s t and a u f s  b e s t e,
z u m  s c h ö n s t e n, i m  g e r i n g s t e n, belong to the absolute
and indefinite class. In other words, while the superlative of adverbs
formed with a m  is definitely and strictly a degree of comparison,
those ending in s t and e n s, or formed with a u f s, z u m and i m,
are not so, but merely express a high degree of anything. — G a n g-
h a f t i g is now out of use and g a n g b a r has taken its place.
D a n k e n is generally a neuter verb, but is sometimes active in the
sense of v e r d a n k e n, and then takes an accusative.

[1] D i e  a n d e r n  S t r a f e n, etc. "The other punishments
and penalties (viz.), suspension," etc.

[2] I r r e g u l a r i t ä t. What sort of penalty is this? Is it de-
priving persons of the privileges which belong to them as *regulares*,
or members of a certain monastic order?

[3] A g g r a v a t i o n. *Aggravatio* est repetita et iterata excommu-
nicatio — Du Cange, Glossarium. R e a g g r a v a t i o n is a still
further repetition.

[4] U n d  w a s  d e r  F ü n d l e i n  m e h r  s i n d, "and whatever more (of) inventions there are." M e h r governs the genitive,
d e r  F ü n d l e i n. See p. 13, Note 3.

[5] D e r  b ö s e  G e i s t, etc. "The evil spirit who is let loose by

ift loß geworden, hat folche greuliche Plage und Jammer in das himmlifche Reich der heiligen Chriftenheit gebracht, und nicht mehr denn Seelen-Verderben und Hindern dadurch zugerichtet daß wohl mag von ihnen verftanden werden das Wort Chrifti Matth. 23: „Wehe euch Schriftgelehrten, ihr" habt euch¹ genommen die Gewalt zu lehren, und „fchließet zu das Himmelreich vor den Menfchen; ihr gehet nicht hinein, und wehret denen, die hinein gehen."

Zum achtzehnten, daß man alle Fefte abthäte, und allein den Sonntag behielte. Wollte man aber je unferer Frau-en² und der großen Heiligen Feft halten, daß fie alle auf

---

the canonical law, has introduced such horrible evil and wretched-ness into the heavenly kingdom of our sacred Christianity, and thereby effected nothing but the hindrance and ruin of souls," etc. H i n d e r n belongs to S e e l e n, in the same way that V e r d e r-b e n does. Though used substantively, they, in the character of verbs, govern the accusative, S e e l e n. On z u r i c h t e n, see p. 50, Note 2, near the end.

¹ E u c h  must not here be taken for the ordinary dative after the verb n e h m e n, (indicating the person *from* whom a thing is taken p. 52, Note 4.), but as a kind of expletive indicating, as usual in such cases, the interest of the agent in what he is said to do.  See Gram. p. 348.

² W o l l t e  m a n  a b e r  j e  u n s e r e r  F r a u e n, etc. " But if men would hold the festival of the Virgin (of our Lady) or of the distinguished saints, (I advise) that they all be transferred (from week-days) to the Sabbath, or that service be held only in the morn-ings, leaving the remainder of the day for business. (The following are the) reasons ;—for, since an abuse is now practised in drinking, amusements, idleness and all sorts of sin, we offend God more on these holy days than on others.  And now they are entirely revers-ed,—the holy days (so called) are not holy, and working-days are holy ; and with these numerous festival days, not only is no service either done to God or to his saints, but great dishonor.  And yet certain senseless prelates think, that if they institute a festival to St. Otilia and St. Barbara, each one (doing so) according to his own blind devotion, they do a very good work ; whereas they would have done much better if they, out of honor to a saint, had turned a festival day

den Sonntag würden verlegt, oder nur des Morgens zur Meſſe gehalten, darnach ließ den ganzen Tag Werktag ſeyn. Urſache: Denn als nun der Mißbrauch mit Saufen, Spielen, Müßiggang und allerlei Sünde gehet, ſo erzürnen wir mehr Gott auf die heiligen Tage, denn auf die andern. Und ſind ganz umgekehrt, daß heilige Tage nicht heilig, Werktage heilig ſind, und Gott, noch ſeinen Heiligen, nicht allein kein Dienſt, ſondern große Unehre geſchieht mit den vielen heiligen Tagen. Wiewohl etliche tolle Prälaten meinen, wenn ſie St. Otilien, St. Barbaren, und ein Jeglicher nach ſeiner blinden Andacht ein Feſt machet, habe gar ein gutes Werk gethan, wo er ein viel Beſſeres thäte, wo er zu Ehren einem Heiligen, aus einem heiligen Tag einen Werktag gemacht.

Dazu nimmt der gemeine Mann[1] zwei leibliche Schaden, über dieſen geiſtlichen Schaden, daß er an ſeiner Arbeit verſäumet wird, dazu mehr verzehret denn ſonſt; ja auch ſeinen Leib ſchwächt und ungeſchickt macht, wie wir das täglich ſehen, und doch Niemand zu beſſern gedenkt. Und hier ſollte man nicht achten, ob der Pabſt die Feſte eingeſetzt hat, oder eine Diſpenſation[2] und Urlaub haben müßte. Was wider Gott iſt,[3] und den Menſchen ſchädlich an Leib und

---

into a working-day."    Frauen. Genitive singular.    Feminine nouns were formerly declined in the singular·

[1] Dazu nimimt der gemeine Mann, etc. "Furthermore, the common people sustain, besides this spiritual injury, two temporal losses, (the one) that they are interrupted in their labor, the other (or in addition to that) they expend more than they would otherwise." Versaūmen means properly *to suffer a thing to pass away through delay*, or negligence, to neglect. In the passive, it means, *to be neglected*, when used of a *thing*, and *to be put behindhand*, or in arrears, *to be hindered*, when used of a *person*.

[2] Oder [man] eine Dispensation, "whether the pope has instituted the festival, or whether one must obtain special permission to hold it."

[3] Was wider Gott ist, etc. "What is opposed to God

Seele, hat nicht allein eine jede Gemeine, Rath oder Obrig=
keit Gewalt abzuthun und zu wehren, ohne Wissen und Wil=
len des Pahsts oder Bischofs ; ja ist auch schuldig bei seiner
Seele Seligkeit, dasselbe zu wehren, ob es gleich Pabst und
Bischöfe nicht wollten, die doch die Ersten sollten seyn,
solches zu wehren.

Zum neunzehnten, daß die Grade oder Glieder[1] würden
geändert, in welchen der eheliche Stand wird verboten, als
da sind Gevatterschaften, der vierte und dritte Grad,[2] daß
wo der Pabst zu Rom darin mag dispensiren um's Geld,
und Schändlichen verkauft,[3] daß auch selbst ein jeder Pfarr=

---

and injurious to man both in soul and body, every parish, common
council or magistrate, has not only the power to abrogate and prevent, without the knowledge or will of the pope and the bishops, but
is bound, upon (peril of) its salvation, to prevent it, notwithstanding
the pope and bishops do not wish it, who ought, however, to be the
first to prevent it."

[1] D i e  G r a d e  o d e r  G l e i d e r, in the canonical law, where
the degrees of relationship within which marriages are lawful, are
definitely pointed out.

[2] D e r  v i e r t e  u n d  d r i t t e  G r a d.  V i e r t e  comes before  d r i t t e, because one would naturally begin with the most remote degree in abrogating the prohibitions.

[3] S c h ä n d l i c h e n  v e r k a u f t, "sells (the privilege of unlawful practices) to scandalous persons."  So this singular expression
must be translated, if there is no error in the text.  But it is almost
beyond a doubt, that by an error of the press, through the addition of
the single letter *t*, the word  v e r k a u f t  was made out of  V e r-
k a u f.  Substitute this word, and everything is simple and easy.
"That where the pope at Rome may in this matter dispense for
money and for scandalous merchandise, that there also every pastor
may dispense for nothing, and for the good of souls."  Thus  u m 's
G e l d, in the first clause, corresponds to  u m — s o n s t  in the
second ; and [u m]  s c h ä n d l i c h e n  V e r k a u f, in the first,
to [u m]  d e r  S e e l e n  S e l i g k e i t, in the second.  Besides,
this is supported by the use of the parallel expression,  d u r c h  s e i-
n e n  s c h ä n d l i c h e n  J a h r m a r k t  z u  v e r k a u f e n, at
the end of the paragraph, where  J a h r m a r k t  is used in the sense

herr möge dispensiren, umsonst und der Seelen Seligkeit. Ja wollte Gott, daß Alles, was man zu Rom muß kaufen, und den Geldstrick das geistliche Gesetz lösen,[1] daß ein jeder Pfarrherr dasselbe ohne Geld möchte thun und lassen; als da sind Ablaß, Ablaßbriefe,[2] Butterbriefe,[3] Meßbriefe,[4] und was Confessionalia[5] oder Bübereien mehr sind zu Rom, da das arme Volk mit wird betrogen und um's Geld gebracht;[6] denn so der Pabst Macht hat seinen Geldstrick und geistliches Netz[7]

of Verkauf. On a subsequent page occurs the expression: Umsonst und [um] Gottes willen.

[1] Und den Geldstrick das geistliche Gesetz lösen, "and loosen that money-shackle, the canonical law," for "obtain by loosening," etc. Luther often calls the canonical law a Geldstrick, a money-fetter.

[2] Ablassbriefe, certificates of indulgence.

[3] Butterbriefe, signified, in the fifteenth century, written documents from the pope, in which permission was granted to eat butter during the church fasts.

[4] Messbriefe is defined, in the lexicons, "bills of exchange available during a public mass or fair." But here it must mean "permission to hold mass," which was abused by the priests for avaricious purposes.

[5] Confessionalia, "writings which contain directions in regard to religious service." On the grammatical construction, see p. 106, Note 5.

[6] Um's Geld gebracht, "ruined in the purse." See umbringen, p. 57, Note 3. Um's Leben bringen means "to take away one's life." So Um's Geld bringen would mean "to take away one's money;" that is, "to deprive one of his money;" and passive, "to be deprived of one's money." This word always implies that the privation or loss is undeserved.

[7] Geistliches Netz. Observe the alliteration, and hence the play upon the word in the last syllable of Gesetz, like, "spiritual cords (re-cords I should say)." "For if the pope has power to sell his money-shackles and spiritual net (or law, I should say) for money (i. e. to dispense one from the obligation to keep it), certainly a preacher has more power to tear it in pieces, and, for the honor of God, trample it under foot." For if there were a moral obligation to do what the canonical law prescribes, no dispensation from that obligation could be given for money. "If he has not power

(Gesetz sollte ich sagen) zu verkaufen um's Geld, hat ge=
wißlich ein Pfarrherr vielmehr Gewalt dieselben zu reißen,
und um Gottes willen mit Füßen zu treten. Hat er aber
das nicht Gewalt, so hat auch der Pabst keine Gewalt, die=
selben durch seinen schändlichen Jahrmarkt zu verkaufen.

Dahin gehöret[1] auch, daß die Fasten würden frei gelassen
einem Jedermann, und allerlei Speise frei gemacht, wie das
Evangelium giebet. Denn sie selbst zu Rom der Fasten
spotten,[2] lassen[3] uns draußen Oele fressen, da sie nicht ihre
Schuhe mit ließen schmieren ; verkaufen uns darnach Frei=
heit, Butter und allerlei zu essen ; so der heilige Apostel sa=
get, daß wir deß Alles[4] zuvor Freiheit haben aus dem
Evangelio. Aber sie haben mit ihrem geistlichen Recht uns
gefangen und gestohlen,[5] auf daß wir es mit Geld wieder
kaufen müssen ; haben damit so blöde[6] schüchterne Gewissen
gemacht, daß nicht gut mehr von derselben Freiheit zu pre=
digen ist, darum, daß sich das gemeine Volk so fast darinnen
ärgert, und achtet für größere Sünde Butter essen, denn
lügen, schwören, oder auch Unkeuschheit treiben. Es ist doch
Menschenwerk,[7] was Menschen gesetzt haben, man lege es

---

(for) that, then the pope has no power to sell the same in his scandalous trade (at his scandalous market)."

[1] G e h ö r e t, agrees with the following clause as its nominative.

[2] D e r  F a s t e n  s p o t t e n, "they ridicule the fasts." In familiar German, the preposition ü b e r, with its case, is more common than the genitive after this verb.

[3] L a s s e n, etc. " they (merely) allow us to eat oil, with which
(d a — m i t) they would not grease their shoes, and afterwards *sell* to
us permission to eat butter and all sorts of things, though (or while,
s o), etc."

[4] D e s s  a l l e s, " of all that," governed by F r e i h e i t.

[5] G e f a n g e n  u n d  g e s t o h l e n, "caught and stolen," probably refers to making captives for the money with which their friends
would redeem them.

[6] H a b e n  d a m i t  s o  b l ö d e, etc. "and they have thereby made
(among the people) such weak and timid consciences, that it is no
longer easy (g u t) to preach respecting that liberty."

[7] E s  i s t  d o c h  M e n s c h e n w e r k e, etc. "Still it is the

wo man hin will, und entsteht nimmer etwas Gutes daraus.

Zum zwanzigsten, daß die wilden Kapellen und Feldkirchen[1] würden zu Boden verstöret; als da sind,[2] da die neuen Wallfahrten hingehen, Welßnacht, Sternberg, Trier, das Grimthal, und jetzt Regensburg, und der Anzahl viel mehr. O wie schwere elende Rechenschaft werden die Bischöfe müssen geben,[3] die solches Teufels-Gespenst[4] zulassen, und Genuß davon empfangen?[5] Sie sollten die Ersten seyn dasselbe zu wehren; so meinen sie[6] es sey göttlich heilig Ding,

---

work of man;—(it is) what man has ordained, do what you will with it, and nothing good ever comes from it."

[1] Die wilden Kapellen und Feldkirchen. "The chapels in the forests and in the open fields," places of superstitious resort.

[2] Als da sind, "such as those, where (da for wo) the new pilgrimages are made (whither they go, da — hingehen), namely, Welsnacht, Sternberg, Triers, Grimthal, and at present Ratisbon and many more (and of that multitude many more)." So Triers had its pretended relics long before the time of Ronge, and is now only sustaining its old character! Grimthal, or Grimmenthal, a little south-east of Meiningen, and not very remote from Erfort, where Luther had resided, was one of the most celebrated places of resort for the superstitious. Anzahl always refers to an actual collection or assemblage of persons or things, and thus differs from Zahl, number.

[3] Werden müssen geben. "Will be obliged to give." See p. 148, Note 3.

[4] Teufels-Gespenst. Gespenst, *ghost*, is figuratively employed for *any imaginary object of fear*. Here it refers to the pretended relics or miracles of these places.

[5] Und Genuss davon empfangen. "And make money out of it." The figurative signification of Genuss, corresponds very nearly with that of the Latin word *fructus*.

[6] So meinen sie, etc. "they (seem to) think, that it is a religious and sacred affair, and do not consider that Satan practises such things in order to strengthen avarice, to uphold false, factitious opinions, to undermine regular religious service (parish churches), to

feheu nicht, baß der Teufel folches treibt, den Geiz zu ftär=
fen, falfche erdichtete Glauben aufrichten, Pfarrfirchen zu
fchwächen, Tabernen und Hurerei zu mehren, unnüß Geld
und Arbeit verlieren, und nur das arme Volf mit der Nafe
umführen. Hätten fie die Schrift fo wahl gelefen, als das
verdammte geiftliche Gefeßt, fie wüßten den Sachen wohl
zu rathen.

Aber was foll ich fagen? Ein Jeder gedenfet nur, wie
er eine folche Wallfahrt¹ in feinem Kreis² aufrichte und
erhalte, gar nichts forgend, wie das Volf recht glaube und
lebe. Die Regenten find wie das Volf, ein Blinder führet

multiply grog-shops and profligacy, to squander money and time (labor), and do nothing but lead at pleasure the poor people by the nose.
Had they studied the Scriptures as much as they have the accursed canonical law, they would have known how to manage the matter."
G l a u b e n is in the plural, which is not very common, and means
*convictions, opinions. Taberna*, in Latin, means a *booth* or *shop*;
T a b e r n e, in German, means a *small tavern* or *grog-shop*. *Tavern*, is the same word, with the ordinary change of the *b* into *v*. See
p. 20, Note 3. We may here remark that many German words are
adopted in English by dropping the liquids *l*, *n*, *r*; thus, a l s be
comes *as* by dropping the *l*; u n s becomes *us* by dropping the *n*;
w i r becomes (w i) *we* by dropping the *r*; s o l c h becomes (s o c h)
*such* by dropping the *l*; w e l c h (Anglo-Saxon *huilc*) becomes
*which* by dropping the *l*; a n d e r, (Gothic a n t h a r, old Saxon
o t h a r), becomes *other*, in the same way, which Webster falsely
derives from o d e r. (*Or* comes from o d e r, by a similar syncope.)
So from s p r e c h e n comes *speak*; from B i e n e, *bee*; from
G a n s (Low Saxon, G a u s) *goose*; from I n s e l, *isle*; from
s a n f t, *soft*; from S p o r n, *spur*; from S t e r n, *star*; from
w ü n s c h - e n, *wish.*

¹ K r e i s. The use of this word here, which properly designates
one of the *Circles* into which Germany was formerly divided, shows
that Luther had not bishops particularly in mind, but princes and
civil rulers, including the archiepiscopal electors.

² W a l l f a h r t, though governed by a u f r i c h t e and e r h a l t e
means the act of performing a pilgrimage, rather than the place of
pilgrimage and whatever gives sanctity to it. See the next note but
one.

ben anbern. Ja, wo bie Wallfahrten nicht wollen ange=
hen,[1] hebt man bie Heiligen an zu erheben ; nicht ben Heili=
gen zu Ehren, bie wohl ohne ihre Erhebung genug geehret
würben, sonbern Geläuf unb ein Gelbbringen aufzurichten.
Da helfen nun Pabst[2] unb Bischöfe bazu, hier regnet es Ab=
laß, ba hat man Gelbes genug bazu ; aber was Gott gebo=
ten hat, ba ist Niemanb sorgfältig, ba läuft Niemanb nach,
ba hat Niemanb Gelb bazu. Ach baß wir so blinb sinb,
unb bem Teufel in seinem Gespensten nicht allein seinen
Muthwillen lassen, sonbern auch stärken unb mehren ![3] Ich
wollte man ließe bie lieben Heiligen mit Frieben, unb bas
arme Volk unverführt. Welcher Geist hat bem Pabst Ge=
walt gegeben, bie Heiligen zu erheben ? Wer sagt es ihm,
ob sie heilig ober nicht heilig sinb ? Sinb sonst nicht[4] Sün=

---

[1] A n g e h e n, *to succeed, to prosper.* " Nay, if pilgrimages will
not succeed (will not go), then men begin to celebrate the memory
of (elevate) saints, not in honor to the saints, etc., but to secure (or
establish a u f r i c h t e n) concourses of people, and pecuniary advantages."

[2] D a  h e l f e n  n u n  P a b s t, etc. " To this the pope and bishops contribute their aid, and here indulgences come in showers ; and
the people have money enough for this. But what God has commanded, no one cares for this ; there is no flocking thither ; no one
has money for this." When d a is separated from z u, it is often
now in colloquial style in Thuringia repeated and prefixed, so that
d a — d a z u is equivalent to d a — z u (i. e. d a z u). So d a — n a c h
stands for d a r n a c h, *thither,* or *towards that.*

[3] S t ä r k e n  u n d  m e h r e n can grammatically govern nothing but M u t h w i l l e n.

[4] S i n d  s o n s t  n i c h t, etc. " Are there not already (otherwise) sins enough in the world, that one must tempt God, interfere
with his decision, and set forth the saints as idols of Mammon ?"
L i e b e cannot be translated in such connections. Everything
which relates to life, or supports it, or gives the least pleasure may
be called l i e b, as d e r  l i e b e  G o t t, *the beneficent God ;* d a s
l i e b e  B r o d t, (*nourishing*) *bread ;* d i e  l i e b e  S o n n e, *the ge-
nial sun ;* d e r  l i e b e  R e g e n, *the refreshing rain.* It cannot be

den genug auf Erden, man muß Gott auch verſuchen, in ſein Urtheil fallen, und die lieben Heiligen zu Geldgötzen aufſetzen?

Darum rathe ich, man laſſe ſich[1] die Heiligen ſelbſt erhe=ben, ja Gott allein ſollte ſie erheben, und Jeder bleibe in ſeiner Pfarre, da er mehr findet,[2] denn in allen Wallkirchen, wenn ſie gleich alle eine Wallkirche wären. Hier findet man Taufe, Sacrament, Predigt und deinen Nächſten; welches größere Dinge ſind, denn alle Heiligen im Himmel. Denn ſie Alle ſind durch das Wort Gottes und Sacrament gehei=ligt worden.

Und obſchon Heiligenerheben vor Zeiten wäre gut gewe=ſen, ſo iſt es doch jetzt nimmer gut; gleichwie viel andere Dinge vor zeiten ſind gut geweſen, und doch nun ärgerlich und ſchädlich, als da ſind Feiertage, Kirchenſchatz und Zier=den. Denn es iſt offenbar, daß durch Heiligen=Erhebung nicht Gottes Ehre noch der Chriſten Beſſerung, ſondern Geld und Ruhm geſucht wird, daß eine Kirche will etwas Beſonderes vor der andern ſeyn und haben, und ihr leid wäre,[3] daß eine andere deßgleichen hätte und ihr Vortheil

---

translated in such expressions as, d e r l i e b e Z u f a l l; m e i n e l i e b e N o t h, where the proper meaning of the word almost van-ishes.

[1] S i c h is not governed by l a s s e, but by e r h e b e n.

[2] D a e r m e h r f i n d e t, etc., " in which he finds more (that is val uable) than in all places (churches) of pilgrimage, if they were all put into one. Here one finds baptism, the eucharist, preaching, and one's neighbor (to serve), — that which (w e l c h e s) constitutes greater things," etc. In w e l c h e s we see the peculiar use of the neuter singular of a pronoun, in an indefinite sense, and yet referring directly to what is plural. See p. 110, Note 3, and p. 111, Note 2.

[3] U n d i h r l e i d w ä r e, etc., " and it would regret (would be painful to it) that another should have the like, and that its advan-tage be common (equally enjoyed by all). To such an extent (s o-g a r) have men perverted spiritual blessings (not *ecclesiastical prop-erty* here as will appear near the close of the paragraph) to improper

gemein wäre ; sogar hat man geistliche Güter zu Mißbrauch
und Gewinn zeitlicher Güter verordnet, in dieser ärgsten
letzten Zeit, daß Alles, was Gott selber ist, muß dem Geiz
dienen. Auch so dienet solcher Vortheil nur zu zweierlei,
Secten[1] und Hoffahrt, daß eine Kirche der andern ungleich,
sich unter einander verachten und erheben ; so doch alle gött=
lichen Güter Allen gemein und gleich nur zur Einigkeit die=
nen sollen. Da hat der Pabst auch Lust dazu, dem leid
wäre, daß alle Christen gleich und Eines wären.

Hier gehöret her,[2] daß man abthun sollte oder verachten,
oder je gemein machen aller Kirchen Freiheit,[3] Bullen, und
was der Pabst verkauft zu Rom auf seinem Schindleich.[4]

---

uses and to worldly gain (gain of worldly goods), in these worst and
latest times, that whatever God himself is, must be subservient to
avarice."

[1] S e c t e n, *divisions.* "And thus, such priviliges serve only to
two ends, to divisions and to arrogance, so that one church being unlike the others, they exalt and depress each other (i. e. depress others
and exalt themselves), whereas all spiritual blessings, being common
and equal to all, should be subservient only to unity. The pope
takes pleasure in this (abuse), to whom it would be a matter of regret, that all Christians should be equal and united." S i c h  u n t e r-
e i n a n d e r, cannnot easily be translated with the two following
verbs, because s i c h is a reciprocal pronoun, with the first verb and
a reflective with the second. "They reciprocally despise each other
and exalt themselves." *Each other*, in English, is simply reciprocal,
and *themselves*, simply reflective. It is a well known principle that,
in German, reflective verbs, may be used as reciprocal. S i c h  h a s-
s e n may mean either, *to hate themselves*, or *to hate each other.*

[2] H i e r  g e h ö r e t  h e r, equivalent to, h i e r h e r  g e h ö r e t.

[3] A l l e r  K i r c h e n  F r e i h e i t, is governed by the last verb,
m a c h e n ; but, only the words K i r c h e n  F r e i h e i t, apart from
the qualification, a l l e r, is governed by a b t h u n and v e r a c h t e n,
"that one should abolish the immunities of (particular) churches, or
despise them, or make them common to (of) all." The next sentence
explains the meaning of this.

[4] S c h i n d l e i c h, a Thuringian word, for which S c h i n d a n g e r
is more common, and sometimes S c h i n d g r u b e (implying *excava-*

Denn ſo er Wittenberg,[1] Halle, Venedig, und zuvor ſeinem
Kom verkauft oder giebt Indulte, Privilegien, Ablaß, Gnade,
Vortheil, Facultäten, warum giebt er es nicht allen Kirchen
ingemein? Iſt er nicht ſchuldig, allen Chriſten zu thun
umſonſt und Gottes willen[2] Alles, was er vermag, ja auch
ſein Blut für ſie zu vergießen? So ſage mir, warum giebt
er oder verkauft dieſer Kirche, und der andern nicht; oder
muß das verfluchte Geld in ſeiner Heiligkeit Augen ſo einen
großen Unterſchied machen unter den Chriſten, die Alle
gleiche Taufe, Wort, Glaube, Chriſtum, Gott und alle
Dinge haben? Will man uns denn[3] aller Dinge mit ſe=
henden Augen blind, und mit reiner Vernunft thöricht mach=
en, daß wir ſolchen Geiz, Büberei und Spiegelfechten ſollen
anbeten? Er iſt ein Hirte, ja wo du Geld haſt und nicht
weiter, und ſchämen ſich dennoch nicht ſolcher Büberei, mit

---

*tion*) is used, means a spot or place (l e i c h) where dead animals are
skinned or flayed. Figuratively, this low word, means a place where
mean dishonesty, and *shaving* are practised.

[1] D e n n  s o  e r  W i t t e n b e r g, etc. " For if he sells or grants
to Wittenberg, Halle, Venice, and especially to his own Rome immunities, privileges, indulgences, favors, advantages and powers (or
permissions)," etc. These substantives are not here used to indicate
so many things specifically different from each other ; they are synonymes, accumulated for rhetorical effect.

[2] U m s o n s t  u n d  [u m]  G o t t e s  w i l l e n. This is a clear instance, where u n d connects a genitive to the second part of a compound, or where u m, is a part of a compound and yet holds the relation of a preposition to a following substantive. Contemplate
s o n s t as a separate word, used substantively, and the construction
will not appear so strange.

[3] W i l l  m a n  u n s  d e n n, etc. " Would they, make us in all
things blind, with our eyes open, and idiotic in the full use of our
reason, in order that we should pay deference to such avarice, knavery, and mockfights? He is a shepherd : — yes ! so far as you have
money, and no farther ; and yet they are not ashamed of such vil-
lany, but lead us about at pleasure with their bulls of indulgence."
A l l e r  D i n g e is a genitive, of an adverbial character.

ihren Bullen uns hin und her zu führen. Es ist ihnen nur um das verfluchte Geld zu thun,[1] und sonst nichts mehr.

So rathe ich das,[2] so solches Narrenwerk nicht wird abgethan, daß ein jeglicher frommer Christen=Mensch seine Augen aufthue, und lasse sich mit den römischen Bullen, Siegel und der Gleißnerei nicht irren,[3] bleibe daheim in seiner Kirche, und lasse ihm seine Taufe, Evangelium, Glaube, Christum und Gott, der an allen Oerten gleich ist, das Beste seyn,[4] und den Pabst bleiben einen blinden Führer der Blinden. Es kann dir weder Engel noch Pabst so viel geben, als dir Gott in deine Pfarrei giebt; ja er verführet[5] dich von den göttlichen Gaben, die du umsonst hast auf seine Gaben, die du kaufen mußt, und giebt dir Blei um's Gold, Fell um's Fleisch, Schnur um den Beutel, Wachs um Honig, Wort um's Gut, Buchstaben um den Geist, wie du vor Augen siehest, und willst's dennoch nicht merken. Sollst du auf seinem Pergament und Wachs gen Himmel fahren, so wird dir der Wagen gar bald zerbrechen, und du in die Hölle fallen, nicht in Gottes Namen.

---

[1] I s t — u m — z u  t h u n.  See p. 35, Note 5, and p. 20, Note 3, middle.

[2] D a s, *this, the following*, namely, " if such foolery be not done away, that each one," etc.

[3] L a s s e  s i c h — n i c h t  i r r e n, "not suffer himself to be misled."

[4] L a s s e  i h m  s e i n e  T a u f e — d a s  B e s t e  s e y n, "and regard (l a s s e  s e y n, *let it be*) his baptism, etc. as the most important to him."

[5] J a  e r  v e r f u h r e t, etc.  " Nay, he seduces you away from God's gifts which are gratuitous, to his own which you must buy, and he gives you lead in exchange for gold, skin for flesh, purse-string for purse, wax for honey, words for goods, the letter for the spirit, as you see before your eyes, and yet will not notice. Should you (attempt to) ride to heaven on his parchments and wax, your chariot would soon go to pieces, and you fall into perdition, and that not in God's name."

Laß dir's[1] nur eine gewisse Regel seyn: Was du vom Pabst kaufen mußt, das ist nicht gut noch von Gott. Denn was aus Gott ist, das wird nicht allein umsonst gegeben, sondern alle Welt wird darum gestraft und verdammt, daß sie es nicht hat wollen[2] umsonst aufnehmen; als da ist das Evangelium und göttliche Werk. Solche Verführung[3] haben wir verdienet um Gott, daß wir sein heiliges Wort, der Taufe Gnade, verachtet haben, wie St. Paulus sagt: „Gott wird senden eine kräftige Irrung allen denen, die die Wahrheit nicht haben aufgenommen zu ihrer Seligkeit, auf daß sie glauben und folgen den Lügen und Bübereien, wie sie würdig sind.

Zum ein und zwanzigsten. Es ist wohl der größten Noth eine, daß alle Bettelei abgethan würde in aller Christenheit, es sollte ja Niemand unter den Christen betteln gehen; es wäre auch eine leichte Ordnung[4] darob zu machen, wenn wir den Muth und Ernst dazu thäten, nämlich, daß eine jegliche Stadt ihre armen Leute versorgte, und keinen fremden Bettler zuließe, sie hießen wie sie wollten, es wären Waldbrüder oder Bettelorden. Es könnte je eine jegliche Stadt die ihren ernähren; und ob sie zu gering wäre, daß

---

[1] Lass dir's, etc. " Let this be an infallible rule for you."

[2] Nicht hat wollen, *was not willing.* See p. 148, Note 3.

[3] Solche Verführung, etc. " Such delusion have we deserved of (with) God, because we have contemned," etc.

[4] Es wäre auch ein leichte Ordnung, etc. " It would be an easy arrangement to be made (to make) respecting it, if we were to apply (suitable) courage and earnestness to the matter, viz. that every town provide for its own poor, and admit no beggars from abroad, be they who they may, whether eremites or mendicant friars. Every city could support its own (poor), or (and) if it were too small (1 would propose) that one direct the people in the adjacent villages to give to that object. If they must otherwise support many vagabonds and worthless fellows under the name of beggars, they might (in the way proposed) ascertain who are really needy and who are not."

**16***

man auf den umliegenden Dörfern auch das Volk vermah=
nete, dazu zu geben.　Müssen sie doch sonst so viel Land=
läufer und böse Buben unter des Bettels Namen ernähren,
so könnte man auch wissen, welche wahrhaftig arm wären
oder nicht.

So müßte da seyn[1] ein Verweser[1] oder Vormund, der alle
die Armen kennete und was ihnen noth wäre, dem Rath
oder Pfarrherrn ansagte, oder wie das auf's beste möchte
verordnet werden.　Es geschieht meines Achtens auf keinem
Handel so viel Büberei und Trugerei, als auf dem Betteln,
die da alle leichtlich[2] wären zu vertreiben.　Auch so geschieht
dem gemeinen Volk wehe durch so frei gemein Betteln.　Ich
hab's überlegt,[3] die fünf oder sechs Bettelorden kommen des
Jahrs an einen Ort, ein jeglicher mehr denn sechs oder sie=
benmal, dazu die gemeinen Bettler, Botschaften und Wall=
brüder, daß sich die Rechnung funden hat, wie eine Stadt
bei sechszig Mal im Jahr geschätzt wird, ohne was der welt=
lichen Obrigkeit gebührt, Aufsätze und Schatzung geben wird,
und der römische Stuhl mit seiner Waare raubet, und sie

---

[1] So müsste da seyn ein Verweser, etc.　"There
would need to be a manager or overseer, who should know all the
poor, and report to the city council or to the pastor, what they were
in want of, or in whatever (other) way the matter might be best arranged."

[2] Leichtlich obsolete for leicht, "all of which might easily be put away."

[3] Ich hab's überlegt, etc.　"I have made the calculation
(have reflected on it); the five or six orders of mendicant friars
come, each one not less than six or seven times a year to one place,
besides the common beggars, (papal) messengers and pilgrims, so
that the account has been found to be (funden for gefunden)
that (how) a city is fleeced about sixty times a year, besides what belongs to the government (and) is given as imposts and taxes, and
(besides what) the Roman see, with its wares (indulgences), plun-
ders and squanders, so that it is to me one of the greatest of God's
wonders, how we can still live and support ourselves."

unnützlich verzehren, daß mir's der größten Gottes Wunder eines ist, wie wir doch bleiben mögen und ernähret werden.

Daß aber etliche meinen, es würden mit der Weise[1] die Armen nicht wohl versorgt und nicht so große steinerne Häuser und Klöster gebaut, auch nicht so reichlich; das glaube ich fast wohl. Ist's doch auch nicht noth. Wer arm will seyn, soll nicht reich seyn; will er aber reich seyn, so greif' er mit der Hand an den Pflug und such's ihm selbst aus der Erden. Es ist genug, daß ziemlich die Armen versorgt seyn, dabei sie nicht Hungers sterben noch erfrieren. Es fügt sich nicht, daß einer auf's Andern Arbeit müssig gehe,[2] reich sey und wohllebe, bei eines Andern Uebel leben,[3] wie jetzt der verkehrte Mißbrauch geht. Denn St. Paulus sagt: „Wer nicht arbeitet, soll auch nicht essen." Es ist Niemand von der Andern Güter zu leben[4] von Gott verordnet, denn allein den predigenden und regierenden Priestern (wie St. Paulus 1. Cor. 9.) um ihrer geistlichen Ar-

---

[1] Es würden mit der Weise, etc. "That some suppose, the poor would not in this (der, demonstrative) manner be so well provided for, and that such great stone buildings and cloisters would not be built, nor so richly (so many of them), that I (as well as they) believe very firmly. Nor is this necessary. He who wishes to be poor (chooses poverty, i. e. a monk) should not be rich. But if he wishes to be rich, let him take hold of the plough with his hand and seek (dig) it (riches) for himself out of the earth."

[2] Auf's (auf des) andern Arbeit müssig gehe, "live idly upon another's labors."

[3] Bei eines Andern Uebel leben. Uebel leben, *ill-living* is used substantively, and is governed by bei and governs the genitive eines andern, *of another.*

[4] Niemand von der Andern Güter zu leben, is a substantive phrase, and nominative to ist verordnet. "(For) no one to live on the property of another, (except priests who actually preach and preside, etc.) is ordained of God." The construction is very irregular. Wirker for Arbeiter is now little used except in composition and applying to manufactures, as Strumpf-wirker, and the like.

beit, wie auch Chriſtus ſagt zu den Apoſteln: „Ein jeglicher
Wirker iſt würdig ſeines Lohns.‟

Zum vier und zwanzigſten, es iſt hohe Zeit, daß wir auch
einmal ernſtlich und mit Wahrheit der Böhmen Sache vor=
nehmen, ſie mit uns und uns mit ihnen zu vereinigen, daß
einmal aufhören[1] die gräulichen Läſterungen, Haß und Neid
auf beiden Seiten. Ich will meiner Thorheit[2] nach der
erſte mein Gutdünken vorlegen, mit Vorbehalt eines je=
glichen beſſern Verſtandes.

Zum erſten müſſen wir wahrlich[3] die Wahrheit bekennen,
und unſer Rechtfertigen laſſen, den Böhmen etwas zugeben,
nemlich daß Johannes Huß und Hieronymus von Prag zu
Coſtnitz, wider päbſtlich, chriſtlich, Kaiſerlich Geleit und Eid
ſind verbrannt, damit wider Gottes Gebot geſchehen,[4] und
die Böhmen hoch zu Bitterkeit verurſacht ſind. Und wie=
wohl ſie ſollten[5] vollkommen geweſen ſeyn, ſolch ſchweres

---

[1] Aufhören, subjunctive.

[2] Ich will meiner Thorheit, etc. "1 will, according
to my indiscretion, give my opinion, the first, with the reservation (to
adopt) any better view (which others may present)."

[3] Wahrlich, *verily*, qualifies, not bekennen, but müssen. "We must, indeed, confess the truth, and not undertake
(and give up) our justification, (but) concede something to the Bohemians, namely, that," etc.

[4] Damit wider Gottes Gebot geschehen, "and in
that act (therewith) something was done (geschehen with ist
understood, and used impersonally) contrary to the command of
God," i. e. and thereby we violated the law of God.

[5] Und wiewohl sie sollten, etc. "And though they
ought to have been faultless (and) to have *endured* such great injustice and such obedience to God on the part of our countrymen ; still,
they were not under obligation to approve of it, and acknowledge it
as done justly ; nay, they ought at this day lose body and life for it
(darüber) sooner than (they ought) acknowledge that it is right
to violate an imperial, papal, and Christian safe-conduct, and act
faithlessly in contravention of it. Therefore, although the Bohemi
ans have been impatient (it is the impatience of the Bohemians), still

Unrecht und Gottes=Ungehorsam von den Unsern gelitten
haben; so sind sie doch nicht schuldig gewesen, solches zu bil=
ligen, und als recht gethan bekennen: ja sie sollten noch
heutiges Tages darüber lassen Leib und Leben, ehe sie be=
kennen sollten, daß Recht sey, kaiserlich päbstlich, christlich
Geleit zu brechen, treulos dawider handeln. Darum, wie=
wohl es der Böhmen Ungeduld ist, so ist's doch mehr des
Pabsts und der Seinen Schuld all' der Jammer, all' der
Irrthum und Seelen=Verderben, das seit demselben Concilio
erfolget ist.

Ich will hier Johannes Huß Artifel nicht richten, noch
seinen Irrthum versechten, wiewohl mein Verstand noch
nichts Irriges bei ihm gefunden hat, und ich mag's[1] fröh=
lich glauben, daß die nichts Gutes gerichtet, noch redlich
verdammt haben, die durch ihren treulosen Handel christlich
Geleit und Gottes Gebot übertreten, ohne Zweifel mehr
vom bösen Geist denn vom heiligen Geist besessen gewesen
sind. Es wird Niemand daran zweifeln, daß der heilige
Geist nicht wider Gottes Gebot handelt; so ist Niemand[2] so
unwissend, daß Geleit und Treue brechen sey wider Gottes
Gebot, ob sie gleich dem Teufel selbst, geschweige einem Ke=
ßer, wäre zugesagt. So ist auch offenbar, daß Johannes
Huß und den Böhmen solches Geleit ist zugesagt, und nicht

---

all the wretchedness, all the errors and ruin of souls, which have followed since that council, are in a greater degree (m e h r) the fault
of the pope and of his party."

[1] U n d  i c h  m a g's, etc., " and I would readily (cheerfully) believe, that they have not judged well at all, nor honestly passed sentence of condemnation, who, through their faithless doings, have
violated a Christian safe-conduct, and God's command, (and who)
were, without doubt, more possessed of the evil spirit than of the
Holy Spirit."

[2] S o  i s t  N i e m a n d, etc, " nor is any one so ignorant (as not
to know) that violating safe-conduct and one's faith, is contrary to
God's command, even though they were pledged to Satan himself,
not to say a heretic."

gehalten, sondern darüber[1] er verbrennet. Ich will auch
Johannes Huß keinen Heiligen noch Märtyrer machen, wie
etliche Böhmen thun, ob ich gleich bekenne, daß ihm Unrecht
geschehen, und sein Buch und Lehre unrecht verdammt ist.
Denn Gottes Gerichte sind heimlich und erschrecklich, die
Niemand denn[2] er selbst allein offenbaren und ausdrucken
soll.

Das will ich nur sagen, er sey ein Ketzer,[3] wie böse er im=
mer möchte seyn, so hat man ihn mit Unrecht und wider Gott
verbrennet; und soll die Böhmen nicht dringen, solches zu
billigen, oder wir kommen sonst nimmermehr zur Einigkeit.
Es muß uns[4] die öffentliche Wahrheit eins machen, und
nicht die Eigensinnigkeit. Es hilft nicht,[5] daß sie zu der Zeit
haben vorgewendet, daß einem Ketzer sey nicht zu halten
das Geleit; das ist eben so viel gesagt, man soll Gottes Ge=
bot nicht halten, auf daß man Gottes Gebot halte. Es hat
sie der Teufel toll und thöricht gemacht, daß sie nicht haben
gesehen, was sie geredet oder gethan haben. Geleit halten[6]
hat Gott geboten, das sollte man halten, ob gleich die Welt
sollte untergehen, geschweige denn ein Ketzer los werden.
So sollte man die Ketzer mit Schriften, nicht mit Feuer
überwinden, wie die alten Väter gethan haben. Wenn es

---

[1] Sondern darüber er verbrennet (ist worden),
but contrary to it (darüber, *over it, across it*) he was burnt."

[2] Niemand, denn, *no one except.* Comp. p. 97, Note 2.

[3] Er sei ein Ketzer, etc., "though he were a heretic, as
bad as he could possibly be."

[4] Es muss uns, etc. "The open truth, and not dogged per-
tinacity, must unite us (the Germans and the Bohemians)."

[5] Es hilft nicht, etc. "It is of no avail, that they then pretended that the safe-conduct is not to be held with a heretic. That is
as much as saying (said), one must not keep the command of God (in
one instance) in order that he may keep the command of God (in
another)."

[6] Geleit halten, a substantive phrase, in the accusative.

Kunſt[1] wäre, mit Feuer Ketzer zu überwinden, ſo wären die Henker die gelehrteſten Doctores auf Erden; dürften wir auch nicht[2] mehr ſtudiren, ſondern welcher den andern mit Gewalt überwände, möchte ihn verbrennen.

Zum andern, daß Kaiſer[3] und Fürſten hineinſchicken etliche fromme verſtändige Biſchöfe und Gelehrten, bei Leib keinen Cardinal noch päbſtliche Botſchaft, noch Ketzermeiſter; denn das Volk iſt mehr denn zu viel ungelehrt in chriſtlichen Sachen, und ſuchen auch nicht der Seelen Heil: ſondern wie des Pabſts Heuchler Alle thun, ihre eigene Gewalt, Nutzen und Ehre. Sie ſind auch die Häupter geweſen dieſes Jammers zu Coſtnitz. Daß dieſelbigen Geſchickten[4] ſollen

---

[1] K u n s t, *an art, an attainment.*

[2] D u r f t e n  w i r  a u c h  n i c h t, etc., "neither should we need to study any more, but whoever should overcome another with force, might burn him."

[3] D a s s  K a i s e r, etc. "(My proposal would be) that the emperor and princes send thither a certain number of pious and intelligent bishops, and learned men, but, for the life of you, no cardinal, nor papal delegate, nor inquisitor; for these people are more than too ignorant in Christian affairs."

[4] G e s c h i c k t e n, is not an adjective here, meaning *skilful*, but the participle of s c h i c k e n, used above, and means *the persons sent*, i. e. the messengers or delegates of the emperor and princes. "That these same persons thus sent, should ascertain of the Bohemians, how matters stand in regard to their faith, whether it would be possible to unite all parties into one. Here ought the pope, out of regard to the souls of men, to lay aside, for a time, his supremacy, and, according to the decision of the most Christian council of Nice, to allow the Bohemians to choose from among themselves an archbishop of Prague, whom the bishop of Olmutz in Moravia, or the bishop of Gran in Hungary, or the bishop of Gnesen in Poland, or the bishop of Magdeburg in Germany, might consecrate (confirm); it is sufficient if he is confirmed by one or two of these, as it was in Cyprian's time. And the pope must not prevent such a course; if he does so, he acts like a wolf and tyrant, and no one should follow him, but return his ban with another." All the bishops here mentioned by Luther, were archbishops.

erkundigen bei den Böhmen, wie es um ihren Glanben stün=
de, ob es möglich wäre, alle ihre Secten in eine zu bringen.
Hier soll sich der Pabst um der Seelen willen eine Zeitlang
seiner Oberkeit entäußern, und nach dem Statut des aller=
christlichsten Concilii Nicäni den Böhmen zulaßen, einen
Erzbischof zu Prag aus ihnen selbst zu erwählen, welchen
bestätige der Bischof zu Olmütz in Mähren, oder der Bischof
zu Gran in Ungarn, oder der Bischof von Gnesen in Polen,
oder der Bischof zu Magdeburg in Deutschland; ist genug,
wenn er von dieser Einem oder Zween bestätiget wird, wie
zu den Zeiten St. Cypriani geschah. Und der Pabst hat
solches keines zu wehren; wehret er es aber, so thut er als
ein Wolf und Tyrann, und soll ihm niemand folgen, und
sein Bannen mit einem Widerbannen zurück treiben.

Zum fünfundzwanzigsten, die Universitäten bedürften auch
wohl einer guten starken Reformation, ich muß es sagen, es
verdrieße wen es will[1]. Ist doch Alles,[2] was das Pabstthum
hat eingesetzet und ordiniret, nur gerichtet auf Sünde und
Irrthum zu mehren, was sind die Universitäten, wo sie nicht
anders, denn bisher, verordnet, denn, wie das Buch Mac=
cabäorum sagt, Gymnasia Ephesorum et Graecae gloriae,
darinnen ein freies Leben geführet, wenig der heiligen
Schrift und christlicher Glaube gelehret wird, und allein der
blinde heidnische Meister Aristoteles regieret auch weiter
denn Christus? Hier wäre nun mein Rath, daß die Bü=

---

[1] Es verdriesse wen es will, *let it offend whom it may.*

[2] Ist doch Alles, etc. "If indeed everything (Is yet everything?) which the papacy has introduced and established, tends only
(is only arranged) to increase sin and error, what are the universities (if not regulated otherwise than heretofore) but *Gymnasia,* etc.,
in which an unrestrained life is led, little of the Holy Scripture and
of the Christian faith taught, and the blind heathen master Aristotle
reigns alone, even more than Christ." G l a u b e, which is here in
the genitive and governed by w e n i g, is used, as it frequently is in
the old German, in the feminine gender.

cher Ariſtotelis, Physicorum, Metaphysicae, de Anima, Ethicorum, welche bisher für die beſten gehalten,[1] ganz würden abgethan, mit allen andern, die von natürlichen Dingen ſich rühmen, ſo doch nichts darinnen mag gelehret werden,[2] weder von natürlichen noch geiſtlichen Dingen; dazu ſeine Meinung bisher Niemand verſtanden, und mit unnützer Arbeit, Studiren und Koſten ſo viel edler Zeit und Seelen umſonſt beladen geweſen ſind. Ich darf's ſagen, daß ein Töpfer mehr Künſt hat der natürlichen Dingen, denn in denen Büchern geſchrieben ſtehet.

Das möchte ich gerne leiden,[3] daß Ariſtotelis Bücher von

---

[1] Für die besten gehalten (worden sind).

[2] So doch nichts darinnen mag gelehret werden, "inasmuch as nothing may be learned from (in) them, either of natural or of spiritual things. Besides, no one has as yet understood his doctrines, and so much valuable time and (so many) minds have been needlessly burdened with useless labor, study and expense (i. e. and much time and strength have been consumed to no purpose in useless, etc.). I may safely affirm that a potter has more knowledge (Kunst for Wissen) than is found (stands) written in those books."

[3] Das möchte ich gerne leiden, etc. "I would desire (would very willingly suffer) that Aristotle's books on logic, rhetoric, and poetry, should be retained (behalten with würden understood). Or, brought into another briefer (brief) form, they would be (have been) useful to exercise the youth in eloquence and preaching (to speak well and to preach). But the (scholastic) comments and party contests (parties) ought to be abolished; and as Cicero's rhetoric (is read) without comment and party-strife, so Aristotle's logic ought to be read (müssten gelesen werden) in a simple (uniform) manner, without such bulky commentaries. But at present neither eloquence nor preaching is taught from it (one teaches neither, etc.), and nothing but disputes and mumbling are made out of it. In connection with these (daneben) one should study (have) the Latin, Greek and Hebrew languages, mathematics and history, which (studies) I recommend to (the attention of) my superiors in knowledge, and which would suggest themselves, if one should seriously meditate a reformation (of the schools). And in-

der Logik, Rhetorik, Poetik, behalten, oder sie in eine andere kurze Form gebracht, nützlich gewesen seyn würden, junge Leute zu üben, wohl reden und predigen; aber die Comment und Secten müßten abgethan, und gleich wie Ciceronis Rhetorik, ohne Comment und Secten, so auch Aristotelis Logik, einförmig, ohne solche große Comment gelesen werden. Aber jetzt lehret man weder reden noch predigen daraus, und ist ganz eine Disputation und Muderei daraus geworden. Daneben hätte man nun die Sprachen Lateinisch, Griechisch und Hebräisch, die Mathematicas, disciplinas, Historien, welches ich befehle Verständigern, und sich selbst wohl geben würde, so man mit Ernst nach einer Reformation trachtete; und fürwahr viel daran gelegen ist. Denn hier soll die christliche Jugend, und unser edles Volk, darinnen die Christenheit bleibet, gelehret und bereitet werden. Darum ich's achte, daß kein päbstlicher noch Kaiserlicher Werk möchte geschehen, denn gute Reformation der Universitäten; wiederum, kein teufelischeres Wesen, denn unreformirte Universitäten.

Die Aerzte lasse ich ihre Facultäten reformiren; die Juristen und Theologen nehme ich für mich und sage zum Ersten,[1] daß es gut wäre, das geistliche Recht, von dem ersten

---

deed this is a matter of great importance. For here should the Christian youth of our noble nation, in which Christianity still has footing, be instructed and prepared (for their duties). Wherefore, I think no act more truly papal and imperial could be performed, than a thorough reform of the universities; and on the other hand, nothing more Satanic than universities unreformed. The physicians I leave to reform their (the medical) faculties; the jurists and theologians I will take (in hand) for myself and say." Papstlicher and kaiserlicher, are in the comparative degree, without the terminations (päpstlicheres, kaiserlicheres) as the substantive is neuter. See teuflicheres a line or two below.

[1] Zum Ersten, etc., "first, that it would be well (that) the canonical law should be expunged utterly (to the ground) from," etc. Dass after wäre is omitted to avoid harshness.

Buchstaben, bis auf den letzten, würde zu Grund ausgetilget, sonderlich die Decretalen. Es ist uns übrig genug[1] in der Bibel geschrieben, wie wir uns in allen Dingen halten sollen; so hindert solches Studiren nur die heilige Schrift, auch das mehrere Theile nach eitel Geiz und Hoffahrt schmeckt. Und ob schon viel Gutes darinnen wäre, sollte es dennoch billig untergehen, darum, daß der Pabst alle geistliche Rechte in seines Herzens Kasten[2] gefangen hat, daß hinfort eitel unnützes Studiren und Betrug darinnen ist. Heut ist geistliches Recht, nicht das in den Büchern, sondern was in des Pabsts und seiner Schmeichler Muthwill stehet. Hast du eine Sache im geistlichen Recht, gegründet auf's Allerbeste, so hat der Pabst darüber Scrinium pectoris, darnach muß sich lenken alles Recht und die ganze Welt. Nun regieret dasselbige Scrinium vielmal ein Bube, und der Teu-

---

[1] Es ist uns übrig genug, etc., " there is quite enough written in the Bible (showing) how we should conduct ourselves in all things. There, such study only stands in the way of the Holy Scriptures; and the greater part of it (canonical law) has the savor (lusts after) of avarice and pride." On übrig, see p. 108, Note 3.

[2] In seines Herzens Kasten, etc., " holds it locked up in his own heart (fastened in the shrine of his heart), so that henceforth there is nothing in it (the canonical law) but useless study and deception. Now-a-days the canonical law is not that which is (stands) in the books, but what is in the arbitrary will of the pope and his flatterers. Though you have a cause, with the best support (founded in the best manner) in the canonical law, still the pope has a *scrinium pectoris* respecting it, to which all law and the whole world mus conform. Now a knave, and even the devil himself often governs that *scrinium*, and yet it receives the praise (it causes itself to be praised) that the Holy Ghost governs it, i. e. it pretends to be governed by the Holy Ghost. So they manage with the suffering people of Christ, impose on them many laws, observe none of them, and yet compel o hers to observe them, or to purchase a dispensation. Now since the pope and his adherents, have set aside even entire canonical laws and do not regard them, and govern themselves everywhere only by their own arbitrary will, we should follow their example."

fel felbst, und läßt sich preisen, der heilige Geist regiere es. So gehet man um mit dem armen Volk Christi, setzt ihm viel Recht, und hält keines, zwingt andere zu halten, oder mit Geld zu lösen.

Dieweil denn der Pabst und die Seinen selbst ganze geist= liche Rechte aufgehoben, nicht achten, und sich nur nach ihrem eigenen Muthwillen halten über alle Welt, sollen wir ihnen folgen, und die Bücher auch verwerfen. Warum soll= ten wir vergebens darinnen studiren? So können wir auch nimmermehr des Pabsts Muthwillen, welches nun geistliches Recht geworden ist, auslernen. Ei so fall' es¹ ja dahin in Gottes Namen, das in's Teufels Namen sich erhoben hat, und sey kein Doctor Decretorum mehr auf Erden; sondern allein Doctores scrinii papalis, das sind des Pabsts Heuchler. Man sagt, daß kein feineres weltliches Regiment irgend sey, denn bei den Türken, die doch weder geistliches noch welt= liches Recht haben, sondern allein ihren Alkoran: so müssen wir bekennen, daß nicht schändlicheres Regiment ist, denn bei uns, durch geistliches und weltliches Recht, daß kein Stand mehr gehet, natürlicher Vernunft, geschweige der heiligen Schrift gemäß.

Das weltliche Recht, hilf Gott, wie ist auch das eine Wildniß geworden! Wiewohl es viel besser, künstlicher, redlicher ist, denn das geistliche, an welchem, über den Na= men,² nichts Gutes ist, so ist sein doch auch viel zu viel ge= worden. Fürwahr, vernünftige Regenten³ neben der heili=

---

¹ Ei so fall' es, etc. "Come, then, in God's name, let that which, in Satan's name has elevated itself, fall (dahin, away)."

² Ueber den Namen, etc., "in which there is nothing good beyond the name. Still it has become far too bulky." Sein, is genitive for seiner and is governed by zu viel. Literally, "Yet if it has become much too much." See p. 46, Note 4.

³ Fürwahr, vernunftige Regenten, etc. "Indeed, sen-sible rulers would be quite competent with (the aid of) the Holy Scriptures. St. Paul says," etc. i. e. would be able to get along without laws. On übrig, see p. 108, Note 3.

gen Schrift, wären übrig recht genug, wie St. Paulus 1. Kor. 6. sagt: „Ist Niemand unter euch, der da möge seines Nächsten Sache richten, daß ihr vor heidnischen Gerichten müsset hadern?„ Es dünkt mich gleich,[1] daß Landrecht und Landsitten den Kaiserlichen gemeinen Rechten werden vorgezogen, und die Kaiserlichen nur zur Noth gebraucht. Und wollte Gott, daß, wie ein jegliches Land seine eigene Art und Gaben hat, also auch mit eigenen kurzen Rechten regiert würden, wie sie regieret sind gewesen, ehe solche Rechte sind erfunden, und noch ohne sie viele Länder regiert werden. Die weitläuftigen und fern gesuchten Rechte sind nur Beschwerung der Leute und mehr Hinderniß denn Förderung der Sachen. Doch ich hoffe, es sey die Sache schon von Andern besser bedacht und angesehen, denn ich's mag anbringen.[2]

Meine lieben Theologen haben sich aus der Mühe und Arbeit gesetzt, lassen die Bibeln wohl ruhen und lesen Sententias.[3]

So wir denn[4] haben den Namen und Titel, daß wir Lehrer der H. Schrift heißen, sollten wir wahrlich gezwungen seyn, dem Namen nach die H. Schrift und keine andere zu lehren. Nun aber, so Sententiae allen herrschen, findet

---

[1] Es dünkt mich gleich, etc. "It seems to me that the laws and usages of the particular State, should be preferred to the imperial (which was a modification of the civil law)." Luther desired — and who will deny his wisdom in this matter? — that each of the States included in the German empire, should be governed as far as possible by laws which grew out of its own necessities, and that the Roman and imperial law be resorted to only when the former was insufficient." Gleich, as, as though, cannot be translated here.

[2] Denn ich's mag anbringen, "than I can present it."

[3] Sententias, the books of the scholastic theologians or Sententiarists, who quoted the sententiae of the Fathers, as authorities.

[4] So wir denn, etc. "Since we have the name and title of being teachers (so that we are called teachers)," etc.

man mehr heidnischen und menschlichen Dünkel,[1] denn
heilige gewisse Lehren der Schrift in den Theologen. Wie
wollen wir ihm nun thun?[2] Ich weiß hier keinen andern
Rath, denn ein demüthiges Gebet zu Gott, daß uns derselbe
Doctores Theologiä gebe. Doctores der Kunst, der Arznei,
der Rechte, der Sententien, mögen der Pabst, Kaiser und
Universitäten machen; aber sey nur gewiß,[3] einen Doctor
der heiligen Schrift wird dir Niemand machen, denn allein
der heilige Geist vom Himmel, wie Christus sagt Joh. 6.:
„Sie müssen alle von Gott selber gelehret seyn." Nun
sragt der heilige Geist nicht nach roth, brann Pareten,[4] oder
was des Prangens ist,[5] auch nicht ob einer jung oder alt,
Laie oder Pfaff, Mönch oder weltlich, Jungfrau oder ehelich
sey.

Die Bücher müßte man auch wenigern, und erlesen die
besten; denn viel Bücher machen nicht gelehrt, viel Lesen
auch nicht;[6] sondern gut Ding und oft lesen, wie wenig sein
ist, das macht gelehrt in der Schrift, und fromm dazu. Ja
es sollten aller heiligen Väter Schrift[7] nur eine Zeitlang

---

[1] Dünkel, from dünken, not to be confounded with Dunkel.

[2] Wie wollen wir ihm nun thun? "How now shall we
manage it (do to it, or in regard to it)?"

[3] Aber sey nur gewiss, "but be well assured." Nur, only
assured, nothing but assured, i. e. well assured.

[4] Paret for Baret, a cap. The p is often used for b in German, especially in the south of Germany, and in the old writers.

[5] Oder, was des Prangen's ist, "or what (anything that)
pertains to show."

[6] Viel Lesen auch nicht, etc., "nor does extensive reading, but valuable matter and frequent reading, however little of it
(sein, genitive for seiner, referring to Ding) there may be,
that makes one learned in the Scriptures and pious too." No modern teacher on this subject has expressed more truth in fewer words.

[7] Väter Schrift, the writings of the Fathers. Luther seems to
use the word Schrift as a collective, with a plural verb.

werden gelesen, dadurch in die Schrift zu kommen;[1] so lesen wir sie nur, daß wir darin bleiben, und nimmer in die Schrift kommen, damit wir gleich denen sind, die die Wege=zeichen ansehen, und wandeln dennoch den Weg nimmer. Die lieben Väter haben uns wollen in die Schrift führen, mit ihrem Schreiben, so führen wir uns damit heraus; so doch allein Schrift unser Weingarten ist,[2] darin wir Alle uns sollten üben und arbeiten.

Vor allen Dingen, sollte in den hohen und niedrigen Schulen die vornehmste und gemeinste Lection seyn: die heilige Schrift,[3] und den jungen Knaben das Evangelium. Und wollte Gott, eine jede Stadt hätte auch eine Mägdlein= Schule, darin des Tages die Mägdlein eine Stunde das Evangelium hörten, es wäre zu deutsch oder lateinisch. Fürwahr die Schulen, Mann= und Frauen=Klöster,[4] sind vor Zeiten darauf angefangen, gar aus löblicher christlicher Meinung, wie wir lesen von St. Agnes und mehr Heiligen; da wurden heilige Jungfrauen und Märtyrer, und stund ganz wohl[5] in der Christenheit; aber nun ist nicht mehr denn Beten und Singen daraus geworden. Sollte nicht

---

[1] Dadurch in die Schrift zu kommen, etc., "to come thereby (i. e. to be introduced by them) to the Scriptures; but we read them (the writings of the Fathers) only to remain in them, and never to come to the Scriptures, whereby we resemble those who look at the guide-boards, and yet never follow the way (they point out)."

[2] So doch allein Schrift unser Weingarten ist, " whereas the Scriptures alone are our vineyard.'

[3] : die heilige Schrift, the semicolon in German is some- times used very much like a dash in English, to give emphasis to a word.

[4] Die Schulen, Mann- und Frauen-Klöster. " In ear- ly times schools, (i. e.) convents for males and those for females, be- gan with this object in view."

[5] Und (es) stand ganz wohl, etc. "and it was very well with Christianity," i. e. the Christian church was in a healthy condi- tion.

billig ein jeder Chriſten=Menſch[1] bei ſeinen neun und zehn=
ten Jahren wiſſen das ganze heilige Evangelium, da ſein
Name und Leben innen ſtehet?[2] Lehret doch eine Spin=
nerin[3] und Näherin ihre Tochter daſſelbe Handwerk in jun=
gen Jahren; aber nun wiſſen das Evangelium auch die
großen gelehrten Prälaten und Biſchöfe ſelbſt nicht.

O wie ungleich fahren wir mit dem armen jungen Han=
ſen, der uns befohlen iſt, zu regieren und unterweiſen?[4]
Und ſchwere Rechnung dafür muß gegeben werden, daß wir
ihnen das Wort Gottes nicht vorlegen: geſchieht ihnen,[5]
wie Jeremias ſagt: Klagel. 2.: „Meine Augen ſind vor
Weinen müde geworden, mein Eingeweide iſt erſchrocken,
meine Leber iſt ausgeſchüttet auf die Erde, um des Ver=
derbens willen der Tochter meines Volks, da die Jungen
und Kindlein verderben, auf allen Gaſſen der ganzen Stadt.
Sie ſprachen zu ihren Müttern: Wo iſt Brod und Wein?
Und verſchmachten als die Verwundeten auf den Straßen
der Stadt, und gaben den Geiſt auf im Schooß ihrer Müt=
ter.“ Dieſen elenden Jammer ſehen wir nicht,[6] wie auch
jetzt das junge Volk mitten in der Chriſtenheit verſchmach=
tet und erbärmlich verdirbt, Gebrechen halben des Evange=
liums,[7] das man mit ihnen immer treiben und üben ſollte.

---

[1] Christen-Mensch. Mensch, like *homo* in Latin, stands
for a human being, and therefore may be applied to a person but nine
or ten years old. Mann could not be so used.

[2] Da sein Name innen steht, for darin sein Name
steht.

[3] Lehret doch eine Spinnerin, etc. is not a hypothetical
clause, but a strong affirmation, as an antithesis to the latter clause.

[4] Der uns befohlen ist, zu regieren und unterwei-
sen, "which is committed to us to be governed and instructed (to
govern and to instruct)." Ungleich, refers to what is done to the
spinster and seamstress.

[5] (Es) geschiet ihnen.

[6] Sehen wir nicht, "we do not see," i. e. we shut our eyes to.

[7] Gebrechen halben des Evangeliums, "on account

Wir follten auch,[1] wo die hohen Schulen fleißig wären in der heiligen Schrift, nicht dahin schicken Jedermann, wie jetzt geschieht, da man nur fraget nach der Menge, und ein Jeder will einen Doctor haben, sondern allein die Allergeschicktesten, in den kleinen Schulen vor wohl erzogen, darüber ein Fürst oder Rath einer Stadt soll Acht haben, und nicht zulassen zu senden, denn wohlgeschickte. Wo aber die heilige Schrift nicht regiert, da rathe ich fürwahr Niemand daß er sein Kind hinthue. Es muß verderben Alles,[2] was nicht Gottes Wort ohne Unterlaß treibet; darum sehen wir auch,[3] was für Volk wird und ist in den hohen Schulen; ist Niemands Schuld denn des Pabstes, Bischöfe und Prälaten, denen solch des jungen Volkes Nutzen befohlen ist. Denn die hohen Schulen sollten erziehen eitel hochverständige Leute in der Schrift, die da möchten Bischöfe und Pfarrherren werden, an der Spitze stehen[4] wider

---

of a deficiency of the Gospel." H a l b e n does not govern E v a n g e l i u m s, but always governs the noun which it follows — G e b r e c h e n, in this instance.

[1] W i r   s o l l t e n   a u c h, etc. "Even if the Universities (that is the meaning of h o h e n   S c h u l e n) were diligent in (the study of) the Scriptures, we ought not to send (indiscriminately) every one thither, — as is now done, inasmuch as men are anxious only about numbers (the universities seek to be much frequented) and every man wishes to have (his son) a doctor — but only the most promising (who have been) previously well trained in the preparatory schools. Respecting this matter the ruler or council of a city should exercise a supervision and not permit (persons) to send (to the universities) any but young men of talents."

[2] E s   m u s s   v e r d e r b e n   A l l e s. A l l e s is in the nominative.

[3] D a r u m   s e h e n   w i r   a u c h, etc. "for this reason do we see what sort of persons are formed (w i r d, become) and now exist (i s t)," i. e. do we see such persons as are now formed and as now exist in the universities.

[4] P f a r r h e r r n   w e r d e n  (u n d)  a n   d e r   S p i t z e   s t e h e n, "become pastors and stand at the head (as leaders)," etc.

die Keßer und Teufel und aller Welt. Aber wo findet man
das? Ich habe große Sorge, die hohen Schulen sind große
Pforten der Hölle, so sie nicht emsiglich die heilige Schrift
üben, und treiben in's junge Volk.

Zum sechs und zwanzigsten, ich weiß wohl, daß der rö=
mische Haufe wird vorwenden und hoch aufblasen,[1] wie der
Pabst habe das heilige römische Reich von dem griechischen
Kaiser genommen, und an die Deutschen gebracht, für welche
Ehre[2] und Wohlthat er billig Unterthänigkeit, Dank und
alles Gutes an den Deutschen verdienet und erlangt haben
soll. Deßhalb sie vielleicht allerlei vornehmen, sie zu refor=
miren, sich unterwinden werden, in den Wind zu schlagen,
und nichts lassen ansehen, denn solches römischen Reiches
Begabungen. Aus diesem Grunde haben sie bisher man=
chen theuern Kaiser so muthwillig und übermüthig verfolgt
und gedruckt, daß Jammer ist es zu sagen,[3] und mit dersel=
ben Behendigkeit sich selbst zu Oberherren gemacht, aller
weltlicher Gewalt und Obrigkeit, wider das heilige Evan=
gelium, darum ich auch davon reden muß.

Es ist ohne Zweifel, daß rechte römische Reich, davon die

---

[1] Vorwenden und hoch aufblasen, pretend and
trumpet aloud that (how)," etc. Vorwenden, see p. 99, Note
7. Aufblasen, *to make a proud display of a thing.* See p. 99,
Note 7.

[2] Für welche Ehre, etc. " for which honor and benefit he
deserves in reason, and should have received, submission, gratitude,
and every favor from (he deserves, etc. *in*) the Germans. Therefore they will, perhaps, venture (sich unterwinden) to disregard (in den Wind zu schlagen) every kind of attempt to
reform them, and allow one to regard nothing but the grant of such a
Roman empire." Sich unterwinden, see p. 155, Note 3.
In den Wind zu schlagen, (*to give to the winds*), *to disregard, to despise.* Begabungen. The plural may refer to the
successive grants of the empire, made to the different emperors.

[3] Dass Jammer ist zu sagen, " that it is painful to speak
of it."

Schrift der Propheten Num. 24. und Daniel verkündiget haben, längst zerstört ist und ein Ende hat, wie Balaam Num. 24. klar verkündiget hat, da er sprach: „Es werden die Römer kommen, und die Juden verstören, und darnach werden sie auch untergehen." Und das ist geschehen[1] durch die Getas, sonderlich aber, da des Türken Reich ist angegangen, bei tausend Jahren, und ist also mit der Zeit abgefallen Asien und Afrika, darnach Frankreich, Spanien, zuletzt Venedig aufgekommen, und nichts mehr zu Rom geblieben von der vorigen Gewalt.

Da nun der Pabst die Griechen und den Kaiser zu Constantinopel, der erblich römischer Kaiser war, nicht mochte nach seinem Muthwillen zwingen, hat er ein solches Fündlein erdacht, ihn desselben Reichs und Namens zu berauben, und den Deutschen, die zu der Zeit streitbar und gutes Geschrei reich[2] waren, zuzuwenden, damit sie des römischen

---

[1] U n d  d a s  i s t  g e s c h e h e n, etc. " And this took place through the Goths, and especially when the kingdom of the Mohammedans arose, about a thousand years ago, and thus in process of time Asia and Africa fell off, and afterwards France and Spain and finally Venice arose, and, at Rome nothing of its former power remained." T ü r k e n is used here in a wide and loose sense. B e i t a u s e n d  J a h r e n qualifies g e s c h e h e n. A n g e h e n (a n g e g a n g e n) is used here, as it often is elsewhere, in the sense of *beginning.* The position of F r a n k r e i c h  u n d  S p a n i e n is ambiguous. But the construction is simple, and the sense better, to connect them with the following rather than with the preceding words. Z u  R o m is not connected with b l e i b e n, but with n i c h t s  m e h r; otherwise the dative without z u would be used.

[2] G u t e s  G e s c h r e i  r e i c h, " rich in good report," i. e. in very high repute. G e s c h r e i was once used as R u f now is, *report,* fame. See p. 42, Note 5, on both words. G e s c h r e i is still used in the sense of *report,* but only of evil report. The extensive use of the word r e i c h to express abundance, is apparent especially in such compounds as, g e i s t r e i c h, l i e b r e i c h, f i s c h r e i c h, which in old German were written separately, with the first part in the genitive. R e i c h is now commonly construed with a n, as r e i c h  a n g u t e n  W e r k e, " rich in good works."

Reichs Gewalt unter sich brächten, und von ihren Händen[1]
zu Lehen gienge.   Und ist auch also geschehen ; dem Kaiser
zu Constantinopel ist es genommen, und uns Deutschen[2] der
Name und Titel desselben zugeschrieben, sind damit des
Pabstes Knechte geworden, und ist nun ein anderes römi=
sches Reich, das der Pabst hat auf die Deutschen gebauet.
Denn jenes, das erste, ist längst, wie gesagt, untergegangen.

Also hat nun[3] der römische Stuhl, seinen Muthwillen,
(Päbste haben allezeit der Deutschen Einfältigkeit miß=
brancht,) Rom eingenommen, den deutschen Kaiser heraus
getrieben, und mit Eiden verpflichtet, nicht in Rom zu woh=
nen.   Soll römischer Kaiser seyn,[4] und dennoch Rom nicht
inne haben ; dazu allezeit in des Pabsts und der Seinen
Muthwillen hangen und weben, daß wir den Namen haben,
und sie das Land und Städte.   Denn sie allezeit unsere
Einfältigkeit mißbraucht haben, zu ihrem Uebermuth und

---

[1] Und von ihren Händen, etc. "and that (it) might proceed from their hands as a fief."   The word ihren, is used by negligence for seiner referring to Pabst.   So sie in the preceding
clause refers to the Romans, whereas, grammatically, it should refer
also to Pabst.

[2] Und uns Deutschen, etc. "and to us Germans the name
and title of it is given (ascribed) and we are (wir, understood)
thereby made slaves of the pope ; and now there is *another* (or
second) Roman empire, which the pope has built up upon the Germans."

[3] Also hat nun, etc. "Thus the apostolical chair has now
its heart's desire (viz. it has) taken Rome," etc.

[4] (Man) soll römischer Kaiser seyn, etc. "One is to
be Roman emperor and yet not have Rome under his control!   Besides, always be dependent on and interwoven with the good pleasure
of the pope and his friends, so that we have the name, and they the
country and cities'"   The preposition in instead of an with
hangen before Muthwillen, gives a peculiar shade to the idea.
It conveys the idea of an internal connection, approaching that expressed by weben, but does not imply any affection. See p. 132,
Note 3.

Tyrannei, und heißen uns[1] tolle Deutsche, die sich äffen und narren laßen, wie sie wollen.

Nun wohlan, Gott dem Herrn ist's ein kleines Ding Reich und Fürstenthum hin und her zu werfen; er ist so mild derselben,[2] daß er zuweilen einem bösen Buben ein Königreich giebt und nimmt es einem Frommen. Zuweilen[3] durch Verrätherei böser untreuer Menschen, zuweilen durch Erben, wie wir das lesen in dem Königreich Persien, Griechenland und fast allen Reichen. Und Daniel 2. und 4. sagt: „Er wohnet im Himmel, der über alle Dinge herrschet, und er allein ist es, der die Königreiche versetzet, hin und her wirft, und macht." Darum, wie Niemand kann das für groß achten, daß ihm ein Reich wird zugetheilet, sonderlich so er ein Christ ist: so mögen wir Deutschen auch nicht hochfahren,[4] daß uns ein neues römisches Reich ist zugewendet. Denn es ist vor seinen Augen eine schlechte Gabe, die er den Alleruntüchtigsten das mehrmal[5] giebt. Wie Daniel 4. sagt: „Alle die auf Erden wohnen, sind vor seinen Augen, als das Nichts ist,[6] und er hat Gewalt in allen Reichen der Menschen, sie zu geben, welchem er will."

Wiewohl nun der Pabst, mit Gewalt und Unrecht das

---

[1] Und heissen uns, etc. "and call us senseless Germans, who suffer themselves to be treated as apes and fools, according to their pleasure." On äffen and narren, see p. 108, Note 7.

[2] Mild derselben, "free or liberal in regard to them," i. e. empire and principality. For this use of mild, see p. 60, Note 2. Derselben is in the genitive, which has a very wide and loose use in the German. See p. 117, Note 1. In old German we meet with such expressions as Dankes milde, *abundant in thanks*.

[3] Zuweilen introduces a sentence, which is properly but a clause of the preceding.

[4] Hochfahren, *to be proud* (to soar high), is now used only in the participial form hochfahrend, *lofty, proud*.

[5] Das mehrmal, *more frequently*, not exactly equivalent to mehrmals, *frequently*. It is no now in use.

[6] Das Nichts ist, "that which is nothing."

römische Reich, oder des römischen Reichs Namen, hat dem rechten Kaiser beraubet, und uns Deutschen zugewendet; so ist es doch gewiß, daß Gott des Pabsts Bosheit hierin hat gebraucht, deutscher Nation ein solches Reich zu geben, und nach Fall des ersten römischen Reichs, ein anderes, das jetzt steht, aufzurichten. Und wiewohl wir der Päbste[1] Bosheit hierin nicht Ursache geben, noch ihre falschen Gesuche und Meinungen verstanden, haben wir doch durch päbstliche Tücke und Schalkheit, mit unzähligem Blutvergießen, mit Unterdrückung unserer Freiheit, mit Zusatz[2] und Raub aller unserer Güter, sonderlich der Kirchen und Pfründen, mit Dulden unerträglicher Trügerei und Schmach, solches Reich leider allzu theuer, bezahlet. Wir haben des Reiches Namen, aber der Pabst hat unser Gut, Ehre, Leib, Leben, Seele, und Alles was wir haben. So soll man die Deutschen täuschen,[3] und mit Täuschen täuschen. Das haben die Päbste gesucht,[4] daß sie gerne Kaiser wären gewesen,

---

[1] Und wiewohl wir der Päbste, etc. "And though we did not wholly give (geben for gegeben, with haben understood) cause (or occasion) to the wickedness of the popes, nor understand their false attempt and designs." Gesuch means properly *seeking through request, visit*, and undoubtedly here refers to the request of the pope that the Franks would deliver Italy.

[2] Zusatz, that which is added to a small income, to piece out a living; and hence any *additional expense.*

[3] Deutschen täuschen, a play upon the words, and hence the repetition: "So must they humbug the Wyttembergers, and give them humbug upon humbug."

[4] Das haben die Päbste gesucht, etc. "That did the popes attempt, because they would gladly have been emperors; and because they could not accomplish this, they (nevertheless) set themselves above the emperors." Das at the beginning of the sentence refers to the whole plan of the popes in respect to the Greek empire in Italy, and the sentence is explanatory of the words Gesuch und Meinungen, above. See also the last sentence of the next paragraph. The use of dass in the sense of *because,* is not very common in modern German; in old German it is more common.

und da sie das nicht haben mögen schicken, haben sie sich doch über die Kaiser gesetzt.

Dieweil denn durch Gottes Geschick und böser Menschen Gesuch,[1] ohne unsere Schuld, das Reich uns gegeben ist, will ich nicht rathen, dasselbe fahren zu lassen, sondern in Gottes Furcht, so lange es ihm gefällt, redlich regieren. Denn wie gesagt ist, es liegt ihm nichts daran,[2] wo ein Reich herkömmt, er will es dennoch[3] regiert haben. Haben es die Päbste unredlich andern genommen, so haben wir es doch nicht unredlich gewonnen. Es ist uns durch böswillige Menschen aus Gottes Willen gegeben, denselben wir mehr ansehen,[4] denn der Päbste falsche Meinung, die sie darin gehabt, selbst Kaiser und mehr denn Kaiser zu seyn, und uns nur mit dem Namen äffen und spotten.

Der König zu Babylon hatte sein Reich auch mit Rauben und Gewalt genommen, dennoch wollte Gott dasselbe regieret haben durch die heiligen Fürsten, Daniel, Anania, Asaria, Misael. Vielmehr will er von den christlichen deutschen Fürsten dieses Reich regieret haben, es habe es der Pabst gestohlen oder geraubt, oder von Neuen an[5] gemacht; es

---

Mögen stands for gemocht. See p. 24, Note 1. Schicken means *to adjust, to make a thing succeed.*

[1] Gottes Geschick und böser Menschen Gesuch. This is an alliteration, bearing some little analogy to the English proverb, "Man appoints, God disappoints."

[2] Es liegt ihm nichts daran. See p. 70, Note 2, and p. 169, Note 4. Wo ein Reich herkömmt, for woher ein Reich kömmt.

[3] Er will es dennoch, etc. "He would nevertheless have it governed (whatever be its origin)."

[4] Denselben wir mehr ansehen, "which (same) we regard more than," etc. After the words "false design of the popes," the clause, "which they had in it," is tautological. "To be themselves emperors and more than emperors," is dependent on Meinung.

[5] Von Neuen an, *anew*, from a new point of time onward. An, *onward*, is not needed here, and cannot so well qualify machen, as the idea of continued existence after it is made.

iſt Alles¹ Gottes Ordnung, welches ehe iſt geſchehen, denn wir darum haben gewußt.

Deßhalb mag ſich der Pabſt und die Seinen nicht rühmen, daß ſie deutſcher Nation haben groß Gutes gethan mit Ver= leihen dieſes römiſchen Reiches.

Zum erſten² darum, daß ſie nichts Gutes uns gegönnet haben, ſondern haben unſere Einfältigkeit darin mißbraucht, ihren Uebermuth, wider den rechten römiſchen Kaiſer zu Conſtantinopel, zu ſtärken, dem der Pabſt ſolches genommen hat, wider Gott und Recht, deß er keine Gewalt hatte.

Zum andern, daß der Pabſt dadurch nicht uns, ſondern ihm ſelbſt das Kaiſerthum zuzueignen geſucht hat, ihm zu unterwerfen³ alle unſere Gewalt, Freiheit, Gut, Leib und Seele, und durch uns (wo es Gott nicht hätte gewehret) alle Welt, wie das klärlich in ſeinen Decretalen er ſelbſt erzählt, und mit manchen böſen Tücken an vielen deutſchen Kaiſern verſucht hat. Alſo ſind wir Deutſchen hübſch deutſch gelehret; da wir vermeinet Herren zu werden, ſind wir der allerliſtigſten Tyrannen Knechte geworden, haben den Na= men, Titel und Wappen des Kaiſerthums; aber den Schatz,

---

¹ E s   i s t   a l l e s, etc. "It is all of God's ordination; it (which) took place before we had any knowledge of it."

² Z u m   e r s t e n, etc. "First they have not done us a favor, but have therein abused our simplicity in order to strengthen themselves (their arrogance) against the rightful Roman emperor at Constantinople, from whom the pope took it (the empire) contrary to (the law of) God and to justice, when he had no power over it." D e s s   genitive governed by G e w a l t.

³ I h m   z u   u n t e r w e r f e n, etc.   I h m   here, as above, for   s i c h. "To subject to himself our power, liberty, property, body and soul, and through us (if God had not prevented) all the world, as he himself has clearly expressed it in his decretals, and has made the attempt with various wicked intrigues upon many German emperors. Thus we Germans are taught in fine German (i. e. as we Germans generally are, by being wheedled). While we expected to become masters, we have become the slaves of the most insidious of tyrants; we have the name," etc.

Gewalt, Recht und Freiheit desselben hat der Pabst; so frißt der Pabst den Kern, so spielen wir mit den ledigen Schalen.

So helfe uns Gott, der solch Reich, (wie gesagt) uns durch listige Tyrannen hat zugeworfen, und zu regieren befohlen, daß wir auch dem Namen, Titel und Wappen Folge thun,[1] und unsere Freiheit, erretten, die Römer einmal lassen sehen, was wir durch sie von Gott empfangen haben. Rühmen sie sich, sie haben uns ein Kaiserthum zugewendet: wohlan,[2] so sey es also, laß ja seyn, so gebe der Pabst her Rom und Alles, was er hat vom Kaiserthum, lasse unser Land frei von seinem unerträglichen Schätzen und Schinden, gebe wieder unsere Freiheit, Gewalt, Gut, Ehre, Leib und Seele, und lasse[3] ein Kaiserthum seyn, wie einem Kaiserthum gebühret, auf daß seinen Worten und Vorgeben genug geschehe.

Will er aber das nicht thun, was spiegelficht[4] er denn mit seinen falschen erdichteten Worten und Gespügnissen? Ist sein nicht genug gewesen,[5] durch so viel hundert Jahre, die edle Nation so gröblich mit der Nase umzuführen, ohne alles Aufhören? Es folget nicht, daß der Pabst sollte über den Kaiser seyn, darum, daß er ihn krönet oder macht. Denn

---

[1] **Folge thun,** *give effect to* the name, title, and coat of arms.

[2] **Wohlan,** etc. "Very well! so be it; let it then take place; let the pope surrender Rome and whatever of the empire he has," etc.

[3] **Und lasse,** etc. "and let an empire exist, as becomes an empire, in order that his words and pretence be fulfilled."

[4] **Was spiegelficht,** etc. "Why does he make a mock-fight with his false, hypocritical words and ghostly terrors?" **Spiegelfichten,** is not now used as a verb, but it occurs as an infinitive used substantively. On **Gespügnissen,** see p. 96, Note 1.

[5] **Ist sein nicht genug gewesen?** "Has there not been enough of it?" **Sein** is in the genitive for **seiner,** and governed by **genug.** "In leading about (to lead about) for so many centuries, so savagely, the noble nation without intermission?"

**18***

der Prophet St. Samuel salbte und krönte den König Saul und David, aus göttlichem Befehl, und war doch ihnen unterthan. Und der Prophet Nathan salbete den König Salomon, war darum nicht über ihn gesetzt. Item, St. Eliseus ließ seiner Knechte Einen[1] salben den König Jehu von Israel; dennoch blieben sie unter ihm gehorsam. Und ist noch nie[2] geschehen in aller Welt, daß der über den König wäre, der ihn weihet oder krönet, denn allein durch den einigen Pabst.

Nun läßt er sich selbst drei Cardinäle krönen zum Pabst, die unter ihm sind, und ist doch nicht desto weniger über sie. Warum sollte er denn[3] wider sein eigenes Exempel und aller Welt und Schrift Uebung der Lehre sich über weltlicher Gewalt oder Kaiserthum erheben, allein darum, daß er ihn krönet oder weihet? Es ist genug, daß er über ihn ist in göttlichen Sachen, d. i.: in Predigen, Lehren, und Sacrament reichen, in welchen auch ein jeder Bischof und Pfarrherr über Jedermann ist; gleichwie St. Ambrosius in dem Stuhl[4] über den Kaiser Theodosius, und der Prophet Nathan über David, und Samuel über Saul. Darum läßt[5]

---

[1] **Liess seiner Knechte Einen**, etc. "caused one of his servants to anoint," etc. **Sie unter ihm,** "they (the prophet and his servants) remained subject to him (Jehu)."

[2] **Und ist noch nie,** etc. "And it never yet happened, in all the world, that he who consecrated or crowned a king, was superior to him, except (**denn** after **nie**) through the pope alone." **Einigen** for **einzigen.** See p. 93, Note 2.

[3] **Warum sollte er denn,** etc. "Why then should he, contrary to his own example and the practice of, all the world and of the Scriptures, exempt himself (**sich erheben**) from the teaching [in the Scriptures] respecting the civil power (i. e. subjection to it) and the empire, merely because he crowns or anoints the emperor?" **Sich erheben** governs the genitive, **der Lehre.** **Ueber** is immediately connected with **Lehre; sich** intervenes to avoid harshness.

[4] **In dem stuhl,** *in the episcopal chair,* or *pulpit,* was superior to the emperor Theodosius (i. e. would not admit him to the communion after a bloody act)," etc.

[5] **Darum lasst,** etc. "Therefore let the German emperor be

ben beutſchen Kaiſer recht und frei Kaiſer ſeyn, und ſeine
Gewalt, noch Schwert, nicht niederbrücken, burch ſolch blin=
des Vorgeben päbſtiſcher Heuchler, als ſollten ſie ausgezo=
gen, über das Schwert regieren in allen Dingen.

Das ſey bießmal genug. Denn was der weltlichen Ge=
walt und bem Abel zu thun ſey, habe ich meines Dünkens
genugſam geſagt im Büchlein von ben guten Werken. Denn
ſie leben auch und regieren, baß es wohl beſſer taugte.[1]
Doch iſt kein Gleichen, weltlicher und geiſtlicher Mißbräuche,
wie ich baſelbſt angezeigt habe.

Ich achte auch wohl,[2] baß ich hoch geſungen habe, viel
Ding vorgegeben, das unmöglich wird angeſehen, viel
Stücke zu ſcharf angegriffen. Wie ſoll ich ihm aber thun?
Ich bin es ſchuldig zu ſagen. Könnte ich, ſo wollte ich auch
alſo thun. Es iſt mir lieber, die Welt zürnet mit mir, benn
Gott; man wird mir je nicht mehr benn das Leben können
nehmen. Ich habe bisher vielmal Friede angeboten meinen
Widerſachern; aber, als ich ſehe, Gott hat mich burch ſie
gezwungen, das Maul immer weiter aufzuthun, und ihnen,

---

a true and free emperor, and let neither his power nor his sword be
trampled down through such blind pretences of the papal hypocrites,
as if they should be made an exception (a u s g e z o g e n with
w e r d e n understood) and should in all things rule over the sword,
or civil power." N i e d e r d r ü c k e n has, perhaps, an accusative,
J e m a n d, understood before it, " let no one put down his power,"
etc. R e g i e r e n is connected, by u n d understood, to a u s-
g e z o g e n w e r d e n.

D a s s e s w o h l b e s s e r t a u g t e, etc. " that the state of
things may be improved, (literally, *that it might, perhaps, better be
worth something*). Still there is no comparison between (of) the civil
and religious abuses."

[2] I c h a c h t e a u c h w o h l, " I am well aware that I have
sung on a high key, and have brought forward many a thing which
will be regarded as impossible (and I shall be considered as) having
assailed many points too severely. But how ought I to act in regard to it? I am bound to speak out. If it were in my power, it
was my wish so to do (to represent the matter truly)."

weil fie unmüffig find, zu reden, bellen, fchreien[1] und fchreien
genug geben.    Wohlan, ich weiß noch ein Liedlein von Rom
und von ihnen; jucket ihnen das Ohr, ich will es ihnen auch
fingen, und die Noten auf's Höchfte ftimmen.    Verftehefft
du mich wohl, liebes Rom, was ich meine?

Auch habe ich mein Schreiben vielmal auf Erkenntniß
und Verhör erboten, das Alles nichts geholfen.[2]    Wiewohl
auch ich weiß, fo meine Sache recht ift, daß fie auf Erden
muß verdammt und allein von Chrifto im Himmel muß ge=
rechtfertiget werden.    Denn das ift die ganze Schrift,[3] daß
der Chriften und Chriftenheit Sache allein von Gott muß
gerichtet werden, ift auch noch nie eine von Menfchen auf
Erden gerechtfertigt, fondern ift allzeit der Widerpart zu
groß und ftark gewefen.    Es ift auch meine allergrößte
Sorge und Furcht daß meine Sache möchte unverdammt
bleiben, daran ich gewißlich erkennet, daß fie Gott noch nicht
gefalle.    Darum laß nur frifch einhergehen, es fey Pabft,
Bifchöfe, Pfaff, Mönch oder Gelehrter; fie find das rechte
Volk, die da follen die Wahrheit verfolgen, wie fie allezeit
gethan haben.    Gott gebe uns Allen einen chriftlichen Ver=
ftand, und fonderlich dem chriftlichen Abel deutfcher Nation,
einen rechten geiftlichen Muth, der armen Kirche das Befte
zu thun, Amen.*

Zu Wittenberg im Jahre 1520.

---

[1] Zu reden, bellen schreien und schreien, are all
dependent on genug geben, "compelled me to open my mouth
wider and wider; and, since they are restless, to give them enough
to say, to bark and to cry and cry."

[2] Das Alles (hat) nichts geholfen. "I have often offered my writings for examination and trial; all that has done no good."

[3] Denn das ist die ganze Schrift, "for this is the
(teaching of the) whole Bible, that the cause of Christians and of
Christianity must be vindicated by God alone; never was one
(cause, etc ) justified by men, but the opposition has always been the
greater and stronger party."

* Before taking leave of this piece, we must quote the following observation from Marheineke :    Wie diese Schrift den Feinden Luthers

## AN ADDRESS TO THE MAGISTRATES AND COMMON COUNCILS OF ALL THE CITIES OF GERMANY IN BEHALF OF PUBLIC SCHOOLS.

𝕾𝖈𝖍𝖗𝖎𝖋𝖙 𝖆𝖓 𝖇𝖎𝖊 𝕭ü𝖗𝖌𝖊𝖗𝖒𝖊𝖎𝖘𝖙𝖊𝖗 𝖚𝖓𝖇 𝕽𝖆𝖙𝖍𝖘𝖍𝖊𝖗𝖗𝖚 𝖆𝖑𝖑𝖊𝖗 𝕾𝖙ä𝖇𝖙𝖊 𝕯𝖊𝖚𝖙𝖘𝖈𝖍𝖑𝖆𝖓𝖇𝖘, 𝖇𝖆𝖘𝖘 𝖘𝖎𝖊 𝖈𝖍𝖗𝖎𝖘𝖙𝖑𝖎𝖈𝖍𝖊 𝕾𝖈𝖍𝖚𝖑𝖊𝖓 𝖆𝖚𝖋𝖗𝖎𝖈𝖍𝖙𝖊𝖓 𝖚𝖓𝖇 𝖍𝖆𝖑𝖙𝖊𝖓 𝖘𝖔𝖑𝖑𝖊𝖓. 𝕬𝖓𝖓𝖔 1525.*

---

𝕲𝖓𝖆𝖇𝖊 𝖚𝖓𝖇 𝕱𝖗𝖎𝖊𝖇𝖊 𝖛𝖔𝖓 𝕲𝖔𝖙𝖙 𝖚𝖓𝖘𝖊𝖗𝖒 𝕹𝖆𝖙𝖊𝖗 𝖚𝖓𝖇 𝕳𝖊𝖗𝖗𝖓

---

eine willkommene Ursach zu neuer Lästerung war, so gereichte sie viel frommen Gemüthern zu wahren Erbauung und Ergötzlichkeit. Sie war in jeder Rücksicht in Ton und Haltung, in Kraft und Lebendigkeit eine wahrhaft teutsche Volksschrift zu nennen. Das reinste und edelste Interesse an dem Wohl des Volks und dem Heil der gemeinen Christenkeit sprach aus ihr und liess in gut gesinnten Gemüthern keinen Misbrauch zu. Die scharfen, hellen, blühenden Farben des Styls gaben ihr einen hohen Reiz. Was Tausende längst dunkel gefühlt, oder sich zu sagen gefürchtet hatten, stand hier in kräftigen, grossen Zügen gezeichnet, vor den Augen der ganzen Welt. Auch war die Aufnahme derselben ihren gewichtvollen Inhalte angemessen; Schon im September (it was written in June) waren viertausend Exemplare davon unter dem Volk verbreitet.—*Geschichte der teutschen Reformation.* I. 162.

* This truly philanthropic and patriotic address is given entire, with the exception of a few short polemic passages. The ablest German writer on education, says : In Luthers Schriften findet sich sehr vieles über Erziehung in Predigten, Bibelerklärungen, Briefen, Tischreden ; einzelne Stücke handeln nur von diesem Thema. Bald wendet er sich an den Aeltern, bald an die Obrigkeit, bald an den Lehrstand und redet allen aufs Eindringlichste zu, sich doch die Kinder auzunehmen, indem er ihnen Segen und Fluch vorlegt, Segen der guten, Fluch der bosen Kinderzucht. Zugleich giebt er die treflichsten Lehren, wie es mit der Zucht zu halten sey, was und wie die Kinder lernen sollen, etc.—Wen sollte es nicht freuen, den grossen Mann auch als Reformator des deutschen Erziehungswesens kennen zu lernen ? Seine Ermahnungen gingen unzähligen Deut-

Jeſu Chriſto. Fürſichtige,[1] weiſe, liebe Herren, wiewohl ich nun[2] wohl drei Jahre verbannet und in die Acht gethan, hätte ſollen ſchweigen, wo ich Menſchen-Gebot mehr, denn Gott, geſcheuet hätte ; wie denn auch viel in deutſchen Län-dern, beide groß und klein, mein Reden und Schreiben, aus derſelben Sache noch immer verfolgen, und viel Blut darü-ber vergießen ; aber weil[2] mir Gott den Mund aufgethan hat, und mich heißen reden, dazu ſo kräftiglich bei mir ſte-het, und meine Sache, ohne meinen Rath und That, ſo viel ſtärker macht, und weiter ausbreitet, ſo viel ſie mehr toben, und ſich gleich ſtellet, als lache und ſpotte er ihres Tobens, wie der 2. Pſalm ſagt. An welchem allein merken mag, wer nicht verſtockt iſt, daß dieſe Sache muß Gottes eigen ſeyn. Sintemal ſich die Art göttliches Worts und Werfs hier ereignet, welches allezeit denn am meiſten zunimmt, wenn man es auf das Höchſte verfolget und dämpfen will :

Darum[2] will ich reden (wie Eſaias ſagt) und nicht ſchwei-

---

ſchen zu Herzen, weckten ſchlafende Gewiſſen und ſtärken müde Hände ; ſeine Urtheile galten bei Fürſten und Völkern wie Gottes Stimmen.—*Karl von Raumer, Geſchichte der Pädagogik.* I. 137, and 189.

[1] Fürsichtige, *prudent,* for vorsichtige. See p. 6, Note 4.

[2] Wiewohl ich nun — Aber weil — Darum. Several im-perfect sentences occur here, which must be joined into one period in order to make out the sense. "Although I, having been put under the ban and outlawed for three years, should be obliged to keep si-lence, had I respected the command of man more than that of God (as many, indeed, both great and small, in the German territories, from that cause, assail incessantly what I have said and written, and shed much blood on that account), yet since God has opened my mouth, and bidden me to speak, and moreover stands by me so firm-ly, and, without any counsel or effort of mine, strengthens and ex-tends my cause the more, the more they rage, and acts as if he held their rage in derision and contempt, as the second Psalm, v. 4, says. (By which alone, one may perceive if he is not rendered obdurate, that this cause must be God's own. For here the peculiar manner of God's word and work appears, which always spreads most when

gen, weil[1] ich lebe, bis daß Christi Gerechtigkeit ausbreche, wie ein Glanz, und seine heilwärtige[2] Gnade wie eine Lampe angezündet werde.  Und bitte euch nun alle, meine lieben Herrn und Freunde, wollet[3] diese meine Schrift und Ermahnung freundlich annehmen und zu Herzen fassen. Denn ich sey gleich[4] an mir selber wie ich sey, so kann ich

men most oppose it and seek to check it) ; therefore will I speak," etc. Hätte sollen. See p. 148, Note 3. — Viel as a neuter is more terse than viele would be. Aus derselben Sache, i. e. Ursache. — Darüber refers to Reden and Schreiben. Mir den Mund, "the mouth to me," is the proper German idiom, for " my mouth." See p. 18, Note 7. — Rath und That. See p. 44, Note 2. — Sich gleich stellen als, " to place or demean one's self as if." — An welchem. See p. 80, Note 3. — Eigen is used after a genitive just as it is after a possessive pronoun, sein eigen, for example. See p. 119, Note 2. — Sich ereignet, *occurs*, is somewhat harsh as applied to Wort. The idea is : " the manner in which God ordinarily disseminates his word and carries on his work is obvious or takes place here." — Denn and wenn, *then* and *when*, are still used with reference to time, though dann and wann are more commonly so used. — Am meisten, *most*, is here clearly distinguished from meistens, *mostly, for the most part.* See p. 171, Note 3, end.

[1] Weil, *while.* This use of the word is obsolete. It now means, *because.* Dieweil underwent a similar change of signification. See p. 104, Note 1.

[2] Heilwärtige, *saving*, obsolete for heilbringend.

[3] Und [ich] bitte — [dass Ihr] wollet.

[4] Ich sei gleich, etc. " be I, in myself, as I may," or " though (gleich) I be as I may, in myself." The proper and literal meaning of the word gleich is *like, equal.* It is, indeed, identical with *like*, being compounded of leich, and the prefix ge. When used with another particle of comparison, it is commonly to be translated, *just, even.* Then, as applied to time, it means *equal in time*, i. e. *instantly, immediately.* See p. 21, Note 3. From this last signification is derived that of *yet*, i. e. an *immediate* consequence, which is expressed by the word itself, and an *adversative* relation to what precedes, which it borrows of course, from the connection. In such cases, the word doch might be substituted for gleich, without affecting the sense.

doch[1] vor Gott mit rechtem Gewiſſen rühmen, daß ich darin=
nen nicht das Meine[2] ſuche, welches viel beſſer möchte mit
Stillſchweigen überkommen;[3] ſondern meine es von Her=
zen[4] treulich mit euch und ganzem deutſchen Lande, dahin
mich Gott verordnet hat, es glaube[5] oder glaube nicht, wer
da will. Und will eure Liebe[6] das frei und getroſt zugeſagt

---

[1] S o   k a n n   i c h   d o c h, etc.  D o c h implies a concession to
the prejudice of the reader. " For be I, in myself, as I may (in the
wrong on other subjects, if you choose), *still* I can," etc.

[2] D a s   M e i n e, *my own, my own interest.*  Comp. p. 70, Note
8.  When the possessive adjective pronouns are used substantively,
which is indicated by their beginning with a capital, the word e i-
g e n cannot be added.  Thus we could not say, m e i n   E i g n e s,
*my own,* instead of d a s   M e i n e.  But when they are used adjectively or as predicates, e i g e n can be added to give them empha-
ses; as m e i n   e i g e n e s   H a u s; d a s s   s i e   s e i n   e i g e n
s e y n   s o l l t e n, *that they should be his own.*  Even to a genitive,
e i g e n may be added merely to give it emphasis, as G o t t e s
e i g e n, *God's own.*  See p. 119, Note 2, end.

[3] U e b e r k o m m e n as an active verb, in the sense of b e k o m-
m e n though now obsolete, is frequently used by Luther.  See Dan.
4: 33.  Rom 9: 31, and 2 Pet. 1: 1, in his version.  In the sense of,
*to fall upon, to overtake, to befall,* it is no longer in common use.  As
a neuter verb, it means, *to cross* or *pass over, to arrive, to come to
hand.*  It is employed provincially in Upper Germany in the sense of,
*to agree, to make a contract.*  It is now beginning to be used of that
which is *handed down to us from antiquity,* as writings, fragments, etc.

[4] ( I c h )   m e i n e   e s   v o n   H e r z e n.  This profession of sin-
cerity stands connected with the conviction that God had raised him
up to be a benefactor to Germany — d a h i n   m i c h   G o t t   v e r-
o r d n e t   h a t.

[5] E s   g l a u b e, etc. " believe (it) or not, whoever will."  E s is
not in the accusative, governed by g l a u b e, but an expletive, employed merely because the nominative comes after its verb.  See p
52, Note 1.  G l a u b e is in the subjunctive.

[6] U n d   ( i c h )   w i l l   e u r e   L i e b e (i. e. e u c h )   d a s, etc.
" And I desire to have this freely and confidently said and declared
to you (or I wish you distinctly to understand this, namely), that, if,"
etc.  E u r e   L i e b e, is a pulpit phrase, used in addressing an au-

und angeſagt haben, daß ihr, wo ihr mir hierin gehorchet, ohne Zweifel nicht mir, ſondern Chriſto gehorchet ; und wer mir nicht gehorchet, nicht mich, ſondern Chriſtum verachtet.

Derohalben[1] bitte ich euch alle, meine lieben Herrn und Freunde, um Gottes willen und der armen Jugend willen, wollet[2] dieſe Sache nicht ſo geringe machen, wie Viele thun, die nicht ſehen, was der Welt Fürſt gedenket.[3] Denn es iſt eine ernſte und große Sache, da Chriſto und aller Welt viel anliegt, daß[4] wir dem jungen Volke helfen und rathen.

---

dience, " your love" instead of " my dear hearers," (m e i n e G e l i e b t e) the abstract for the concrete. If the punctuation of the text is correct, it is necessary to regard the words as the indirect object of the following participles, and as being, from negligence, put in the accusative instead of the dative, so that the sense would be given by substituting e u c h.— A n g e s a g t, *announced to*, is a more formal and elevated expression than z u g e s a g t, *said to*. This difference of meaning arises from the different nature and use of the two prepositions, a n and z u. These participles are not connected with h a b e n as their auxiliary, but they are used adjectively with d a s, which is governed by h a b e n. Comp. p. 15, Note 6.

[1] D e r o h a l b e n, *therefore*, is an obsolete word, used only in formal or solemn style. It is derived from h a l b e n, *on account of*, and d e r o (an old genitive plural of d e r,) *these things*. D e s w e g e n is now used in both numbers in place of it. Compare d e r h a l b e n p. 8, Note 2, and p. 4, Note 2.

[2] (D a s s i h r) w o l l e t.— D e r W e l t F ü r s t, " the prince of the world," or satan. In such constructions, the article (d e r) always belongs to the first of the two substantives, and is consequently in the genitive. See p. 17, Note 1.

[3] G e d e n k e t. G e d e n k e n was in the Middle Ages equivalent to d e n k e n, *to think*. But from the collective or frequentative force of the particle g e, it came to signify, *to have in mind, to keep in mind, to intend*, as in this passage. Thence, the derivative signification, to show by some act, whether kind or unkind, that one kept in mind, or remembered something past, i. e. *to requite a favor*, or *an injury*. To these leading significations of the word it is easy to trace all those which are to be found in the lexicons.

[4] D e n n e s i s t— d a s s, etc. E s refers to the clause introduced by d a s s. " It (namely, that we aid and counsel the young)

19

Damit ist denn auch uns und allen geholfen[1] und gerathen. Und deuket, daß solchen,[2] stillen, heimlichen tückischen An= fechtungen des Teufels will mit dem großem christlichen Ernst gewehret seyn.[3] Liebe Herrn, muß man jährlich[4] so

is a serious and important matter in which (d a) Christ and all the world are deeply concerned." Comp. p. 103, Note 1.

[1] D a m i t   i s t — u n s — g e h o l f e n.   The German abounds much more than the English in the *impersonal* use of passive verbs, as does also the Latin.

[2] S o l c h e n, refers to a description in a passage, which is omit- ted here.

[3] W i l l — g e w e h r e t   s e y n, "it is necessary to ward off." It is impossible to represent the structure of this highly idiomatic sen- tence by anything corresponding to it in English. W i l l   g e w e h- r e t   s e y n is impersonal, and governs the dative A n f e c h t u n- g e n. — There are many idiomatic expressions formed, from the pe- culiar use of the word w o l l e n.   It expresses 1. *a wish*, as, W a s w i l l s t   d u   v o n   m i r ?   "What do you wish of me ?" or *inclina- tion*, as, E r   w i l l   n i c h t   d a r a n, "he has no inclination to do it;" E r   w o l l e   o d e r   w o l l e   n i c h t, *nolens, volens;* E s   w i l l s i e   N i e m a n d, "nobody will have her." 2. *Intention*, as, W a s w i l l   e r   d a m i t   h a b e n ?   "What is he after?" "What is he seeking for?" W a s   w o l l e n   S i e   d a m i t   s a g e n ?   "What do you mean by that?" 3. *Assertion*, or *affirmation ;* as, E r   w i l l e s   s e l b s t   g e h ö r t   h a b e n.   "He declares that he heard it himself," or *belief*, as, D a s   w o l l e n   j e n e   g a r   n i c h t, "They will not admit that." 4. *On the point of doing something ;* as, E r w o l l t e   e b e n   w e g g e h e n, "He was just on the point of go- ing away." E r   w i l l   s t e r b e n, "He is at the point of death." 5. *Demand, requisition*, as, D e r   K r i e g   w i l l   v i e l   G e l d, "War requires much money." 6. *Supposition*, or *concession for ar- gument's sake ;* as, I c h   w i l l   m i c h   e i n m a l   g e i r r t   h a b e n, "Suppose, then, that I am mistaken." 7. *Contingency*, or *indiffer- ence ;* as, D e m   s e i,   w i e   i h m   w o l l e, "be that as it may" (let it be in respect to that, as it will). 8. *It is used pleonastically ;* as, D a s   w i l l   v i e l   s a g e n, "That is much, or is important." H u n d e r t   T h a l e r   w o l l e n   w e n i g   s a g e n, "A hundred dollars are but little."

[4] M u s s   m a n   j ä h r l i c h, etc.   "If we (one) must annually ex- pend so much on rifles, roads, bridges, dams and many other similar

viel wenden an Büchsen, Wege, Stege, Dämme und der=
gleichen unzählige Stücke mehr, damit eine Stadt zeitlichen
Frieden und Gemach[1] habe ; warum sollte man nicht viel=
mehr doch auch[2] so viel wenden an die dürftige arme Ju=
gend, daß man einen geschickten Mann oder zwei zu Schul=
meistern hielte.

Denn Gott der Allmächtige hat fürwahr uns Deutschen[3]

---

things, etc., why should we not, etc. ?'' W e n d e n signifies *to turn*,
in general; k e h r e n, *to turn*, more commonly in the specific
sense of *turning about*, or assuming the opposite direction; d r e -
h e n, *to turn around a centre or axis.* S i c h a n j e m a n d e n
w e n d e n means *to apply to one*, to come to him for something.
D e n R ü c k e n w e n d e n, *to go away from one, to turn from him
and leave him.* G e l d a u f e t w a s w e n d e n, *to expend money
for a thing ;* G e l d a n e t w a s w e n d e n, *to expend money on
or for anything.* F l i n t e is the ordinary word for *gun*, and
B ü c h s e, the name for a *rifle.* The former is so named from the
*flint* used in striking fire ; the latter from the barrel of the gun, regarded as a *box.* S t e g properly means *any long and narrow piece
of wood*, which will explain several uses of the word in the mechanical arts. Next it signifies *a plank or narrow bridge* across a ditch,
or river. It is sometimes used for S t e i g, *a path.* D e r g l e i c h e n,
though used adverbially, is properly a genitive plural, governed by
S t ü c k e.

[1] G e m a c h, in the old German, means *convenience, repose.* Compare the adjective g e m a c h, and the compound, U n g e m a c h.
It now signifies an *apartment for repose, or convenience*, and hence is
used mostly of palaces, or poetically when applied to ordinary rooms
or apartments. Luther here uses it in its ancient signification, *repose, quiet.*

[2] V i e l m e h r d o c h a u c h. Such an exuberance of particles
would hardly be admitted in English ; and yet they all have their
force in German. Omitting them all, we should translate the passage, " Why not apply as much ?" A u c h, modifies the expression
to *even as much.* D o c h added, makes it, " Why not, however, apply," etc. ; and v i e l m e h r, " Why not, however, rather apply
even as much," etc. But this is tautological in English.

[3] U n s D e u t s c h e n. D e u t s c h e n, coming after the pronoun u n s, is of the new, or third declension. In themselves con

jeßt gnädiglich daheim gesuchet, und ein rechtes goldenes
Jahr[1] aufgerichtet.[2]  Da[3] haben wir jeßt die feinsten,[4] ge=
lehrtesten, jungen Gesellen[5] und Männer, mit Sprachen
und aller Kunst gezieret, welche so wohl Nußen schaffen[6]
könnten, wo man ihr brauchen wollte, das junge Volk zu

---

sidered, these two words might be either in the dative or in the accusative.  But h e i m s u c h e n, and its equivalent d a h e i m  s u -
c h e n, govern the accusative.  This verb was formerly used in an
indifferent sense, *to visit either with good or with evil.*  Here it is
used in the former sense.  But, at the present day, it is used only in
the latter sense, as, " to visit with a rod."

[1] G o l d e n e s  J a h r, *a golden year*, is here used indefinitely of
time.

[2] A u f g e r i c h t e t.  A u f r i c h t e n signifies literally *to raise,
to erect, to build.*  See p. 5, Note 2.  Applied to things of an imma-
terial, or abstract nature, as a *covenant, doctrine*, etc., it means *to
establish, to bring into existence.*  See Ezek. 16: 60.  Rom. 1: 5, and
2 Cor. 5: 19, in Luther's version.  Also, *to raise up, to support, to
comfort.*

[3] D a  is here an expletive.

[4] D i e  f e i n s t e n.  See p. 24, Note 4.

[5] G e s e l l e n is derived from s a l, *a hall*, or in the old German houses, " a large lower room, where persons ate, played and
lept together."  G e s e l l, therefore, meant originally *an inmate ;*
and afterwards, *an associate.*  Hence, S c h l a f g e s e l l, *a bed-fel-
low ;*  S p i e l g e s e l l, *a playmate ;*  S t u b e n g e s e l l, *a room-
mate ;*  J u n g g e s e l l, *a bachelor, an unmarried man* (originally, as
in this passage, *a young gentleman*) ;  G e s e l l s c h a f t, *society.*
In early times, the word G e s e l l was used in an honorable sense ;
but now it is more commonly used in a low sense ; as, D i e b s g e-
s e l l, *an associate with thieves.*  In a restricted sense, it means a
*journeyman mechanic.*  G e f ä h r t e, *an associate*, literally means *a
traveling companion ;* and in its wider signification, it means, *an
associate in any enterprise.*  G e n o s s, from G e n i e s s e n, *to enjoy*, means *an associate in something agreeable*, though in many ap-
plications of the word, the idea of enjoyment is nearly lost.

[6] N u t z e n  s c h a f f e n does not mean *to derive benefit to one's
self*, but *to be useful to others.*  S o  w o h l, *so well*, i. e. *very well.*

lehren.[1] Iſts nicht vor Augen,[2] daß man jetzt einen Knaben in drei Jahren zurichten[3] kann, daß er in ſeinem fünfzehnten Jahre oder achtzehnten Jahre mehr kann,[4] denn
bisher alle hohe Schulen[5] und Klöſter gekonnt haben? Ja,
was hat man gelernet in hohen Schulen und Klöſtern bisher, denn nur[6] Eſel, Klötze und Blocke werden? Zwanzig,
vierzig Jahre hat einer gelernet, und hat noch weder lateiniſch noch deutſch gewußt. Ich ſchweige das ſchändliche lä-
ſterliche Leben, darinnen die edle[7] Jugend ſo jämmerlich verdorben iſt.

---

[1] Z u  l e h r e n, is dependent on N u t z e n  s c h a ff e n, "which
could be so useful in teaching (to teach) the young, if one would employ them."

[2] V o r  A u g e n, like *ante oculos*, in Latin, *before one's eyes, obvious.*  A u s  d e n  A u g e n, *out of sight.*  I n  d i e  A u g e n, *in
one's sight or observation.*  But a n  d e n  A u g e n, refers to
something as *observable in the eye itself, physically.*  One may dis-
cover another's emotion a n  d e n  A u g e n, as the place where it
is betrayed.  This meaning grows out of the peculiar nature and use
of the preposition, a n.  See p. 80, Note 3.

[3] Z u r i c h t e n.  See p. 50, Note 2, near the end.  This word,
which generally signifies *to prepare*, is sometimes employed in the
sense of instructing or qualifying a person for a certain place or service.  Isa. 43: 21, and Eph. 4: 12, in Luther's version.  It is often
used in a bad sense, like the vulgar English phrase, " to fix one out,"
i. e. to beat him severely, or to injure his person or appearance in any
way.

[4] K a n n is frequently used, as it is here, in the sense of *knowing.*
See the lexicons.

[5] H o h e  S c h u l e n signifies *universities*, as distinguished from
gymnasia and other schools.  *High School*, in English, has a very
different import.

[6] W a s — d e n n  n u r, *what but.*

[7] E d l e.  E d e l is generally, as here, used in a moral sense,
*noble, generous;* when applied to persons of rank, it includes both
the higher and the lower nobility.  A d e l i g, *noble*, designates the
lower nobility, or those lower than a G r a f and higher than a
B ü r g e r.

**19\***

Aber nun[1] uns Gott so reichlich begnadet,[2] und solcher Leute die Menge[3] gegeben hat, die das junge Volk sein lehren und ziehen mögen, wahrlich so ist's Noth, daß wir die Gnade Gottes nicht in Wind schlagen[4] und lassen ihn nicht umsonst anklopfen. Er stehet vor der Thür, wohl uns, so[5] wir ihm aufthun; er grüßet uns, selig der ihm antwortet. Versehen wir es,[6] daß er vorüber gehet, wer will ihn wiederholen?

Lasset uns unsern vorigen Jammer ansehen und die Finsterniß, darinnen wir gewesen sind. Ich achte, daß Deutschland noch nie so viel von Gottes Wort gehöret habe, als jetzt, man spüret je nichts in der Historie davon. Lassen wir es[7] denn so hingehen ohne Dank und Ehre, so ist's zu besorgen,[8] wir werden noch gräulicher Finsterniß und Plage

---

[1] N u n. See p. 12, Note 4.

[2] B e g n a d e t.  B e g n a d e n is an obsolete word, for which b e g n a d i g e n is now in common use. It means *to show favor to*. It is an active verb, as nearly all which have the prefix b e, are, and, of course, u n s is in the accusative.   This prefix not only converts neuter verbs into active verbs, but is used in forming verbs from substantives and adjectives, as in English.

[3] S o l c h e r  L e u t e  d i e  M e n g e, *an abundance of such people*.   Observe the peculiar use of the word M e n g e with the *definite* article.   Z i e h e n is frequently used by Luther where e r z i e h e n, *to educate*, would now be employed.

[4] I n  W i n d  s c h l a g e n.  See p. 202, Note 2.

[5] W o h l  u n s, s o, etc. "happy are we, if we open to him." S e l i g  d e r, "happy is he who."

[6] V e r s e h e n  w i r  e s, etc. "If we disregard it, so that he pass by, who will recall him (bring him back)?" V e r s e h e n, *to see wrong*, means also, *to overlook, to neglect;* and hence, as a substantive, it means *an oversight, an error.*

[7] L a s s e n  w i r  e s, not here in the sense of l a s s e t  u n s, as it is sometimes, but of w e n n  w i r  l a s s e n.

[8] S o  i s t  e s  z u  b e s o r g e n, *then it is to be feared.*   In such expressions, where the passive form of the verb is more commonly required in English, the active form is employed in German.   Thus, E r  i s t  n i r g e n d s  z u  f i n d e n, "he is nowhere to be found;"

leiden. Lieben Deutschen,[1] kaufet weil der Markt vor der Thüre ist, sammlet ein, weil es scheinet und gut Wetter ist, brauchet Gottes Gnade und Wort, weil es da ist.[2] Denn das[3] sollt ihr wissen, Gottes Wort und Gnade ist[4] ein fahrender Platzregen, der nicht wieder kommt, wo er einmal gewesen ist. Er ist bei den Juden gewesen, aber hin ist hin,[5] sie haben nun nichts. Paulus brachte ihn in Griechenland, hin ist auch hin; nun haben sie[6] den Türken. Rom und Lateinischland hat ihn auch gehabt, hin ist hin; sie[6] haben nun den Pabst. Und ihr Deutschen[7] dürft nicht denken,

---

er ist zu loben, "he is to be praised." It is probably out of this use of the infinitive that the present participle, as a future passive, sprung; as der zu lobende Schüler, "the praiseworthy scholar," the scholar that is to be commended; die zu fürchtende Gefahr, "the danger that is to be feared." E s, in this passage, refers to the clause immediately following. For the omission of the conjunction dass, and the corresponding change of the construction, see p. 11, Note 4.

[1] Lieben Deutschen. Present usage would require liebe Deutschen, in the vocative plural. The addition of the *n*, is a Thuringian peculiarity. See p. 169, Note 3.

[2] Weil es da ist, "while it is here at hand." Da, has a signification intermediate between hier and dort; that is, it points out a place not so near as hier, nor so remote as dort. Therefore, it *may* stand for either of those.

[3] Das, *this*, refers to the following clause. As dass is omitted in this clause, the latter is not inverted. Comp. p. 11, Note 4.

[4] Ist with two nominatives. See p. 93, Note 4, and p. 112, Note 5. Fahrender Platzregen, *a moving shower*. Platzregen, *a heavy local shower*, in opposition to Landregen, *a wide-spread rain*.

[5] Hin ist hin, literally, *gone is gone*, or *lost is lost*, i. e. what is lost is lost, or *he is gone*.

[6] Sie refers to the inhabitants of Griechenland and Lateinischland. This latter word is antiquated, for which Italien is now used.

[7] Ihr Deutschen, *ye Germans*. The old or full form of declension is necessary to the adjective, whenever no declinable article, adjective, or pronoun precedes it, or when these are themselves im-

daß ihr ihn ewig haben werdet, denn der Undank und Verachtung wird ihn nicht laſſen bleiben.[1]  Darum greifet zu[2] und haltet zu, wer greifen und halten kann, faule Hände müſſen ein böſes Jahr haben.

Gottes Gebot treibet durch Moſes ſo oft und fordert, die Eltern ſollen die Kinder lehren, daß[3] auch der 78. Pſalm ſpricht: „Wie hat er ſo hoch[4] unſern Vätern geboten, den Kindern kund zu thun, und zu lehren Kindes Kind.“  Und das weiſet auch aus[5] das vierte Gebot Gottes, da er der Eltern Gehorſam den Kindern ſo hoch gebeut,[6] daß man auch durchs Gericht tödten ſoll ungehorſame Kinder.  Und warum leben wir Alten anders, denn daß wir des jungen Volks warten,[7] lehren und aufziehen ?  Es iſt nicht möglich, daß ſich das tolle Volk[8] ſollte ſelbſt lehren und warten ; dar-

---

perfect in their declension.  In all other cases, the new or imperfect form of declension may be used.  Here D e u t s c h e n  is preceded by the personal pronoun  I h r,  which clearly indicates the case, and hence the form  D e u t s c h e  is not needed.  See Gram. p. 118, 3.

[1]  N i c h t   l a s s e n   b l e i b e n,  "will not let it remain,"  will drive it away.  In such expressions,  l a s s e n  ordinarily stands at the end of the sentence.

[2]  D a r u m   g r e i f e t   z u,  etc.  "Therefore seize and hold, whoever can."  W e r,  on account of its indefinite sense, *whoever*, is referred to in the preceding imperatives, as though it were a plural. The reader will not fail to perceive the stirring eloquence of this passage.

[3]  S o   o f t — d a s s,  *so often that.*

[4]  H o c h,  *above what is ordinary*, in a high degree, or earnestly. The word, in this sense, is now but little used.  S o   h o c h,  is not here a direct comparison, but indirect—*so earnestly* (i. e. as he does). This idiom is common to the German and the English.

[5]  W e i s e t — a u s,  a compound verb,  a u s w e i s e n,  *to show, to prove.*  "And the fourth commandment of God shows this, where," etc.

[6]  G e b e u t,  obsolete for  g e b i e t e t.  See Gram. p. 203 supra.

[7]  W a r t e n.  See p. 39, Note 2.  From the primary signification, *to watch*, is derived that of *attending to, taking care of.*

[8]  D a s   t o l l e   V o l k,  that is, *the giddy youth.*  W a r t e n  does

um hat sie uns Gott befohlen,[1] die wir alt und erfahren sind, was ihnen gut ist, und wird gar schwere Rechnung von uns für dieselben fordern. Darum auch Moses befiehlt Deut. 32. und spricht: „Frage deinen Vater, der wird dir es sagen, die Alten werden dir es zeigen."

Wiewohl es Sünde und Schande ist, daß dahin[2] mit uns kommen ist, daß wir allererst[3] reizen und uns reißen lassen

---

not, like l e h r e n, govern s i c h, but it stands without its object, s e i n e r or s e i n being understood.

[1] S i e u n s — b e f o h l e n, etc. " has commended them to us, who are old and experienced as to what (or, who know what) is good for them." D i e w i r, *who.* See Gram. p. 157.

[2] D a s s d a h i n, etc. " that it has come to this with us, that we must now arouse (ourselves) and be aroused, to educate our children and youth, and to consider their interests; whereas, nature itself should move us to this, and the example of the heathen variously instruct us." K o m m e n for g e k o m m e n.

[3] A l l e r e r s t, (*first of all*) *not till now.* See p. 16, Note 2. E r s t stands connected with the old English *erst,* as e h e r does with *ere.* But the manner in which the words e r s t and a l l e r-e r s t are sometimes used is very peculiar. " E r s t, s c h o n and n o c h, when they qualify the predicate itself, are all adverbs of *time.* E r s t then indicates the priority of one act to another; as, m a n s o l l e r s t d e n k e n, d a n n s p r e c h e n, "one should first think, then speak." S c h o n means *already.* N o c h means *still.* But when these words do not qualify the predicate itself, but relate to some other word, e r s t expresses limitation, and is synonymous with n i c h t f r ü h e r or n i c h t m e h r; as, E r i s t e r s t g e s t e r n a n g e k o m m e n, " he did not arrive till yesterday;" E r i s t e r s t z e h n J a h r a l t, " he is but ten years old." But s c h o n, in such a use of it, means *not later than, not less than;* while n o c h, if it relates to *time,* limits the duration of an occurrence; as, E r w i r d n o c h h e u t e k o m m e n, " he will yet come to-day (not later)." I c h h a b e i h n n o c h g e s t e r n g e s e h e n, " I saw him as late as yesterday." Where n o c h refers to quantity, it conveys the idea of a climax, like the English word *still.—Heyse's Schulgrammatik,* p. 292. We add a few more examples of the use of e r s t, as it is difficult to explain it sufficiently by rules. J e t z t a l l e r e r s t b i n i c h g e k o m m e n, " I have but just

ſollen, unſere Kinder und junges Volk zu ziehen, und ihr
Beſtes bedenken, ſo doch daſſelbe uns die Natur ſelbſt ſollte
treiben, und auch der Heiden Exempel uns mannigfäl=
tig weiſen. Es iſt kein unvernünftig Thier, das ſeiner
Jungen nicht wartet und lehret, was ihnen gebühret;[1]
ohne der Strauß,[2] davon Gott ſagt Hiob 39.: „Daß er
gegen ſeine Jungen ſo hart iſt, als wären ſie nicht ſein,
und läßt ſeine Eier auf der Erde liegen."[3] Und was hilft

now come." Jetzt erst, "not till now." Er hat erst angefangen, "he has just begun (not before)." Erst jetzt
merke ich's, "I just begin to perceive it." Erst übers
Jahr, "not till next year." Er ist erst auf der Hinrei-
se, "he has just started on a journey." In the passage before us,
allererst conveys the idea that there has been negligence,—
" that we must now (in regard to that which ought to have been done
long ago), after all that God and nature have taught, need, or begin,
to arouse ourselves and to be aroused." Ziehen, in the sense of
erziehen.

[1] Gebühret, *belongs to them*, in the sense of, " it is due to or
from them." Gehören, *to belong*, as a part does to the whole.
Hence, " to be essentially, properly, or justly connected with." Zu-
stehen, *to belong to*, i. e. to be the proper part of, to be fitting to a
*voluntary agent*. Dem Alter gebühret Ehrerbeitung
und es steht der Jugend zu diese jenem zu weisen.

[2] Ohne der Strauss, da Gott von, "Except the ostrich, of
which," etc. Ohne, see p. 147, Note 1.—Da—von, see p. 130,
Note 3.

[3] Als wären sie nicht sein, und lässt seine Eier liegen. According to present usage, when the possessive adjective
pronouns are used as a *predicate*, and the subject to which they belong, is a *substantive* or a *distinct and definite personal pronoun*, they
are not declined. See sein in the sentence above. But if they are
not in direct agreement with the subject, but merely refer to it in an
*indefinite* way, especially by the use of the indefinite pronoun es,
they are then declined; as, Wem gehöret der Hut—die
Feder—das Buch? Er—sie—es ist mein. Here es is a
neuter pronoun referring to a *neuter* substantive. But let es be used
indefinitely referring to any one of the three genders, and then the

es,[1] daß wir sonst[2] alles hätten und thäten, und wären gleich eitel Heiligen, so wir das unterwegs laſſen, darum wir allermeist leben, nämlich : des jungen Volks pflegen. Ich halte auch, daß unter den äußerlichen Sünden die Welt vor Gott von keiner[3] so hoch beſchweret iſt, und so gräuliche Strafe verdienet, als eben von dieſer, die wir an den Kindern thun, daß wir ſie nicht ziehen.

O wehe der Welt immer und ewiglich. Da werden täglich Kinder geboren und wachſen bei uns daher,[4] und iſt

answer will be; es ist meiner—meine—meines. But the forms der meine, der meinige, etc. with the definite article, never *agree* with a substantive expressed or understood, but *merely refer to one going before*; or they are used as substantives and are written with a capital; es dein Bruder ist mit dem meinigen ausgegangen; or Du hast das Deinige gethan, "you have done your part;" die Meinigen lassen sich Ihnen und den Ihrigen empfehlen, "my family (parents, children, relations) send their respects to you and yours."

[1] Und was hilft es, etc. "And of what avail will it be, that we should have and do everything else, and be like pure saints, if we neglect that for which we chiefly live, namely, to take charge of the young?" Etwas unterwegen lassen, is the same as unterlassen, but is now a provincialism. Was hilft's? is equivalent to, "What good will it do?"

[2] Sonst and anders are both rendered by the word *otherwise ;* but they are very different words.—Anders means, *in another manner.* Sonst means, *aside from this*, and hence, *in other respects*, or *at another time.*

[3] Von keiner (Sünde). Hoch, *highly, in a great degree.* See p. 224, Note 4. "I consider, that among outward offences, the world is, in God's view, so heavily laden with none, and, for none deserves so severe punishment, as for this which we commit against children in that we do not educate them." How strong the author's convictions, and how just his views of the necessity of popular education!

[4] Wachsen—daher, *grow up.* Daher, *hence*, in composition with verbs has the accent on the second syllable (her) and conveys the idea of approach, — *hither*, or motion *from* another place and *towards* us. Sometimes the idea of approach is nearly lost, and

leiber Niemand, der sich des armen jungen Volks annehme und regiere, da lässet man es¹ gehen, wie es gehet.

Ja sprichst du, solches alles² ist den Eltern gesagt, was gehet das die Rathsherrn und Obrigkeit an ; ist recht gere= det,³ ja, wie wenn die Eltern aber solches nicht thun ? Wer soll es denn thun ? Soll es darum nach bleiben,⁴ und die

---

along, without particular reference to the *direction*, expresses nearly the force of the word, when applied in its literal sense to motion, and *up* or *off*, when used figuratively ; as d a h e r f a h r e n, *to drive along ;* d a h e r p r a n g e n, *to show off.*

¹ E s is not here a personal pronoun referring definitely to V o l k, but it is used indefinitely and impersonally ;—" and things are suffered to go as they do." See p. 164, Note 1.

² S o l c h e s  a l l e s, etc. " all that is said to parents ; what does that concern the members of the council, and the magistrates ?" R a t h s h e r r, in the time of Luther, meant, *a senator,* or *a member of the city council.* This council was originally a kind of senate, consisting ordinarily of about twenty or thirty persons, chosen from the higher or noble families. Not far from Luther's time, the wealthy classes of burghers had been admitted, and thus this senate sunk to the character of a common city council. The B ü r g e r m e i s t e r sometimes one, and sometimes two in a city, was the head of this council, and chief magistrate, to whom the abstract term, O b r i g k e i t is often applied. Below this smaller council stood a larger council or popular assembly, whose concurrence was necessary on certain subjects of common interest.

³ I s t  r e c h t  g e r e d e t, etc. " That is all true (that is rightly said, namely, that parents are under obligation to educate their children) ; but how, if parents do not attend to it ? Who shall do it then ?" J a, can be omitted in the translation, when there is an adversative particle, like a b e r or a l l e i n, in the sentence. If there be no adversative particle, in such interrogative clauses after a concessive clause, j a itself must be regarded as an adversative, and translated by *but.* Literally, j a corresponds nearly to the word *well,* used concessively, as " *Well,* but how if parents do not attend to it." But it is redundant in English.

⁴ N a c h  b l e i b e n, *to remain unnoticed, to be passed by.* But it is used in familiar phrase, and the corresponding English expression would be, " Shall we therefore let it alone ?" So the words, s o

Kinder versäumet werden? Wo will sich da die Obrigkeit und Rath entschuldigen,[1] daß ihnen solches nicht sollte gebühren? Daß es von den Eltern nicht geschieht, hat mancherlei Ursache:

Auf's Erste, sind auch etliche nicht so fromm und redlich,[2] daß sie es thäten,[3] ob sie es gleich könnten, sondern, wie die Straußen härten sie sich auch gegen ihre Jungen, und lassen es dabei bleiben,[4] daß sie die Eier von sich geworfen und Kinder gezeuget haben, nicht mehr thun sie dazu. Nun diese Kinder[5] sollen dennoch unter uns und bei uns leben in gemeiner Stadt. Wie will denn nun Vernunft und sonderlich christliche Liebe das leiden, daß sie ungezogen[6] aufwachsen, und den andern Kindern Gift und Geschmeiße[7] seyn,

---

mag's nachbleiben, "well, then, let it alone." Versäumet, see p. 174, Note 1.

[1] Wo will sich da—entschuldigen, etc. "How will the magistrates and council excuse themselves [and make it appear] that such a duty does not belong to them?" Wo for wie is now provincial. On will in the singular, see p. 93, Note 4. After entschuldigen, there is no ellipsis in German. But the word *excuse*, in English, cannot be immediately followed by such a phrase as, "that it should not."

[2] Fromm und redlich. See p. 49, Note 2, and p. 22, Note 5. Sondern, p. 2, Note 7.

[3] Dass sie es thäten, *as to do it*, that they should do it.

[4] Dabei bleiben, "stop, or break off with this, viz. that," etc. Damit could not be used for dabei, in such connections. Mit diesem would be an equally gross Anglicism.

[5] Nun diese Kinder, etc. "Now these children must nevertheless live in the same town among us and with us. How then can reason and, most of all, Christian charity suffer (this) that," etc. A free translation in order to give the sense more fully.

[6] Ungezogen means, *ill-bred;* unerzogen, *uneducated*, and sometimes, *not yet grown up, not an adult.*

[7] Geschmeisse, *the eggs of vermin.* In its widest sense, it means whatever is cast forth from the body. Hence it means either *filth*, or the *eggs* or *brood of winged-insects*. It therefore often stands for *vermin*, for which, however, the more modern word Ungezie-

damit zuletzt eine ganze Stadt verderbet, wie es denn zu
Sodom und Gomorrä und Gaba, und etlichen mehr Städ=
ten ergangen ist.

Auf's Andere,[1] so ist der größte Haufen der Eltern leider!
ungeschickt dazu,[2] und nicht wissen, wie man Kinder ziehen
und lehren soll. Denn sie selbst[3] nichts gelernet haben,
ohne den Bauch versorgen; und gehören sonderliche Leute
dazu, die Kinder wohl und recht lehren und ziehen sollen.

Auf's Dritte, obgleich die Eltern geschickt wären, und woll=
ten es gerne selbst thun, so haben sie vor[4] anderen Geschäfte
und Haushaltung weder Zeit noch Raum dazu, also daß die
Noth zwinget, gemeine Zuchtmeister für die Kinder zu hal=
ten. Es wollte denn ein Jeglicher für sich selbst einen Eig=
enen halten. Aber das würde dem gemeinen Mann zu
schwer, und würde abermal[5] mancher seiner Knabe um Ar=
muths willen versäumet. Dazu sterben so viele Eltern,
und lassen Waisen hinter sich, und wie dieselben durch Vor=
münde versorget werden, ob uns die Erfahrung[6] zu wenig

---

fer is more commonly employed. The latter is less expressive of
loathsomeness than the former when both relate to vermin. Luther
compares uneducated children to *a nest of young vermin.*

[1] A u f's  a n d e r e. "In the second place." See p. 2, Note 6.

[2] U n g e s c h i c k t  d a z u, "unqualified for it." See p. 145,
Note 2.—N i c h t  w i s s e n, would by present usage be required to
stand thus; w i s s e n  n i c h t.

[3] D e n n  s i e  s e l b s t, etc. "For they themselves have learned nothing except to provide for their stomachs; and a distinct class
of persons are required for this purpose, who shall," etc.

[4] V o r. *On account of.* This preposition often denotes a cause acting upon the subject or agent and obstructing his activity. See Gram.
p. 356. "Still, on account of business and household affairs they
have neither time nor space for it, so that necessity requires," etc.—
E s  w o l l t e  d e n n, *unless each one would.*

[5] A b e r m a l, *again, on the other hand.* See p. 35, Note 6.

[6] O b  u n s  d i e  E r f a h r u n g, etc. "even if experience did not
sufficiently teach us (were not enough), this (circumstance, viz.) that
God calls himself the father of the orphans, as of those who are neglected by every body else, should teach us."

wäre, follte uns das wohl zeigen, daß sich Gott selbst der
Waisen Vater nennet, als derer, die von Jedermann sonst
verlassen sind. Auch sind etliche, die keine Kinder haben,
die nehmen sich auch darum nichts an.[1]

Darum will es hier dem Rath und der Obrigkeit gebüh=
ren,[2] die allergrößeste Sorge und Fleiß auf das junge Volk
zu haben. Denn weil der ganzen Stadt Gut, Ehre, Leib
und Leben ihnen zu treuer Hand befohlen ist,[3] so thäten sie
nicht reichlich[4] vor Gott und der Welt, wo sie der Stadt
Gedeihen und Besserung nicht suchten mit allem Vermögen
Tag und Nacht. Nun liegt einer Stadt Gedeihen nicht al=
lein darin, daß man große Schätze sammle, feste Mauern,
schöne Häuser, viele Büchsen und Harnischzeuge;[5] ja, wo
deß viel[6] ist, und tolle Narren daruber kommen,[7] ist so viel

---

[1] Nehmen sich — an.  See p. 55, Note 2.

[2] Gebühren.  See p. 226, Note 1.

[3] Ihnen zu treuer Hand befohlen ist, "is committed to
their trust." This is an idiomatic expression. The pronoun in the
dative expresses the persons to whom, and zu the object for which,
it was committed. Stadt is governed by the following substantives,
all which, being regarded as constituting a whole, are construed with
a verb in the singular number.

[4] So thäten sie nicht reichlich, etc. "they would not
do enough (richly, sufficiently), i. e. they would be held recreant before God and the world, if they should not seek," etc.

[5] Harnisch (harness), "what is worn upon the body for pro-
tecting it in battle." It includes everything below the helmet.
Panzer, *a coat of mail*, is a part of a Harnisch, covering the
body, but not the limbs. Kürass, for which Luther and the older
writers often use Krebs, is a *breast-plate*. Harnischzeuge,
means the various coverings worn as armor.

[6] Dess viel, *much of this.*

[7] Darüber kommen, *come upon them, come in possession of
them.* Darüber itself means, *about, concerning* or *for that; upon*
or *during that; over and above that;* and *across;* and generally modifies the verb to which it is prefixed by adding to it one or more of
these significations. Examples; darüber arbeiten, 1. *to labor
beyond* (what is required). 2. *to labor on a thing;* darüber bauen,

deſto ärger und deſto größerer Schade derſelben Stadt,
ſondern das iſt einer Stadt beſtes und allerreichſtes Gedei=
hen, Heil und Kraft, daß ſie ſo viel[1] feiner, gelehrter, ver=
nünftiger, ehrbarer, wohlgezogener Bürger hat, die können
darnach wohl Schätze, und alles Gut ſammeln, halten und
recht brauchen.

Weil denn eine Stadt ſoll und muß Leute[2] haben, und
allenthalben der größte Gebreche, Mangel und Klage iſt,
daß es an Leuten fehle, ſo muß man nicht harren, bis ſie

---

to build (active) *upon a thing,* or (neuter) *during a time;* d a r ü b e r
b i e t e n, *to overbid, outbid;* d a r ü b e r b r i n g e n, 1. *to bring over*
or *across.* 2. *to bring more* (than is necessary); d a r ü b e r g e h e n,
1. to *pass* or *go over* or *across.* 2. *to go about a work.* 3. *to excel* or
*surpass;* d a r ü b e r h a l t e n, 1. *to hold* one thing *over* another. 2.
*to estimate highly.* 3. *to hold on to, to observe* (a usage), *to preserve, to
cherish;* d a r ü b e r h e r g e h e n, 1. *to go at or about a work.* 2. *to
blame, to assail;* d a r ü b e r h i n g e h e n, *to pass over* (ordinarily
*in silence*); d a r ü b e r h i n m a c h e n, *to run over a work hastily and
lightly;* d a r ü b e r h i n s e h e n, 1. *to look beyond a thing.* 2. *to overlook* or *neglect;* d a r ü b e r m a c h e n, *to do over and above;* d a r ü-
b e r s i c h m a c h e n, like d a r ü b e r g e h e n, or h e r g e h e n, *to
apply one's self to, to begin a work;* d a r ü b e r s c h r e i b e n, 1. *to
superscribe.* 2. *to write about,* or *treat upon;* d a r ü b e r s c h w i m-
m e n, 1. *to swim at the top.* 2. *to swim across;* d a r ü b e r s e t z e n,
1. *to set* or *place one upon a thing* or *over a business.* 2. *to carry one
across a place.* 3. *to prefer one to another;* d a r ü b e r s e y n, 1. *to excel.* 2. *to be busied with;* d a r ü b e r w e g s e y n, 1. *to be,* or *to have
gone through a business or trouble.* 2 *not to need a thing, not to be
troubled about it;* d a r ü b e r k o m m e n, 1. *to rise above, to excel.* 2.
*to go beyond, to rise* (in price). 3. *to fall upon, to happen to come to.*
4. *to begin, to take in hand, to take away.* With these illustrations, it
will not be difficult to make out any other similar combinations.—
" Where there is much of this, and reckless fools come into possession of them (upon them), it is so much the worse." V i e l appears to be redundant.

[1] D a s s (s i e) s o v i e l, etc. " that it have many — citizens who,"
etc. S o merely gives intensity to v i e l.

[2] L e u t e, (*skilful*) *people.*—G e b r e c h e for which d a s G e-
b r e c h e n is now used.

ſelbſt wachſen ; man wird ſie auch weder aus Steinen hauen, noch aus Holz ſchnitzeln ; ſo wird Gott nicht Wunder thun, ſo lange man der Sachen durch andere ſeine dargethane Güter gerathen[1] kann.   Darum müſſen wir dazu thun,[2] und Mühe und Koſt daran wenden, ſie ſelbſt[3] erziehen und machen.   Denn wes iſt die Schuld, daß es jetzt in allen Städten ſo dünne ſiehet[4] von geſchickten Leuten, ohne der Obrigkeit, die das junge Volk hat laſſen aufwachſen, wie das Holz im Walde wächſet, und nicht zugeſehen, wie man es lehre und ziehe ?   Darum iſt[5] es auch ſo unordentlich ge-

---

[1] G e r a t h e n.   See p. 156, Note 2.   "God will not perform a miracle, so long as men can attain their object (things) through his other benefits shown."   At present the preposition z u generally fol-lows this verb, instead of the genitive.

[2] D a z u   t h u n.   See p. 94, Note 4.   D a z u, when prefixed to verbs, generally signifies, 1. *to that.* 2. *in addition to that.* 3. *to that end.* E. g.   d a z u   b r a u c h e n means, 1. *to need for that.* 2. *to apply to that object.* 3. *to use at the same time,* or *in addition to ;*  d a z u   e s s e n, 1. (neuter) *to eat while doing something else.* 2. (active) *to eat one ar-ticle of food with,* or *in addition to another ;*  d a z u   h a l t e n, 1. (ac-tive) *to keep or employ a person for a certain object or business.* 2. (re-flective), *to hasten.* 3. *to follow, to belong to the sect or party of.*  D a-z u   k a u f e n, 1. *to purchase in addition to.* 2. *to purchase for a spe-cific object ;*  d a z u   k o m m e n, *to come to, to fall upon, to happen ;* e s k o m m t   d a z u   d a s s, *accedit quod* or *ut,* add to this *;*  d a z u   g e-h e n, 1. *to go to.* 2. (in music) *to fall,* or *strike in with.*   Nearly all other instances of the use of this particle with verbs may be ex-plain-ed after the analogy of these examples.

[3] S e l b s t, belongs not to  s i e, which is in the accusative, but to the subject of the verb, " to educate them and form them ourselves."

[4] D a s s   e s — s o   d ü n n e   s i e h e t.   " Whose fault is it that at present, in all the cities so few skilful people are seen (it looks so thin of skillful people) except of the magistrates, who have left the youth to grow up like wood in the forest, and have not taken notice how they are taught and educated ?   L e h r e and z i e h e are in the sub-junctive, because they refer not to the view of the *author* which was definite, but to the *ignorance* and *uncertainty of the magistrates.*

[5] D a r u m   i s t's, etc.   " Therefore has it grown so irregularly

**20\***

wachſen, daß zu keinem Bau, ſondern nur ein unnützes Ge=
hege, und nur zum Feuerwerk tüchtig iſt.

Es muß doch weltlich Regiment bleiben. Soll man denn[1]
zulaſſen, daß eitel Rülzen und Knebel regieren, ſo man es
wohl beſſern kann, iſt je ein wildes unvernünftiges Fürneh=
men. So laß man eben ſo mehr[2] Säne und Wölfe zu
Herrn machen, und ſetzen über die, ſo nicht denken wollen,
wie ſie von Menſchen regieret werden. So iſt es auch eine
unmenſchliche Bosheit, ſo man nicht weiter denkt; denn al=
ſo: wir wollen jetzt regieren, was gehet uns an, wie es de=
nen gehen werde, die nach uns kommen. Nicht über Men=
ſchen, ſondern über Säue und Hunde ſollten ſolche Leute re=
gieren, die nicht mehr denn ihren Nutzen und Ehre im Regi=

---

that it furnishes no timber (is good for no building), but is a useless
hedge, and good only for fuel."

[1] So ll m a n d e n n, etc. "If then we should permit that perfect dolts and stocks should rule, when we can prevent it (make it
better), it would be a barbarous and brutal undertaking." R ü l s for
R ü l p s, *belching; one that belches, a sottish fellow.*

[2] So' l a s s m a n e b e n s o m e h r, etc. "Then let us rather
make swine and wolves rulers, and set them over those who will not
think how they are [to be] governed by men (i. e. under what rulers
they shall live). It is a barbarous crime, if one thinks of nothing
farther than this; viz. We will now reign; — what does it concern
us how it shall be with those who come after us?"—G e h e t — a n.
A n g e h e n, as an active verb, means 1. *to address one's self to a
thing or to a person to take hold of, to apply to.* 2. (impersonally, for
the most part), *to concern, to relate to.* As a neuter verb, it means, *to
begin, to go on, to succeed, or prosper.*—d e n e n g e h e n. See p. 23,
Note 5.—The word s o at the beginning of these two sentences, may
be rendered by *thus,* or *then,* or they may be omitted in the English.
At the commencement of several of the clauses which occur here, it
menns, *if,* and in one of them (d i e, s o n i c h t d e n k e n) it is a relative pronoun. This word, in its various uses, and with the various intonations which it receives in conversation (expressing, assent, surprise, doubt, etc.), has a great diversity of significations.
It would of itself be no mean test of one's knowledge of German.

ment ſuchen. Wenn man gleich den höchſten Fleiß fürwen=
det,[1] daß man eitel ſeine gelehrte, geſchickte Leute erzöge zu
regieren, es würde dennoch Mühe und Sorge genug haben,
daß es wohl zuginge.[2] Wie ſoll es denn zugehen, wenn man
da gar nichts zuthut?[3]

Ja, ſprichſt du abermal,[4] ob man gleich ſollte und müßte
Schulen haben ; was iſt uns aber nütze lateiniſche, grie=
chiſche und ebräiſche Zungen und andere ſreie Künſte zu leh=
ren ? Könnten wir doch[5] wohl deutſch die Bibel und Got=
tes Wort lehren, die uns genugſam iſt zur Seligkeit? Ant=
wort : ja ich weiß leider wohl, daß wir Deutſchen müſſen
immer Beſtien und tolle Thiere ſeyn und bleiben,[6] wie uns
denn die umliegenden Länder nennen, und wir auch wohl
verdienen. Mich wundert aber, warum wir nicht auch ein=
mal[7] ſagen : was ſoll[8] uns Seide, Wein, Gewürze, und der

---

[1] Fürwendet for vorwendet. See p. 136, Note 1.—Eitel,
see p. 110, Note 4.

[2] Zuginge. See p. 130, Note 2.

[3] Zu thut. See p. 163, Note 5.

[4] Ja, sprichst du abermal. See p. 228, Note 3, and p. 230,
Note 5.

[5] Könnten wir doch, etc. is not a direct question, but an affirmation, with a point of interrogation, which is equivalent to the interrogation, " Should we not ?" in English. " We could still teach
the Bible and the word of God in German, which is enough for our
salvation, [could we not ?]." Such sentences are common in German.

[6] Seyn und bleiben. These two words are very often coupled
together in German for the sake of emphasis, though they express
but one idea.

[7] Einmal. See p. 48, Note 2.

[8] Sollen. See p. 123, Note 2. " Of what use to us are silk,
wine, spices and [other] foreign articles, since we ourselves have
wine, corn, wool, flax, wood and stone in the German States not only an abundance of it for sustenance, but a choice and selection of it
for embellishment and ornament." Die Fülle is construed like
die Menge. See p. 222, Note 3. When it is preceded by words
expressing the material to which it refers, these words may be either
n the genitive or in the accusative. The former is the more eleva-

fremben ausländischen Waaren, so wir doch selbst Wein, Korn, Wolle, Flachs, Holz und Steine in deutschen Ländern nicht allein die Fülle haben zur Nahrung, sondern auch die Kühr[1] und Wahl zu Ehren und Schmuck? Die Künste und Sprachen, die uns ohne Schaden, ja größerer Schmuck, Nutzen, Ehre und Frommen sind,[2] beide zur heiligen Schrift zu verstehen und weltlich Regiment zu führen, wollen wir verachten; und die ausländischen Waaren, die uns weder noth noch nütze sind, dazu uns schinden bis auf den Grath, der wollen wir nicht entrathen; heißen das nicht billig deutsche Narren und Bestien?

Zwar,[3] wenn kein anderer Nutzen an den Sprachen wäre,

---

ted, the latter more colloquial; as, B r o d e s u n d W e i n e s d i e F ü l l e, "an abundance of bread and wine," or B r o d u n d W e i n d i e F ü l l e, "bread and wine [in] abundance."

[1] K ü h r or K ü r, *choice, election*, is now most frequently found in compounds, as W i l l k ü r, *arbitrium*, and K ü r f ü r s t, *elector*.

[2] D i e u n s o h n e S c h a d e n—s i n d, etc. "which are harmless, nay a greater ornament, benefit, honor and advantage [than are those things] both for the understanding of the Scriptures and for managing the civil government, we are disposed to despise; and with foreign articles, which are neither necessary nor useful to us, [and which] besides strip us to the very back bone, with these we are unwilling to dispense. Does not that make us deserve the name of German duncemany and brutes?"—O h n e S c h a d e n is used as a predicate after s i n d, much as the following nominatives are.—F r o m m e n, see p. 49, Note 2.—Z u r h e i l i g e n S c h r i f t, "for the Holy Scriptures, to understand them," i. e. for understanding the Scriptures and for managing the civil government.—G r a t h or G r a t, for which R ü c k g r a t is now more common. D e r is for d e r e r.—H e i s s e n d a s n i c h t b i l l i g d e u t s c h e N a r r e n u n d B e s t i e n. On the use of d a s, see p. 110, Note 3, and Gram. p. 303. "Are not these reasonably called," etc. equivalent in sense to, "Do they not deserve to be called," or "Is that not being German fools and brutes."

[3] Z w a r is compounded of z u w a h r, *in truth*, and is written separately in old German. Z w a r, f r e i l i c h and w o h l are used

ſollte doch uns das[1] billig erfreuen und anzünden, daß er[2] ſo eine edle, ſeine Gabe Gottes iſt, damit uns Deutſchen Gott jetzt ſo reichlich, faſt über alle Länder, heimſuchet[3] und begnadet.    Man ſiehet nicht viel,[4] daß der Teufel dieſelben hätte laſſen durch die hohen Schulen und Klöſter auffkommen ; ja ſie haben allezeit auf das Höchſte dawider getobet, und auch noch toben.    Denn der Teufel roch den Braten wohl : wo die Sprachen hervor kämen, würde ſein Reich ein Fach gewinnen, das er nicht wieder leicht könnte zuſtopfen. Weil er nun nicht·hat mögen wehren, daß ſie hervor kämen, denket er doch ſie nun alſo ſchmal zu halten, daß ſie von

---

as concessive particles, meaning, *indeed* or *to be sure*, and are generally followed by an adversative (d o c h, a b e r, etc.) in the next clause.  They differ thus ; Z w a r, expresses *certainty;* f r e i l i c h, *unhesitating concession,* or *obviousness ;* w o h l, *probability.*

[1] D a s, like *hoc* in Latin, refers often to a following clause.  See p. 223, Note 3.

[2] E r refers *grammatically* to N u t z e n.  In sense, it is more general.

[3] H e i m s u c h e t.  See p. 219, Note 3.  B e g n a d e t.  See p. 222, Note 2.

[4] V i e l, *much, in many instances.*  The sense is ; " We do not find in many instances, that Satan allowed them (the languages) to flourish by means of the universities and cloisters ; nay more, they have always raged most violently against them, and do so still ; for Satan got the scent of it, that if the languages should come into vogue, his kingdom would have a hole made in it, which he could not easily stop up again.  But as he could not prevent them from coming up, he intends, at least, to keep them within such narrow limits, that they will of themselves waste away and fall.    In these, no welcome guest has entered his house ; therefore, he desires to give him such dry picking, that he will not stay long.  Very few, dear sirs, of our people perceive this mischievous trick of Satan."—R o c h  d e n B r a t e n is a phrase corresponding to the French, *sentir de loin la fricassée,* and the English, *to smell a rat.*—F a c h has here a peculiar meaning and is used in the sense of L o c h.—W e h r e n  d a s s.  See p. 98, Note 7.—U n s e r, *of us,* is governed by w e n i g.

ihnen selbst wieder sollen vergehen und fallen. Es ist ihm nicht ein lieber Gast damit ins Haus gekommen, darum will er ihn auch also speisen, daß er nicht lange solle bleiben. Diesen bösen Tück des Teufels sehen nnser gar wenig, lieben Herrn.

Darum, lieben Deutschen, lasset uns hier die Augen auf= thun, Gott danken für das edle Kleinod, und fest darauf halten,[1] daß es uns nicht wieder entzogen werde, und der Teufel nicht seinen Muthwillen büsse. Denn das können wir nicht leugnen, daß, wiewohl das Evangelium allein durch den heiligen Geist ist gekommen, und täglich kömmt, so ist es doch durch Mittel der Sprachen gekommen, und hat auch daburch zugenommen, muß auch daburch behalten werden. Denn gleich als da[2] Gott durch die Apostel wollte in alle Welt das Evangelium lassen kommen, gab er die Zungen dazu ; und hatte auch zuvor durch der Römer Regi= ment die griechische und lateinische Sprache so weit in alle Länder ausgebreitet, auf daß sein Evangelium je bald fern und weit Frucht brächte. Also hat er jetzt auch gethan. Niemand hat gewußt, warum Gott die Sprachen hervor ließ kommen,[3] bis daß man nun allererst[4] siehet, daß es um des Evangelii willen geschehen ist, welches er hernach hat wollen[5] offenbaren, und daburch des Endechrists Regiment

---

[1] Fest darauf halten, *hold on to it, take pains to preserve it, to cherish it.*—Büsse. This verb not only signifies *to mend, to make good, to atone for*, but also *to satiate, to gratify ;* and so here.

[2] Gleich als da, *immediately when.*

[3] Hervor liess kommen, instead of hervor kommen liess.

[4] Allererst. See p. 225, Note 3.

[5] Hat wollen. The verbs dürfen, können, mögen, müssen, sollen, wollen, lassen, as also heissen, helfen, hören, sehen, and sometimes lehren and lernen, have this peculiarity that the *infinitive* is used in the place of the *perfect parti- ciple* (after an auxiliary) when another verb in the infinitive is de- pendent on them. See p. 24, Note 1, end.

aufdecken und zerſtören. Darum hat er auch Griechenland den Türken gegeben, auf daß die Griechen, verjaget und zerſtreuet,[1] die griechiſche Sprache ausbrächten, und ein Anfang würde, auch andere Sprachen mit zu lernen.

So lieb nun als uns das Evangelium iſt, ſo hart laſſet uns über den Sprachen halten.[2] Denn Gott hat ſeine Schrift nicht umſonſt allein in die zwei Sprachen ſchreiben laſſen, das alte Teſtament in die Ebräiſche, daß Neue in die Griechiſche. Welche nun Gott nicht verachtet, ſondern zu ſeinem Wort erwählet hat vor allen andern, ſollen auch wir dieſelben[3] vor allen andern ehren. Denn St. Paulus rühmet das für eine ſonderliche Ehre und Vortheil der ebräiſchen Sprache, daß Gottes Wort darinnen gegeben iſt, da er ſprach Röm. 3: „Was hat die Beſchneidung Vortheil oder Nutzen? Faſt[4] viel. Auf's Erſte, ſo ſind ihnen Gottes Rede befohlen." Das rühmet auch der König David, Pſ. 147: „Er verkündiget ſein Wort Jakob, und ſeine Gebote und Rechte Iſrael. Er hat keinem Volk alſo gethan, noch ſeine Rechte ihnen offenbaret." Daher auch die ebräiſche Sprache heilig heißet. Und St. Paulus Röm. 1. nennet ſie die heilige Schrift, ohne Zweifel um des heiligen Worts Gottes willen, das darinnen verfaſſet iſt. Alſo mag

---

[1] Verjaget und zerstreuet, participles used adjectively. " In order that the Greeks, driven away and dispersed, should carry the Greek language abroad, and that a beginning be made to learn other languages also at the same time (mit)."

[2] Hart—über den Sprachen halten. Ueber etwas halten is the same in sense as auf etwas halten. Compare darauf halten p. 238, Note 1, and darüber halten p. 231, Note 7. " So dear as the gospel is to us, so zealously let us cherish the languages."

[3] Welche—dieselben. " What languages (or such languages as) God has not despised, but chosen for his word in preference to all others, *these* we also should honor more than all other languages." See p. 44, Note 3.

[4] Fast. See p. 153, Note 4.

auch die griechische Sprache wohl heilig heißen, daß[1] dieselbe
vor andern dazu erwählet ist, daß das neue Testament dar=
innen geschrieben würde. Und aus derselben,[2] als aus
einem Brunnen, in andere Sprache durchs Dolmetschen ge=
flossen, und sie auch geheiliget hat.

Und lasset uns das gesagt seyn,[3] daß wir das Evangelium
nicht wohl werden erhalten ohne die Sprachen. Die
Sprachen sind die Scheide, darinnen dieß Messer des Geistes
steckt. Sie sind der Schrein,[4] darinnen man dieß Kleinod
trägt. Sie sind das Gefäß, darinnen man diesen Trank
fasset. Sie sind die Kemnot,[5] darinnen diese Speise liegt.
Und wie das Evangelium selbst zeigt, sie sind die Körbe, da=
rinnen man diese Brodte, und Fische und Brocken behält.
Ja wo wir es versehen,[6] daß wir (da Gott vor sey)[7] die
Sprachen fahren lassen, so werden wir nicht allein das
Evangelium verlieren, sondern wird auch endlich dahin ge=

---

[1] D a s s, *because.*

[2] U n d  a u s  d e r s e l b e n, etc. " and from this language as from
a fountain it (the New Testament) has flowed into other languages
and sanctified them also."

[3] U n d  l a s s e t  u n s  d a s  g e s a g t  s e y n, "and let this be kept
in mind ; literally, " and let this be said to us." But g e s a g t is not
a *passive* with s e y n, which would require g e s a g t  w o r d e n
s e y n, but it is used adjectively. "Let this be regarded as said or
settled."

[4] S c h r e i n, (English *shrine*, Latin *scrinium*), *a box*, or *casket*, is
more used in poetry than in prose.

[5] K e m n o t, or K e m n a t e, *a store-house*, so used only in the
old German. It commonly means, *a house, room*, or *chamber*.

[6] V e r s e h e n. See p. 222, Note 6.

[7] D a  G o t t  v o r  s e y, *which may God forbid.* D a — v o r for
d a v o r. One is represented as hindering a thing *by being before it.*
See p. 230, Note 4. Compare the word *prevent.* " Indeed, if we are
so negligent as to let the languages go, (if we neglect it, so that we
let, etc.)—which may God prevent—then we shall not only lose the
gospel, but it will finally turn out (or come to this) that," etc. D a=
h i n  g e r a t h e n. See p. 38, Note 3.

rathen, daß wir weder Lateinisch noch Deutsch recht reden oder schreiben können. Deß laßt uns[1] das elende gräuliche Erempel zur Beweisung und Warnung nehmen in den ho=. hen Schulen und Klöstern, darinnen man nicht allein das Evangelium verlernet, sondern auch lateinische und deutsche Sprache verderbet hat, daß die elenden Leute schier zu lauter Bestien geworden sind, weder deutsch noch lateinisch recht reden oder schreiben können, und beinahe auch die na= türliche Vernunft verloren haben.

Darum haben es die Apostel auch selbst für nöthig an= gesehen, daß sie das neue Testament in die griechische Sprache fasseten und anbänden, ohne Zweifel, daß sie es uns daselbst sicher und gewiß verwahrten, wie in einer heili= gen Lade. Denn sie haben gesehen[2] alle dasjenige, das zu= künftig war, und nun also ergangen ist; wo es allein in die Köpfe gefasset würde, wie manche wilde, wüste, Unordnung und Gemenge, so mancherlei Sinnen, Dünkel und Lehren sich erheben würden in der Christenheit, welchen in keinem Wege zu wehren, noch die Einfältigen zu schützen wären, wo nicht das neue Testament gewiß in Schrift und Sprache ge= fasset wäre. Darum ist es gewiß, wo nicht die Sprachen bleiben,[3] da muß zuletzt das Evangelium untergehen.[4]

---

[1] D e s s  l a s s t  u n s, etc. " Of this let us take as a proof and as a warning, the wretched and shocking example [presented] in the universities," etc. L a s s t for l a s s e t. On z u, see p. 78, Note 4, and p. 104, Note 6.

[2] D e n n  s i e  h a b e n  g e s e h e n, etc. " For they all foresaw that which was then future, and which now has taken place accor-dingly ; namely, that as much wild and strange disorder and con-fusion so also various views, opinions and doctrines would spring up in Christendom, if it (divine revelation) were to be received mere-ly into the *mind ;* which it would be impossible to prevent."

[3] W o  n i c h t  d i e  S p r a c h e n  b l e i b e n, etc. " Therefore it is certain that where the languages are not preserved (do not re-main) there the gospel must at length become extinct." By the lan-guages is meant the study of the languages. We might expect the word d a s s before w o ; but it is not necessary in German.

[4] U n t e r g e h e n, *to sink, to go to the bottom, to perish.* In order

21

Das hat auch bewiesen,[1] und zeiget noch an die Erfahrung. Denn sobald nach der Apostel Zeit, da die Sprachen

---

to distinguish this word from n i e d e r g e h e n, it will be necessary
to form a precise idea of the difference between u n t e r and n i e-
d e r. It is well known that u n t e r has two significations, expressed in Latin by *sub* and *inter*. With this last signification, *inter*,
*among*, and sometimes *between*, we have here nothing to do. In the
former signification, in which it bears a close analogy to the adverb
u n t e n, *below*, *beneath*, it is properly the opposite of ü b e r. Thus,
placed antithetically, the words would stand, ü b e r  u n d  u n t e r,
*over and under*, o b e r  u n d  n i e d e r, *upper and lower*. U n t e r-
g e h e n is therefore a much stronger expression than n i e d e r g e-
h e n. As applied to the sun, the former would imply that *it is set-
ting* or *passing below the horizon*, whereas the latter would mean that
*it is declining*, i. e. either *approaching the horizon*, or *sinking below it*.
Any descent is expressed by n i e d e r g e h e n; but u n t e r g e-
h e n means *to descend so far as to be under something else*. U n t e r
is also used frequently in composition as the opposite of o b e r.
Thus we have not only O b e r d e u t s c h l a n d and N e i d e r-
d e u t s c h l a n d; O b e r h e s s e n and N i e d e r h e s s e n; O b e r-
r h e i n and N i e d e r r h e i n, *Upper Germany* and *Lower Germany; Upper Hesse* and *Lower Hesse; the Upper Rhine* and the *Lower Rhine;* but
O b e r i t a l i e n and U n t e r i t a l i e n; O b e r ä g y p t e n and Un-
t e r ä g y p t e n, *Upper Italy* and *Under Italy; Upper Egypt* and *Under
Egypt*. In those compound verbs in which either u n t e r or n i e d e r
are used in nearly the same sense, such as n i e d e r t a u c h e n and
u n t e r t a u c h e n;   n i e d e r l i e g e n   and   u n t e r l i e g e n,
the latter, or those compounded with u n t e r, are more elevated and
dignified.   N i e d e r is etymologically the same as the English
word *nether*, and enters into the compounds *beneath*, *underneath*.

[1] D a s  h a t  a u c h  b e w i e s e n, etc. "Experience has proved
that, and still shows it; for immediately (s o b a l d) after the times
of the apostles, when the languages (gift of tongues) ceased, the gospel, and the [true] faith, and Christianity itself (entire) declined more
and more, until they entirely vanished under the pope; and since the
time that the languages disappeared, not much that is special or good
(b e s o n d e r s) has been seen in Christendom, but very many shocking abominations (very much shocking abomination) have found
place."   S o b a l d, does not necessarily imply any comparison, that
is, it may signify not only *as soon as*, but *immediately, directly*. But

aufhörten, nahm auch das Evangelium und der Glaube und
ganze Christenheit je mehr und mehr ab, bis daß sie unter
dem Pabst gar versunken ist, und ist, seit der Zeit die Spra=
chen gefallen sind, nicht viel besonders in der Christenheit
ersehen; aber gar viel gräulicher Gräuel aus unwissenheit
der Sprachen geschehen. Also wiederum:[1] weil jetzt die
Sprachen hervor gekommen sind, bringen sie ein solches Licht
mit sich, und thun solche große Dinge, daß sich alle Welt
verwundert, und muß bekennen, daß wir das Evangelium
so lauter und rein haben, fast als die Apostel gehabt haben,
und ganz in seine erste Reinigkeit gekommen ist, und gar viel
reiner, denn es zur Zeit St. Hieronymi oder Augustini ge=
wesen ist. Und Summa,[2] der heilige Geist ist kein Narr,[3]
gehet auch nicht mit leichtfertigen unnöthigen Sachen um;
der[4] hat die Sprachen so nütze und noth geachtet in der Chri=
stenheit, daß er sie oftmals vom Himmel mit sich gebracht
hat. Welches uns allein sollte genugsam bewegen, diesel=

---

s o  b a l d, written separately always implies some comparison.
N a h m — a b. See p. 26, Note 5. It indicates *gradual decrease*.
Applied to one's declining health, it means *to pine away*, whereas
a b f a l l e n means that the flesh *falls away more rapidly*, and e i n-
f a l l e n that it *falls in* or *leaves visible marks or cavities.*—E r s e-
h e n is a participle, forming the perfect tense with i s t. B e s o n-
d e r s is probably here used for B e s o n d e r e s by a negligence
in the orthography. On the word C h r i s t e n h e i t, see p. 11,
Note 3.

[1] A l s o  w i e d e r u m, "So on the contrary." See p. 3, Note 2.

[2] S u m m a, or i n  S u m m a, *in a word.* Adopted from the Latin.

[3] D e r  h e i l i g e  G e i s t  i s t  k e i n  N a r r. The argument
is this : ' Since the Holy Ghost does no foolish or useless thing ; and
yet has bestowed the gift of tongues, it is evidently our duty to cultivate a knowledge of the languages as a useful and Christian attainment.'

[4] D e r, a demonstrative is more emphatic than e r in the next
clause. The form of both may be given by the word, *he*, italicised
in the former case and not in the latter.

ben mit Fleiß und Ehren zu suchen, und nicht zu verachten, weil er[1] sie nun selbst wieder auf Erden erwecket.

Ja sprichst du: es sind viele Väter selig geworden, haben auch gelehret ohne Sprachen.[2] Das ist wahr. Wo rechnest du aber auch das hin,[3] daß sie so oft in der Schrift gefehlet haben? Wie oft fehlet St. Augustinus im Psalter und andern Auslegungen, so wohl als Hilarius, ja auch alle, die ohne die Sprachen sich die Schrift haben unterwunden[4] auszulegen?[5] Und ob sie gleich[6]

[1] **Weil er**, etc. The Holy Ghost or divine Providence, is here represented as having produced the revival of learning.

[2] **Ohne Sprachen** belongs not only to **haben gelehrt** but also to **sind selig geworden**. In such sentences the punctuation is different in the German from what it is in the English.—**Ja** at the beginning of the sentence, is to be rendered *nay but*, or simply *but*. See p. 228, Note 3. The German **ja** and the English *yea* are the same word.

[3] **Wo rechnest du aber auch das hin**, etc. "But to what (**wo—hin**, *whither*) do you ascribe this, namely, that they have so often mistaken the meaning of the Scriptures?"

[4] **Unterwunden**. See p. 155, Note 3.

[5] **Auszulegen**. **Auslegen**, in its literal sense, is equivalent to **hinaus legen**, *to put out to show* (as goods), *to expose to view*. Figuratively, it means *to set forth a subject so that all its parts may be seen and understood*. The leading idea is to bring from a state of *concealment*. Applied to language, it means to explain or interpret the sense of the words by unfolding the grammatical construction.—**Erklären** is originally the same as **klar machen**, and relates to what was before **dunkel**, *obscure;* and hence, *to make clear by giving the reasons or grounds of a thing*.—**Deuten**, means *to indicate, to point out, to intimate by a sign*, a wink, nod, etc. **Auslegen** and **deuten** relate only to things as *signs* or *symbols* of something else (words as signs of ideas, and prognostics as signs of events), whereas **erklären** relates to *things in themselves*. Thus **einen Traum auslegen** or **deuten**, is to interpret or tell the meaning of a dream; but **einen Traum erklären**, is to explain the cause of the dream. Hence **Sterne deuten** is the office of an *astrologer;* but **Sterne erklären** is that of an *astronomer*.

[6] **Ob sie gleich**. **Ob**, in old German is nearly equivalent to

etwa[1] recht geredet haben, ſind ſie doch der Sachen nicht gewiß geweſen, ob daſſelbe[2] recht an dem Orte ſtehe, da ſie es hin deuten? Als, daß ich deß ein Erempel zeige, recht iſt es geredet, daß Chriſtus Gottes Sohn iſt. Aber wie ſpöttiſch lautet es in den Ohren der Widerſacher, da ſie deß Grund führeten aus dem 110. Pſalm: Tecum principium in die virtutis tuae, ſo doch daſelbſt in der ebräiſchen Sprache nichts von der Gottheit geſchrieben ſtehet. Wenn man aber alſo mit ungewiſſen Gründen und Fehlſprüchen[3] den Glau‐ ben ſchützet, iſt es nicht eine Schmach und Spott der

---

wenn. See p. 16, Note 1. But it now means *whether.* Conse-quently, obgleich, obwohl, ob auch, obschon, and ob-zwar have substantially the same signification as the simpler and easier forms, wenn gleich, wenn auch, wenn schon, and wenn zwar. Obgleich and wenn gleich are frequently separated by personal pronouns and other intervening words; the others are less frequently separated. Ob auch is poetical; and ob-zwar is obsolete. The etymological differences of these words are not regarded by writers at the present day. They are that ob, as a concessive particle, expresses more of *doubt* than wenn, which *pre-supposes* the condition expressed. Gleich implies that the condi-may follow *immediately* or *without hindrance;* schon implies that it has *already* taken place; wohl implies the *possibility* of the condi-tion; zwar implies the *certainty* of it; auch implies that the con-dition follows *also,* or follows as a consequence of something else.

[1] Etwa properly means *apparently* or *according to one's* opinion. Hence its two leading significations, 1. *about, nearly,* like unge-fähr; that is, *about or nearly so, if we may judge from appearances.* 2. *perhaps, perchance,* like vielleicht; that is, *it may be so, judging from appearances.* But Ungefahr, *about, nearly,* expresses *mere indefiniteness,* without reference to any *uncertainty,* arising from the *grounds* on which the judgment is formed; and vielleicht means literally *very easily* (viel in old German means the same as sehr); and hence, *very likely, perhaps.*

[2] Dasselbe, neuter singular, referring in an indefinite way to the plural Sachen. " And though they said what was not far from the truth (nearly right), still they were not sure (of the things) whether it belonged to the place, where they intimated it."

[3] Fehlsprüchen, *false proof-texts.*

21*

Christen bei den Widerfechtern,[1] die der Sprache kundig
sind? Und werden[2] nur halsstarriger im Irthum, und
halten unsern Glauben mit gutem Schein für einen Men=
schen=Traum.

Weß ist nun die Schuld,[3] daß unser Glaube also zu
Schanden wird? Nämlich: daß wir die Sprachen nicht
wissen, und ist hier keine Hülfe, denn die Sprachen wissen.
Ward nicht St. Hieronymus gezwungen, den Psalter von
neuem aus dem Ebräischen zu verdolmetschen, um deß wil=
len,[4] daß, wo man mit den Juden aus unserm[5] Psalter han=

---

[1] Widerfechter, can easily be explained from its etymology.
It differs from Widersacher, as *antagonist* in English differs
from *adversary*. It means, literally one who *fights* against another.
It is not now in common use.

[2] Und [sie] werden, etc. "And they are only made the more
obstinate in their error," etc.

[3] Wess ist nun die Schuld, etc.? "What is the cause,
that our faith is brought into such disgrace, or is so disgraced? It
is our ignorance of the languages; and here there is no remedy but
a knowledge of the languages." Literally, it would be, "Of what
is it the fault, that our faith becomes so disgraced (to disgrace)?
Namely, or forsooth [the circumstance] that we do not know the languages, and there is here no help than knowing the languages."—
Wess the genitive of was is now mostly out of use except in such
compounds as wesshalb and wesswegen.—Schuld is often
employed where the word *cause* would be, in English; but it differs
widely from Ursache, by being only an *evil* cause, and is hence
often to be rendered by the word *fault.*—Zu Schanden. See p.
56, Note 3.—Nämlich is here used in the sense of, *to be sure.*—
Die Sprachen wissen is a substantive phrase. See p. 68,
Note 2.

[4] Um desswillen, *because, on this account.* This word differs
from desswegen and desshalb, as ἵνα does from ὅτι. Strictly
speaking, desswegen, *because,* denotes *grounds* or *motives of action;* desshalb, *because,* indicates *that in regard to which, in consideration of which,* one *acts;* um desswillen, *because,* expresses
*personal intention,* or it is used in the sense of desswegen.

[5] Unserm, *our,* i. e. the Christian or Latin version of the Psalms
then in use.

delte,[1] spotteten fie unfer,[2] daß es nicht alfo ftünde im Ebrä=
ifchen, wie es die Unfern[3] führten? Nun find[4] aller alten
Väter Auslegung, die ohne Sprachen die Schrift haben ge=
handelt (ob fie wohl nichts unrechtes lehren) doch dergeftalt,
daß fie faft oft ungewiffe, unebene, und unzeitige Sprüche
führen, und tappen wie ein Blinder an der Wand, daß fie
gar oft des rechten Tertes fehlen, und machen ihm eine
Nafe nach ihrer Andacht, wie dem Vers oben angezeiget:
tecum principium, etc. Daß auch St. Auguftinus felbft
muß bekennen, wie er fchreibet de doctrina Christiana, daß
einem chriftlichen Lehrer, der die Schrift foll auslegen, Noth
find über die Lateinifche, auch die griechifche und ebräifche
Sprache; es ift fonft unmöglich, daß er nicht allenthalben
anftoffe, ja noch Noth und Arbeit da ift, ob einer die Spra=
chen fchon wohl kann.

Darum ift es gar viel[5] ein ander Ding um einen fchlech=
ten Prediger[6] des Glaubens, und um einen Ausleger der

---

[1] Handelte. See p. 29, Note 2.

[2] Spotteten sie unser. See p. 177, Note 2. Comp. p. 46,
Note 4.

[3] Die Unsern, our party, i. e. the Christians. Comp. p. 70,
Note 8.

[4] Nun sind, etc. " Now the interpretation of all the ancient
fathers, who, without a knowledge of the languages, have treated of
the Scriptures, (though they teach nothing heretical) is still of such
a character that they very often employ uncertain, variable and un-
timely expressions and grope like a blind man along the wall, so that
they often fail of the right [sense of the] text, and shape it (make a
waxen rose of it) to their pious fancy, so that even St. Augustine
himself was obliged to confess — that the Greek and Hebrew languages are necessary over and above the Latin to a Christian teacher,
who is to interpret the Bible. It is otherwise (i. e. without this aid)
impossible that he should not everywhere stumble; indeed, there is
trouble and labor, even though one be well acquainted with the languages."—Einem—noth sind—die Sprachen. See p. 162
Note 1.

[5] Gar viel, *very much*, or *quite.*

[6] Um einen schlechten Prediger, etc., with a simple or

Schrift, oder, wie es St. Paulus nennet: einen Propheten. Ein schlechter Prediger[1] (ist wahr) hat so viel heller Sprüche und Terte durchs dolmetschen, daß er Christum versteshen, lehren und heiliglich leben und andern predigen kann. Aber die Schrift auszulegen, und zu handeln für sich

---

mere preacher of the gospel (faith) from what it is with an interpreter," etc. Literally, It is quite another (i. e. it is not the same) thing with a preacher and with (or, as with) an interpreter. On the word s c h l e c h t, see p. 39, Note 5, and p. 78, Note 3. Perhaps all the significations of u m can be brought under the following heads, 1. *circum, circa, circiter.* 2. *de.* Here a few phrases. I c h r e d e w i e es m i r u m s H e r z i s t. " I speak my mind, (as it is in or respecting my heart)." E s s i e h t ü b e l u m i h n a u s, " He appears to be in a bad way (either as to his health or as to his affairs). Literally, " it appears ill respecting him." E r t h u t s e h r u m s e i n e n F r e u n d, " He feels much for his friend." Comp p. 20, Note 3, med. and p. 35, Note 5. E s i s t u m m i c h g e s c h e h e n, *de me actnm est.* E s i s t e i n s o n d e r b a r e s D i n g u m d i e L e i b e, " There is something singular about love, or love is a strange thing." S i c h u m E i n e n v e r d i e n t m a c h e n, " to gain one's favor by some service (to make one's self deserving of another)." 3. *For*, that is, n a c h when a certain end or object is sought; and f ü r, when there is reference to price in trade. See p. 133, Note 1. 4. As marking measure of time, space and degree, where it may be omitted in the translation, or rendered by the word *by* when it is a measure of excess. See p. 41, Note 1.—5. *To ruin* with k o m m e n, b r i n g e n, etc. See p. 106, Note 6, and p. 57, Note 3.—6. *Every other*, or *alternately.* See p. 116, Note 1.—7. *In order to* with the infinitive.—8. *Right about, over, prostrate*, as an adverb.

[1] E i n s c h l e c h t e r P r e d i g e r, etc. " An ordinary preacher, it is true, has so many clear passages and texts through interpretation (in translations) that he can understand and teach Christ, lead a holy life, and preach to others." Where several words in the same regimen succeed without the conjunction u n d expressed, they all belong to one category ; but when u n d is inserted, as it is here after l e h r e n and l e b e n, it implies that the following words belong to a new class. Hence the rule for the omission or insertion of this conjunction is very different in German from what it is respecting the word *and*, in English.

hin,[1] und zu streiten wider die irrigen Einführer der Schrift,
ist er zu geringe,[2] das lässet sich ohne Sprachen nicht thun.[3]
Nun muß man je in der Christenheit solche Propheten ha=
ben, die die Schrift treiben[4] und auslegen, und auch zum
Streit tangen, und ist nicht genug am heiligen Leben und
recht lehren. Darum sind die Sprachen stracks und aller
Dinge vonnöthen in der Christenheit, gleichwie die Prophe=
ten oder Ausleger, ob es gleich nicht Noth ist, noch seyn
muß, daß ein jeglicher Christ oder Prediger ein solcher Pro=
phet sey, wie St. Paulus sagt 1. Cor. 12, 8. und 9., Ephes.
4, 11.

Daher kömmt es, daß seit der Apostel Zeit die Schrift so
finster ist geblieben, und nirgends gewisse,[5] beständige Ausle=
gungen darüber geschrieben sind. Denn auch die heiligen
Väter (wie gesagt) oft gefehlet, und weil sie der Sprachen

---

[1] Für sich hin, *from one's own view, independently.* Comp. p.
16, Note 8.

[2] Gering means *small* with special reference to *quality* or *value*,
and hence often means *inferior, weak.* Klein, *small,* relates strictly to *dimensions,* or *size.*

[3] Lässt sich — nicht thun, *cannot be done.* So the phrases,
Das lässt sich hören, *that may be listened to,* i. e. is reasonable; das lässt sich denken, *that is conceivable.*

[4] Die die Schrift treiben, etc. " who study and interpret
the Scriptures, and are competent to controversy ; nor is holy living
and orthodoxy enough (for the defender of Christianity). Therefore
the languages are strictly and altogether necessary to the Christian
church, as are prophets, or interpreters, although it is not necessary
nor indispensable that every Christian or preacher should be a prophet."—Treiben, see p. 29, Note 1, and p. 109, Note 2.—Taugen,
*to be good, useful* or *fit for.* Compare tauglich, p 145, Note 2.—
Ist nicht genug, etc. literally, " there is not enough in holy living and correct teaching," meaning, that, " a pious life and orthodox
teaching are not all that is requisite."—Aller Dinge which is
now out of use, differs from allerdings only by being in the genitive plural instead of the genitive singular. See p. 183, Note 3.

[5] Gewisse, like the English word *certain,* is used in the two
senses of *sure,* and *some.*

unwiſſend geweſen,[1] ſind ſie gar ſelten eins, der fähret ſonſt, der fähret ſo. St. Bernhard iſt ein Mann von größem Geiſt geweſen, daß ich ihn ſchier[2] dürfte über alle Lehrer ſetzen, die berühmt ſind, beide alte und neue; aber ſiehe, wie er mit der Schrift ſo oft (wiewohl geiſtlich)[3] ſpielet, und ſie außer dem rechten Sinn führt. Derhalben haben auch die Sophiſten geſagt: die Schrift ſey finſter, haben gemei‐ net,[4] Gottes Wort ſey von Art ſo finſter, und rede ſeltſam. Aber ſie ſehen nicht, daß aller Mangel an den Sprachen liegt,[5] ſonſt[6] wäre nichts leichters je geredet, denn Gottes Wort, wo wir die Sprachen verſtünden. Ein Türke muß mir wohl finſter reden, welchen doch ein türkiſch Kind von ſieben Jahren wohl vernimmt,[7] dieweil ich die Sprache nicht kenne.

Darum iſt das auch ein tolles Vornehmen geweſen, daß man die Schrift hat wollen lernen durch der Väter Ausle‐

---

[1] [Haben] oft gefehlet — gewesen [sind]. "For even the holy fathers, as we have said, have often failed, and because they were not versed in the languages, they are very seldom agreed; one goes this way, the other that." See on this last expression, p. 74, Note 7.

[2] Schier, *almost.* See p. 25, Note 5.

[3] Geistlich, *spiritually.*

[4] Haben gemeint, etc. "They have supposed that the word of God was (so) obscure in its nature, and speaks in (such) a singu‐ lar manner."

[5] Dass aller Mangel an den Sprachen liegt, "that all the fault lies in the languages," i. e. ignorance of the languages is the cause. On this use of the preposition an, see p. 169, Note 4, med.

[6] Sonst, *aside from this,* referring to Mangel, renders the close of the sentence a little tautological. "But for this, nothing easier (simpler) could ever be spoken, than the word of God, if we understood the languages."

[7] Vernimmt, *perceives,* is here used in the obsolete sense of *understands.*

gen, und viel Bücher und Glossen Lesen.[1] Man sollte sich
dafür auf die Sprachen begeben haben.[2] Denn die lieben
Väter, weil sie ohne Sprachen gewesen sind, haben sie
zuweilen mit vielen Worten an einem Spruch gearbeitet,
und dennoch nur kaum hienach geahmet,[3] und halb gerathen,
halb gefehlet. So läufest du demselbigen[4] nach mit vieler
Mühe, und könntest dieweil durch die Sprachen demselben
viel besser selbst rathen, denn der, dem du folgest. Denn
wie die Sonne gegen dem Schatten ist, so ist die Sprache
gegen aller Väter Glossen.

Weil denn nun den Christen gebühret, die heilige Schrift
zu üben, als ihr eigen einiges[5] Buch, und eine Sünde und

---

[1] V i e l  B ü c h e r  u n d  G l o s s e n  L e s e n is a substantive
phrase, and L e s e n itself governs v i e l in the accusative. " Reading many books and glosses." Comp. p. 68, Note 2.

[2] S i c h — a u f — b e g e b e n  h a b e n, *to have given themselves
to.* S i c h  b e g e b e n, *to give one's self, to put one's self,* which is
no longer used in a metaphorical sense, may generally be translated
by *to go, to resort.* With the prepositions a u f, n a c h and i n it
implies *motion to,* whereas with the genitive it indicates *motion from,*
or *the surrender of a thing.* See p. 165, Note 7.

[3] H i e n a c h  g e a h m e t, *approached it in resemblance.* N a c h -
a h m e n, for which h i e n a c h  a h m e n seems here to be used
with a slight modification, properly signifies *to imitate.* On g e r a -
t h e n, see p. 38, Note 3.

[4] D e m s e l b i g e n, refers indefinitely to some one of the fathers;
and d e m s e l b e n, refers to S p r u c h. R a t h e n with the dative, *to arrive at,* is unusual. " You pursue him (one of the fathers)
with great trouble, and yet might, with the aid of the languages,
yourself better reach your object, than he whom you pursue."

[5] E i n i g e s in the sense of e i n z i g e s. See p. 93, Note 2, and
p. 149, Note 1. " Since, then, it is proper for Christians to use the
Bible as their own [and] only book, and [since] it is a sin and shame
that we do not know our own book, nor understand the language
and word of God, it is the greater sin and shame that we do not learn
the languages, especially as God is now both offering and giving us
men and books and whatever else is serviceable to that end, and is
even inciting us to it, and would gladly have his book [made] open."

Schande iſt, daß wir unſer eigen Buch nicht wiſſen, noch unſers Gottes Sprache und Wort nicht kennen, ſo iſt es noch viel mehr Sünde und Schande, das wir nicht Spra=chen lernen, ſonderlich, ſo uns jetzt Gott darbeut, und giebt Leute und Bücher, und allerlei was dazu dienet, und uns gleich dazu reizet, und ſein Buch gerne wollte offen haben. O wie froh ſollten die lieben Väter geweſen ſeyn, wenn ſie hätten ſo können zur heiligen Schrift kommen und die Spra=chen lernen, als wir könnten. Wie haben ſie mit großer Mühe und Fleiß kaum die Brocken erlanget, da wir mit halber,[1] ja ſchier ohne alle Arbeit, das ganze Brod gewin=nen könnten. O wie ſchändet ihr Fleiß unſere Faulheit, ja, wie hart wird Gott auch rächen ſolchen unſern Unfleiß und Undankbarkeit.

Daher[2] gehöret auch, daß St. Paulus 1. Cor. 14. will, daß in der Chriſtenheit ſoll das Urtheil ſeyn über allerlei Lehre, dazu aller Dinge von Nöthen iſt, die Sprachen zu wiſſen. Denn der Prediger oder Lehrer mag wohl die Bibel durch und durch leſen,[3] wie er will, er treffe oder fehle, wenn Riemand da iſt, der da urtheile, ob er es recht mache oder nicht. Soll man denn urtheilen, ſo muß Kunſt[4] der Sprachen da ſeyn, ſonſt iſt es verloren. Darum, obwohl der Glaube und das Evangelium durch ſchlechte[5] Prediger

---

[1] H a l b e r is an adjective agreeing with A r b e i t in the dative. "Whereas we with half—or rather almost without any, labor, might obtain the whole loaf."

[2] D a h e r, which commonly means *hence*, sometimes means *hither* or *here*, as in this passage.

[3] L e s e n, here means the public reading and exposition of the Scriptures. "For the preacher or teacher may read [from the pulpit] the whole Bible (or, the Bible through and through) as he choses, right or wrong (hit or miss), unless there be some one to judge whether he does it correctly or not."

[4] K u n s t. See p. 191, Note 1, and p. 193, Note 2.

[5] S c h l e c h t e. The use of this word here, illustrates the con-nection between its two significations *simple* and *bad* or *poor*. The

mag ohne Sprachen geprediget werden, so gehet's doch faul[1]
und schwach, und man wird zuletzt müde und überdrüßig,
und fället doch zu Boden. Aber wo die Sprachen sind, da
gehet es frisch und stark, und wird die Schrift durchtrieben,[2]
und findet sich der Glaube immer neu, durch andere und
aber andere Worte und Werke.

Es soll uns auch nicht irren,[3] daß Etliche sich des Geistes
rühmen, und die Schrift geringe achten. Etliche auch, wie
die Brüder Valdenses, die Sprachen nicht nützlich achten.
Aber lieber Freund, Geist hin, Geist her,[4] ich bin auch im
Geist gewesen, und habe auch Geister gesehen (wenn's je
gelten soll von eigenem Fleisch rühmen) vielleicht mehr,
denn eben dieselbigen noch im Jahr sehen werden, wie fast
sie auch sich rühmen. Auch hat mein Geist sich etwas be=
weiset, so doch ihr Geist im Winkel gar stille ist, und nicht
viel mehr thut, denn seinen Ruhm aufwirft. Das weiß ich
aber wohl,[5] wie fast der Geist alles allein thut. Wäre ich

word *simple* has two significations connected in the same way. See
p. 39, Note 5.

[1] So ge het's doch faul, etc. "still it goes on sluggishly
and feebly, and one finally becomes weary and sick at heart, and falls
to the ground."

[2] Durchtrieben, for durchgetrieben, *carried through
to the end* as contrasted with "falling to the ground" before coming
to the end.

[3] Irren is sometimes, as here, used in an active signification,
for which irre machen is commonly employed.

[4] Geist hin, Geist her, "the spirit here and the spirit
there," i. e. what signifies the spirit? It is all nothing. "I also
have been in the spirit, and have seen perhaps more spirits (if it is
ever allowable to boast of one's own flesh) than these same persons
will see in a year, however much they boast. My spirit has also dis-
played itself somewhat, while theirs is stock-still in its hiding-place
and does little more than boast." Aufwerfen see, p. 151, Note 5.

[5] Dass weiss ich aber wohl. Here Luther speaks more
seriously of the spirit, referring to its ordinary influences, but still
maintaining that spiritual influences without study, will not make

doch allen Büſchen zu ferne geweſen, wo mir nicht die Spra=
chen geholfen, und mich der Schrift ſicher und gewiß gemacht
hätten.    Ich hä te auch wohl können fromm ſeyn, und in
der Stille recht predigen; aber den Pabſt und die Sophiſten
mit dem ganzen endechriſtiſchen Regiment würde ich wohl
haben laſſen ſeyn, was ſie ſind.    Der Teufel achtet meinen
Geiſt[1] nicht ſo faſt, als meine Sprache und Feder in der
Schrift.    Denn mein Geiſt nimmt ihm nichts, denn mich
allein ; aber die heilige Schrift und Sprachen machen ihm
die Welt zu enge, und thut ihm Schad:n in ſeinem Reiche.

So kann ich auch die Brüder Valdenſes darinnen gar
nicht loben, daß ſie die S rachen verachten.    Denn ob ſie
gleich recht lehrten,[2] ſo müſſen ſie doch gar oft des rechten
Textes fehlen, und auch ungerüſtet und ungeſchickt bleiben
zu fechten für den Glauben wider den Irrthum.    Dazu iſt
ihr Ding ſo finſter,[3] und auf eine eigene Weiſe gezogen, au=

---

one a sound teacher.  "But I know full well, how the spirit does almost everything.  Still I should have been out of reach of my object
(too far from the bush) had not the languages come to my aid, and
made me sure and certain respecting (of) the Scripture.  I might
also have been pious, and have preached the true faith in sentiment."

[1] G e i s t  here does not mean talent, but *spiritual gift* or *influence.*
—M e i n e  S p r a c h e  u n d  F e d e r  i n  d e r  S c h r i f t, "my
philology and my pen in connection with the Bible," i. e. his languages or philology in studying the Bible and his pen in explaining and
enforcing it.  "For my spirit (i. e. the grace of God in me) takes
nothing but myself away from him ; but the Holy Scriptures and the
[knowledge of the] languages drive him out of the world (make the
world too narrow or uncomfortable for him) and inflict an injury
upon his kingdom."

[2] R e c h t  l e h r t e n, *taught no heresy.*  Though their *doctrines*
were correct, they necessarily failed very often in applying the right
proof-texts.

[3] D a z u  i s t  i h r  D i n g  s o  f i n s t e r, etc.  "Besides, their
views are so unenlightened, and are represented under such peculiar
forms, not following the language of the  Scriptures, that I fear they
are not, or will not continue to be right."  This sentence will hardly

ßer der Schrift Weise zu reden, daß ich besorge, es sey oder werde nicht lauter bleiben. Denn es gar gefährlich ist, von Gottes Sachen anders reden, oder mit andern Worten, denn Gott selbst brauchet. Kürzlich, sie mögen bei ihnen selbst heilig leben und lehren; aber weil sie ohne Sprachen bleiben, wird ihnen mangeln müssen, das[1] allen andern mangelt, nämlich: daß sie die Schrift gewiß und gründlich nicht handeln noch andern Völkern nützlich seyn mögen. Weil sie aber das wohl könnten thun, und nicht thun wollen, mögen sie zusehen,[2] wie es vor Gott zu verantworten sey.

Nun das sey gesagt[3] von Nutzen und Noth der Sprachen und christlichen Schulen, für das geistliche Wesen und zur Seelen Heil. Nun lasset uns[4] auch den Leib vornehmen

---

admit of a literal translation. D i n g does not mean *cause* or *enterprise*, which would be expressed by the word S a c h e, but their whole character and manner, as uncultivated and partaking largely of cant. F i n s t e r, means *dark*, i. e. not luminous, not enlightened; d u n k e l, *dark*, i. e. not clear, obscure; d ü s t e r, *dark*, i. e. not cheerful, gloomy, melancholy. Without a nice observance of these synonymes, there would be a liability to misinterpret the writer, and to understand him as saying that the Waldenses were vague in their thoughts and obscure (d u n k e l) in their language, like Böhme, or that they were gloomy and sad (d ü s t e r), like some of the more rigid puritans.

[1] D a s, used like w a s, *that which*. See p. 15, Note 4. The negatives n i c h t and n o c h, seem hardly necessary after m a n g e l t. The want or defect *consists* in not treating the Scriptures with certainty and thoroughness. A l l e n a n d e r n, *all other people*,—a complaint against the general neglect of the Scriptures.

[2] M ö g e n s i e z u s e h e n, " let them see to it, how they are to answer for it before God."

[3] D a s s e i g e s a g t, " so much for the utility and necessity of the languages, etc." Literally, " let this be said," i. e. considered or received as said. Hence a similar form is used in commands or threats, meaning, " give attention to this." See p. 240, Note 3.

[4] N u n l a s s e t u n s, etc. " Now let us consider the body and inquire (s e t z e n, *suppose*, *propose*): though there were no soul nor heaven, nor hell, and [we] should regard merely the civil gov-

und ſetzen: ob ſchon keine Seele noch Himmel oder Hölle
wäre, und ſollten allein das zeitliche Regiment anſehen nach
der Welt, ob daſſelbe nicht bedürfte vielmehr guter Schulen
und gelehrter Leute, denn das Geiſtliche? Denn bisher
ſich deſſelben die Sophiſten ſo gar nichts haben angenommen,
und die Schulen ſo gar auf den geiſtlichen Stand gerichtet,
daß gleich eine Schande geweſen iſt, ſo ein Gelehrter iſt
ehelich geworden, und hat müſſen hören ſagen: ſiehe, der
wird weltlich, und will nicht geiſtlich werden; gerade, als
wäre allein ihr geiſtlicher Stand Gott angenehm, und der
weltliche (wie ſie ihn nennen) gar des Teufels und unchriſtlich.

Nun iſt hier nicht Noth zu ſagen, wie das weltliche Regiment eine göttliche Ordnung und Stand iſt, davon ich ſonſt
viel geſagt habe, daß ich hoffe,[1] es zweifelt Niemand daran,
ſondern iſt zu handeln, wie man ſeine geſchickte Leute darein
kriege.[2]    Und hier bieten uns[3] die Heiden einen großen Trotz

---

ernment in reference to the present world, whether this do not require good schools and learned men, even more than our spiritual interests do.   For hitherto the sophists (Papists) have not taken the
least interest in it (z e i t l i c h  R e g i m e n t), and have arranged the
schools so exclusively for the priesthood that it has become a matter
of reproach, if a learned man marries, and he has been obliged to
hear it said, ' Behold, he has become a man of the world, and desires
not the clerical state,' as though their priestly condition alone were
acceptable to God, and the secular classes, as they are called, belonged to Satan, and were unchristian.  On sich desselben
angenommen haben, see p. 55, Note 2.

[1] D a s s  i c h  h o f e, " so that I hope, no one will doubt respecting it."

[2] K r i e g e.   This word signifies properly to catch with the hand.
In the sense of b e k o m m e n, to obtain, as used here and often by
Luther, it is now employed only in common life, among the unedu-
cated.

[3] U n d  h i e r  b i e t e n  u n s, etc.  " And here the heathen offer
us a challenge and put us to shame."   On the peculiar use of the
word T r o t z, see p. 120, Note 1.  The force of the word must be

und Schmach an, die vor Zeiten, sonderlich die Römer und Griechen, gar nichts gewußt haben, ob solcher Stand Gott gefiele oder nicht, und haben doch mit solchem[1] Ernst und Fleiß die jungen Knaben und Mädchen lassen lehren und aufziehen, daß[1] sie dazu geschickt wurden, daß[1] ich mich unserer Christen schämen muß, wenn ich daran gedenke, und sonderlich unserer Deutschen, die wir sogar Stöcke und Thiere sind, und sagen dürfen: ja, was sollen die Schulen, so man nicht soll geistlich werden? Die wir doch wissen,[2] oder je wissen sollen, wie ein nöthiges und nützliches Ding es ist, und Gott so angenehm, wo ein Fürst, Herr, Rathsmann, oder was regieren soll, gelehrt und geschickt ist, denselben Stand christlich zu führen.

Wenn nun gleich (wie ich gesagt habe) keine Seele wäre, und man der Schulen und Sprachen gar nicht bedürfte, um der Schrift und Gottes willen, so wäre doch[3] allein diese

---

variously expressed in English, according to the connection.—V o r Z e i t e n, see p. 113, Note 1. Here v o r  A l t e r s might also be used; but that would modify the representation, though the idea would remain the same.

[1] After s o l c h e m  E r n s t, the first d a s s refers to l e h r e n u n d  a u f z i e h e n, and the second (d a s s  i c h  m i c h, etc.) to s o l c h e m. "That, when I think of it, I am ashamed of Christians, and especially of our Germans, who are very blockheads and brutes, and can say, "pray, what is the use of schools, if one is not to become a priest?" W a s  s o l l e n is explained p. 123, Note 2.

[2] D i e  w i r  d o c h  w i s s e n, "who, notwithstanding, know, or ought to know, how necessary and useful a thing it is, and so (or how) acceptable to God, if a prince, lord, counsellor, or whatever else that exercises authority, is instructed and skilled in discharging, in a Christian manner, the functions of the office."

[3] S o  w ä r e  d o c h, etc. "still, for the establishment of the very best schools everywhere both for boys and girls, this, of itself, would be a sufficient reason, namely, that society (the world), even for the maintenance of civil order, needs accomplished and well-trained men and women."—G e n u g s a m "that which can or may be enough;" g e n u g, "that which is enough," may frequently be

Urſache genugſam, die allerbeſten Schulen, beide für Knaben und Mädchen, an allen Orten aufzurichten, daß die Welt auch ihren weltlichen Stand äußerlich zu halten doch bedarf ſeiner geſchickter Männer und Frauen, daß die Männer wohl könnten regieren Land und Leute, die Frauen wohl ziehen und halten könnten Haus, Kinder und Geſinde. Nun ſolche Männer müſſen aus Knaben werden, und ſolche Frauen müſſen aus Mädchen werden; darum iſts zu thun, daß man Knaben und Mädchen dazu recht lehre und aufziehe. Nun habe ich oben geſagt: der gemeine Mann thut hier nichts zu, kann es auch nicht, will es auch nicht, weiß auch nichts. Fürſten und Herren ſollten es thun; aber ſie haben auf Schlitten[1] zu fahren, zu trinken und in der Mummerei zu laufen, und ſind beladen[2] mit hohen merkli= chen Geſchäften des Kellers, der Küche und der Kammer. Und ob es Etliche gerne thäten, müſſen ſie die Andern ſcheuen, daß ſie nicht für Narren oder Ketzer gehalten wer= den. Darum will[3] es euch, liebe Rathsherren, allein in

---

used for each other. The adjective termination s a m corresponds to the English ending *able* or *ible*.

[1] S c h l i t t e n. This word, and the English words *sled* and *sledge* and the American word *sleigh*, all have one common origin, and are only different dialectical forms, derived, probably, from the old Sax- on and Anglo-Saxon word s l i d a n, *to slide*. The connection be- tween the words *sled* and *sleigh* is indicated in Low German where the same word is sometimes written S l e d e, and sometimes S l e e.

[2] U n d s i n d b e l a d e n, "and are burdened with the high special (remarkable) duties (or employments) of the cellar, kitchen, and chamber (drinking, eating and sleeping). And though some would be glad to do it (would gladly do it), they must stand in fear of the rest, lest they should be held as fools or heretics." S c h e u e n, to fear, to be s c h e u, *shy* of.

[3] W i l l, does not like w i r d with the infinitive, express mere fu- turity, but implies either that a person *wills*, or that circumstances *demand*, a thing to be. See p 32, Note 2.—E u c h a l l e i n i n d e r H a n d b l e i b e n, "remain in your hands alone." On this use of the dative (e u c h) see p. 18, Note 7, and Gram. p. 347 infra.

der Hand bleiben; ihr habt auch Raum und Fug[1] dazu,
beſſer denn Fürſten und Herren.

Ja, ſprichſt du:[2] ein Jeglicher mag ſeine Söhne und

---

[1] R a u m   u n d   F u g.   R a n m, like the English word *space*, is frequently used with reference to time.   F u g, which may commonly
be rendered by the word, *right*, properly means *propriety*, i. e. a thing
which it is *proper* for one to do, and which he therefore, and in that
sense, has a right to do.   A right which is founded in the nature of
things or in law is R e c h t; a right which is derived from a special
decision or decree is B e f u g n i s s.   This last word comes from b e-
f u g e n, *to authorize, to empower*.   But F u g is derived from fü-
g e n, 1. to connect or join; 2. to connect so as to put a thing in its
*fitting* or *proper* place.   M i t   F u g e in the old German is the same
in sense as p a s s e n d, *fitting*.   "Therefore, respected members of
the city councils, this business must be left in your hands.   You have
the leisure for it and the right to it, better than princes and lords."

[2] J a,   s p r i c h s t   d u, etc.   "But nay, say you.   Each one may
himself teach his sons and daughters, or discipline them.   Reply.
Yes, we see how it goes with teaching and training!   And even if
discipline is carried to the highest point, and succeeds (turns out)
well, it amounts to no more than that, in some measure (e i n   w e-
n i g), a forced and respectable mien is acquired (is there); in other
respects (s o n s t) they nevertheless remain mere dunces, who can
say nothing of this or that (or of one thing or of another), and are
able neither to advise nor to aid any one.   But if they should be
taught and educated (if one should teach and educate them) in the
schools or elsewhere, where there should be educated and well-bred
instructors and instructresses, who should teach languages and other
arts and history (histories) then they (the pupils) would learn the
histories and maxims of all the world, how things went with this
city, this kingdom, this prince, this man, this woman; and thus they
would be able in a very short time (short time immediately) to contemplate (apprehend) for themselves, as in a mirror, the character
(W e s e n), life, counsels, proposals, successes and failures of the
whole world from the beginning.   From this (d a r a u s) they could
adjust their views, and with piety regulate themselves in the course
of the world (i. e. in life); and moreover (d a z u) from the same histories become wise and prudent [as to] what is to be sought and
what avoided in this (outward) life, and advise and direct others accordingly.   But the training which it is proposed to give at home

Töchter wohl selber lehren oder sie ziehen mit Zucht. Antwort: Ja man siehet wohl, wie sich's lehret und ziehet. Und wenn die Zucht auf's höchste getrieben wird, und wohl geräth, so kommt es nicht weiter, denn daß ein wenig eine eingezwungene und ehrbare Geberde da ist; sonst bleiben es gleichwohl eitel Holzblöcke, die weder hievon noch davon wissen zu sagen, Niemand weder rathen noch hilfen können. Wo man sie aber lehrete, und zöge in Schulen oder sonst, da gelehrte und züchtige Meister und Meisterinnen wären, die da Sprachen und andere Künste und Historien lehreten, da würden sie hören die Geschichten und Sprüche aller Welt, wie es dieser Stadt, diesem Reiche, diesem Fürsten, diesem Manne, diesem Weibe gegangen wäre; und könnten also in kurzer Zeit gleich der ganzen Welt von Anbeginn Wesen, Leben, Rath und Anschläge, Gelingen und Ungelingen für sich fassen, wie in einem Spiegel; daraus sie denn ihren Sinn schicken, und sich in der Welt Lauf richten könnten mit Gottesfurcht, dazu witzig und klug werden aus denselben Historien, was zu suchen und zu meiden wäre in diesem äußerlichen Leben, und Andern auch darnach rathen und regieren. Die Zucht aber, die man daheim ohne solche Schulen vornimmt, die will uns weise machen durch eigene Erfahrung. Ehe das geschieht, so sind wir hundertmal

---

without such schools, *that* would [attempt to] make us wise by our own experience. [But] before that would take place, we should die a hundred times, and should have acted (done everything) all our lives long inconsiderately; for our own experience would require much time."—J a is explained p. 228, Note 3; S e l b e r p. 103, Note 3, end.—S i c h's l e h r e t u n d z i e h e t, literally, "how it teaches and trains itself," i. e. how teaching and training are performed. Compare p. 128, Note I, end.—I h r e n S i n n s c h i c k e n, literally, "to fix or adjust their sense," means "to form their views," or to acquire practical principles.—Z u m e i d e n w ä r e, "is to be avoided." Compare p. 12, Note 3.—G e s c h i e t and s i n d t o d t, the present for the future, is much more common in German than in English. See Gram. p. 308, (1).

tobt, unb haben unfer Lebenlang alles unbebächtig gehan=
belt: benn zu eigener Erfahrung gehöret viel Zeit.

Weil benn bas junge Volk muß lecken[1] unb fpringen, ober
je[2] etwas zu fchaffen haben, ba es Luft innen hat, unb ihm
barin nicht zu wehren ift,[3] es auch nicht gut wäre,baß man
Alles wehrete; warum follte man benn ihm nicht folche
Schulen zurichten, unb folche Kunft vorlegen? Sintemal
es jetzt von Gottes Gnabe alles alfo zugerichtet ift, baß bie
Kinber mit Luft unb Spiel lernen können, es feyen Spra=

---

[1] L e c k e n, old German, *to leap and run.* In modern German
it is entirely out of use in this sense.

[2] J e, like the English word ever, (See p. 41, Note 2) has a variety of derived significations which are difficult to be traced. Here,
it is used nearly in the sense of d o c h. What is true *always*, or *at
any time* (j e) is true *in any case*, or *at least*, or *certainly ;* and so the
signification approaches to that of d o c h. In je z u Z e i t e n
(always at times), it means (at intervals, z u Z e i t e n) *without any
entire cessation.* Hence the phrase, like j e b i s w e i l e n, signifies,
*now and then.* It is frequently used as a mere particle of affirmation,
meaning *indeed, truly*, resembling w o h l, or j a, and may be entirely omitted in English. What is said, p. 16, Note 5, and p. 151,
Note 2, on the use of j e for j a may be explained in this way. The
following, though somewhat obsolete, may serve as examples. D a s
h e u r i g e G e w ä c h s ist je s o r e i c h a l s d a s v o r i g e,
" this year's crop is (indeed) as plentiful as the last year's." D a s
ist je e i n W u n d e r - d i n g, " That is truly a strange thing."
D a s ist je g e w i s s l i c h w a h r, " That is (indeed) certainly
true." W i r m ü s s e n je b e k e n n e n, " We must indeed confess." Compare the force of the word *ever*, in *whoever ;* also in the
word *every*, as illustrating derived but remote significations.

[3] I h m n i c h t z u w e h r e n ist means, *ei non resistendum
est.* I s t is impersonal ; z u w e h r e n, *to restrain*, after i s t (see
p. 259, Note 2, near the end) governing the dative i h m, means " it
is proper to restrain it," i. e. the youth. " Now since the young
must leap and jump, or at least have something to do, because they
desire it and ought not therein to be restrained, and it would not be
well to check them in everything, why should we not provide for
them such schools and lay before them such knowledge ?"

chen oder andere Künste oder Historien. Und ist jetzt[7] nicht
mehr die Hölle und das Fegfeuer unsere Schule, darinnen
wir gemartert sind über den Casualibus und Temporalibus,
da wir doch nichts, denn eitel nichts gelernet haben durch
so viel Stäupen, Zittern, Angst und Jammer. Nimmt
man doch so viel Zeit und Mühe, daß man die Kinder spie=
len auf Karten, singen und tanzen lehret; warum nimmt
man nicht auch so viel Zeit, daß man sie lesen und andere
Künste lehret, weil sie jung und müssig, geschickt und lustig
dazu sind? Ich rede für mich, wenn ich Kinder hätte und
vermöchte es, sie müßten mir nicht allein die Sprachen und
Historien hören, sondern auch singen, und die Musik mit
der ganzen Mathematik lernen. Denn was ist dieß Alles,
denn eitel Kinderspiel, darinnen die Griechen ihre Kinder
vor Zeiten erzogen, dadurch doch wunder geschickte Leute
daraus geworden, zu allerlei hernach tüchtig? Ja wie leid
ist mir's jetzt, daß ich nicht mehr Poeten und Historien ge=

---

[7] **Und ist jetzt,** etc. "And our schools are now no longer
a hell and purgatory, in which we are tortured over cases and tenses,
in which, by the way, we learned nothing but mere nothing by so
much flogging, trembling, anguish and wretchedness. If men take
so much time and trouble to teach their children to play at cards,
sing and dance, why should they not take as much time to teach
(that they teach) them to read and other branches of knowledge,
while they are young and have leisure, are adapted to it and take
pleasure in it? I speak for myself. If I had children [Luther was
not yet married], and were able, I would have them learn (they must
learn for me) not only languages and history, but singing and (in-
strumental) music and the entire course of mathematics. For what
is all this but mere children's play in which the Greeks in former
ages trained their children, whereby wonderfully skilful people
were made of them, afterwards capable of all sorts of things. How
sorry I now am, that I did not read the poets and histories more, and
that no one taught me those. Instead of these, I was obliged to read
the devil's filth, the philosophers and sophists (the Aristotelian and
scholastic philosophy) at great expense, labor and injury, so that I
now have enough to do to unlearn it."

lefen habe, und mich auch diefelben Niemand gelehret hat.
Und habe dafür müffen lefen des Teufels Dreck, die Philo=
fophen und Sophiften mit großen Koften, Arbeit und Scha=
den, daß ich genug habe daran auszufegen.

So fprichft du: Ja, wer kann feiner Kinder fo entbeh=
ren,[1] und alle zu Junkern ziehen?[2] fie müffen im Haufe der
Arbeit warten[3] 2c. Antwort: Ift's[4] doch auch nicht meine
Meinung, daß man folche Schulen anrichte[5], wie fie bisher
gewefen find, da ein Knabe zwanzig oder dreißig Jahre hat
über dem Donat[6] und Alexander[7] gelernet, und dennoch
nichts gelernet. Es ift jetzt eine andere Welt, und gehet

---

[1] Entbehren, entrathen, missen and vermissen
all signify to be without something. Entrathen means this simply, and in the most general sense. Entbehren adds to that
signification the idea of bearing, or suffering the want as an evil.
These two words do not intimate whether that which is wanting was
ever possessed or not. The other two words imply that there is a
loss of what was once possessed ; and this loss when slightly felt or
merely perceived, is expressed by missen ; and when keenly felt
by vermissen.

[2] Alle zu Junkern ziehen. If no regard were paid to
the German idiom, this phrase might be supposed to mean, " lead or
conduct them all to [other] young gentlemen." But on zu see p.
94, Note 2, and p. 104, Note 6—"bring them all up as gentlemen."
On the etymology of Junker, see p. 58, Note 1, end.

[3] Warten, see p. 224, Note 7.

[4] Ist's for es ist, see p. 16, Note 7.

[5] Anrichten, see p. 50, Note 2, near the beginning.

[6] Donat. "Among the later Roman grammarians is to be mentioned Aelius Donatus in particular, who lived at Rome as teacher
of grammar about the year 250 of the Christian era, who introduced
a new method and whose book was used in the schools for more than
a thousand years." Schwartz, Geschichte der Erziehung, Vol. II. p. 200.

[7] Alexander. " But the Grammar of the Franciscan monk,
Alexander of Brittany, who flourished about 1250, written in hex-
ameter verse and in rhymes and called Doctrinale, had the most influence and was most used in schools. The pupils were obliged to
learn it by heart from beginning to end." Schwartz. II. 201.

anders zu[1]. Meine Meinung[2] ist, daß, man die Knaben des
Tages eine Stunde[3] oder zwei lasse zu solcher Schule gehen,
und nichts desto weniger die andere Zeit im Hause schaffen,
Handwerke lernen, und wozu man sie haben will, daß beides
mit einander gehe, weil das Volk jung ist, und gewarten
kann.   Bringen sie doch sonst wohl zehnmal so viel Zeit zu
mit Keulchen schießen, Ball spielen, Laufen und Rammeln.
Also kann ein Mägdlein[4] ja so viel Zeit haben, daß sie

---

[1] U n d   g e h e t   a n d e r s   z u, " and things go differently (now)."
See p. 130, Note 2.

[2] M e i n u n g, *opinion, sentiment.*  It corresponds exactly in signification with the verb, m e i n e n, which see, p. 47, Note 2.

[3] D e s   T a g e s   e i n e   S t u n d e, etc.  This passage illustrates
well the difference between the genitive and accusative when they
designate time.  D e s   T a g e s, signifies at some point, during
some part, or within the day.  E i n e   S t u n d e means, *an hour
long*, or *for an hour*.  " My view is that one send (l a s s e   g e h e n)
boys to such a school one or two hours a day, and yet make them
work (l a s s e   s c h a ff e n, the rest of the time, learn some employment (manual exercise) and [do] whatever one shall wish, that both
[study and labor] may be carried on together, while the children
(folks) are young and can attend to them.  They spend now (s o n s t
*otherwise*, i. e. not in school, or as they now are) ten times as much
time in shooting with cross-bows, in playing ball, in running and
tumbling about."  S c h a ff e n, *to do*, properly governs e t w a s,
which was omitted, in familiar style, as it is now in the South of
Germany.  It then corresponds to our word *work*, as familiarly
used in common life.  U n d   w o z u   m a n   s i e   h a b e n   w i l l,
is elliptical, " and [attend] to whatever one will have them," or
desires them.  G e w a r t e n when, as here, it means, " to attend to any business," requires the genitive ; which is understood,
or to be supplied in this sentence.  Compare w a r t e five or six
lines below.  The word also means, *to expect, to wait for*.  B r i n-
g e n — z u (z u b r i n g e n) *to pass*, or *spend time*.  K e u l c h e n,
*a dart*, or *arrow*, a diminutive of K e u l e, *a club*, is not in common
use.

[4] M a g d l e i n, *girl*, the obsolete diminutive of M a g d.  The
modern word is M ä d c h e n.

des Tages eine Stunde zur Schule gehe,[1] und dennoch ihres Geschäfts im Hause wohl warte; sie verschläft[2] und vertanzt es, und verspielet doch wohl mehr Zeit. Es fehlet allein daran,[3] daß man nicht Lust noch Ernst dazu hat, das junge Volk zu ziehen, noch der Welt zu helfen und zu rathen mit feinen Leuten. Der Teufel hat viel lieber grobe Blöcke und unnütze Leute, daß es den Menschen ja nicht so wohl gehe auf Erden.

Welche[4] aber der Ausbund[5] darunter wären, der man sich verhofft[6], daß es geschickte Leute sollen werden zu Lehrern und Lehrerinnen, zu Predigern und andern geistlichen Aemtern, die soll man desto mehr und länger dabei lassen, oder selbst ganz dazu verordnen. Wie wir lesen von den heili=

---

[1] **Dass sie — gehe,** "that she may go," or, as we should say in English, "as to go."

[2] **Sie verschläft,** etc. "She sleeps it (the hour's time) away, and dances it away, and plays away (consumes in play) more time." On the force of the prefix, **ver,** see Gram. p. 250, 1, and 2.

[3] **Es fehlet allein daran,** etc. "Herein alone lies the difficulty (fault) viz. that we have no desire nor solicitude to educate the young, nor to aid mankind (**der Welt**) and to benefit them with accomplished citizens." **Rathen** is often coupled with **helfen** and has a similar signification; which comes from the idea of helping one out of difficulty by giving good counsel.

[4] **Welche,** *what persons,* i. e. "such persons among them as would be a choice selection, etc." See p. 239, Note 3.

[5] **Ausbund** literally means a specimen or pattern which shop-keepers put out (**aus**) for show, and bind or fasten (**binden**) upon a frame. As such specimens are generally *the best of their kind,* the word has come to signify commonly *a choice* or *selection.* When applied to anything bad, it means *the worst of the kind.*

[6] **Der man sich verhofft,** "of whom one entertains the hope that they will become suitable persons for instructors and instructresses, preachers and other clerical offices, these we ought to retain (leave) there so much the more, and the longer, or even direct them wholly to this employment," etc. **Der,** for **derer** in the genitive plural, is governed by **sich verhoft.** The construction is obsolete.

gen Märtyrern, die St. Agnes und Agata und Lucian du
dergleichen aufgezogen haben; daher auch die Klöster und
Stifte gekommen sind, aber nun gar in einen andern ver=
dammten Brauch verkehret. Und das will auch wohl Noth
seyn, denn der beschorene Haufe nimmt sehr ab: so ist auch
der größere Theil untüchtig zu lehren und zu regieren; denn
sie könnten nichts ohne des Bauchs pflegen, welches man
auch sie allein gelehret hat. So müssen wir ja Leute haben,
die uns Gottes Wort und Sacramente reichen, und Seelen=
wärter sind im Volk. Wo wollen wir sie aber nehmen, so
man die Schulen vergehen läßt, und nicht andere christlichere
aufrichtet? Sintemal die Schulen bisher gehalten, ob
sie gleich nicht vergiengen, doch nichts geben mögen, denn
eitel verlorene, schädliche Verführer.

Darum es hohe Noth ist,[1] nicht allein der jungen Leute
halben, sondern auch beider unserer Stände, geistlichen und
weltlichen, zu erhalten, daß man in unserer Sache mit Ernst
und in der Zeit dazu thue, auf daß wir's nicht hinten nach,
wenn wir's versäumet haben, vielleicht müssen lassen, ob
wir's denn gerne thun wollten, und umsonst den Reuling
uns mit Schaden beißen lassen ewiglich. Sehet an zum
Erempel, welch' einen großen Fleiß der König Salomo
hierinnen gethan hat,[2] wie hat er sich des jungen Volkes

---

[1] D a r u m  e s  h o h e  N o t h  i s t, etc. "Therefore there is
an urgent necessity, not only on account of the youth, but in order
to sustain both of our orders, the spiritual and the temporal, that men
take hold of this our cause with earnestness and in season, lest afterwards, when we have neglected it, we should be obliged to omit it,
though we would be glad then to attend to it, and should, to no purpose, forever cause remorse to gnaw us to our detriment. Z n  e r -
h a l t e n is used in the sense of um  zu  erhalten. H i n t e n
n a c h, means *after a thing is done*, or *when it is too late*. H i n t e n
d r e i n is used in the same sense. R e u l i n g, for R e u e is entirely out of use.

[2] G e t h a n  h a t, *used*. This word is often employed in connections where neither *to do*, nor *to make*, could be employed in English.

angenommen,[1] daß er unter seinen königlichen Geschäften auch ein Buch für das junge Volk gemacht hat, das da[2] heißet Proverbiorum. Und Christus selbst, wie zieht er die jungen Kindlein zu sich? Wie fleißig befiehlet er sie uns, und rühmet auch die Engel, die ihrer warten, Matth. 18.; daß er uns anzeige, wie ein großer Dienst[3] es ist, wenn man das junge Volk wohl ziehet: wiederum, wie gräulich er zürnet, so man sie ärgert und verderben lässet.

Darum, liebe Herrn, lasset euch das Werk angelegen[4] seyn, das Gott so hoch[5] von euch fordert, das euer Amt schuldig ist, das der Jugend so Noth ist, und das weder Welt noch Geist entbehren kann. Wir sind leider lange genug in Finsterniß verfaulet und verdorben, wir sind allzu lange genug[6] deutsche Bestien gewesen. Lasset uns auch einmal die Vernunft brauchen, daß Gott merke die Dankbarkeit seiner Güter,[7] und andere Länder sehen, daß wir auch Menschen und Leute sind, die etwas Nützliches entweder von ihnen lernen oder sie lehren könnten, damit auch durch uns die Welt gebessert werde. Ich habe das Meine gethan, ich wollte den deutschen Ländern gerne gerathen und geholfen haben,[8] ob mich gleich Etliche darüber werden verachten,

---

In such cases, it may be rendered by, *to use, to exercise, to apply*, etc.  Compare p. 20, Note 3.

[1] S i c h   d e s   j u n g e n   V o l k e s   a n g e n o m m e n.   See p. 55, Note 2.

[2] D a s   d a.  See p. 43, Note 4, end, and Gram. p. 157, infra.

[3] W i e   e i n   g r o s s e r   D i e n s t.  The German does not allow the article to follow the adjective except in exclamations, as in the English *how great a service.*

[4] A n g e l e g e n.  See p. 70, Note 2.

[5] H o c h.  See p. 152, Note 4.

[6] G e n u g  is redundant here.

[7] D a n k b a r k e i t   s e i n e r   G ü t e r, " that God may observe [in us] gratitude *for* his mercies."

[8] G e r a t h e n   u n d   g e h o l f e n   h a b e n.  See p. 265, Note 3.

und solchen truen Rath in Wind schlagen,[1] und besser wissen
wollen, das muß ich geschehen lassen.[2] Ich weiß wohl, daß
es Andere könnten besser ausgerichtet haben, aber weil sie
schweigen, richte ich's aus, so gut als ich's kann. Es ist je
besser dazu geredet, wie ungeschickt es auch sey, denn aller
Dinge[3] davon geschwiegen. Und bin der Hoffnung,[4] Gott
werde je eurer Etliche erwecken, daß mein treuer Rath nicht
gar in Asche falle, und werden ansehen nicht Den, der es
geredet, sondern die Sache selbst[5] bewegen, und sich bewegen
lassen.

Zum letzten[6] ist auch das wohl zu bedenken allen denjeni‑
gen, so Liebe und Lust haben, daß solche Schulen und Spra‑
chen in deutschen Ländern aufgerichtet und erhalten werden,
daß man Fleiß und Kosten nicht spare, gute Libereien und
Bücherhäuser, sonderlich in den großen Städten, die solches
wohl vermögen, zu verschaffen. Denn so das[7] Evangelium

---

[1] In Wind schlagen. See p. 202, Note 2.

[2] Dass muss ich geschehen lassen, "to that I must
submit."

[3] Aller Dinge, *wholly*. See p. 249, Note 4. Geredet—
geschwiegen [zu haben].

[4] Bin der Hoffnung, *am of the hope*, or entertain the hope.
Compare p. 68, Note 3.

[5] Die Sache selbst, etc. "agitate the subject itself and be
moved by it,"—a very peculiar form of expression.

[6] Znm letzten, etc. "Finally this must be considered by all
those who have a solicitude (love) and desire that such schools
should be established and such languages preserved in the German
states, that one should spare neither labor nor expense to procure
good libraries, and buildings to contain them, especially in large
cities, which can well afford it." Ist das zu bedenken al‑
len denjenigen, is highly idiomatic. The dative points out
the persons who ought to consider, as in the Latin, *id omnibus con‑
siderandum est.*

[7] Denn so das, etc. "For, if the gospel and knowledge of
every kind are to be preserved (to remain), they must be embraced
in and attached to books and writings."

und allerlei Kunst soll bleiben, muß es je in Bücher und Schriften verfasset und angebunden seyn; wie die Propheten und Apostel selbst gethan haben, als ich droben gesagt habe. Und das nicht allein darum, daß diejenigen, so uns geistlich und weltlich vorstehen, sollen zu lesen[1] und zu studiren haben: sondern daß auch die guten Bücher behalten und nicht verloren werden, sammt der Kunst und Sprache, so wir jetzt von GOttes Gnade haben. Hierinnen ist auch St. Paulus fleißig gewesen, da er Timotheo befiehlt: „Er solle anhalten am Lesen," und auch befiehlt: „Er solle das Pergament, das er zu Troada gelassen, mit sich bringen."

Ja, solches[2] haben sich beflissen alle Königreiche, die etwas sonderliches gewesen sind, und zuvor das israelitische Volk, unter welchen solches Werk Mose anfieng, der erste, und ließ das Buch des Gesetzes in die Lade GOttes verwahren, und that es unter die Hand der Leviten, daß man bei denselben sollte holen Abschriften, wer es bedürfe, also, daß er auch dem Könige gebeut, er solle von den Leviten solches Buches Abschrift nehmen. Daß man wohl siehet, wie Gott das Levitische Priesterthum unter andern Geschäften auch dazu verordnet hat, daß sie der Bücher hüten und warten sollten. Nachdem hat diese Liberei gemehret und gebessert Josua, darnach Samuel, David, Salomo, Jesajas, und so

---

[1] Sollen zu lesen, etc. " should have *something* to read and to study." See p. 111, Note 3, and p. 151, Note 3.

[2] Solches is in the genitive. " All kingdoms which have been distinguished, have bestowed care upon this (such); and first of all the Israelites, among whom Moses was the first to begin such a work, and commanded [them] to preserve the book of the law in the ark of God, and put it under the care (hand) of the Levites, that from (by) them persons should procure (go and get) copies, whoever needed them. He even commands the king (so that he commands the king) to take of the Levites a copy of this book. Thus one may see (so that one may see) that (how that) God directed the Levitical priesthood, to this among other duties, namely that they should preserve, and give attention to the books.

**23\***

fortan viel mehr Könige und Propheten. Daher ist gekommen die heilige Schrift des alten Testaments, welche sonst nimmermehr wäre zusammengebracht[1] oder geblieben, wo Gott nicht hätte solchen Fleiß darauf heißen haben.

Dem Exempel nach[2] haben auch die Stifte und Klöster vor Zeiten Libereien angerichtet, wiewohl mit wenig guten Büchern. Und was es für Schaden gethan hat, daß man zu der Zeit nicht darob gehalten hat, Bücher und gute Libereien zu verschaffen, da man Bücher und Leute genug dazu hatte, ist man darnach wohl gewahr worden, daß leider mit der Zeit dahin gefallen sind alle Künste und Sprachen, und anstatt rechtschaffenen Büchern die tollen, unnützen, schädlichen Mönchbücher Catholicon, Florista, Græcista, Labyrinthus, Dormi secure, und dergleichen vom Teufel eingeführet sind, daß damit die lateinische Sprache zu Boden ist gegangen, und nirgends keine geschickte Schule, noch Lehre, noch Weise zu studiren ist übriggeblieben. Und wie wir er-

---

[1] Zusammengebracht [werden], etc. "which would otherwise never have been collected, or have been preserved (remained) if God had not required (commanded) such diligence [in regard] to it."

[2] Dem Exempel nach, etc. "After this example did the collegiate churches and convents formerly found libraries, although with few good books. And what harm it has done, than men were not at that time intent upon procuring books and good libraries, when there were hooks and persons enough for that purpose, was afterwards perceived, namely, that, in time, all the arts, and languages declined, and, instead of good books, the senseless, useless, and infecting books of the monks, the catholicon, Florista, Graecista, Labyrinthus, Dormi secure, and the like were introduced by Satan, so that the Latin language was destroyed by them, and neither good schools, good instruction nor good modes of study remained." Darob (darüber) halten. See p. 239, Note 2.—Dahin gefallen, *fallen away*. On the use of dahin, see p. 80, Note 1. The monastic productions here censured were miserable school books, lexicons, grammars, etc. with these quaint titles.

fahren¹ und gesehen haben, daß mit so viel Mühe und Ar=
beit man die Sprachen und Kunst dennoch gar unvollkom=
men aus etlichen Brocken und Stücken alter Bücher aus
dem Staube und den Würmern wieder hervorgebracht hat,
und noch täglich daran sucht und arbeitet, gleichwie man in
einer zerstörten Stadt in der Asche nach den Schätzen und
Kleinodien gräbet.

Darin ist uns auch recht geschehen,² und Gott hat unsere

---

¹ Und wie wir erfahren, etc. This is an irregular construction. Und properly connects dass mit so viel Mühe
with dass damit die lateinische Sprache in the preceding sentence, which with the clause, dass leider mit der
Zeit, depend on the words gewahr worden.

² Darin ist uns auch recht geschehen, etc. There-
in we have received our just due, and God has paid us well (recht
wohl, *right well*) for our ingratitude, in that we did not consider
his benefits, and make provision at the proper time (when it was
time) and when we easily might, with which to have kept in possession of good books and learned men, but let it pass, as though it did
not concern us. So did he [to us] in turn, and suffered, instead of
the Bible and good books, Aristotle and numberless pernicious books
to come into vogue, which only led us farther and farther (immer
weiter) from the Bible. To these [were added] Satan's grim vis-
ages, the monks and the university ghosts, which we founded at an
inhuman expense, and [besides these,] many doctors, preachers, mag-
isters, priests and monks, i. e. great, coarse, fat asses, adorned with
red and brown caps, like swine led by a golden chain provided with
pearls, and we have burdened ourselves with these, who have taught
us nothing useful, but made us more and more blind, and senseless,
and as a reward (dafür) have consumed all our property, and have
filled all the cloisters, and indeed every corner (sammelten alle
Klöster, ja alle Winkel voll) with the dregs and filth of
their dirty, noxious (poisonous) books, on which one cannot think
without horror (on which it is horrid to think)." Ist uns recht
geschehen, corresponds to our phrase "It, or he served him
right;" and Es geschiet ihm Unrecht, to, "Injustice is
done him."—Als gienge es uns nicht an. Angehen,
is explained p. 234, Note 2.—So that er wiederum. This
last word often indicates *reciprocity*, whereas wieder without the

Undankbarkeit recht wohl bezahlet, daß wir nicht bedachten seine Wohlthat, und Vorrath schafften, da es Zeit war, und wohl konnten, damit wir gute Bücher und gelehrte Leute hätten behalten, und ließen es so fahren, als gienge es uns nicht an; so that er auch wiederum und ließ, anstatt der heiligen Schrift und guter Bücher, den Aristoteles kommen mit unzähligen schädlichen Büchern, die uns nur immer weiter von der Bibel führeten; dazu die Teufelslarven, die Mönche und der Hohenschulen Gespenst, die wir mit unmenschlichem Gut gestiftet, und viele Doctoren, Predicatoren, Magister, Pfaffen und Mönche, das ist große, grobe, fette Esel, mit rothen und braunen Baretten geschmückt, wie die Säue mit einer goldnen Kette und Perle erhalten, und auf uns selbst geladen haben, die uns nichts Gutes lehreten, sondern nur immer mehr blinder und toller machten, und dafür all' unser Gut fraßen, und sammelten nur des Drecks und Mistes ihrer unflätigen, giftigen Bücher alle Klöster, ja alle Winkel voll, daran gräulich zu denken ist.

Ist's nicht ein elender Jammer bisher gewesen, daß ein Knabe hat müssen[1] zwanzig Jahre oder länger studiren, allein, daß er so viel böses Lateinisch hat gelernt, daß er möchte Pfaffe werden und Messe lesen? Und welcher dahin gekommen ist, der ist selig gewesen, selig ist die Mutter gewesen, die ein solches Kind getragen hat. Und ist doch[2]

---

addition of u m expresses *repetition* merely. For this force of u m, see p. 133, Note 1.—D e s  D r e c k s is governed by v o l l, and the whole phrase a l l e  K l ö s t e r ,  j a  a l l e  W i n k e l  v o l l, as the object of the verb s a m m e l t e n expresses a *measure* or *quantity.*

[1] H a t  m ü s s e n, *has been obliged.* See p. 148, Note 3.

[2] U n d  i s t  d o c h, etc. "And yet he has continued to be a poor, ignorant man all his life long, who has been good for nothing either to cluck or to lay eggs. Z u m belongs not to E i e r (for d e m in z u m or z u  d e m could not belong to a plural noun) but to l e g e n. The article is used because the infinitive here assumes the nature of a substantive,—*egg-laying.* See p. 14, Note 3.

ein armer, ungelehrter Mensch sein Lebenlang geblieben, der weder zu glucken, noch zum Eier legen getaugt hat. Solche Lehrer und Meister haben wir müssen allenthalben haben, die selbst nichts gekonnt[1] und nichts Gutes noch Rechtes haben mögen lehren, ja auch die Weise nicht gewußt, wie man doch lernen und lehren sollte. Was ist die Schuld? Es sind keine andere Bücher vorhanden gewesen, denn solche tolle Mönchs= und Sophisten=Bücher. Was sollten denn anders daraus werden, denn eitel[2] tolle Schüler und Lehrer, wie die Bücher waren, die sie lehreten?[3] Eine Dohle hecket keine Taube, und ein Narr macht keinen Klugen. Das ist der Lohn der Undankbarkeit, daß man nicht hat Fleiß an Libereien gewendet, sondern hat die guten Bücher vergehen lassen und die unnützen behalten.

Aber mein Rath ist nicht, daß man ohne Unterschied allerlei Bücher zu Haufe raffe, und nicht mehr gedenke, denn nur auf die Menge und den Haufen der Bücher. Ich wollte die Wahl darunter haben, daß[4] es nicht Noth sey, aller Juristen Comment, aller Theologen Sententiarien,[5] und aller Philosophen Questionen und aller Mönche Sermone zu sammeln. Ja ich wollte solchen Mist ganz ausstoßen, und mit rechtschaffenen Büchern meine Liberei versorgen, und gelehrte Leute darüber zu Rath nehmen.

Erstlich sollte die heilige Schrift beide auf Lateinisch, Griechisch, Hebräisch und Deutsch, und ob sie noch[6] in mehr

---

[1] Gekonnt, *known.* See p. 221, Note 4.

[2] Eitel. See p. 10, Note 4.

[3] Die sie lehreten. Grammatically, either d i e or s i e might be the nominative ; but both usage and the sense require d i e to be the nominative.

[4] D a s s, *because.*

[5] Sententarien. Sententiarier (sententiarii) were those who wrote Sententiarien (sententiaria) on the Sentenzen (sententiae) of Peter Lombardus.

[6] Und ob sie noch, etc. " and if it be still in other langua-

Sprachen wäre, darinnen ſeyn. Darnach die beſten Auslleger und die Aelteſten, beide Griechiſch, Hebräiſch und Lateiniſch, wo ich ſie finden könnte.

Darnach ſolche Bücher, die zu den Sprachen zu lernen dienen,[1] als die Poeten und Oratoren, nicht angeſehen,[2] ob ſie Heiden oder Chriſten wären, griechiſch oder lateiniſch. Denn aus ſolchen muß man die Grammatica lernen.

Darnach ſollten ſeyn die Bücher von den freien Künſten, und ſonſt von allen andern Künſten.

Zuletzt auch Bücher der Rechte und Arznei, wiewohl auch hier unter den Commenten eine gute Wahl nöthig iſt.

Mit unter den vornehmſten aber ſollten ſeyn die Chroniken und Hiſtorien, welcherlei Sprachen man haben könnte :[3] denn dieſelben[4] wundernützlich ſind, der Welt Lauf zu erkennen und zu regieren, ja auch Gottes Wunder und Werke zu ſehen. O wie manche ſeine Geſchichten[5] und Sprüche ſollte man jetzt haben, die in deutſchen Ländern geſchehen und ergangen ſind, deren wir jetzt gar keines wiſſen. Das macht :[6] Niemand iſt da geweſen, der ſie beſchrieben, oder ob ſie ſchon[7] beſchrieben geweſen wären, Niemand die Bü-

---

ges," is elliptical for, " and in other languages, if it existed in any other."

[1] D i e  z u  d e n  S p r a c h e n  z u  l e r n e n  d i e n e n, a peculiar expression, " which serve for the languages to learn (them)."

[2] A n g e s e h e n.  See p. 15, Note 8, and p. 7, Note 6.

[3] W e l c h e r l e i  S p r a c h e n  m a n  h a b e n  k ö n n t e for i n  w e l c h e r l e i  S p r a c h e n  m a n  s i e  h a b e n  k o n n t e.

[4] D e n n  d i e s e l b e n, etc. " for they are wonderfully useful for learning and regulating the course of the world."

[5] G e s c h i c h t e n (not H i s t o r i e n) can be said to g e s c h e - h e n because the former properly indicates *events* (w a s  g e s c h i - e t), whereas the latter properly means the *narratives* of those events.

[6] D a s  m a c h t.  D a s is in the accusative, and the following sentence is nominative to m a c h t.  In a free translation, it would be, " The cause is that no one," etc.—D e r  s i e  b e s c h r i e b e n [h a t].

[7] O b—s c h o n, *if.*  Literally it means *although.*

cher behalten hat; darum man auch von uns Deutschen nichts weiß in andern Ländern, und müssen[1] in aller Welt die deutschen Bestien heißen, die nichts mehr können,[2] denn kriegen, fressen und saufen. Aber die Griechen und Lateiner, ja auch die Hebräer, haben ihr Ding[3] so genau und fleißig beschrieben, daß, wo auch ein Weib oder Kind etwas Son= derliches gethan oder geredet hat, das muß alle Welt lesen und wissen: dieweil sind wir Deutsche noch immer Deutsche, und wollen Deutsche bleiben.

Weil uns denn jetzt Gott so gnädiglich berathen hat mit aller Fülle, beide der Kunst, gelehrter Leute und Bücher, so ist's Zeit, daß wir ernten und einschneiden das Beste, das wir können, und Schätze sammeln, damit wir etwas behal= ten auf das Zukünftige von diesen goldnen Jahren, und nicht diese reiche Ernte versäumen. Denn es zu besorgen ist,[4] und jetzt schon wieder anfängt, daß man immer neue und andere Bücher macht, daß es zuletzt dahin komme, daß durch des Teufels Werk die guten Bücher, so jetzt durch den Druck hervorgebracht sind, wiederum unterdrückt werden, und die losen, heillosen Bücher von unnützen und tollen Dingen wieder einreißen und alle Winkel füllen. Denn damit gehet der Teufel gewißlich um, daß man sich wieder= um mit eitel Catholicen, Floristen, Wodernisten,[5] und dem

---

[1] Und [wir] müssen.

[2] Die nichts mehr können, etc. "who know nothing but how to fight, eat and drink." On the words fressen and saufen, see p. 51, Note 1

[3] Ding. See p. 254, Note 3.

[4] Denn es zu besorgen ist, etc. "For it is to be feared, and even now has begun again [to take place], that new and differ- ent books will not cease to be made, so that at least it will come to this, that through Satan's influence the good books which," etc.

[5] Catholicen, Floristen, Modernisten, *Catholicons, Florists, Modernists*. It would be amusing to see a list of all the fanciful names which the monks gave to the school-books which they wrote.

verdammten Mönchen= und Sophiften=Mift tragen und
martern[1] müffe, wie vorhin, und immer lernen, und doch im=
mer nichts erlernen.[2]

Derohalben bitte ich euch, meine lieben Herrn, daß ihr
wollet diefe meine True und Fleiß bei euch laffen Frucht
fchaffen. Und ob Etliche wären,[3] die mich zu geringe dafür
hielten, daß fie meines Raths follten leben, oder mich, als
den Verdammten von den Tyrannen, verachten: die woll=
ten doch das anfehen, daß ich nicht das meine, fondern al=
lein des ganzen deutfchen Landes Glück und Heil fuche.
Und ob ich fchon ein Narr wäre, und träfe doch etwas
Gutes,[4] follte es je keinem Weifen eine Schande dünken,
mir zu folgen. Und ob ich gleich ein Türke und Heide wäre,
fo[5] man doch fiehet, daß nicht mir daraus kann der Nutzen
kommen, fondern den Chriften, fo[5] follen fie doch billig[6] mei=

---

[1] S i c h   m i t —t r a g e n   u n d   m a r t e r n, *to busy and torture
one's self with.* See the lexicons on the reflective verb s i c h   t r a-
g e n, when used of a person. Of a garment, it means *to sit, to fit.*

[2] E r l e r n e n. The prefix e r implies *success,* in the act expressed by the verb. See Gram. p. 249. 2. "To be ever learning, and
yet never acquire anything."

[3] U n d   o b   E t l i c h e   w ä r e n, etc. "And though there
should be some, who regard me as so insignificant that they will not
accept of my advice (hold me as too insignificant for this, namely,
that they should take my advice) or contemn me as one condemned
by the tyrants, still let them (they should) consider this, that I am
not seeking my own interest but merely that of all Germany."—
R a t h s is governed by l e b e n. Compare p. 68, Note 3.—W o l l-
t e n, imperfect subjunctive, *they should be willing.*—G l ü c k   u n d
H e i l are regarded as one and the same, and hence d a s   m e i n e,
in the singular, can agree with them.

[4] U n d   t r ä f e   d o c h   e t w a s   G u t e s, etc. "and should yet
hit upon something good, no wise man should think it a disgrace to
follow me. On d ü n k e n, see p. 22, Note 3. The rule of the grammarians there referred to is often disregarded, and so here.

[5] S o, in the first instance is conditional (if); in the second, illative and not to be translated.

[6] B i l l i g. See p. 102, Note 3.

nen Dienſt nicht verachten. Es hat wohl jemals[1] ein Narr beſſer gerathen, denn ein ganzer Rath der Klugen. Moſe mußte ſich von Jethro lehren laſſen.[2]

Hiemit befehle ich[3] euch Alle Gottes Gnade, der wolle eure Herzen erweichen und anzünden, daß ſie ſich der armen, elenden, verlaſſenen Jugend mit Ernſt annehmen, und durch göttliche Hülfe ihnen rathen und helfen zu ſeligem und chriſtlichem Regiment des deutſchen Landes an Leib und Seele, mit aller Fülle und Ueberfluß, zu Lob und Ehren Gott dem Vater, durch JEſum Chriſtum, unſern Heiland, Amen. Datum Wittenberg, Anno 1524.

---

[1] J e m a l s properly signifies *ever* in the sense of *at any time.* It seems here to mean, *at times, sometimes.*

[2] S i c h  v o n  J e t h r o  l e h r e n  l a s s e n, "seek instruction from Jethro," (cause himself to be taught by Jethro).

[3] H i e m i t  b e f e h l e  i c h, etc. " Herewith I commend you all to the grace of God. May he (who may) soften and kindle your hearts, that they may interest themselves in behalf of the poor, wretched, and abandoned youth, and with the blessing of God counsel and aid them on to a happy and Christian state of social order (government) in respect both to body and to soul, will all fulness and plenty to the praise and honor of God the Father through Jesus Christ our Saviour." Welche herzliche Seelsorgerliebe Luthers spricht aus dieser Schrift! Wie vertritt er, als ein kräftiger Vormund, die Sache der Jugend bei den Eltern und Obrigkeiten!—wie die Sache der Gelehrsamkeit, besonders das Erlernen der Sprachen gegen rohe, eigennützige Philister einerseits, und gegen *freres ignorantins* andrerseits!—Raumer, Geschichte der Pädagogik I. 169.

**24**

## EXPOSITION OF THE FOURTEENTH CHAPTER OF THE GOSPEL OF JOHN.

Auslegung des 14 Capitels Johannis *

---

### Vorrede.

In diesem und zweyen folgenden Capiteln des Evange=
listen St. Johannis, haben wir die schöne Predigt des Herrn
Christi, welche er gethan hat nach dem letzten Abendmahl,
da er jetzt an sein Leiden treten und seine liebe Jünger hin=
ter ihm lassen sollte, sie damit zu trösten[1] und zu stärcken,
beyde, wider die gegenwärtige Traurigkeit über seinem Ab=
scheiden, und wider das zukünftige Leiden, so sie überfallen
würde vom Teufel, von der Welt und ihrem eignen Gewis=
sen.

Und ist freylich diß die beste und tröstlichste Predigt, so der
Herr' Christus auf Erden gethan, und St. Johannes diß[2]
Stücks halber insonderheit zu preisen ist vor andern Evan=

---

* Several paragraphs, not essential to the connection, have been omitted for the sake of brevity. The orthography has not been conformed strictly to that of the preceding part of the work; but, as Luther himself was by no means uniform in this respect, it has been thought best, in order better to prepare one to read Luther and other old writers, to let the orthography, in the present piece, stand as it is in the edition from which we copy. The peculiarity consists mostly in using the vowel *i* single, when it is long, for the diphthong *ie*, as, in d i s s instead of d i e s s; double consonants instead of single consonants, as in k l o p f f e n, instead of k l o p f e n; *y* for *i*, as in b e y instead of b e i; and r e n and l e n in certain verbs instead of e r n and e l n, as in t r a u r e n instead of t r a u e r n.

[1] S i e d a m i t z u t r ö s t e n in the sense of u m s i e d a m i t z u t r ö s t e n. "In order therewith to comfort and strengthen them both against," etc.

[2] D i s s for d i e s e s, "on account of this piece."

geliſten, daß er ſolche Predigt gefaſſet, und der Chriſtenheit zu Troſt nach ihm gelaſſen,[1] als einen Schatz und Kleinod, ſo mit der Welt Gut nicht zu bezahlen,[2] und ja immer Schade und hoch zu beklagen wäre, wo ſolche Predigt ſollte unbeſchrieben, und wir ſolches Schatzes beraubet blieben ſeyn.[3]

Denn es ſind doch hierinn[4] die allerlieblichſten, freund= lichſten Tröſtungen und ſüſſeſten Worte des treuen, lieben Heilandes Chriſti, ſo er ſeinen lieben Jüngern, als er von ihnen ſcheidet, zur Letze[5] gibt, dergleichen nimmer kein Menſch[6] auf Erden gegen ſeinen liebſten und beſten Freun= den thun und reden kann. Daß[7] man ſiehet, wie er aus

---

[1] Gelassen [hat]. And so a little above, gethan [hat].

[2] So mit der Welt Gut nicht zu bezahlen [wäre], " which (so) it would not be possible to repay (nicht zu bezahlen wäre) with [all] the goods of the world."

[3] Beraubet [ge] blieben seyn [sollten].

[4] Hierinn. According to present usage, this word would end in a single *n*. Short unaccented monosyllabic terminations, particles, and auxiliaries double their final consonants only when they receive an accession, forming a new syllable, thus giving some degree of accent to the former; as hierin, hierinnen; Fürstin, Fürstinnen; des, dessen; hat, hatte. There are a few exceptions. See Gram. p. 80.

[5] Zur Letze, *as a token of affection on parting.* It is now provincial.

[6] Dergleichen nimmer kein Mensch, " such as (the like of which) no man ever." See p. 4, Note 2, and p. 148, Note 6.

[7] Dass, *so that,* is dependent on the preceding assertion. " So that one perceives how he, from the pure, overflowing, indescribable love with which his heart burned towards them, cared for them, and took a heartier interest in them, than the greatest peril and distress of one's nearest friend can give him, so that over it he forgets his own sorrow and anguish (in order that he may support them with his consolation), of which, however, his heart was, at this hour, full (as he himself says to them : My soul is sorrowful even unto death) and was already in the sternest conflict with death and the devil."—Einem zu Hertzen gehen is *to go near one's heart.* Instead of höheste, höchste is now used.

eitel voller unausſprechlicher Liebe, damit ſein Hertz gegen
ihnen gebrannt, für ſie ſorget, und ſich ihrer annimmt, hertz=
licher, denn keinem Menſchen ſeines nächſten Freunds hö=
heſte Gefahr und Noth mag zu Hertzen gehen, daß er auch
darob ſeines eigenen Leibs und Angſt vergiſſet, (damit er
nur ſie durch ſeinen Troſt erhalte,) welcher doch auf dieſe
Stunde ſein Hertz voll war, (wie er ſelbſt zu ihnen ſagt:
Meine Seele iſt betrübt bis auf den Tod,) und bereits in
dem höheſten Kampf ſtund wider den Tod und Teufel. Und
hat allhie reichlich ausſchüttet alle den hohen, hertzlichen
Troſt, ſo die gantze Chriſtenheit hat, und ſo ein Menſch in
allen Nöthen und Leiden begehren ſollte.

---

1. Und er ſprach zu ſeinen Jüngern: Ener
Herz erſchrecke nicht.

Hier ſieheſt du erſtlich, wie hertzlich und treulich der freund=
liche Herr Chriſtus ſich ſeiner lieben Jünger annimmt, und
für ſie ſorget, daß er ſie nicht ohne Troſt laſſe, weil es jetzt
an dem war,[1] daß er eben in derſelben Nacht ſollte von
ihnen geſchieden werden durch ſein bitter Leiden und Creutz,
(wie er ihnen bisher mannigfaltiglich zuvor geſagt hatte,)
und ſie allein hinter ihm laſſen in groſſer Gefahr, Furcht
und Schrecken.

Denn bis daher[2] waren ſie allezeit ſicher, getroſt und ohne
Furcht geweſt,[3] weil er ſelbſt perſönlich bey ihnen war, und
ſie ſahen, wie er ſich ſo gewaltiglich beweiſete in dem Volck
mit Predigen und Wundern, daß ſie alle Aufſehen auf ihn

---

[1] An dem war dass er sollte, "was on the point of (was
at the point that he should separate,) being separated." An dem
is often so used.

[2] Bis daher, *up to that point;* bisher, *hitherto.* Daher, in
the former expression, does not mean *hence,* but *at that place,* as it
frequently does.

[3] Gewest, obsolete for gewesen.

haben mußten,[1] und die Hohenpriester und Obersten[2] selbst
sich müßten fürchten, und sorgen, wo sie ihn angriffen,[3]
möchte sich das ganze Volck wider sie erregen.  Darum die
Apostel, ob sie wol arme, geringe[4] Leute waren, doch waren
sie ohne Sorge und Furcht, gingen dahin, als[5] müßten sich
ehe die andern vor ihnen fürchten.  Denn sie dachten, weil
uns dieser Mann lebet,[6] so hat es keine Noth, er kann uns
wohl schützen und retten rc.  Daher war auch St. Petrus
so ein[7] trefflich kühner Mann und unerschrockener Apostel,
daß er sich darbent[8] und vermisset,[9] mit Christo auch in Tod

---

[1] Dass sie alle Aufsehen auf ihn haben mussten,
"that they (das Volk) must all be amazed (have amazement) at
him," or that he created a great sensation among them.

[2] Obersten.  Der Oberste, from ober, *over*, means *the
highest in authority*, and varies in signification according to the class
of individuals to whom it refers, as *ruler, chief, captain*, etc.  Obrigkeit (or Oberkeit) means *the civil authorities*, the magistracy,
and admits of the distinction höchste Obrigkeit and Unter-
Obrigkeit.

[3] Angriffen, imperfect subjunctive.  "If they should apprehend him."

[4] Geringe, *weak, insignificant*,  See p. 249, Note 2.

[5] Gingen dahin, als, etc.  "went on, as if the others were
sooner to stand in fear of them."

[6] Weil uns dieser Mann lebet, "while this man (Christ)
is alive with us (for us).  Uns is *dativus commodi*.

[7] So ein.  See p. 25, Note 7.

[8] Darbeut, obsolete for darbietet.  See Gram. p. 203, supra.

[9] Vermisset.  Sich vermessen, from messen, *to measure*, and ver, *wrong*, means *to presume, promise or affirm too much
in consequence of over-estimating one's self*.  In the old writers and
in common life, it means, *to affirm with an oath, or solemnly*; and so
here.  "That he volunteered and solemnly averred that he would die
with Christ, though all the others should deny him, and began to
show it (his courage or the truth of what he said) with his action.
When the Jews would apprehend Christ, he put himself at once on
the defensive, and began to lay on with the sword, not intimidated
(by the circumstance) that a great and armed multitude had come to

zu gehn, ob ihn gleich die andern alle verleugneten, und fing auch an, solches mit der That zu beweisen: als die Juden Christum wollten fahen, stellt er sich sobald zur Gegenwehr, und fähet an, mit dem Schwerdt drein zu schlagen, unge=scheuet, daß der Haufe groß und mit Waffen gerüstet zu ihnen kommen war. Und Summa,[1] so lange sie Christum bey sich hatten, durften sie sich nichts besorgen, wären auch wol vor jedermann sicher blieben.

Nun aber Christus ihnen verkündiget, daß er muß von ihnen scheiden, zeigt und weissaget er ihnen zuvor, daß es ihnen viel anders, denn bis daher, gehen werde, und nun dazu kommen, daß ihr Hertz mit Schrecken und Zagen ver=sucht werde. Wie es denn geschah, als[2] er hinweg war, so schändlich, jämmerlich und ärgerlich hingerichtet; da entfiel ihnen bald das Hertz, daß sie sich[3] vor Furcht verschlossen und versteckten, und nicht herfür durften.

---

them."—Fahen is obsolete for fangen, and fahet an, for fängt an.—Drein zu schlagen. See p. 166, Note 1. Un-gescheuet is formed from scheu, *timid*. Gescheut has come to have the secondary or derived signification, *cautious, prudent, wise*, and is often confounded with gescheit. With the prefix un, the word sometimes, as here, has its original signification, *fearless*, though it more commonly means, *heedless, impudent*.—Kommen stands for gekommen.

[1] Summa, *in a word*. See p. 243, Note 2. " And, in a word, so long as they had Christ with them, they ought to fear nothing; they would, no doubt have remained safe before any man." Blieben for geblieben.

[2] Als. There is confusion in this sentence. Either als here performs improperly the two-fold office of introducing the *apodosis* (Nachsatz) to the preceding words, and, at the same time, of stand-ing at the beginning of the *protasis* (Vordersatz) to the clause beginning with da entfiel (As it happened, when he went away. When he went away, etc. their hearts failed them), or, wie es denn geschah belongs to the preceding sentence, and als should begin a new one. The latter is probably the case.

[3] Dass sie sich, etc. " so that they shut themselves up, and

Denn es war auch gar zu ein schrecklicher,[1] scheuslicher Fall, daß der Christus, so zuvor gefürchtet und schrecklich war allen Rathsherren und Priestern zu Jerusalem, der wird[2] plötzlich so schwach und so gar verlassen, daß er kommt in die Hände seiner Feinde, die ihn haudeln aufs allerärgste, und des schändlichsten Todes dahin richten.[3] Da ist nicht mehr der Christus, der die Todten auferwecket,[4] die Käufer und Verkäufer aus dem Tempel stieß, und so wunderte daß sich jedermann dafür entsetzet; sondern so schwach und veracht, als der ärgeste, elendeste Mensch auf Erden, den jedermann mit Füssen trit, und die Allergeringsten ihn[5] anspeyen. Das war ja weit und tief gefallen[6] von der vorigen herrlichen Gestalt, daß die lieben Jünger, als die auch noch schwach[7] im Glauben, und solche Püffe nicht mehr erfahren hatten, mußten sorgen und zagen: O, wo wollen

---

hid themselves, and did not dare come forth." Herfür, for hervor kommen. See p. 35, Note 3, and p. 6, Note 4.

[1] Gar zu ein schrecklicher, "quite too frightful an occurrence," is obsolete for ein gar zu schrecklicher.

[2] Der wird, etc. Der is not needed here; it merely resumes the beginning of the clause der Christus." " That Christ, who was formerly so feared, and so terrible to all the elders (counsellors) and priests at Jerusalem, he becomes (instead of, " that he should become") all of a sudden so weak," etc.

[3] Des schändlichsten Todes dahin richten. Dahin richten (to put out of the way) is nearly the same as hinrichten, to execute. See p. 50, Note 2 near the end, and p. 57, Note 1. Todes is a genitive of manner. See p. 68, Note 3.

[4] Auferwecket [hat]. Wunderte for Wonder that, used in this sense, in the old German only.

[5] Ihn, is not necessary, as without it, den is sufficient.

[6] Das war—gefallen, a peculiar German idiom, by which a preterite participle (that was far fallen) is used where we should use a present participle substantively. " That was falling far," i. e. was a great fall. See p. 9, Note 5.

[7] Als die noch schwach, "as those still weak," or those who are still weak.

wir nun bleiben ?¹ Er iſt unſer Troſt und Trotz geweſt,
der² iſt nun dahin, und haben niemand mehr, der uns ſchütz=
en oder beyſtehen könnte ; jetzt ſind unſere Feinde ſtarck und
mächtig, wir aber ſchwach und verlaſſen von aller Welt, ꝛc.

Wider ſolche künftige Angſt und Schrecken kommt er zu=
vor, als ein frommer, treuer Herr, mit dieſem Troſt und
Vermahnung, daß ſie dennoch³ bleiben können und nicht ver=
zagen, fähet ſolches eben an von dem, das ihnen begegnen
ſollte und mußte, daß, wenn es alſo geſchehen würde, ſie
daran gedächten, daß ers ihnen zuvor geſagt und dagegen
vermahnet hätte, und ſpricht zum allererſten : Euer Hertz
erſchrecke nicht. Als ſollte er ſagen : Ich weiß wohl,⁴
meine lieben Jünger, wie es euch gehen wird, wenn ich von
euch kommen und euch allein laſſen werde, daß euch eitel
Schrecken und Furcht wird überfallen, und werdet ſolch
Ding an mir erſehen, das euch groſſe Urſach wird geben, zu

---

¹ W o  w o l l e n  w i r  n u n  b l e i b e n. "Where now shall we
keep ourselves (remain)?"  What shall we do with ourselves?
With the word b l e i b e n several idioms are formed besides those
mentioned p. 63, Note 5. See the larger lexicons.

² D e r, as a demonstrative is more emphatic than e r would be
here, and is equivalent to *he* italicized in English.  See p. 243, Note
4.—U n d  [w i r]  h a b e n  n i e m a n d.

³ D a s s  s i e  d e n n o c h, etc.  It may seem a little doubtful what
the relation of this clause is to the preceding, whether d a s s is to be
rendered, *namely that*, or *to the end that*.  The latter is undoubtedly
the right construction.

⁴ I c h  w i e s s  w o h l, etc.  "I know full well, my dear disciples,
how it will be (go) with you, when I shall go away from you and
leave you alone, viz. that nothing but (e i t e l) terror and fear will
come (fall) upon you, and that you will behold in respect to me (not,
*in me*) things that will give you great occasion to be alarmed, so that
your heart might be shut up within you, and that you will not know
what will become of you (where you shall keep yourselves).—S o l c h
D i n g—d a s, "such things as," or "things which."—A n  m i r,
*upon me*, or relating to me externally (not to his *character*). See p.
80, Note 3. Z u s c h m e l z e n, means to *solder, to seal*, or close up
by melting.

zagen, daß euch das Hertz im Leib möcht zuschmeltzen, und nicht wissen werdet, wo ihr bleiben sollet. Das sage ich euch zuvor und eben darum, daß ihr euch nicht so bald lasset das Hertz gar nehmen,[1] sondern seyd keck, und rüstet euch zu dem Kampf; und wenn es dazu kommt, so denckt dieser meiner Vermahnung, daß ihr darum nicht so bald verzagt und verzweifelt 2c.

Also wollte er ihnen gerne das Hertz aufrichten und erhalten, als der da wohl wußte, wo es ihnen liegen würde :[2] daß, ob sie gleich Schrecken und Angst fühlen würden, sich dennoch könnten aufhalten und desto leichter dawider bestehen. Denn es liegt gar viel daran, wie das Hertz gerüstet sey : ob Unglück[3] und Schrecken daher gehet, daß man dennoch möge Aufenthalt wissen, oder jemand habe, der ihm ein tröstlich Wort einrede oder erinnere ; so ist es alles desto leichter zu tragen. Darum thut er ihnen diese Predigt zuvor, beyde, das künftige Schrecken anzuzeigen, und daneben[4]

---

[1] Euch—das Hertz nehmen, " take away your courage." See p. 52, Note 4. " That you do not at once allow your courage to be taken away, but that you be bold, and arm yourselves for the conflict; and when it comes (to it)," etc.

[2] Wo es ihnen liegen würde, " where the difficulty would lie with them." Wo is here used nearly in the sense of woran. Compare es liegt gar viel daran, at the beginning of the next sentence, and p. 169, Note 4.

[3] Ob Unglück, etc. " [that] if calamity and terror come, one may still know where to find support, or have some one, who," etc. Though the English idiom requires the word, that, at the beginning of this sentence (before, if), in the German, dass properly comes after the clause.—Aufenthalt commonly signifies abode. But the word aufhalten in the preceding sentence, (for which Luther sometimes uses enthalten. See p. 83, Note 2,) and erhalten a little below, and furthermore the circumstance that the old writers use the verb anfenthalten in the sense of to sustain, to support, make the meaning evident here, as given in the translation.

[4] Daneben, " in connection with that," or, " at the same time." See p. 94, Note 4, and p. 193, Note 3, near the middle.

zu tröſten, auf daß ſie ſich hernach derſelben erinnern und damit erhalten ſollten; wiewol dieſe Tröſtung[1] zu der Stunde ſobald nicht half, noch zu Kräften kam, bis ſo lang der Heilige Geiſt kam. Aber zu der Zeit, als Chriſtus hinweg war, da war es gar aus und kein Hertz noch Muth mehr bey ihnen, daß auch ihrer keiner für einer ohnmächtigen Magd konnte ſtehen; da waren alle ſein Wort und Werck dahin, und dieſes Troſts gantz und gar vergeſſen. Alſo hat er dißmal ſeine lieben Apoſteln vermahnet und getröſtet, als die[2] auch des Troſts wohl bedurften.

Es iſt aber nicht um ihrentwillen, ſondern uns[3] geſchrieben, daß wir auch dieſes Troſtes lernen gebrauchen auf gegenwärtige und künftige Noth, und daß ein jeglicher Chriſt, wenn er getauft iſt, und ſich hat zu Chriſto begeben, mag und ſoll ſich[4] auch alſo drein ſchicken, und gewißlich deß verſehen, daß ihm auch begegnen wird Schrecken und Angſt, die ihm das Hertz blöd und verzagt machen, es ſey durch eine oder mancherley Feindſchaft und Widerſtand.

Denn ein Chriſt hat aus der Maaſſe viel Feinde,[5] wo er

---

[1] Wiewohl diese Tröstung, etc. "although this consolation did not at the moment immediately aid, and take effect, until the Holy Spirit came; but at the time that Christ was [taken] away, then all was over (out), and no heart nor courage was in them, so that none of them could stand before (für for vor) a feeble maid; all his (Christ's) words and works were away (out of mind), etc.— Aus as an adverb after ist, war, etc. is used just like our word, *over*, in similar constructions. Alle, with Wort and Werk as collectives.

[2] Als die, *as those who.*

[3] Uns, is not governed by um—willen, which requires the genitive, but the construction is changed to the dative, uns instead of unsertwillen. "But it is written not on their account, but for us."

[4] Mag und soll sich, etc. "he may and should accommodate himself to it, and confidently expect it that fear," etc.

[5] Aus der Maasse viel Feinde, etc. "has surpassingly numerous enemies, if he will stand (abide) by his Lord; the world with the devil daily seeks his (body and) life, furthermore his own

bey seinem Herrn bleiben will, die Welt samt dem Teufel steht ihm täglich nach Leib und Leben, dazu sein eigen Fleisch und Vernunft und Gewissen, so ihn stets plagt, daß ihm leichtlich Schrecken und Zagen widerfähret, auch von seinem eignen Hertzen.

Darum, willst du auch ein Christ seyn,[1] den Aposteln und allen Heiligen gleich, so rüste dich, und warte deß gewiß, daß einmal ein Stündlein kommen wird, und dein Hertz treffen, daß du erschrecken und zagen wirst. Denn solches ist allen Christen verkündiget, auf daß sie lernen[2] sich ge= wöhnen, und kurtz ihre Sachen also richten, wenn sie jetzt

flesh, reason and conscience, which constantly tortures him, so that terror and fear easily invade him, even from his own heart." B l e i - b e n with b e i, in a figurative sense, often means *to adhere to one, to stand by him.*—S t e h e n followed by n a c h, (different from n a c h s t e h e n meaning *to be inferior*), signifies, *to seek*, like the Latin *petere*, generally in a hostile sense. L e i b, *the body*, i. e. to kill it. L e i c h t l i c h, see p. 186, Note 2.

[1] W i l l s t  d u  a u c h  e i n  C h r i s t  s e y n, etc. " If you will also be a Christian like the Apostles and all the saints, arm yourself, and assuredly expect (it) that an [evil] hour will come and pierce your heart so that you," etc.

[2] A u f  d a s s  s i e  l e r n e n, etc. " in order that they may learn [in their thoughts] to accustom themselves, and immediately so dis-pose their affairs (if they at present feel secure) and that they so ap-prehend and regard it as if (that) their state (it) will soon change, and that they may say to themselves (think) : ' let things continue as they are, just as long as it is God's will ; to-day, joyful and in good spirits, to-morrow sad ; to-day alive, to-morrow dead ; to-day in prosperity and security, to-morrow in all sorts of calamity,'—and that they do not slumber (snore) ever on, as though there never were to be any calamity." A l s o in both instances relates to a l s  d a s s. The latter indicates how it will be with Christians *in fact*, the former points out a corresponding feeling. In good English, we should vary the form of comparison and say ; " In order that they may regulate their plans, and adjust their affairs, and all their views and feelings as though they were certain that a change would take place." W ü r d e  e s, is impersonal, and refers to the idea of *life, condition,* etc.

ſicher ſind, daß ſie es alſo annehmen und anſehen, als daß
es ſich bald ändern werde, und dencken: es währe, wie
lange Gott will; hent fröhlich und gutes Muths, morgen
traurig; hent lebend, morgen todt; hent in Glück und
Sicherheit, morgen in aller Noth, und nicht ſo gar für und
für dahin ſchnarchen, als würde es keine Noth haben.

Das weiß nun Chriſtus wohl, wenn wir wollen ſein blei‐
ben, an der Taufe, Sacrament und Evangelio halten, daß
es nicht anders ſeyn kann, wir müſſen[1] den Teufel zum
Feind haben, der uns ohn Unterlaß zuſetzet mit aller ſeiner
Macht und uns nach Leib und Seele ſtehet: und wo ihm
Gott nicht wehret,[2] daß er dich nicht kann in einem Tage
erwürgen, ſo läßt er doch nicht ab mit allerley Liſten und
Tücken, daß er dir zum wenigſten deinen Muth und Sicher‐
heit nehme, und zu Unruhe und Traurigkeit, darnach auch
in andere Gefahr und Noth bringe. Weil es denn alſo
gehen muß, daß wir müſſen dem Teufel unter die Spieſſe
lauffen,[3] und uns von ihm plagen und martern laſſen; ſo

---

[1] [Als dass] wir müssen. Such ellipses are not uncommon.

[2] Und wo ihm Gott wehret, etc. "and though (if) God
hinders him from destroying you (so that he cannot destroy you) in
a single day, still he (Satan) does not cease (leave off) from his de-
vices and tricks, in order that he may, at least, take away your courage and security and bring you into disquiet," etc. Nicht before
wehret injures the sense as the construction now is. Undoubtedly the writer unconsciously changed the construction, forgetting
when he came to the close, how he commenced it.

[3] Dem Teufel unter die Spiesse laufen, etc.
"expose ourselves to the darts of Satan (run under the darts to Satan), and be vexed and tormented by him, still Christ, would hereby
warn us against them and comfort us, in order that we may not yield
to them, nor be greatly terrified nor easily let Satan capture us, that
he may bring us into [a state of] melancholy and despondency."—
Uns von ihm plagen lassen, literally, "suffer ourselves
to be vexed by him." Uns vermahnet haben, "have us
warned." This idiom is also found in English; as, "I would have
you," for "I wish you would." Uns dazu schicken, "ac-

will uns Christus dagegen hiemit vermahnet und getröstet
haben, daß wir uns dazu schicken sollen, nicht so sehr er=
schrecken, noch den Teufel so leichtlich uns einnehmen lassen,
daß er uns in Schwermuth und Verzweiflung bringe.

Darum laßt uns diesen Trost auch gesagt seyn,[1] und also
einbilden und fassen, daß wir ihn brauchen, und damit uns
stärcken können, wenn wir Trübsal und Angst fühlen, als
höreten wir alsdenn Christum solche Worte zu uns sagen:
Was thust du? Willt du darum zu tode erschrecken und za=
gen? Sey doch getrost und fasse ein Hertz;[2] ist darum noch
nicht aus,[3] ob dich der Teufel, die Welt, oder dein eigen Ge=
wissen plagt und schreckt, und mich nicht gegenwärtig fühlest.
Weißt du nicht, daß ich dirs lang zuvor gesagt habe, und
den Trost hinter mir gelassen, der dich stärcken und erhalten
soll? Siehe, also sollten wir lernen und uns gewöhnen,
diese Tröstung des Herrn Christi zu nutze zu machen durch
tägliche Uebung, in allen unsern Anfechtungen, daß wir uns
solches nicht liessen vergeblich gesagt und geschrieben seyn.

Und aus diesen und dergleichen Worten und Vermahnun=
gen Christi sollen wir auch lernen den Herrn Christum recht

commodate ourselves, i. e. yield to it." D a s s here refers to s o.
S o s e h r and s o l e i c h t l i c h are used absolutely in the sense
of *very much* and *easily*, and d a s s means *in order that*.

[1] L a s s t  u n s  d i e s e n  T r o s t  a u c h  g e s a g t  s e y n, "let
this consolation be said to us," i. e. let us receive it. See p. 240,
Note 3. E i n b i l d e n  u n d  f a s s e n, "and let us so apprehend
and understand it, that we can use it," etc. L a s s t  u n s is used
in two distinct senses here. In the first clause the verb governs
T r o s t, and u n s is in the dative; in the second (u n d [l a s s t
u n s] a l s o  e i n b i l d e n), u n s is in the accusative. "And let
us so apprehend "

[2] F a s s e  e i n  H e r t z, "to take courage," "to pluck up courage." Compare the English word *dishearten*.

[3] I s t  d a r u m  n o c h  n i c h t  a n s, etc. "All is not therefore over,
even though the devil, the world and their own conscience distress
and terrify thee, and thou dost not feel my presence (me present)."
See p. 236, Note 1.

kennen, daß wir deſto herßlichere, tröſtlichere Zuverſicht
zu ihm gewinnen mögen, und mehr auf ſein Wort achten,
denn auf alles, ſo uns mag vor Augen, Ohren und
Sinne kommen. Denn ſo ich ein Chriſt bin,[1] und mich
zu ihm halte, ſo weiß ich je, daß er mit mir redet. Nun
höre ich ja hie und anderswo, daß alle ſeine Worte dahin
gehen, daß er mich tröſte, ja alles, was er redet und thut
oder gedencket, eitel freundliche, tröſtliche Worte und Wercke
ſind.

Darum muß das gewiß ſeyn und nicht fehlen: Wenn ein
Menſch trauert und ein blödes erſchrecken Herß hat, das
muß nicht von Chriſto ſeyn. Denn er iſt nicht der Mann,
der die Herßen erſchrecket, oder traurig und ſchwermüthig
machen will. Denn er iſt eben dazu kommen, und hat alles
gethan, ſich auch darum hinauf gen Himmel geſetzt, daß er
Traurigkeit und Schrecken des Herßens hinweg nehme, und
dafür ein fröhlich Herß, Gewiſſen und Gedancken gebe, und
verheißt auch darum, ſeinen Jüngern und Chriſten den
Heiligen Geiſt zu ſenden, und nennet ihn einen Tröſter, da=
durch er ſie ſtärcken und erhalten will, nachdem er leiblich
von ihnen gehen mußte.

Wer nun das könnte lernen und wohl ins Herß faſſen,
wie Chriſtus mit ſeinem Mund redet und zenget, daß es
ihm zuwider und leid ſey, wenn eines Chriſten Herß traurig
oder erſchrocken iſt, der wäre wohl bran,[2] und hätte mehr

---

[1] Denn so ich ein Christ bin, etc. "For if I am a
Christian, and adhere to him, then I always know that he [in these
words] speaks to me. Now I learn in this very passage and elsewhere that all his words tend to this, to comfort me (that he comfort
me);—indeed all that he says and does or thinks are nothing but
kind and consoling words and works."—[Ge]kommen in line 14.

[2] Der wäre wohl daran, he is (would be) in a good way,
or is doing well, (in the matter, daran) or is well off, and has more
than half conquered." Daran, in such cases, is indefinite, as in
English, at it, in such familiar phrases as to go at it.

denn halb gewonnen.   Denn wenn es so weit kommt,[1] daß ich den Feind, so mich erschrecken und betrüben will, kenne, und weiß, woher solche Gedancken und Einfälle kommen, so habe ich bereits einen festen Trit und Fels, darauf ich gründen und stehen kann, und mich sein erwehren, und sagen: Das ist nicht mein Herr Christus, sondern Christi Feind, der leidige Teufel.[2]   Denn er betreugt auch wol die frommen Hertzen damit, daß er sich verstellt (wie St. Paulus sagt, 2 Cor. 11, 14.) in einen Engel des Lichts, und sich also bildet und vorgibt, als sey er Christus selbst.

Ein Christ aber lebet wol auch also,[3] daß er äusserlich viel Leiden und Anfechtung hat; aber doch kann er ein getrost, fröhlich Hertz und Muth zu Gott haben, und sich des allerbesten zu ihm versehen.   Darum lasset uns solches wohl lernen: es komme über uns, was für Unglück kommen mag, Pestilentz, Krieg, theure Zeit, Armuth, Verfolgung, schwere Gedancken, so den Kopf niederschlagen und das Hertz klopfend und zappelnd machen, daß[4] wir doch so viel wissen und

---

[1] Denn wenn es so weit kommt, etc. "For, if so much progress has been made (it has gone so far) that I know the enemy who would terrify and distress me, and understand whence such thoughts and fancies come, I have already a firm footing and a rock," etc.   Denn wenn, must not be confounded with dann wenn, *then if* or *then when*.   On the difference between kennen and wissen, see p. 54, Note 6.   Einfall means *the act of falling into*, which when it relates to the territories of an enemy, means an *invasion*, or *assault;* when it relates to the mind, it means *the thoughts that fall accidentally or pop into the mind,—whims, conceits, fancies.*—Mich sein erwehren, *ward him off.*

[2] In der leidige Teufel, as in der liebe Gott is a peculiarity which distinguishes the German language from ours. We do not say, *the wicked devil*, and *the dear God.*   Betreugt for betriegt. See p. 281, Note 8.

[3] Lebet wohl auch also.   Wohl here softens the affirmation.   Not, "lives well also thus," but "lives commonly (or, probably) in such a way that," etc.

[4] Dass refers to solches, near the beginning of the sentence.

schliessen können, daß solches nicht von Christo sey, und hüten uns für dem Teufel, der sich kann bilden und darstellen in Christi Gestalt und Namen.

Das wäre[1] wol die rechte Kunst eines Christen, wer also könnte unterscheiden im rechten Kampf, was Christi oder des Teufels Eingeben sey? Aber, wie schwer es ist, das gläubet niemand, denn er es erfahren hat.[2] Denn der Teufel kann sich so kleiden und schmücken mit Christi Namen und Worten, und so bilden und stellen, daß einer wol tausend Eyde schwüre, es wäre wahrhaftig Christus selbst, so es doch der Ertzfeind und rechte Ertzwiderchrist[3] ist.

Darum lerne[4] hieraus, so du ein Christe bist, wer dich will schrecken und das Hertz blöde machen, daß du gewißlich könnest schliessen, daß er des Teufels Bote ist. Denn wo auch Christus jemand schrecket zur Busse und Bekehrung vom Unglauben und sündlichen Leben, (wie er St. Paulum vor der Bekehrung, item St. Paulus[5] von Christi wegen die zu Corintho, item die Galater schrecket,) so währet es doch nicht lange. Denn er thuts nicht darum, daß du sollt trang rig bleiben, sondern führet dich bald heraus, und tröstet dich

---

[1] Das wäre, etc. "That would be a Christian's true knowledge when one (whoever) could, in the real conflict, distinguish between the suggestions (what is the suggestion) of Christ and of Satan." Wer has this indefinite meaning in itself and in consequence of subjunctive mode, which represents not *real* but *supposed* cases. This idiom frequently occurs in Luther's writings.

[2] Denn er [der] es erfahren hat.—Und [sich] so bilden und stellen.

[3] Ertzwiderchrist, *arch-antichrist*. Endechrist also occurs, ende standing for *anti*.

[4] Darum lerne, etc. "Learn therefore from this, if you are a Christian, that whoever would terrify you, and make your heart fearful, you may certainly infer that he is Satan's messenger." Dass before du gewisslich must, in the translation, be placed at the beginning of the preceding clause. See p. 285, Note 3.

[5] Item St. Paulus, etc. "Also St. Paul, on Christ's account terrified those at Corinth, and the Galatians.

wieder. Das thut der Teufel nicht, sondern läßt keinen[1] Stolzen und Unbußfertigen verzagt werden, oder wo er ans letzte in Schrecken und Angst fällt (wie denn zuletzt solchen allen geschieht): so läßt er ihn darinn stecken, macht desselben kein Ende, treibt und drückt so hart, daß er ewiglich verzweifeln muß, wo er nicht wieder durch Christum aufgerichtet wird.

Siehe, das will Christus allhie lehren, da er spricht: Euer Hertz erschrecke nicht 2c. Als sollte er sagen: Ich sterbe und fahre davon aus euern Augen, und lasse euch hinter mir in der Welt, da ihr mich nicht sehen noch hören werdet, sondern müsset nur sehen, hören und fühlen allerley Plage und Unglück, das euch allenthalben wird schrecken und angst machen.[2] Aber laßt euch darum das Hertz nicht matt und seig machen,[3] sondern haltet euch dagegen deß,[4] so ihr von mir höret, daß ihr sollet getrost und guten Muths seyn. Denn ich wills nicht seyn, der[5] euch schrecket und betrübet, sondern, wo ihr solches höret oder fühlet, so schliesset flugs, daß es des Teufels Gespenst und Trug[6] sey. Meine Stim-

---

[1] Sondern lässt keinen, etc. "but [ordinarily] causes no haughty or impenitent one to become discouraged, or if the latter at last falls into [a state of] fear and distress (as happens to all in the end), he leaves him there (lets him stay or stick there), makes no end to (of) it, pursues (urges) and presses him so hard," etc.

[2] Angst machen. Angst with machen, seyn and werden is an indeclinable word, meaning, *anxious*, *distressed*. These verbs are, when so employed, followed by a dative. The word angst, when not a substantive, is limited to these expressions.

[3] Aber lasst euch, etc. "But do not therefore become faint hearted and timid (suffer one to make your heart faint and cowardly) but, on the contrary, rely on that which you have heard of me," etc.

[4] Haltet euch dess, "hold yourselves or adhere to that." This verb is now always followed by a n with the accusative, instead of the genitive, as here.

[5] Denn ich wills nicht seyn, der, etc. "For I would not be one to terrify and trouble you, (I will not be it who, etc.)"

[6] Gespenst und Trug, "grim visage and illusion."

me (dabey ihr mich follt kennen, als die Schafe ihren rech=
ten Hirten,) foll alfo heiffen: Fürchte dich nicht und er=
fchrick nicht! Das find[1] meine Worte und Gedancken.
Höreft du ein anders, fo höreft du nicht meine Stimme, ob
fich3 gleich in meinem Namen und Geftalt dir vorbildet.
Darum follt du folchem nicht glauben, noch folgen.

Glaubet ihr an Gott, fo glaubet auch an
mich.

Da fetzt er Urfachen der vorigen Worte, damit[2] er ange=
fangen hat, fie zu vermahnen, getroft und unerfchrocken zu
feyn. Laßt euch nicht erfchrecken (fpricht er), noch das
Hertz feig machen, ob ich wol leiblich von euch komme und
euch ftecken laffe mitten unter der Welt und Teufels Gewalt,
die euch drücken und klemmen, und alles Unglück anlegen
werden; fondern ftehet keck und veft wider alles, das euch
mag begegnen. Denn ihr, als Chriften, follet ja nicht tran=
ren noch zagen, weil ihr nicht feyd,[3] wie die, welche, fo fie
in Leiden, Unglück und Widerwärtigkeit kommen, keinen
Troft noch Zuverficht haben, als da find, die da nicht gläu=
ben, noch Gottes Wort wiffen, fondern ihren Troft auf zeit=
liche Dinge fetzen und mit dem Hertzen nur an dem hangen,
das da gegenwärtig und fichtbar ift, und wo daffelbe wendet,
da wendet auch ihr Muth und Zuverficht. Darum, wenn
fich das Glück wandelt in Unglück; fo fallen fie plötzlich da=

---

[1] Das sind, *these are.* See Gram. p. 348.—Ein anders, *any
other.*

[2] Damit in the sense of womit, *with which.* Comp. p. 105,
Note 1.

[3] Weil ihr nicht seyd, etc. "because ye are not like those,
who, if they come into suffering, misfortune and adversity, have no
consolation or confidence, as is the case with those (as are those) who
do not believe, who are not acquainted with the word of God, but put
their trust (consolation) in temporal things, and in their hearts are
attached only to what is present and visible, and if that fails (turns
away), their spirits and confidence also fail."—Vest, three lines
above, for fest.

hin, und verzagen, als sey es alles mit ihnen aus. Das
sind Leute, die keinen Gott haben, und nichts wissen, noch
erfahren von solchem Trost, der da bestehen und siegen kann
mitten in[1] höchster Noth und Unglück, obgleich alles Zeitliche und Vergängliche, so man sich zu versehen und zu hoffen hat, aufhöret. Solche Leute (spricht er,) sollet ihr
nicht seyn. Denn ihr habt ja Gottes Wort, dadurch ihr
ihn habt kennen lernen[2] und an ihn gläuben. Darum sollet ihr euch kein Schrecken überwältigen noch überwinden
lassen, sondern kecklich und männlich widerstehen, und euch
erzeigen, als die viel andern,[3] gewissern, höhern Trost und
Trotz wissen, denn alle Welt hat, und grösser Stärcke und
Macht, darauf ihr euch zu verlassen habt, denn der Welt
und des Teufels Gewalt und Macht ist. Lasset andere auf
ihre zeitliche Gewalt und Glück trotzen und pochen; ihr
aber tröstet euch,[4] daß ihr einen Gott habt und ihn kennet,
und verlasset euch darauf, daß er bey euch ist, und euch helfen kann, wie er euch durchs Wort zugesagt hat, und gewißlich nicht fehlen wird, obgleich alles wider euch ist, sondern
euch beystehen, beschirmen und aushelfenwird, dieweil ihr
um seinetwillen alles leidet.

Gläubet ihr nun, und verlasset euch auf Gott, so gläubet

---

[1] Mitten in. In English the order is always reversed, *in the
midst of*, instead of *middle in*.

[2] Lernen for gelernt. See p. 238, Note 5. " By which
you have learned to know him and to believe on him."

[3] Als die viel andern, etc. "as those who have (know)
very different (not " much other"), surer and higher consolation and
assurance, than all the world has, and greater strength and power to
rely on (on which you have to rely) than," etc.

[4] Ihr aber tröstet euch, etc. " but console ye yourselves
that you have a *God* and that you know him, and rely (imperative)
on it that he will be with you and help you, as he has promised you
through his word, and certainly will not fail [to fulfil it] though
everything be against you, but will stand by you, defend you and deliver you, because you have suffered everything for his sake."

auch an mich. Iſt euer Glaube recht, daß ihr euch zu Gott alles Guten verſehet,[1] ſo verſehet euch deſſelben auch zu mir. Was ihr bey ihm Troſts und Hülfe ſuchet und gewartet, das gewartet auch von mir; ich will euch gewißlich nicht fehlen, ſo wenig als Gott ſelbſt. Habe ich euch bisher geholfen, und alles bey euch gethan, was ihr bedürft habt, und mich alſo erzeigt, beyde, mit Worten und Wercken, daß ihr euch mein habt dürfen tröſten,[2] und kühnlich auf mich verlaſſen, und ich euch noch nie nicht habe laſſen fehlen: ſo will ichs auch hinfort thun, und euch nicht laſſen, ob ich gleich nicht leiblich bey euch bleibe. Denn ich habe noch dieſelbige Kraft[3] und Macht, beyde, von und mit Gott, daß ichs thun kann und will; allein, zweifelt und zagt nicht, als hättet ihr, beyde, Gott und mich verloren, ſondern ſtehet veſt im Glau= ben, und laſſet eure Zuverſicht nicht ſincken noch ſchwächen, ob ihr gleich ſehet mich leiden und ſterben, und euch hinter mir allein laſſen. Und wie ihr bisher bey mir geſehen und erfahren habt leiblichen Beyſtand und Schutz: alſo glaubet nun auch, ob ihrs gleich nicht vor Augen ſehen werdet. Denn ſo ihr meine Jünger und rechte Chriſten ſeyd, müſſet

---

[1] Dass ihr euch zu Gott alles Guten versehet, " that you look confidently to God for every good thing, then look confidently to me for the same." Sich versehen, with the genitive, means *to expect a thing confidently;* and with the addition of a dative of the person with z u, *to look to one for a thing*, or *to expect it of one.*—W a s—T r o s t s und H ü l l e, *what of consolation and aid.*

[2] Dass ihr euch mein habt dürfen trösten, "that you have been able to comfort yourselves in me." M e i n is in the genitive for m e i n e r. S i c h t r ö s t e n which is now in common language followed by the preposition ü b e r, m i t or i n, formerly governed a genitive in the same sense, *to comfort one's self over, with* or *in.*—N o c h n i e n i c h t is obsolete for n o c h n i e.

[3] Denn ich habe noch dieselbige Kraft, etc. "For I have the same efficacy and power still from God and the same with him, (i. e. with his aid, or through him,) so that I have both the power and the will to do it, (both can and will do it).

ihr nicht¹ immerdar bleiben hangen an dem Sehen und Fühlen äusserlichen Trosts, sondern fortfahren und die Kunst lernen, (welches ist der Christen Kunst,) daß ihr ungezweifelt gläubet, daß ich euch helfen kann und will, da ihrs nicht sehen noch fühlen könnet, sondern das Widerspiel sehet und fühlet, nemlich im Leiden und allen Nöthen, und dennoch allezeit den Trost behaltet, daß ihr Gott und mich habt, obgleich sonst alles euch absagt und entfället.

2—4. In meines Vaters Hause sind viel Wohnungen; wo aber das nicht wäre, so sage ich euch doch, daß ich hingehe, euch die Stätte zu bereiten. Und ob ich hingehe, will ich doch wiederkommen, und euch zu mir nehmen, auf daß ihr seyd, wo ich bin; und wo ich hingehe, das wisset ihr, und den Weg wisset ihr auch.

Er tröstet alhier seine lieben Jünger und Christen auf dreyerley Weise: Die erste ist, daß sie wissen sollen, daß bey seinem Vater viel Wohnungen für sie sind. Das setzet er gegen andere zweyerley² Haus oder Wohnungen; als sollte er sagen: Auf Erden werdet ihr nicht viel Häuser, noch gewisse Wohnung haben. Denn alhier hat der Teufel sein Reich, sein Haus und Wohnung, da er Herr ist, und

---

¹ Müsset ihr nicht, etc. "You must not always continue to cling to seeing and feeling outward consolation, but make progress and learn the art (and this is the Christians's art) of believing unhesitatingly, that I have the ability and disposition to aid you, even when you can neither see it nor feel it, but see and feel just the contrary, viz. are in suffering and distress. Still you always have the consolation, that you have God and myself, though everything else forsakes (renounces) you and flies from you."

² Zweyerley. "This he represents in comparison with others in a two-fold manner," i. e. in saying this, he compares *two kinds* of houses or dwellings. The construction is harsh and not very clear.

ſitzet in dem Seinen ;[1] darum wird er euch, weil ihr wider ihn und ſein Reich ſtrebet, nicht lang alhier wohnen und hauſen laſſen.

Aber ſeyd[2] deß unerſchrocken, (ſpricht Chriſtus,) es ſoll euch nichts ſchaden ; könnt ihr hier kein Haus und Wohnung haben, und euch der Teufel mit ſeinen Tyrannen aus der Welt jagt : ſo ſollt ihr dennoch Raums genug haben, da ihr bleiben ſollt.[3] Wollen ſie euch nicht leiden[4] zu Bürgern und Nachbarn, oder auch zu Gäſten, und ſie die Welt allein behalten : ſo laſſet ſie behalten, und wiſſet, daß ihr dennoch auch ſollt Wohnung, und derer viel haben.

Diß ſoll alhier aufs einfältigſte die Weynung ſeyn, eben wie er an einem andern Ort ſpricht, Matth. 13, 29 : Wer da verläßt Häuſer, Brüder oder Schweſter, oder Vater, oder Mutter, oder Weib, oder Kind, oder Aecker, um meinetwillen und um des Evangelii willen, der wirds hundertfältig empfahen in dieſer Zeit, und in der zukünftigen Welt das ewige Leben ꝛc., alſo ſey auch hier die Meynung : Wenn man euch aus einem Hauſe verjagt, ſo ſollt ihr viel Häuſer dafür haben ; nimmt man euch einerley,[5] ſo ſollt ihr viel-

---

[1] **Sitzet in dem Seinen.** "He is in possession of his own," or what belongs to him. On this use of **sitzen**, see p. 63, last line and the note to it, and p. 64, lines 6 and 7.

[2] **Aber seyd dess unerschrocken**, etc. "But be not afraid of that ; it shall do you no harm." **Unerschrocken**, here followed by the genitive, is now almost always followed by the preposition **vor**.

[3] **Da ihr bleiben sollt**, "to remain in," where you may remain.

[4] **Wollen sie euch nicht leiden**, etc. "If they will not endure you as citizens and neighbors, or even as guests, but will have the world to themselves, let them have it, and be assured yourselves that you will still have a dwelling-place, and enough of them."

[5] **Einerley.** See p. 77, Note 2.—**Empfahen** obsolete for **empfangen**. "If they should not act so wickedly, and should not take so much away from you, still you shall have a hundred-fold and more [for what you shall have lost]."

fältig wieder dagegen empfahen; und sollens so böse nicht machen und euch so viel nicht nehmen, ihr sollets hundert= mal so gut und viel besser haben. Habt ihrs hier nicht, so krigt ihrs gewißlich dort reichlich. Denn er hat noch so großen Vorrath, daß er euer jeglichem[1] kann geben hundert Wohnungen für eine. Darum nur getrost[2] und frisch dahin gesetzt, was euch die Welt nehmen kann: die Wohnungen des Lebens sind viel weiter, denn die Wohnung des Todes. Ob sie euch nun hier in Kercker und Gefängniß stecken, oder auch ausjagen, das laßt euch nicht kümmern, es sind häuser, die der Welt zugehören; ihr aber sehet auf ein anders, wo= rauf ihr zu warten habt, und was ihr dort krigen und be= sitzen sollet.

Also ist dieser Text zu Trost geredt den Christen, daß sie sich nicht irren lassen, ob ihnen die Welt alle Plage anlegt, und nicht allein dieser Wohnung beraubt, sondern alles nimmt, was sie alhier haben, Gut, Ehre, Leben, und wirft sie ins Elend, Armuth, Blöße, Schande, Schmach und Tod; sondern daß sie dagegen halten,[3] was sie gegen diesen gerin= gen Verlust gewinnen, wo sie jetzt einer Wohnung beraubet werden, daß sie dafür viel bessere Wohnungen krigen sollen, nemlich an dem Ort, das da heißt: In meines Vaters

---

[1] **Euer jeglichem**, "to each one of you."

[2] **Darum nur getrost**, etc. The preterite participle is often employed for the imperative. See Gram. p. 262 infra. "Therefore be firm and resign yourself (**dahin gesetzt**, *bring your mind to it*) cheerfully in respect to what the world can take from you. The mansions of life (heaven) are much more spacious than those of death (this world). Whether, now, they thrust you into dungeons and imprisonment, or banish you, let that not trouble you; they are houses [those from which you are driven] which belong to the world. Look to something widely different, which you are to expect, and which, in another world (**dort**), you shall acquire and retain."

[3] **Dagegen halten**, "that they compare with this (hold side by side with this) that which they obtain in return for this small loss if they are now robbed of a dwelling." See p. 152, Note 1.

Haufe. Wo der ift[1] und bleibet, da werde ich und ihr auch bleiben, (wie er hernach fagen wird,) daß ihr nicht weltliche und menfchliche, fondern himmlifch, göttliche Wohnungen und Häufer haben follet; das ift, für eine unflätige, vergängliche, unfichere und unftäte Wohnung, (die ihr und alle Welt ohne das[2] bald laffen müffet,) eitel fchöne, herrliche, weite, ewige, fichere und gewiffe Wohnungen, die euch nicht können genommen werden, und vor jedermann friedlich behalten werdet.

Der andere Troft ift, daß er weiter fpricht: Wo das nicht wäre,[3] fo fage ich euch doch, daß ich hingehe, euch die Stätte zu bereiten 2c. Summa, Wohnungen follt ihr gewißlich haben; und ob ihrer noch nicht genug wären, fo will ich ihrer genug fchaffen, daß, ob es zu wenig wäre, daß ihr hundert für eine krigt, wollte ich ihr hundert taufend und noch mehr fchaffen, daß da kein Mangel noch Gebrechen foll feyn und allerley Wohnungen, wie es euer Hertz begehren mag.

Alfo redet er mit ihnen aufs allereinfältigfte und gleichfam kindlich, nach ihren Gedancken, (wie man muß Einfältige reitzen und locken,) damit er fie von demfelbigen hinauf ziehe, daß fie können einen Muth und Troft fchöpfen.

Aber das wäre die Kunft,[4] wer folches auch könnte gläuben. Denn es ift ja wahr, daß ein jeglicher Chrift, der das

---

[1] **Wo der ist**, etc. "Where he (**mein Vater**) dwells, there will we (I, i. e. Christ and you, i. e. my disciples) dwell." **Ist und bleibt**, *is and remains* conveys an idea which is best expressed in English, by *continue to be.*

[2] **Ohne das**, *aside from this.*

[3] **Wo das nicht wäre**, "If that were not so (if there were no mansions ready) still I would say that I go to prepare places for you." So many of the old interpreters understood this passage. The English version is undoubtedly more correct.

[4] **Aber das wäre Kunst**, etc "But that would be an attainment, if one (or, whoever) could believe all this." See p. 292, Note 1, and p. 14, Note 5.

Wort bekennen will, entweder mit predigen, oder, sonst vor Gericht, der stehet sehr übel auf Erden, alle Stunden unsicher und in Gefahr, daß man ihn von Gut, Weib und Kind jage, da die andern alles vollauf[1] haben, im Sause und gutem Gemach leben. Aber, wenn wir auch ansehen, was uns vorbehalten ist, und wozu wir kommen sollen, sollten wir ja fröhlich darzu seyn, und uns vielmehr jammern[2] lassen der armen, elenden Welt. Denn was ists, ob sie uns mit Füssen trit, und aufs höheste uns plaget und Leid thut, wir können doch nichts verlieren. Verlieren wir aber, so verlieren wir den Sack, so wir am Halse tragen, das ist nicht mehr, denn die Hülsen verloren;[3] indeß bleibt uns gleichwol der Schatz, daß wir beyde, dieses, so wir hier lassen, reichlich wieder kriegen, und dazu viel mehr ewiger, göttlicher Güter.

Zum dritten spricht er: Ob ich jetzt von euch gehe, (euch die Wohnung zu bereiten,) sollt ihr nicht erschrecken noch trauren, daß ihr mich nicht habt; sondern sollt den Trost auch haben, daß ich euch nicht will lassen, sondern wieder zu euch kommen, und euch zu mir holen ꝛc., daß ihr meines Ganges[4] oder Abschieds nicht sollt Schaden haben; sondern wisset, daß es euch zu gute geschehe, daß ich euch die Wohnungen beym Vater bereite und bestelle, und darzu auch wieder zu euch kommen, und selbst euch mit mir dahin bringen will, daß ihr die Wohnungen einnehmet, und also bey mir

---

[1] Alles vollauf "all, in abundance."

[2] Uns vielmehr jammern, "and rather bewail the [condition of] the poor, miserable world." Literally, "cause ourselves to be distressed." Jammern in the first person may take über after it. In the second and third persons, it takes the accusative of the person.

[3] Denn die Hülsen verloren, "than losing the husk." See p. 240, Note 3.

[4] Dass ihr meines Ganges, etc. "that ye may not loose by my going or departure (have the loss of my going, etc.)."

bleibet, wo ich bin: also, daß ihr beydes gewiß habt, die Wohnungen im Himmel und mich in Ewigkeit bey euch.

Das sind die drey Stücke, die uns trösten sollen wider Teufel und Welt, und alles, was uns Böses mag widerfahren, daß wir einen solchen Herrn und treuen Heiland haben, der dahin gefahren ist, und uns schon Wohnung bereitet, und gleichwol bey uns seyn und bleiben will. Es ist aber noch sehr verborgen, und scheinet nicht; denn wir sehen und fühlen, daß dennoch die Welt und Tyrannen üben ihren Troß und Frevel immerfort wider das Evangelium und die Christen. Aber darum heisset er uns, an ihn gläuben. Als sollte er sagen: Wenn ihr nur könntet die kleine Weile Geduld haben, und an meinem Wort hangen, sie werdens[1] doch nicht hinaus singen, ob sie jeßt alle noch viel böser wären; denn es ist schon beschlossen, und das Urtheil ist zu starck gegangen, sie wird das Stündlein treffen, das sie schrecken und ihnen so bange und angst machen wird, das sie nirgend werden zu bleiben haben. Allein ists darum zu thun, daß ihr die Augen recht aufthut, und nicht ansehet, wie es vor denselben gehet und stehet, sondern, was ich rede und sage, daß ich euch nicht will lassen, noch von euch bleiben, sondern zu euch kommen und euch zu mir nehmen, also, daß ich bey euch, und ihr bey mir bleibet 2c.

Zum vierten beschleußt[2] er: Es soll nicht genug seyn, daß ihr wisset, daß ich hingehe, euch die Wohnung zu bereiten, und wieder zu euch kommen und bey euch bleiben will, daß ihr seyd, wo ich bin 2c., sondern darüber habt ihr auch den

---

[1] S i e  w e r d e n s, etc. "they could (would) not carry it out (sing their song out), even if they were much worse than they now are; for it is already decreed, and the decree too firmly made [for that]. The evil time will come upon them, which will terrify them and make them fearful and anxious, so that they will have no quiet abode (will nowhere have a place to stay in). This alone is to be attended to," etc. On D a r u m  z u  t h u n, see p. 20, Note 3. med.

[2] B e s c h l e u s s t, for b e s c h l i e s s t.

Vortheil, daß ihr bereits wiſſet, wo ich hingehe, und wiſſet auch den Weg.

Das iſt nun der Weg ſeines heiligen Leidens, davon er ihnen bereits viel und oft geſagt hatte, ſonderlich an demſelbigen letzten Abend ; wiewol ſie es doch nicht verſtehen konnten, und ihnen diß Wort noch dunckel war, daß ſie ihn[1] bald darauf fragen, iſt aber ſo viel geſagt: Was ſoll ich euch viel ſagen ? Ich will euch nicht flabbern noch ſchweben laſſen mit Gedancken ; ihr wiſſets und ſehets ſchon alles. Denn wenn ihr mich habt, ſo habt ihr Gott und alles, und wenn ihr mich ſehet hingehen, ſo ſehet ihr ſchon den Weg. Ich will euch keinen andern Weg weiſen, noch andere Weiſe vorſchlagen, es iſt ſchon alles da ;[2] allein, daß ener Hertz nur zufrieden ſey, und ſich nicht dafür entſetze, ob euch die Welt ſchrecket und bekümmert, daß ihr in mir Freude und Friede habet ꝛc.

5, 6. **S p r i c h t  z u  i h m  T h o m a s ,  d e r  d a  h e i ß t Z w i l l i n g :  H e r r ,  w i r  w i ſ ſ e n  n i c h t ,  w o  d u  h i n - g e h e ſ t ,  u n d  w i e  k ö n n e n  w i r  d e n  W e g  w i ſ ſ e n ? J e ſ u s  ſ p r i c h t  z u  i h m :  I c h  b i n  d e r  W e g ,  u n d d i e  W a h r h e i t ,  u n d  d a s  L e b e n .**

Sie hatten gehöret,[3] die lieben Jünger, daß er wollte hin-

---

[1] D a s s  s i e  i h n, etc. " so that they soon ask him about it." But this is what was meant (so much as this was said): ' Why should I use many words ?  I wish not to make you flutter and fly all about with your speculations.'

[2] E s  i s t  s c h o n  a l l e s  d a, etc. " Everything is contained in this (i. e. nothing else is necessary).  Only let your heart be quiet (only that your heart may be quiet) and not be alarmed, though the world terrify and trouble you.  Have (or seek) joy and peace in me."

[3] S i e  h a t t e n  g e h ö r e t, etc. " The beloved disciples had heard that he would go away and prepare dwellings for them ; and not only so (that), but that they themselves already knew the way, where he would go and stay, and [that] they also should follow him thither, that he could not [now] say much to them, and [that] they ought

gehen, und ihnen die Wohnungen bestellen ; und nicht allein
das, sondern daß sie auch schon selbst den Weg wüßten, wo
er hingehen und bleiben würde, und sie ihm auch dahin fol=
gen sollten, daß er nicht viel predigen dürfte, und sie sich
desto weniger bekümmern und erschrecken sollten, daß er jetzt
von ihnen scheiden müßte. Darauf fähet[1] St. Thomas an
zu wundern, und ist ihm ebentheuerlich geredt, daß er sagt :
sie wissen, wo er hinwolle, und wissen dazu den Weg, so er
ihnen doch nichts davon gesagt habe, wohin oder welches

---

not (ought so much the less) to be troubled and alarmed at his leaving them now (that he must now part with them)."—D i e  l i e b e n
J ü n g e r, in apposition with s i e, is a forcible mode of expression.
—All the principal clauses, after the word  g e h ö r e t, are dependent
on that word, as is indicated in the translation, whether the word
d a s s  is inserted or omitted.—B e s t e l l e n  is a difficult  word to
explain, particularly if all its significations are to be  referred  to one
radical signification.  The objects to which it relates, however, give
it this diversity of meanings.  The word itself in its common, i. e.
figurative sense, means, *to put in its place*.  1. To direct a *person* to
his proper place (e i n e n  w o h i n  b e s t e l l e n).  2. To commis-
sion a *person* with a certain *business*, or  impose  some  duty  on  him
(e i n e n  z u  e t w a s  b e s t e l l e n).  3. To order (also, engage),
direct (also, deliver) or prepare something (e t w a s  b e s t e l l e n).
Consider therefore whether the object is a person (e i n e n) or a
thing (e t w a s), and then, whether there be also an *indirect* object,
and whether that relates to a place (w o h i n) or to a thing or duty
(z u  e t w a s).  The literal meaning of the word, *to cover a place
over*, is obsolete.  The third signification is very broad, and admits
of a variety of modifications.  Compare the miscellaneous examples
in the larger lexicons.

[1] D a r a u f  f ä h e t  (f ä n g t), etc.  "Thereupon Thomas begins to wonder ; to him the remark appears strange (to him it is
spoken strangely) when Christ says (that he says), 'they know
whether he intends to go (h i n w o l l e) and they know the way
thither,' though (s o - d o c h) he has said nothing about (it) whither
or what way (W e g e s, genitive of manner) he will go from them.
Therefore he begins, in a gross, carnal manner (W e i s e, genitive),
to inquire in his mind (d e n c k e n) after the road," etc.

Weges er von ihnen gehen wollte, fähet also an zu dencken, grober, fleischlicher Weise, nach der Straffe, darauf man leiblich gehet oder fähret von einer Stadt zur andern, und nach dem Wege, darauf die Füffe treten. Deffelben,[1] spre= chen sie, wiffen wir keines, wo oder zu welchem Thor und wo hinaus du willst. Wie sollten wir denn Weg wiffen?

Auf diese grobe, fleischliche Gedancken antwortet nun Chri= stus: Ich meyne es also,[2] daß ihr den Weg wiffet, das ist, ihr kennet ja den, welcher der Weg ist, nemlich mich; denn ihr sehet und wiffet, daß ich bin Christus, euer Herr und Heiland, und ihr meine Jünger, die ihr[3] so lange meine Pre= digt gehört und meine Wunderwercke gesehen habt. So ihr nun mich kennet, so kennet und wiffet ihr den Weg, und alles, was ihr wiffen sollt.

Das ist nun abermal[4] ein sonderliches, und eben, das der Evangelist St. Johannis pflegt immer zu schreiben und zu treiben, daß alle unsere Lehre und Glauben soll auf Chri= stum gehen, und allein an dieser einigen Person hangen, und daß wir (alle Kunst und Weisheit beyseite gethan,) schlechts

---

[1] Desselben, etc. "We know, say they, nothing of this desselben-keines), when or at what gate [of the city], and at what passage (wo hinaus) thou wouldest go out." Wo hi-naus du willst, "you will go out," is here peculiar on ac-count of the connection of hinaus not only with wo, but with willst, analogous to hinwolle a few lines above. Such a twofold use of a particle is not unusual with Luther.

[2] Ich meyne es also, "I mean as follows" (I mean it thus).

[3] Und ihr meine Jünger, die ihr, "and that you [are] my disciples who," etc.

[4] Das ist nun abermal, etc. "That again is a peculiarity (peculiar) and precisely [the one] which the Evangelist John is al-ways accustomed to write and treat of, namely that all our teaching and faith should relate to Christ and be attached to this peculiar per-son alone, and that we (all human knowledge and wisdom apart) should know nothing at all (simply, or purely nothing) except," etc. —Beyseite gethan is put absolute with Kunst und Weis-heit.

nichts wissen sollen, denn, wie St. Paulus. 1 Cor. 2, 23 ; 2, 2. sagt, den gecreußigten Christum.

Aber, wie groß[1] und schwer diese Lehre und Kunst ist, auch den rechten Schülern Christi, das beweiset wohl alhier St. Thomas und bald hernach St. Phillippus, (wie wir hören werden,) welche vor den andern allerwegen herausfahren mit ihrem Unverstande, und lassen sich mercken, daß sie noch seiner Rede wenig oder nichts verstehen: so sie doch den Herrn Christum so lange gehöret, und auch jetzt über Tische hören, wie er ihnen saget von seines Vaters Hause, da er wolle hingehen, und ihnen die Wahnung bereiten ꝛc., lassen ihn da hinter dem Tische sitzen, und solches vorpredigen zu ihrem Trost, so flabbern sie dieweil anders wohin mit Gedancken und machen ihnen einen andern Weg, und scheiden Christum weit von ihnen.

Darum rücket er sie herum,[2] doch mit seinen, freundlichen

---

[1] A b e r, w i e g r o s s, etc. "But how great and difficult this doctrine (and knowledge) is, even to the true disciples of Christ, (that) is shown by Thomas here (shows Thomas here) and soon after (as we shall hear) Philip, who always dash on before the rest with their foolishness, and show (and cause themselves to give indications, or to be observed) that, as yet, they understand little or nothing of his discourse. Though they have so long heard Christ their Lord, and even now hear at table, as he speaks to them of his Father's house, to which he will go and prepare mansions for them, [still] they leave him sitting there by the table and giving them beforehand such instruction for their [future] consolation, and meanwhile they fly off with their own thoughts, and strike out another track for themselves and separate themselves widely from Christ (Christ widely from themselves)."—A l l e r w e g e n, *everywhere*, is here used in the obsolete sense of *always*, which word is of the same etymology.— H i n t e r d e m T i s c h e s i t z e n is a form of expression which admirably intimates the disrespect which is here censured. The latter part of this paragraph is highly idiomatic, and is easier felt than explained. An attempt is made to give the force of it in the translation.

[2] D a r u m r ü c k e t e r s i e h e r u m, etc "Therefore he censures them (pulls or jerks them around), though with delicate and

Worten, als ein gütiger Herr und Meister, so der Seinen Unwissenheit und Schwachheit wohl kann versehen und zu gut halten, und will sie schlecht allein an sich hefften und binden mit Augen, Ohren und Hertzen, daß sie nicht weiter sehen noch dencken sollen. Als sollte er hiermit sagen: Thoma, Thoma, wo gaffest oder denckest du hin? Also muß man nicht speculiren und flabbern; hierher auf mich müsset ihr sehen. Ihr kennet und wisset ja mich; so ihr nun mich kennet und sehet, so kennet und sehet ihr den Weg, und dürfet nicht weiter suchen noch sorgen. Denn ihr müsset[1] mich nicht also ansehen, wie die Kuh ein neu Thor ansiehet, oder wie mich die ungläubigen Jünger ansehen, wie ich Augen, Maul und Nasen habe, als euer einer; sondern müßt die Augen läutern, die Ohren fegen, und anders sehen, hören, dencken und verstehen, denn nach fleischlichem Sinn und Verstand.

Siehe, auf solche Weise will er hier sich angesehen haben, nicht also, wie die Augen sehen, daß er leiblich mit den Füßen vor ihnen gehe an einen andern Ort, eines Wegs, den sie nicht wissen, wo er hinfährt oder bleibt, und sie also hinter ihm lasse, daß sie sich sein nichts mehr trösten[2] können;

---

gentle words, as a kind lord and master, who can overlook and leniently construe the ignorance and weakness of his dependents, and will fasten and bind them directly to himself alone, with their eyes, ears and hearts, that they should neither look nor think farther; as if he would thereby say, ' Thomas, Thomas, whither are you gaping and wandering with your thoughts! One must not speculate and fly about so. You must look hither at me ' " R ü c k e n is used here in the obsolete sense, equivalent to z i e h e n, or r e i s s e n.

[1] D e n n  i h r  m ü s s e t, etc. "For you must not stare at me as a cow does at a new gate, or as my unbelieving followers do, to see what sort of eyes, mouth and nose I have, as one of you; but you must purge your eyes and clear out your ears, and see, hear, think and understand otherwise than after carnal sense and understanding."

[2] S i c h  s e i n - t r ö s t e n, "console themselves in respect to him." S e i n genitive for s e i n e r. See p. 296, Note 2.

fonbern, wie er geiftlich gehet und fähret, welches er recht
heißt zum Vater gehen, dadurch, daß er leidet und ftirbt,
und doch nicht im Tode bleibt, fondern eben dadurch dahin
kömmt, daß er in fein Reich trit und herrfchet, dazu, daß fie
durch ihn zum Vater kommen, und er fie fchütze, rette und
helfe in allen Nöthen. Darum fpricht er : Wer mich alfo
anfiehet, wie ich zum Vater gehe, der hat alfo viel gefehen,
daß ich den Tod leide nach meines Vaters Willen, und dar=
nach ewiglich lebe und regiere, und alfo gehe ich euch vor
und breche die Bahn, daß ihr auch follet nachfolgen. Das
thue ich und kein andrer, und muß es thun, fonft würdet ihr
nimmermehr dazu kommen. Darum, fo ihr folches wiffet,[1]
fo wiffet ihr beydes, wo ich hin will, und wiffet auch den
Weg, daß ich dahin komme, und ihr mir folgen müffet, nem=
lich, daß ichs felbft bin, und ihr alles in mir habt, was ihr
bedürfet, als der für euch ftirbt, den Vater verföhnet, die
Sünde tilget, den Tod verfchlinget, und alfo alles zu mir
ziehe, daß ihr in mir alles habt.

Dieß heißt nun Chriftum viel anders anfehen, denn ihn
alle Welt anfiehet, und die Jünger felbft zuvor ihn anfahen.
Denn jetzt find die Augen geläutert durch den Glauben, und
ift gar eine neue Erkenntniß. Gleich als wenn[2] ich eines

---

[1] Darum, so ihr solches wisset, etc. "Therefore if
you know this, you know both where I intend going, and you know
also the way (that I may go there and you must follow me), viz.
that it is I myself, and you have everything you need, in me, as [in
one] who dies, reconciles the Father, blots out sin, swallows death
for you, and thus attract everything to myself, that in me ye may
have everything." There is great freedom here in the use of parenthetical observations.

[2] Gleich als wenn, etc. " Just as if I should see a king's
son captured and in wretchedness, in a gray coat or in pilgrim's cos-
tume (form) [and should regard him] as a poor man, and not otherwise
than as (for) a poor beggar, as my eyes direct me ; but if I hear that
he is a king's son, then the gray coat, the staff and every such beg-
garly appearance disappear so that I bow the knee before him and
call him gracious lord," etc.

Königes Sohn gefangen und im Elend sehe, in einem grauen
Rocke oder Pilgrims Gestalt, als einen armen Mann, und
nichts anders, denn für einen Bettler, wie mich die Augen
weisen: wenn ich aber höre, daß er eines Königes Sohn
ist, so fället sobald der graue Rock und der Stab und alle
solche Bettlergestalt aus den Augen, daß ich die Knie gegen
ihm benge, und ihn gnädigen Herrn heisse, ob gleich noch
keine güldene Krone, noch Majestät an ihm gesehen wird.
Also, da St. Thomas und die Andern Christum sehen hin=
ter dem Tische sitzend, als mit fleischlichen Augen, sehen sie
noch nicht, was er für ein Mann ist. Aber hernach krigen
sie ein ander Gesicht, nemlich, daß er sey der Weg, und durch
seinen Tod zum Vater gehe, und (dadurch, daß sie an ihn
gläuben,) sie auch dahin durch ihn gebracht werden.

Darum, wenn das Stündlein kömmt, da unser Thun und
Werck aufhören muß, und wir nicht länger alhie zu bleiben
haben, und diese Disputation[1] angehet: Wo nehme ich nun
eine Brücke oder Steg, der mir gewiß ist, dadurch ich hinü=
ber in jenes Leben komme? wenn man dahin kommt, (sage
ich,) so siehe dich nur nach keinem Weg um, so da heissen
menschliche Wege und unser eigen Gut, heilig Leben oder
Werck; sondern laß solches[2] alles zugedeckt seyn mit dem
Vater Unser, und drüber gesprochen: Vergib uns unsre
Schuld 2c., und halte dich allein zu diesem, der da sagt: Ich
bin der Weg 2c. Und siehe, daß du diß Wort alsdenn dir
vest und tief eingebildet habest, und also, als hörtest du
Christum gegenwärtig dir sagen, wie er hier zu Thoma sagt:
Was suchest und gaffest du nach andern Wegen? Hieher,
auf mich, mußt du sehen und bleiben, und dir keinen andern

---

[1] Disputation, *soliloquy.* — Wenn man dahin kommt,
" when one comes to that," or when that time arrives.

[2] Sondern lass solches, etc. " let all that be overspread
with the Lord's Prayer, and over it (all your good works) let the
words be spoken, ' Forgive us our sins,' and cleave alone to this one,
who says," etc.

Gedancken laſſen machen, wie du mögeſt gen Himmel kom=
men ; ſondern alles rein[1] ab und weit aus dem Hertzen ge=
ſetzt, und nicht anders gedacht, denn, wie ich dir ſage : Ich
bin der Weg. Siehe nur, daß du auf mich treteſt, das iſt,
halte dich mit veſtem Glauben und aller Zuverſicht des
Hertzens an mich ; ich will die Brücke ſeyn und dich übertra=
gen, daß du ſollt in einem Augenblick aus dem Tode und
der Höllenangſt in jenes Leben kommen. Denn ich bins,[2]
der den Weg oder Bahn ſelbſt gepeflaſtert, und ſelbſt gegan=
gen und übergefahren bin, auf daß ich dich und alle, ſo an
mir hangen, hinüber bringe ; allein, daß du dich ungezwei=
ſelt auf mich ſetzeſt, friſch auf mich wageſt, und getroſt und
fröhlich dahin fahreſt und ſterbeſt in meinem Namen.

So will er hiemit ſeine Jünger und Chriſten dazu zurü=
ſten und bereiten, daß ſie immerdar gewarten des Ganges[3]
zu jenem Leben. Alſo ſollte er ſagen : Es wird nun viel
anders mit euch werden, weil ich von euch ſcheide. Der
Tod wird[4] euch täglich unter Augen ſtoſſen, und werdet alle

---

[1] S o n d e r n   a l l e s   r e i n, etc. "but [let] everything [be] put
entirely away (r e i n   a b) and far from your heart, and nothing else
[be] thought than," etc. The participle for the imperative. See p.
297, Note 1.

[2] D e n n   i c h   b i n s, "For it is I who have myself paved the
way or path, and have myself gone and passed over it, in order that
I may convey across thee and all who cleave to me. Only [be sure]
that you surrender yourself unhesitatingly to me, that you cheerfully
venture upon me, and that you go confidently and joyfully and die
in my name."

[3] D a s s   s i e   i m m e r d a r   g e w a r t e n   d e s   G a n g e s, etc.
"that they may be ever awaiting their passage to that other life."
G e w a r t e n   like   w a r t e n, governs the genitive. See p. 224,
Note 7.

[4] D e r   T o d   w i r d, etc. "Death will daily stare you in the
face (rush upon your view) and you will needs expect every hour
that men will torment you, murder you and hunt you from the world,
so that you must go the way that I go out of this life. Therefore
see to it, that you know then where first to set your foot, and find

Stunden warten müssen, daß man euch wird martern, würgen und aus der Welt jagen, daß ihr auch müsset den Weg gehen, den ich jetzt gehe aus diesem Leben. Darum sehet zu, daß ihr alsdenn wisset, wohin ihr den Fuß zum ersten setzen sollet, und den Weg treffet, der euch tragen kann, das ist, daß ihr veste an mir hanget, daß ihr nicht also zappelt und zaget, wie die, so von mir nichts wissen und ihren Reim führen :

Ich lebe, und weiß nicht, wie lang.
Ich sterbe, und weiß nicht, wann.
Ich fahr, und weiß nicht, wohin.
Mich wundert, daß ich fröhlich bin.

So sollten die sagen, die diese Lehre nicht wollen hören, noch den Weg annehmen, und ihr Lebenlang vergeblich andere Wege suchen. Denn also stehet[1] und muß des Menschen Hertz, (so es ohne Christo ist,) daß es immerdar hanget und pampelt in solchem ewigen Zweifel, Schrecken und Zagen, wenn es des Todes gedenckt, daß es nicht weiß, wo aus, wollte gerne dem Tode und der Höllen entfliehen, und weiß doch nicht, wie, wie sie selbst mit diesem Reim bekennen. Aber ein Christ, als der diesen Weg kennet, und schon angefangen hat, darauf zu gehen, soll das Blat umwenden[2] und fröhlich also sagen :

the way that can support you, i. e. that you cleave fast to me, and that you therefore do not struggle and shrink back with fear (z a g e t), as those who know nothing of me, and say in their song," etc.

[1] D e n n  a l s o  s t e h e t, etc. "For so it is (stands) and must be with the heart (so is and must be the heart) of man, if it is without Christ, that it ever hangs and swings (dangles) in such doubt, terror and fear, when it thinks of death, that it knows no way out; it would gladly escape death and hell, and yet knows not how, as they themselves acknowledge in this stanza." P a m p e l n is provincial for b a m m e l n, or rather for b a u m e l n which is a better word.—W o  a u s [z u  k o m m e n].

[2] D a s  B l a t t  u m w e n d e n.  See p. 135, Note 2.  Compare p. 124, Note 6.

Ich lebe, und weiß, wie lang.
Ich sterbe, und weiß wohl, wie und wann.
(nemlich alle Tage und Stunden vor der Welt.)
Ich fahr, und weiß, Gott Lob! wohin,
Mich wundert, daß ich traurig bin.

Denn ein Christ soll ja[1] seiner Sachen gewiß seyn, und weil er Christum hat, so hat ers alles, daß er billig soll alle Stunden in Sprüngen gehen; aber solches alles nach dem Geist und Glauben in Christo, damit er angefangen hat, auf diesem Wege zu gehen. Denn nach dem Fleisch und leiblichen Fühlen ist es noch zugedeckt und gar verborgen. Denn, wie gesagt, menschliche Vernunft und Sinne können nichts weniger verstehen noch begreiffen, denn daß diß sollte ein Weg seyn, da sie nichts siehet noch fühlet, daran sie sich halten könne, sondern schlecht über und ausser ihr Fühlen und Verstehen sich so bloß dahin begeben und wagen, als in eine grosse Wildniß oder weites Meer, da sie keinen Aufenthalt bey sich selbst findet. Darum muß hier der Glaube seyn, der das Wort ergreiffe und sich daran halten könne, und getrost auf denn Mann dahin fahre, obgleich der alte Adam darüber zu scheitern gehet.

---

[1] Denn ein Christ soll ja, etc. "For a Christian should be sure of his case, and, since he possesses Christ he possesses everything, so that he should, by good rights (billig) go leaping [with joy] every hour. But all this [should be done] according to the spirit and the faith in Christ with which he began to walk in this way. For according to the flesh and natural feeling it is still covered and quite concealed. For, as I said, human reason and sense can understand anything sooner (nothing less) than that this should be a way where it can neither see nor feel anything to which it can cleave, but [must] yield itself up and venture above and beyond feeling and knowledge, as if into a great desert or wide ocean, where it finds no dwelling-place (by itself). Therefore there must be a faith which will seize the promise (word) and be able to hold on to it, and confidently commit all (go away) to Christ (the man), though the old Adam meanwhile goes to wreck."

Also auch ihr, (will Christus hier sagen,) wenn ihr mich durch den Glauben ergriffen habt, so seyd ihr auf dem rechten Wege, der euch gewiß ist und nicht verführet. Aber sehet allein zu, daß ihr darauf bleibet und fortfahret; denn es wird euch gar mancherley Anstoß und Hinderniß begegnen, beyde, zur rechten und lincken Seite. Darum müßt ihr gerüst seyn,[1] daß ihr vest an mir haltet, und euch nichts lasset anfechten, was euch grausames oder schreckliches vor Augen kömmt, so euch von mir will abschrecken oder mit schönem Schein zur Seite ausreißen und locken will, und wissen, daß solches alles eitel Lügen und Betrug des Teufels ist, dadurch er euch ins Verderben führet. Ich aber will euch gewiß seyn, und durch dieses weite Meer, aus dem Tode ins ewige Leben, aus der Welt und Teufels Reich zum Vater bringen. Darum will ich nicht allein selbst der Weg, sondern auch die Wahrheit und das Leben seyn und heissen.

Siehe, also verstehe ich diesen Spruch aufs einfältigste, daß es immer bleibe auf einerley Meynung von dem einigen Christo, daß er heisse der Weg,[2] um des Anfangs willen; die Wahrheit, von wegen des Mittels und Fortfahrens, und auch das Leben, von wegen des Endes. Denn er muß doch alles seyn, der Anfang, Mittel und Ende unserer Seligkeit: daß man ihn zum ersten Stein lege und die andern und

---

[1] Darum müsst ihr gerüst[et] seyn, etc. "Therefore you must be armed, that you may cleave fast to me, and let nothing that appears (vor Augen kommt) cruel or fearful, which would frighten you away from me, or [which] would draw you aside and allure you with an attractive appearance, tempt you, and be assured that all this is nothing but Satan's lies and deception, by which he would lead you (leads you) to destruction."

[2] Dass er heisse der Weg, etc. "that he is called the way, on account of the beginning; the truth, because of the middle and progress; and the life, because of the end. For he must be everything, the beginning, middle and end of our salvation, so that one must make him the foundation stone, lay the others, the intermediate ones upon it, and then crown it with the vaulted summit or roof."

mittlern darauf ſetze, und auch das Gewölbe oder Dach dar=
auf ſchlieſſe. Er iſt, beyde, die erſte, mittel und letzte
Stuſe an der Leiter gen Himmel, 1. Moſ. 28, 12. Denn
durch ihn müſſen wir anfahen, fortfahren und hindurch zum
Leben kommen.

Niemand kömmt zum Vater, denn durch mich.

Da nimmt er die drey Stücke auf einen Haufen, und faſ=
ſets alles in Eins, deutet mit unverblümten, klaren Worten,
was er meyne, und wozu er ſich alſo genennet habe: den
Weg, Wahrheit und Leben, nemlich alſo und dazu,[1] daß
man zum Vater komme. Summa, (will er ſagen,) ich bins
allein alles; ſoll jemand zum Vater kommen, ſo muß es
allein durch mich geſchehen, Anfang, Mittel und Ende.

Was iſt aber zum Vater kommen? Nichts anders,
denn, wie nun oft geſagt, aus dem Tode ins Leben, aus der
Sünde und Verdammniß zur Unſchuld und Frömmigkeit,
aus dem Jammer und Hertzeleid zur ewigen Freude und
Seligkeit kommen, Solches (ſagt er,)[2] nehme ihm niemand
vor, auf andere Weiſe dazu zu kommen, denn durch mich.
Denn ich bin allein der Weg, die Wahrheit und das Leben.
Das heißt ja klar und deutlich genug geredt, rein ausge=
ſchloſſen und gewaltiglich niedergelegt alle Lehre vom Ver=
dienſt der Wercke und eigener Gerechtigkeit, und ſchlecht ver=
neint und verſagt allen andern Troſt und Vertrauen, da=
durch man vermeynet, gen Himmel zu kommen. Denn es
heißt kurtz: Niemand, niemand kommt zum Vater, denn
durch mich; es iſt kein ander Schiff noch Ueberfahrt.

---

[1] Nemlich also und dazu, "namely thus, and to this end."

[2] Solches (sagt er), etc. "This (such), says he, let no one
attempt to arrive at (take before or upon him to come to it) in
any other manner than through me. For I alone am the way, the
truth and the life. This is speaking plainly and distinctly enough;
[it is] excluding and putting down with a strong hand all doctrine of
the merit of works and of our own righteousness, and directly denying and prohibiting any other consolation or confidence through

7. Wenn ihr mich kennetet, so kennetet ihr auch meinen Vater, und von nun an kennet ihr ihn und habt ihn gesehen.

Hie machet der Herr Christus abermal eine neue Parabel und verdeckte Rede vor den Jüngern, daß sie erst anfahen zu fragen von dem Vater, was und wo er sey? Denn, wiewol er deutlich genug davon geredt und sich erkläret hat, wie er sey der Weg, die Wahrheit und das Leben 2c., damit, daß er sagt: „Niemand kommt zum Vater, ohne durch mich," so sind doch die lieben Jünger noch unverständig, hören diese Worte alle: Weg, Wahrheit, Leben, zum Vater kommen 2c., so gar mit lauter Vernunft und fleischlichem Sinn, daß sie sich nicht können drein richten. Darum läßt er sie freundlich anlauffen,[1] und wirft ihnen einen Klotz in den Weg, daran sie sich stoffen sollen, und verursacht werden, weiter zu fragen.

Darum fähet er also an: Wenn ihr mich kennetet 2c. Wie? Kennen sie denn nun Christum nicht, so sie ihn doch

which many fancy that they are going (to go) to heaven." See p. 283, Note 6.

[1] Darum lässt er sie freundlich anlaufen, etc. "Therefore he kindly lets them trip, and throws a stumbling-block in the way, against which they should dash and be induced to inquire farther." Einen anlaufen lassen is now used only in a figurative sense, *to treat one as he deserves, to treat one coldly.* But originally, it meant, *to make one run against something and stumble,* and that was considered as treating a wrong-headed man as he deserved. This signification is very obvious from several passages in Luther's version of the Scriptures, as Ps. 27: 2. " If the wicked, mine enemies come upon me they must stumble (müssen sie anlaufen) and fall." Ezek. 3: 20. " If a righteous man turn from his righteousness and do evil, I will lay a stumbling-block before him (so werde ich ihn lassen anlaufen), so that he shall die." See also Rom. 11: 11, and on the substantive Anlaufen, *stumbling,* see Rom. 9: 32 and 33.—Nearly all the significations of the verb can be derived from the literal one laufen, *to run,* an, *against, upon* or *up.* Thus this otherwise difficult word is made to appear quite simple.

vor ihnen gegenwärtig sehen und hören, und so lange Zeit[1] mit ihm umher gezogen sind? Das ists aber, das ich gesagt habe, daß: Christum kennen, heißt hier nicht, nach dem Angesicht und (wie St. Paulus sagt,) fleischlich ihn kennen, sondern wissen, wofür er zu halten, was wir an ihm haben und wie wir sein brauchen sollen. Denn das ist in Summa seine Meynung, daß es alles daran liege, und allein das soll der Christen Kunst seyn, daß wir ihn recht kennen lernen und ausmahlen[2] von allen Gedancken, Wesen, Lehren und Leben, und was man vornehmen kann, und also an ihm allein hangen mit dem Glauben, und von gantzem Hertzen sagen: Ich weiß nichts und will nichts wissen in göttlichen Sachen, ohne allein von meinem Herrn Christo; der solls allein alles seyn, was meine Seligkeit betrifft und zwischen Gott und mir zu handeln ist.[3] Und ob ich wol mancherley Anfechtung und Widerstand habe vom Teufel, Welt und meinem eigenen Gewissen, dazu den Tod muß drüber leiden,[4] noch will ich dabei bleiben, leben und sterben. Das hiesse denn[5] (spricht er,) mich recht gekennet, und durch mich auch den Vater.

---

[1] Und so lange Zeit, etc. "and have gone about with him so long." Umherziehen, as an active verb with the auxiliary haben, means *to drag about*, etc. As a neuter verb with seyn, it means *to move or stroll about.* Herumziehen as an active, and as a reflective verb has very nearly the same significations.

[2] Und ausmahlen, etc. "and separate him from all [human] thoughts, qualities (Wesen, those things which constitute a whole) teachings and practices (life), and whatever one can propose, and so cling to him alone," etc.—Ausmahlen, *to grind out, to sift out,* and thus *to separate,* must not be confounded with a similar word, now commonly written ausmalen, *to fill out* or *complete a painting.* The participle of the former is ansgemahlen, that of the latter, ausgemalt.

[3] Zu handeln ist, *is to be transacted.*

[4] Dazu den Tod muss drüber leiden, "and besides must die from it (over it)."

[5] Das hiesse denn, etc. "For this, says he, is rightly know-

8, 9. Spricht zu ihm Philippus, Herr, zeige uns den Vater, so genüget uns. Jesus spricht zu ihm: So lange bin ich bey euch, und du kennest mich nicht? Philippe, wer mich siehet, der siehet auch den Vater. Wie sprichst du denn: Zeige uns den Vater.

Das ist eine sehr schöne Disputation oder Gespräch und Predigt des Herrn Christi. Denn, nachdem er ihnen viel gesagt hat von seinem Vater, wie er zu ihm gehen wolle, und sie auch zu ihm bringen, daß sie ihn auch sehen sollen, ja auch bereits ihn kennen und gesehen haben: da fährt der Apostel Philippus, als etwas verständiger und schärfer, denn die andern, heraus mit der hohen Frage, damit sich allezeit die höhesten, weisesten Leute viel und hoch bekümmert, fleißig gesucht und geforschet haben; was doch Gott sey, und wie man Gott erkennen und erlangen möge, aber nie keiner hat treffen können, und auch unmöglich ist der Natur und menschlicher Vernunft zu treffen, wie Philippus selbst hie zeuget und zeiget, daß, wiewol er Christum gehöret vom Vater predigen und sagen, doch desselben noch nie nichts[1] überall verstanden habe, oder noch verstehe. Das macht, daß ers noch mit Vernunft fassen und durch eigene Gedanken erlangen will.

Darum, obwohl Christus ihn allein auf sein Wort weiset und an sich hängen will,[2] und sagt, er kenne ihn bereits und

---

ing me and, through me, the Father." See p. 48, Note 5, and p. 283, Note 6.

[1] Doch desselben noch nie nichts, etc. "still he never understood anything (nichts) at all (überall) of it (desselben)."

[2] Und an sich hängen will, etc. "and wishes to attach him to himself, and says that he (Philip) already knows him (Christ) and has seen him, still there is yet no cleaving to him, but (Philip) freely acknowledges what is passing in his mind (how he has it in his heart)," etc.—Hängen, as causative of hangen is an active verb. See p. 132, Note 3.—Haftet es, is impersonal, but refers, of course, to Philip.

habe ihn gesehen, doch hafftet es noch nicht bey ihm, sondern bekennet frey zu, wie ers im Hertzen hat, und spricht: Ach zeige uns doch den Vater, so gnüget uns. Also sollte er sa= gen: Du sagest uns wol vom Vater, wie wir ihn kennen; hab ich ihn doch trann mein Lebtag[1] nie gesehen, und wüßte nichts liebers zu wünschen, denn daß ich möchte so selig seyn, und einmal ihn sehen.

Also läßt sich der liebe Apostel hören, daß er noch ist ein wanckender, unbeständiger Gläubiger, gleichwie die andern alle, wiewol sie nicht so herausfahren. Denn er glaubet auch an Gott und hat viel von ihm gehöret. Nun er aber höret Christum sagen: Wenn ihr mich kennet, so kennet ihr den Vater, und jetzt kennet ihr ihn,—das ist ihm gar eine fremde, unverständige Sprache. So weit kommt er[2] mit

---

[1] **Traun mein Lebtag. Traun**, *certainly*, from **trauen**, *to* r*ely upon it*, is obsolete. **Mein Lebtag**, *all my life*, is, in modern German, always in the plural, **meine Lebtage**. Probably **mein Lebtag** is not designed as a singular, which would hardly make sense, but is an abbreviation, as is common in familiar language, of the plural form. " Yet I have certainly never seen him in all my life, and I could wish nothing more fondly than that I might be so happy as once (one day) to see him." **Und wüste nichts liebers zu wünschen**, literally, " and I should know nothing more agreeable to wish or to be wished." **Liebers** for **Lieberes** is used in the sense of **Angenehmeres**, as the positive **Liebes**, *something agreeable*, is used for **Angenehmes**. Such adjectives when appended to **nichts, etwas alles, wenig, viel**, etc. are, in modern German, generally written with a capital, as **nichts Gutes**, *nothing good;* **nichts Neues**, *nothing new*.

[2] **So weit kommt er**, etc. " Thus far does he wander away (**davon**, from the true meaning of Christ's words); he lets Christ set there and talk by the table (i. e. leaves him there talking), as Thomas did (see above v. 5), [and] is utterly unable (can directly not) to cleave to Christ, who is talking with him, but, notwithstanding that, sallies out one side with his own thoughts, and flies up into the clouds, ' O that we might but see him, as he sets above among the angels.'" **Desselben** with **ungeachtet** is used as **dessen** is. See p. 7, Note 6.

feinen Gedancken davon, läßt Christum da sitzen und reden,
gleichwie St. Thomas droben (B. 5.) auch thut, kann
schlechts nicht hafften an dem Christo, so mit ihm redet;
sondern, desselben ungeachtet, spazieret er beyseit aus mit
eigenen Gedancken, und flabbert hinauf in die Wolcken:
Ach, daß wir ihn doch sehen möchten, wie er droben sitzet
unter den Engeln!

Aber das Sehen und Kennen mußt du nicht also grob
und fleischlich verstehen, daß, wer Christum siehet, (wie die
Kuh ein Thor ansiehet,) daß der den Vater also mit Augen
sehe, wie er gestalt[1] ist, sondern nach des Geists und Glaubens Gesicht, und doch wahrhaftig also, wie die Worte deuten. Sonst haben ihn auch gesehen und gekennet Caiphas,
Pilatus, Herodes und fast das gantze Jüdische Volck, und
doch weder ihn noch den Vater erkennet. Denn ob sie wohl
die Person Christi sehen und kennen: doch sehen sie noch
nicht, wie der Vater in Christo, und Christus in ihm, und
beyder ein Hertz, Sinn und Wille, ja, auch ein einig, unzertrennlich, göttlich Wesen ist.

Siehe, also will er hiemit Philippum und die andern
Apostel zurück ziehen, als die[2] hin und her wancken und flabbern mit Gedancken, und so weit kommen vom Glauben, daß
sie nicht wissen, wo und wie sie Gott suchen oder finden sollen, ob sie wol Christum vor ihrer Nase sehen. Wo gaffest
du hin, spricht er, und was flabberst du und fährest mit Gedancken, wie ein unstät Queckfilber? Wie sprichst du noch,
ich soll dir den Vater zeigen? Ich meynete, du kennetest
ihn sehr wohl. Hörest du nicht, wer mich siehet, der siehet
den Vater ꝛc. Das ist, willt du wissen, wie du mit Gott
dran seyst,[3] und wie er gegen dich gesinnet sey, oder über

---

[1] Gestalt for gestaltet, "how he is formed," or of what
form he is.

[2] Als die, "as [those] who."

[3] Wie du mit Gott dran seyst, "how you are off (dran,
or daran, *on it*) with God," or how you stand with him.

dich gedencket, und Summa, wie du zu ihm kommen mögest, (denn solches wissen,[1] heißt eigentlich, den Vater kennen,) so frage nur dein eigen Hertz,[2] noch Vernunft und Gedancken, auch keinen Mosen oder andern Lehrer nicht darum ; sondern allein mich siehe an, und höre, was Ich rede. Auf mich (sage ich) mußt du sehen und hören. Wenn du solches, so du an mir siehest und von mir hörest, ins Hertz fassest, wie ich mich gegen dir erzeige und hören lassen, so triffst du gewißlich den Vater, und hast ihn recht gesehen und erkannt, wie man ihn sehen und kennen soll.

Denn an dieser Person Christi siehest du, daß er niemand sauer ansiehet, noch unfreundlich handelt, oder schrecket und von sich jagt, sondern jedermann, beyde, mit Worten und Geberden aufs freundlichste zu sich locket und reitzet, erzeiget sich nicht anders, denn als ein Diener, der, jedermann gerne helfen will : also auch, daß er sich um deinetwillen läßt ans Creutz schlagen, und sein Blut mildiglich vergeußt. Das siehest du mit Augen ; dazu hörest du mit Ohren nichts anders, denn eitel solche freundliche, süsse, tröstliche Worte : Euer Hertz erschrecke nicht rc. Kommt zu mir alle, die ihr mühselig und beladen seyd, Matth. 11, 28. Wer an mich gläubet, soll nicht verloren werden, sondern das ewige Leben haben rc., Joh. 3, 16, und was solcher Sprüche mehr sind,[3] welcher das gantze Evangelium Johannis voll ist. Daraus kannst du gewißlich schliessen, daß er dir nicht feind ist, sondern alle Gnade und Wohlthat erzeigen will. Da bleibe

---

[1] Denn solches wissen. Solches can grammatically be either an accusative governed by wissen, as den Vater is by kennen, or it can be used adjectively agreeing with wissen as a substantive,—"to know such," or "such knowledge." The latter is much the simpler construction.

[2] Eigen Hertz must be connected with nicht darum. "Consult not thine own heart about it, nor thy reason and thoughts, nor any Moses or other teacher."

[3] Solcher Sprüche mehr sind. See p. 106, Note 5.

bey und halte veſt dran, dencke und ſiehe nicht weiter, und laß dich nichts irren,[1] was dir anders vorkommt.

Wie du nun Chriſtum höreſt und ſieheſt, alſo höreſt du und ſieheſt gewißlich auch den Vater ſich gegen dir erzeigen. Denn die Worte, ſo ich zu euch rede, ſpricht er bald hernach, (V. 10.) ſind nicht mein, ſondern meines Vaters, daß wer den Sohn ſiehet und gläubet an ihn, habe das ewige Leben ꝛc., Joh. 6, 39. 40. Wer nun ſolches mit dem Glauben faſſet, der kann ja nicht dencken, daß Gott mit ihm zürne, oder ihn von ſich ſtoſſen und verdammen wolle. Denn es iſt ja hier kein Wort noch Zeichen einiger Ungnade, ſondern eitel freundliche, holdſelige Worte und lieblicher, freundlicher Anblick, und Summa, eitel Brunſt und Glut unausſprech=licher, väterlicher, hertzlicher Liebe.

**10. Gläubeſt du nicht, daß ich im Vater und der Vater in mir iſt? Die Worte, die ich rede, die rede ich nicht von mir ſelbſt. Der Vater aber, der in mir wohnet, der thut die Wercke.**

Das iſt alles dahin geredet, daß er dieſen Hauptartickel, wie ich geſagt habe, wohl einbilde und einbläue,[2] daß man lerne aus den Augen und Hertzen thun alles, was da mag

---

[1] Irren, in the sense of irre machen. See p. 253, Note 3.

[2] Einbläue, *beat into*, from blaüen, *to beat black and blue.* It is now no longer an elevated word. "That is all said to this end, that he might impress and beat in this leading principle, as I have said, that men should learn to put away from their eyes and from their hearts whatever may be taught and preached even in the law of Moses, and much more [what proceeds] from human reason and from one's own thoughts, when it relates to this that one is to have to do with God and ascertain his will. He must be established in this one point, namely that he can bring before him [the image of] this Jesus Christ, and let nothing tempt him to the contrary or lead him astray, whether it be called doing and living right or wrong, holiness or sin."

gelehret und geprediget werden, auch im Geſetz Moſis, viel=
mehr aus menſchlichem Verſtande und eigenen Gedancken,
wenn es dazu kömmt, daß der Menſch ſich mit Gott beküm=
mern ſoll und ſeinen Willen erkundigen will, und allein das
einige Stück faſſe, daß er ihm könne dieſen Jeſum Chriſtum
fürbilden, und nichts laſſe dagegen anfechten noch irren, es
heiſſe wohl oder übel gethan und gelebt, Heiligkeit oder
Sünde.

Diß iſt die Kunſt, davon St. Johannes, als ein ausbün=
diger[1] Evangeliſt in dieſem Stücke, und St. Paulus vor an=
dern lehren, daß ſie ſo veſt in einander binden und hefften
Chriſtum und den Vater: auf daß man lerne, von Gott
nichts zu dencken, denn in Chriſto, und ſo bald wir hören
Gottes Namen nennen, oder von ſeinem Willen, Wercken,
Gnade oder Ungnade ſagen, daß wir nicht darnach richten,
wie es in unſerm Hertzen iſt, oder einiges Menſchen Weis=
heit davon diſputiret, oder auch das Geſetz vorgibt; ſondern
allein in dieſen Chriſtum uns wickeln und hüllen, und nichts
anders wollen ſehen noch hören, denn, wie er ſich uns zei=
get als ein liebliches Kindlein an der Mutter Armen und
Schoos, item, als ein treuer Heiland an dem Creutz ſein
Blut für uns mildiglich vergeußt, item, wie er wider auf=
ſtehet, den Teufel und Hölle unter ſich wirft und den Tod
mit Füſſen trit, und dir ſolches, beyde, ſelbſt und durch ſeine
Apoſtel verkündiget und ſchencket, damit er genugſam zeuget,
daß er keinen Zorn noch Ungnade gegen dir hat, ſondern
alles dir zu Hülfe und Troſt thut, was er thun ſoll und
thun kann, ſo du es allein willt gläuben und annehmen.

Ja, ſprichſt du, das ſehe und höre ich wohl, wer weiß
aber, wo es Gott auch alſo mit mir meynet? Antwort:
Da hüte dich für;[2] denn das heißt Chriſtum und Gott ge=

---

[1] A u s b ü n d i g e r, *most excellent*, an obsolete word. See p. 265,
Note 5.

[2] D a  h ü t e  d i c h  f ü r [v o r], etc. " Beware of that; for that is
dividing and separating Christ and God."

theilet und getrennet. Gleichwie Philippus alhier thut, der da Christum läßt fahren, und Gott oben im Himmel sucht, und dencket: Ich höre wol, daß Christus mit mir redet; wie weiß ich aber, was Gott droben im Himmel über mich gedencket oder beschlossen hat? Was ist das anders, denn ein Unglaube und heimliche Verleugnung Gottes, daß ihn Christus hiermit strafen muß, auf daß er ihn von solchem schändlichen Wahn reisse, und spricht: Philippe, was soll das seyn,[1] daß du den Vater und mich von einander reissest, kletterst hinauf in die Wolcken mit Gedancken, und läßt mich hier vergebens mit dir reden? Hörest du nicht, was ich dir sage, daß, wer mich siehet, der siehet den Vater selbst, und gläubest nicht, daß ich im Vater und der Vater in mir ist; item: Die Worte, die ich rede, sind nicht meine, sondern des Vaters Worte? Das sind wol freundliche, aber doch ernste Worte des Herrn. Denn er wills nicht leiden, daß man also vergeblich und ungewiß hin und her gaffe und umher flabbere; sondern will uns gantz und gar an sich und an sein Wort gebunden haben, daß man Gott nirgend, denn in ihm, suche.

Siehe, das ist[2] diß schöne Gespräch und Predigt auf die Frage des Apostels Philippi, damit ihm nicht allein geantwortet, sondern aller Menschen fliegenden Gedancken, damit sie sich unterstehen, Gott zu ergreiffen, also, daß dir und aller Welt hiermit durch Christum gesagt sey: Was machest du, daß du willst Gott anders suchen, denn in mir; oder

---

[1] Was soll das seyn, etc. "what does this mean, that you rend the Father and me asunder, and clamber up into the clouds in your thoughts, and leave me here talking with you to no purpose?"

[2] Siehe, das ist, etc. "Behold, such (that) is this fine dialogue and discourse on the question of the apostle Philip, with which a reply is made not only to him but to the towering thoughts of all men with which they presume to comprehend God, so that herewith it is said by Christ to you and to all the world."—Geantwortet [ist] is impersonal, like gesagt sey below. See p. 155, Note 3.

auber Wort unb Werck, denn die ich rede unb schaffe, sehen
unb hören? Weißt du nicht, daß ich im Vater unb der
Vater in mir ist ec.? Darnach hörest du mich in St Paulo,
Paulum in Tito ober anbern Predigern, unb also fort in
allen, so diß Wort predigen, daß es alles Ein Küchen[1] ist
in dem Herrn Christo. Wo Paulus ist, da bin ich; wo ich
bin, da ist Paulus unb alle Prediger. Alles in Christo
durch unb durch; Christus aber in unb mit dem Vater;
unb wiederum, Christus in allen, der Vater aber in Christo.
Was fragest du dennoch, spricht er, aus der unverständigen
Vernunft, wo doch der Vater sey? Also soll kein Jünger
Christi nicht[2] fragen. Laß die anbern Unchristen, Heyden,
Jüben, Türcken, Ketzer, Mönche unb Sophisten also for=
schen unb suchen; du aber hüte dich, daß du nicht anßer mir
fahrest. Denn also findest du nicht Gott, sondern den leidi=
gen Teufel, welcher, wie gesagt ist, kann nicht die Leute an=
bers betrügen, er muß der Majestät Namen an seine Lügen
schmieren.

**11.** Gläubet mir, daß ich im Vater bin,
unb der Vater in mir ist; wo nicht, so gläu=
bet mir doch um der Wercke willen.

Wollet ihr nicht gläuben, spricht er, um meiner Predigt
willen, daß Gott in mir wohne unb sey, unb ich in ihm: so
gläubets doch um der Wercke willen, so ihr vor Augen sehet,
unb kein Mensch leugnen kann, daß es nicht menschliche,
sondern, göttliche Wercke sind, unb starck genug beweisen
unb zengen, daß er in mir unb durch mich rede unb wircke.
Das sind nun die Wercke unb Wunder, die er vor aller
Welt erzeigt hat, da er die Blinden sehend, die Tauben hö=
rend, allerley Krancke gesund,[3] die Teufel ausgetrieben unb

---

[1] K ü c h e n, *cake*, used here to indicate "one and the same thing."
[2] K e i n — n i c h t, a double for a single negative.
[3] Gesund [gemacht].

die Todten auferwecket hat, allein mit dem Wort, welches[1] sind nicht allein göttliche Wercke, sondern auch Zeugen von Gott dem Vater, daß man nicht allein den Glauben daraus schöpffen, (daß er in Christo und Christus in ihm ist,) sondern auch den Trost fassen kann der väterlichen Liebe und Gnade gegen uns.

Denn wo er Lust hätte zu zürnen, verdammen, strafen und plagen, würde er nicht durch Christum Sünde vergeben, und die Strafe derselbigen wegnehmen an dem Gichtbrüchigen, Aussätzigen und andern, die vom Teufel besessen und geplaget waren 2c. Item, wo er Lust hätte zum Tode, würde er nicht die Todten auferwecken und lebendig machen. Nun aber hat er solches in Christo gethan und uns gezeiget, daß wir ihn lernen recht ansehen und erkennen, als einen gnädigen Vater, der uns gerne helfen und selig machen will. Und zwar beweiset ers auch täglich an allen seinen Wercken, so er in der gantzen Welt thut, daß er seine Creaturen stets erhält, und aller Welt so viel Wohlthaten thut, und seine Güter reichlich ausschüttet, ohne, wo[2] er aus Noth und um der Frommen willen strafen und den Bösen steuren muß. Doch regieret er also, daß wir auch leiblich allzeit mehr seiner Gnaden und Wohlthaten sehen, denn Zorn und Strafe. Denn, wo einer kranck, blind, taub, gichtbrüchig, aussätzig ist, da sind dagegen hundert tausend gesund; und ob ein Glied am Leibe einen Fehl hat, so ist dagegen der gantze Mensch, so noch Leib und Seele hat, eitel Gottes Güte.

12. Wahrlich, wahrlich, ich sage euch, wer an mich gläubet, der wird die Wercke auch thun, die ich thue, und wird grössere, denn diese thun; denn ich gehe zum Vater.

---

[1] Welches refers not to Wort, but to the whole clause.

[2] Ohne, wo, etc. "except where he must of necessity and on account of the righteous punish and govern the wicked." See p. 147, Note 1.

Hier kömmt er wieder auf den Trost, so er hat angefangen den Jüngern zu geben, daß sie nicht sollten darum erschrecken noch trauren, daß er würde leiblich oder sichtbarlich von ihnen gehen, und sie in der Welt lassen, sondern dagegen ansehen und zum Trost fassen, was sie des für Nutzen und Frommen[1] haben sollen für den geringen leiblichen Mangel: nemlich, daß er ihnen viel herrlichere Wohnungen bereiten will, und doch bey ihnen seyn, daß er sie auch dahin bringe,[2] da er ist, dahin sie sonst nicht kommen könnten, item, daß sie schon den Weg wüßten und den Vater kenneten; also, daß er nun das ausgerichtet, darum er bey ihnen gewesen war, und nicht mehr sie durfte lehren, ohne daß ers nun vollbringe und ihnen helfe, dahin sie kommen sollen. Zudem setzet er nun das auch, damit sie desto mehr Trosts haben und spüren, daß sie gar keinen Mangel noch Schaden seines Abschieds haben, sondern viel reichlicher und herrlicher, denn bisher, begnadet werden: nemlich, daß sie dadurch solches überkommen,[3] daß sie eben dieselben Wercke thun sollen, so er gethan hat, und dazu grössere, denn er leiblich bey ihnen gethan hat, oder noch thun werde. Und wie er jetzt gesagt hat, daß er solche Wercke thue, dadurch sie sollen glauben, daß der Vater in ihm und er im Vater sey: also führet ers hie herab[4] und sagt, daß sie auch sollen

---

[1] Was—des für Nutzen und Frommen, "what kind of (was für) use and advantage from it (des, of it) they should have," etc.

[2] Dass er sie auch dahin bringe, etc. "that he bring them to that place where he is, whither they could not otherwise come ; also, that they have now ascertained the way and known the Father; likewise that he has now accomplished that for which (darum) he was with them, and could not [consistently] teach them any more without doing the work itself (es) and giving them the aid [by which] they should come thither."

[3] Solches überkommen, "come into possession of such [power]."

[4] Also führet ers hie herab, etc. "thus he brings it down

folche Wercke thun, dabey man fpüren werde, daß auch fie in Chrifto und Chriftus in ihnen fey, wie er hernach weiter fagen wird. Denn er hiermit anzeigt, was er in ihnen und durch fie thun und ausrichten will in der Chriftenheit, wie wir hören werden.

Was foll man aber dazu fagen, daß er nicht allein von den Apofteln folches redet, fondern von allen, die an ihn gläuben? Und was mögen das für Wercke feyn, die da follen gröffer feyn, denn des Herrn Chrifti? Was kann gröffers genennet werden, denn Todte lebendig machen, die Seelen aus des Teufels und des Todes Gewalt erlöfen und das ewige Leben geben? Sind das nicht allein feine eigene Wercke, fo er durch feine göttliche Kraft und Macht an uns thut? Wer kann denn fagen daß wir follen gröffere thun?

Hier laß ich mir gefallen den gemeinen Verftand diefes Spruchs, wie es denn nicht kann anders feyn, daß es darum gröffere Wercke gethan heiffe durch feine Chriften, daß die Apoftel und Chriften weiter kommen mit ihren Wercken, denn er kommen ift, und mehr zu Chrifto bringen, denn er leiblich auf Erden gethan hat. Denn er hat[1] nur einen kleinen Winckel vor fich genommen, da er geprediget und gewundert hat, dazu eine kleine Zeit. Die Apoftel aber und ihre Nachkommen find durch die gantze Welt kommen, und hat gewähret,[2] fo lange die Chriftenheit geftanden ift: alfo, daß es Chriftus nur perfönlich angefangen hat, aber durch

---

to [this further] application." That is, the works performed by them, will not only prove, by the fulfilment of his promise, that he is in the Father, but also that they are in him.

[1] Denn er hat, etc. "For he entered upon a small district (corner) only, in which he preached and wrought miracles, and that for a short time." Wundern, see p. 283, Note 4.

[2] [Ge]kommen, und [es] hat gewähret "went into all the world and it, i. e. their work, has been going on as long as Christianity has existed."

die Apostel und folgenden Prediger hat müssen immer weiter
ausgebreitet werden bis an den Jüngsten Tag. Also ists
wahr, daß die Christen grössere Wercke, das ist, mehr und
weiter thun, denn Christus selbst; doch sind es einerley und
eben dieselbigen Wercke. Denn damit, daß er spricht: Wer
an mich gläubet, der wird grössere Wercke thun, verneinet
er nicht, daß solche Wercke durch seine Kraft müssen gesche=
hen, und aus ihm, als dem Haupte, herfliessen; sondern
zeiget selbst, beyde, hier, da er spricht: „Wer an mich
gläubet", und in folgenden Worten: Denn ich gehe zum
Vater; item V. 14: Was ihr bitten werdet, das will ich
thun 2c., daß[1] solche nicht geschehen, denn allein von denen,
so durch den Glauben an ihm hangen, und er seine Kraft in
ihnen wircket und durch sie beweiset.

Das sage ich, daß man diesen Text desto baß[2] verstehe,
wie durch die Christen ohne Unterlaß die allergrössesten
Wercke geschehen in der Welt, ob sie wol nicht anzusehen
sind, noch erkannt werden, beyde, im geistlichen und auch im
leiblichen Wesen und Regiment, als nemlich: Zustörung
des Teufels Reichs, Erlösung der Seelen, Bekehrung der

---

[1] Sondern zeiget selbst beide, hier — und in folgenden Worten — dass. Beide refers to hier and to in folgenden Worten, "but he even intimates both here when he
says, ' He who believeth on me,' and in the following words, etc.
that such things do not take place except with those who," etc.

[2] Bass, *good*, *well*, an obsolete word in the positive degree from
which the comparative besser (bässer) is formed. In Luther's
time, it was commonly used as a comparative, *better*. " This I say
in order that one may the better understand the text, how that,
though they are not obvious (to be seen) nor perceived, the very
greatest works are effected in the world through Christians continually both in spiritual and in secular matters and government, as, for
example, the overthrow of Satan's kingdom, the redemption of souls,
the conversion of men (hearts), the triumph and maintenance of
peace in countries and among nations, aid, protection and deliverance
in all kinds of calamity and distress." This translation is given as
the easiest way of explaining the construction.

Herßen, Sieg und Erhaltung des Friedens bey Landen und Lenten, Hülfe, Schuß und Rettung in allerley Plagen und Nöthen. Solches alles spricht er, soll durch die Christen geschehen, weil sie an Christum gläuben und alles von ihm, als dem Haupt, hergehet, ja, auch durch einen jeglichen insonderheit, daß er möchte sagen: Die Wercke, die ich thue, die thue ein jeglicher Christ, so heute getauft ist.

Weil wir denn solchen Schaß haben, so haben wir alles, und sind Herren über alle Herren. Bettler sind wir auf Erden, wie Christus auch selbst gewest ist, aber vor Gott,[1] sind wir überschüttet mit allen Gütern: daß die Welt gegen uns elend und bloß ist, und ohne uns auch ihre Güter nicht behalten kann, ich aber, wenn ich sterbe, habe ich doch solche Güter, die mir bleiben sollen; denn ich habe den Herrn Christum selbst, so droben im Himmel sißet, du aber mußt alsdenn nacket und bloß davon scheiden und nicht einen Faden mit nehmen, und dort auch alles Guten beraubt seyn, ob du gleich ein mächtiger König wärest, und aller Welt Gut hattest. Aber ein Christ soll seiner Güter nicht ein Härlein[2] hinter ihm lassen; denn er hat bereits seinen Schaß droben im Himmel in und mit Christo, wie St. Paulus, Ephes. 2, 6., sagt, daß wir schon durch ihn gesezt sind in das himmlische Wesen. Jeßt ist es wol nicht offenbar; aber am Jüngsten Tage wird alle Welt müssen sehen, was der arme Lazarus, der vor des Reichen Thüre nicht die Brosamlein hatte, so von seinem Tische fielen, für Reichthum und ewige Herrlichkeit haben wird im Himmel, da der

---

[1] A b e r  v o r  G o t t, etc. "but before God we are overwhelmed with all good things (possessions); so that the world in comparison with us (see p. 151, Note 1.) is miserable and destitute (bare. See 2 Chron. 28: 19), and without our aid (us), cannot hold its possessions, whereas I, if I die, have such goods as (or goods which) must remain with me."

[2] H ä r l e i n diminutive of H a a r, like B r o s a m l e i n a little below, from B r o s a m, *a crumb*, from an old verb b r o s e n, *to break*.

reiche Wanſt ſamt aller ungläubigen Welt wird in ewiger Glut liegen und brennen. Luc. 16, 19. ff.

Nun, was iſt denn die Urſache, warum die Chriſten ſollen eben ſo gröſſere Wercke thun, denn er ſelbſt? Keine andere,[1] ſpricht er, ohne dieſe: Denn ich gehe zum Vater. Wie reimet ſich doch das? Iſt der Mann truncken, oder redet im Traum? Aber das iſts, das ich geſagt habe, daß wir ſolche Wercke nicht thun von uns ſelber. Daß aber die Chriſtenheit ſo groſſe Wercke thut durch die gantze Welt, die er auf Erden nur in dem kleinen Völcklein gethan, das kömmt daher, will er ſagen, daß ich zum Vater gehe, und mein Reich einnehme, das iſt, durch mein Leiden, Sterben und Auferſtehen überwinde ich den Teufel, Tod, Fleiſch und Blut, Welt und alles, was drinnen iſt, und ſetze mich hinauf zur Rechten des Vaters, daß ich gewaltiglich regiere und mir alles unterthan mache, und könne ſagen zum Tode, Sünde, Teufel, Welt und allem, das da böſe iſt: Da liege mir zun Füſſen und ſey nimmer Tod, Sünde, Teufel und böſe Welt, wie du geweſen biſt.

13, 14. Und was ihr bitten werdet in meinem Namen, das will ich thun, auf daß der Vater geehret werde in dem Sohn. Was ihr bitten werdet in meinem Namen, das will ich thun.

Er zeiget mit dieſen und folgenden Worten, was da ſey[2]

---

[1] Keine andere, etc. "No other, says he, but this, 'For I go to my Father.' But what sense is there in that (how does that agree)? Is the man intoxicated, or is he dreaming? But that is what I have said, that we do not perform such works of ourselves. But that the church performs such great works in all the world, which he [while] on earth performed only among a small nation, comes from this (he wishes to say)," etc.

[2] Was da ſey, etc. "what is the proper office and work of Christians, and how necessary the same is in the church."

der Christen eigentlich Amt und Werck, und wie noth daſſel=
bige in der Christenheit sey, davon der Prophet Zacharias
12, 10. sagt, daß Christus soll ausgieſſen und geben den
Geiſt, der da heißt ein Geiſt der Gnaden und des Gebets.
Denn dieſe zwey Stücke soll er ausrichten und schaffen in
allen Christen : erſtlich, daß ihr Hertz verſichert und gewiß
sey, daß sie einem gnädigen Gott haben ; zum andern, daß
sie auch können andern helfen durch das Gebet.   Das erſte
Stück machet, daß sie mit Gott verſöhnet werden, und für
sich alles haben, was sie bedürfen.   Wenn sie das haben,
sollen sie darnach auch Götter werden[1] und der Welt Hei=
laube durch das Gebet, und also durch den Geiſt der Gna=
den selbſt Gottes Kinder werden, darnach als Gottes Kind=
er zwischen ihm und dem Nächſten handeln und andern die=
nen und helfen, daß sie auch dazu kommen mögen.

Denn wenn ein Christ anfähet, Christum zu kennen als
seinen Herrn und Heiland, durch welchen er iſt erlöſet aus
dem Tode und in seine Herrschaft[2] und Erbe gebracht, so
wird sein Hertz gar durchgöttert, daß er gerne wollte jeder=
mann auch dazu helfen.   Denn er hat keine höhere Freude,
denn an diesem Schatz, daß er Christum erkennet.   Darum
fähret er heraus, lehret und vermahnet die andern, rühmet
und bekennet daſſelbige vor jedermann, bittet und seufzet,
daß sie auch möchten zu solcher Gnade kommen.   Das iſt

---

[1] Götter werden, etc. " become gods and saviors of the world
through prayer, and thus by the spirit of grace become themselves
children of God, and then as children of God mediate between him
and their neighbor, and serve and aid others so that they may come
to the same state (dazu)."

[2] Und in seine Herrschaft, etc. "and is introduced into
his (the Christian's) dominion and inheritance, his heart is pervaded
with divinity, so that [like God] he would gladly help every one [to
come] to the same."   Durchgöttern, formed after the analogy
of vergöttern, admirably expresses the apostolic idea of our " being made partakers of the divine nature" by the infusion of the divine
Spirit as a pervading element of our character.

ein unruhiger Geist in der höheſten Rühe,[1] das iſt in Gottes
Gnade und Friede, daß er nicht kann ſtille noch müßig ſeyn,
ſondern immerdar darnach ringet und ſtrebet mit allen
Kräften, als der allein darum lebt, daß er Gottes Ehre
und Lob weiter unter die Lente bringe, daß andere ſolchen
Geiſt der Gnaden auch empfahen, und durch denſelbigen
auch ihm helfen beten.   Denn wo der Geiſt der Gnaden
iſt, der machet, daß wir auch können und dürfen, ja müſſen
anfahen, zu beten.

Aber ein recht Chriſtlich Gebet[2] ſoll und muß alſo gehen
aus dem Gnadengeiſt, der da ſaget: Ich habe gelebt, wie
ich kann, ſo bitte ich, du wolleſt ja nicht mein Leben und
Thun anſehen, ſondern deine Barmherßigkeit und Güte,
durch Chriſtum verheiſſen, und um derſelben willen mir ge=
ben, was ich bitte.   Alſo, daß man in dem Gebet in rechter
herßlicher Demuth von uns ſelbſt falle, und allein hange an
der Verheiſſung der Gnade, mit veſtem Vertrauen, daß er
uns wolle erhören, wie er zu beten befohlen und Erhörung
zugeſagt hat.

Darum ſeßet er auch ſelbſt deutlich dazu diß Wörtlein:
in meinem Namen, zu lehren, daß ohne den Glauben
kein recht Gebet geſchehen kann, und auſſer Chriſto niemand
vermag einen Buchſtaben zu beten, das vor Gott gelte und
angenehm ſey.

Alſo lerne hier, daß wir durch den Herrn Chriſtum allein

---

[1] In der höhesten (höchsten) Ruhe, etc. "in the greatest repose, i. e. in the grace and peace of God, so that," etc.

[2] Aber ein recht christlicher Gebet, etc. "But a truly
Christian prayer should and must thus proceed from the spirit of
grace, which says : ' I have lived, as l could ; but I pray that thou
wouldest not look upon my life and works, but upon thy mercy and
kindness, promised in Christ, and on account of these grant me what
I request." Soll und muss is an idiomatic phrase not unlike ist
und bleibt, and handeln und wandeln. In English, the
word *must* renders the word *should* unnecessary.

haben die zwey Stück: Gnade und Erhörung des Gebets, daß wir erſtlich Kinder Gottes werden, damit wir ihn können anruffen, und darnach auch für uns und andere erlangen, was wir bedürfen. Darum, wo ein Chriſt iſt, da iſt eigentlich der Heilige Geiſt, der da nichts anders thut, denn immerdar betet. Denn ob er gleich nicht immerdar den Mund reget, oder Worte machet, dennoch gehet und ſchlägt das Hertz, gleichwie die Pulsadern und das Hertz im Leibe, ohne Unterlaß mit ſolchem Seufzen: Ach lieber Vater, daß doch Dein Name geheiliget werde, Dein Reich komme, Dein Wille geſchehe bey uns und jedermann ꝛc. Und darnach[1] die Püffe oder Anfechtung und Noth härter drücken und treiben, darnach gehet ſolch Seufzen und Bitten deſto ſtärcker, auch münblich: daß man keinen Chriſten kann finden ohn beten, ſo wenig, als einen lebendigen Menſchen ohne den Puls, welcher ſtehet nimmer ſtill, reget und ſchläget immerdar für ſich, ob gleich der Menſch ſchläft oder anders thut, daß er ſein nicht gewahr wird.[2]

Auf daß der Vater geehret werde in dem Sohn.

Was heißt nun, der Vater werde geehret in dem Sohn? Nichts anders, denn daß der Vater alſo erkannt und für den gehalten werde, der da ſey ein gnädiger, barmhertziger Vater, der da nicht mit uns zürnet, noch zur Höllen verdammen will, ſondern die Sünde vergibt, und alle ſeine Gnade uns ſchencket, um ſeines Sohnes Chriſti willen, wie bisher genug geſagt iſt. Das iſt die rechte Ehre, damit Gott geehret wird. Denn daher erwächſet im Hertzen rechtes Vertrauen, das es zu ihm Zuflucht hat, und ihn kann tröſtlich

---

[1] **Und darnach, etc.** "And (according) as assaults (blows) or temptation and trial (distress) press and urge us the harder, so (accordingly) go forth such sighs," etc.

[2] **Dass er sein (seiner) nicht gewahr wird,** "so that he is not aware of it."

anruffen in allen Nöthen, item für seine Gnade und Wohl=
that dancket, seinen Namen und Wort vor jedermann beken=
net und kund machet, welches sind die rechten Gottesdienste,
so ihm gefallen und dadurch er gepreiset wird. Solche aber
können nicht geschehen, ohne allein, wie er sagt, in dem
Sohne, das ist, wo Christus also erkannt und gegläubt wird,
wie gesagt ist, daß wir durch ihn lernen, Gott sehen und
seine Gnade und väterlich Hertz erkennen, und wissen, was
wir in seinem Namen bitten von Gott, gewißlich gewähret
seyn und empfahen sollen.

**15. Liebet ihr mich, so haltet meine Worte.**

Denn ich will nicht ein Moses seyn, der euch treibe und
plage• mit Dräuen[1] und Schrecken, sondern gebe euch solche
Gebote, welche ihr wohl ohne Gebieten könnet und werdet
halten, so ihr mich anders lieb habt. Denn wo das nicht
ist, da ist doch vergebens, daß ich euch viel gebieten wollte;
denn es bleibet doch ungehalten. Darum sehet nur darauf;
Wollt ihr mein Gebot halten, daß ihr mich lieb habt, und
bedencket, was ich euch gethan habe, daß ihr mich billig sollt
lieben, als der ich mein Leib und Leben für euch setze und
mein Blut für euch vergieße; so thuts doch um meinetwillen,
und bleibt unter einander einig und freundlich, daß ihr zu=
gleich an mir haltet mit euerer Predigt, und einer den an=
dern durch die Liebe trage, und nicht Trennung und Rotten
anrichtet. Denn ich habe es auch redlich und wohl verdie=
net; es wird mir ja hertzlich sauer und kostet mich mein
Leib und Leben, daß ich euch erlöse. Ich werfe mich selbst
unter den Tod und in des Teufels Rachen, daß ich die
Sünde und Tod von euch nehme, die Hölle und des Teufels
Gewalt zerstöre, und schencke euch den Himmel und alles,
was ich habe, und will euch gerne zu gut halten, ob ihr un=
terweilen irret und fehlet, oder auch gröblich fallet, schwach

---

[1] **Dräuen.** See p. 95, Note 1.—**Anders,** *otherwise,* is often
better omitted in the translation.

und gebrechlich ſeyd, allein, daß ihr euch wieder an mich haltet und in die Liebe tretet, und unter einander einer dem andern auch vergebe, wie ich auch gegen euch thue, auf daß die Liebe unter euch nicht zutrennet werde.

**16. Und ich will den Vater bitten.**

Denn ich will nicht müßig ſitzen droben im Himmel, und euer vergeſſen, ſondern nichts anders thun, denn euer lieber Prieſter und Mittler ſeyn, den Vater für euch bitten und flehen, daß er euch den Heiligen Geiſt gebe, der euch in allen Nöthen tröſten, ſtärcken und erhalten ſoll, daß ihr in meiner Liebe bleibet, und alles fröhlich ertragen könnet, was euch um meinetwillen widerfähret.

**Und er ſoll euch einen andern Tröſter ge= ben, daß er bey euch bleibe ewiglich.**

Alſo fähet er nun an zu predigen von dem Heiligen Geiſt, ſo der Chriſtenheit ſollte gegeben werden, und dadurch[1] ſie ſollte erhalten werden bis an den Jüngſten Tag. und iſt hier ſonderlich zu mercken, wie der Herr Chriſtus ſo freund= lich und tröſtlich redet für alle arme, betrübte Hertzen und furchtſame, blöde Gewiſſen, und uns zeiget, wie wir den Hei= ligen Geiſt recht erkennen und ſeines Troſts empfinden ſollen.

Denn hier iſt beſchloſſen, daß er will den Vater bitten, und alſo bitten, daß er uns nicht ſoll ſchrecken, noch in die Hölle ſtoſſen, ſondern daß er ſoll einen andern Tröſter geben, und einen ſolchen Tröſter, der da ewiglich bey uns ſey, und nichts bey uns thue, denn ohn Unterlaß uns ſtärcke und tröſte. Nun iſt kein Zweifel, daß des Herrn Chriſti Gebet gewißlich erhöret iſt, und der Vater alles thut, was er ihn bittet ; dar= um muß es nicht Gottes Willen und Meynung ſeyn, was uns will ſchrecken und betrüben. Denn Chriſtus thut es ja nicht, wie er, beyde, mit Worten und Wercken allenthalben

---

[1] D a d u r c h in the sense of w o d u r c h, *through which.*

beweiſet; der Vater thut es auch nicht, als der mit Chriſto ein Hertz und Willen hat; der Heilige Geiſt auch nicht, denn er iſt[1] und ſoll heiſſen, wie ihn Chriſtus allhier nennet und mahlet, ein Tröſter. Nun verſtehet jedermann, was da heißt diß Wort: Troſt und Tröſter, daß man nicht kann dafür ſich ſcheuen oder fürchten, ſondern eben das iſt, das ein elend, betrübt Hertz am allerhöchſten begehret.

## 17. Den Geiſt der Wahrheit.

Nicht allein iſt der Heil. Geiſt ein Tröſter, der die Chriſten trotzig und muthig machet wider allerley Schrecken, ſondern iſt dazu auch ein Geiſt der Wahrheit, das iſt, ein wahrhafti= ger, gewiſſer Geiſt, der nicht treugt[2] noch fehlen läßt. Denn diß gehöret auch dazu, daß ſie keck und unerſchrocken werden. Denn es muß nicht ſeyn ein ſolcher tummer Sinn, Durſt[3] und Trotz, als da iſt der tollen Kriegsleute und Wagehälſe, die freudig dahin treten gegen die Schwerter, Spieſſe und Büchſen. Das iſt auch wol eine Freudigkeit, aber ein falſch= er Troſt und Trotz, denn er verläßt ſich entweder auf eigene Kraft, oder auf eitele Ehre und Ruhm. Darum iſt wol da ein Geiſt, aber doch nicht ein rechter wahrhaftiger Geiſt.

Welchen die Welt nicht kann empfahen; denn ſie ſiehet ihn nicht und kennet ihn nicht.

Das gehöret auch zur Tröſtung der Chriſtenheit. Denn wenn ſie ſich umſehen[4] in die weite Welt, weil ihr unzählig

---

[1] Denn er iſt, etc. "for he is, and deserves (ought) to be called, (as Christ here terms and represents him), a comforter."

[2] Treugt, obsolete for triegt or trägt, for which betragt is now used.

[3] Durſt, not thirst, but *daring*, from dürfen in the old sense of wagen.—Tummer for dummer.

[4] Denn wenn ſie ſich umſehen, etc. "For where they look about them in the wide world (because there are very many of

viel ſind, die unſere Lehre verachten, läſtern und verfolgen, und nicht ſchlechte, geringe Leute, ſondern allermeiſt die Hochverſtändigſten, Gelehrteſten, Gewaltigſten, und auch, die da wollen die Frömmſten und Heiligſten ſeyn, das ſtöſſet ein ſchwachgläubig Hertz vor den Kopf, daß es anfähet zu dencken: Sollten denn ſo groſſe Lente allzumal irren, und alles falſch und verdammt ſeyn, was ſie thun und ſagen, ſetzen und ſchlieſſen? Dawider ſtellet er hiemit das Urtheil dürr und klar, daß wir deß ſollen gewiß ſeyn, daß es nicht anders gehet noch gehen kann, und ſchleuſt, daß ſie es nicht können verſtehen, noch zu warten oder zu hoffen ſey, daß der groſſe Haufe, welche ſind die Größten, Edelſten, Beſten, und der rechte Kern der Welt, ſollten die Wahrheiten haben.

Alſo ſiehet Chriſtus in dieſer Predigt immer beyſeits auf

---

it (the world) who despise, reproach and oppose our teaching and [are] not simple, insignificant people, but the most intelligent, learned and powerful, and those, too, who would pass for the most pious and holy), that strikes down (strikes in the head) one who (a heart which) is weak in faith, so that he begins to think, ' Is it likely (s o l l t e n) that such great persons should all err, and everything that they do and say, decide and conclude upon, is false and damnable ? Against this he gives hereby the plain (dry) and clear decision, that we must be certain of this, that it is not, and cannot be otherwise, and concludes that they [men of the world] cannot understand, nor is it to be expected or hoped, that the great mass, who are the greatest, noblest and best [of mankind], and the very cream (kernel) of the world should possess the truth.''

" Thus Christ, in this discourse, glances at those who would frighten his little flock, and make them timid and fearful, so that they should fall into doubts and think [within themselves and soliloquize thus] ; Shouldst thou alone be wise, prudent and holy, and so many excellent persons be and know nothing ? What can I do alone, or with so few ; [how can I] endure persecution and suffer myself to be condemned and given over to Satan by so many distinguished and excellent people ?' ' Take courage, says he, you must be prepared (g e r ü s t, for g e r ü s t e t, *armed*) for that, and not let it tempt you, but he assured, that you have the spirit of truth, of which the others, who persecute you, are not worthy,' '' etc.

die, so sein kleines Häuflein wollen erschrecken, blöde und verzagt machen, daß sie sollen zweifeln und dencken: Solltest du allein weise, klug und heilig seyn, und so viel trefflicher Leute alle nichts seyn noch wissen? Was soll ich allein oder mit so wenigen machen und Verfolgung leiden, und mich lassen von so viel hohen, trefflichen Leuten verdammen und dem Teufel geben? Wolan, dazu (spricht er) mußt du gerüst seyn, und dich solches nicht lassen anfechten, sondern gewiß seyn, daß du habest den Geist der Wahrheit, welches die andern, so dich verfolgen, nicht werth seyn, ja ihn nicht können sehen noch kennen, wenn sie noch viel gelehrtere, weisere und höhere Leute wären, und daß dein Thun und Wesen soll gelten und recht seyn und bleiben vor Gott, und ihres dagegen verdammt seyn. Also deutet ers nun selbst, so er spricht:

Ihr aber kennet ihn; denn er bleibet bey euch und wird in euch seyn.

Woher kennen und haben sie den Heiligen Geist, daß er bey ihnen bleibet? Allein daher, wie gesaget ist, das sie an Christo bleiben hangen durch den Glauben, sein Wort lieb und werth haben. Darum, was sie thun, leiden und leben, das ist alles des Heiligen Geistes Thun und Werck, und heißt[1] recht und wohl gelebt, gethan und gelitten, und ist

---

[1] U n d  h e i s s t, etc. " and consists in (or is) right and well living, doing and suffering, and is purely a precious thing before God. One will at the same time (d a b e y) perceive, says he, if it is done (goes) in my name, and relates to me, that the name of Christ creates the difficulty (dispute) and that the game has respect to (arises respecting) him, as (thank God) we now see acts of violence (G r e i f e n) pass before our eyes. Therefore we have consolation, though we are poor, frail persons, and sinners besides. Although, in respect to our lives, we might, in comparison with them make our boast, and they have in reality as gross faults (things) attached to them, as they accuse us of, so that they might well come to a pause with us. But

eitel koſtlich Ding der Gott. Das wird man dabey erken=
nen, (ſpricht er,) ſo es in meinem Namen gehet, und um
mich zu thun iſt, das der Name Chriſti den Haber mache,
und das Spiel ſich über ihm erhebe, wie (Gott Lob!) wir
jetzt ſehen greiffen vor Augen gehen ; daher wir auch haben
den Troſt, ob wir wol arme gebrechliche Lente ſind, und
Sünder dazn. Wiewol wir des Lebens halben anch wol
gegen unſere Feinde rühmen können, und ſie ja ſo grobe
Stücke auf ihnen haben, als ſie uns Schuld geben, daß ſie
wol mögen mit uns gleich aufheben. Aber, weil es um des
Herrn Chriſti willen zu thun iſt, daß wir den predigen und
hoch heben, ſo wollen wir dabey bleiben und ſtehen wider
alle Welt, und ſie ſollen uns den Rnhm laſſen, anch ohne
ihren Danck, daß unſer Geiſt der Geiſt der Wahrheit ſey,
und wollens darauf mit ihnen ausfechten und unſere Köpffe
an ihre ſetzen.

Denn unſer Herr hat auch Stahl und Eiſen im Kopf und
Marck in Fäuſten und Beinen, daß ers kann ausſtehen, wie
er bereits an vielen gethan hat, die den Kopf an ihm abge=
lauffen und zubrochen haben und noch zubrechen ſollen, aber
den unſern unzubrochen laſſen.

---

because it concerns Christ our Lord that we proclaim and exalt him,
we will abide by our cause (stand by) and face all the world, and
they must yield to us the credit (no thanks to them) that our spirit
is the spirit of truth, and we will fight it out with them, and beat
our heads against theirs. For our Lord has a head of steel and iron,
and nerve (marrow) in his hands and legs, so that he can stand it
through, as he has already done towards many who have lost their
heads in running against him (run off their heads against him) and
broken them, but have left ours unbroken." On um zu thun,
which occurs twice in this passage, see p. 20, Note 3 med. and p. 35,
Note 5. On gelebt, gethan und gelitten, see p. 283, Note
6.—Greiffen, or greifen is an infinitive used substantively, *the
act of seizing.* The closing sentences are in the old German warlike
and feudal spirit, so forcibly expressed in the word Faust-recht,
*club-law.*

18. Jch will euch nicht Wäysen[1] laſſen, ich komme zu euch.

Es ſcheinet wol alſo,[2] beyde, nach der Welt Achten und nach unſerm eigenen Fühlen, als ſey diß Häuflein der Chriſten arme, verlaſſene Wäyſen, beyde, von Gott und Chriſto, und habe unſer vergeſſen, weil er das leidet, daß ſie geläſtert und geſchändet, verdammt, verfolget und ermordet werden, und jedermanns Fußtuch ſind, dazu von dem Teuſfel im Hertzen immerdar erſchreckt, betrübt und geplaget werden, daß ſie wohl und recht Wäyſen, mögen heiſſen vor allen andern Wäyſen und verlaſſenen Menſchen auf Erden, von welchen die Schrift ſagt, daß ſich Gott derſelben muß ſelbſt annehmen, als ſonſt von jedermann verlaſſen, Pſalm 27, 10., und ein Vater derſelben ſich nennen läßt, Pſalm 68, 6. Aber ich will euch nicht alſo verlaſſen, wie es ſich anſiehet und fühlet,[3] (ſpricht Chriſtus,) ſondern will euch den Tröſter geben, der euch ſolchen Muth mache, daß ihr deß gewiß ſeyd, daß ihr meine rechte Chriſten und die rechte Kirche ſeyd. Dazu will ich ſelbſt gewißlich bey euch ſeyn und bleiben mit meinem Schutz und Oberhand, ſo ich wol jetzt leiblich und ſichtbarlich von euch gehe, daß ihr müſſet allein ſeyn, des Teufels und der Welt Boßheit und Macht vorgeworfen. Aber ſo mächtig[4] ſoll die Welt nicht ſeyn,

---

[1] Wäysen, or Waisen.

[2] Es scheint wol also, etc. "It seems indeed both according to the view of the world and according to our own feelings, as if this handful of Christians were poor, forsaken orphans, [forsaken] both of God and of Christ, and [as if] he had forgotten us," etc.

[3] Wie es sich ansiehet und fühlet, is explained by the first clause in the paragraph. The verbs are both impersonal, "as it appears and is felt."

[4] Aber so mächtig, etc. "But so powerful [as you or others imagine] shall the world not be, nor so much mischief shall Satan make; so prudent shall all the learned and wise not be; but my baptism and preaching about me shall continue and be carried on," etc.

noch der Teufel so böse machen; so klug sollen alle Gelehr=
ten und Weisen nicht seyn: es soll dennoch meine Taufe
und Predigt von mir bleiben und getrieben werden, und
mein Heiliger Geist in euch regieren und wircken, ob es im=
merdar angefochten wird, und auch bey euch selbst schwäch=
lich scheinet.

19. Es ist noch um ein kleines, so wird mich
die Welt nicht mehr sehen, ihr aber sollt
mich sehen; denn ich lebe, und ihr sollt auch
leben.

Er fähret immer fort, der liebe Herr Christus, mit freund=
lichen, tröstlichen Worten, daß er sie bereite und geschickt
mache, sich in ihrem Trübsal, Trauren und Leiden sein zu
trösten,[1] und auf ihn einen Muth zu schöpffen wider alles,
das sie anfichtet.

Darum spricht er nun: Es soll bald angehen,[2] und ist
noch um eine Nacht zu thun, so wird mich die Welt nicht
mehr sehen. Als sollte er sagen: Es ist so böse,[3] gifftig
Ding um die Welt, daß, wer sein Trost und Heil auf die
Leute will setzen, der ist schon verloren. Denn ich habs ver=
sucht und erfahren. Ich bin kommen, ihr zu helfen, und
habe alles gethan, was ich an ihr thun sollte: so will sie
mich nicht leiden, und des Vaters Zeugniß und des Heiligen
Geistes Predigt und Werck weder annehmen, noch wissen,
sondern schlechts des Teufels seyn und bleiben.

Darum will ich auch ihr aus den Augen[4] gehen, daß sie

---

[1] Sein zu trösten, "to comfort themselves in him." See
p. 307, Note 2.

[2] Es soll bald angehen, etc. "This should soon begin,
and there is but one night first (and one night is still concerned)."

[3] Es ist so böse, etc. "The world is so malicious and
deadly." Literally, "It is so malicious and poisonous with the
world." See p. 247, Note 6.

[4] Ihr aus den Augen, *out of its sight,* "out of the eyes to
it, or of it."

mich nicht ſehen ſoll, und doch alſo machen, daß ſie mich muß auf Erden leiden und laſſen regieren. Denn ob ich wol mich creutzigen laſſe und dieſem Leben abſterbe, will ich doch dadurch in ein ander unſterblich Leben gehen und kommen, darinne ich ewig regieren werde; alsdenn ſoll erſt mein Reich recht angehen. Denn weil ich[1] alſo gehe ſterblich vor ihren Augen, ſo iſt kein Aufhören des Tobens und Wütens wider mich, wollen und können mich nicht lebendig ſehen noch leiden, bis ſie mich zum Tode bracht haben. Aber ich wills bald ein Ende machen, daß ſie an mir thun, was ſie wollen, und mich nicht mehr, ſehen, wie ſie begehren, und doch eben, damit das ausrichten, daß ſie mich ohne ihren Danck[2] in meine Herrlichkeit und Regiment bringen, welches ſie müſſen leiden, und ſoll es niemand wehren. Alſo iſt diß[3] zu hohem Trotz geredet der ſchändlichen, böſen Welt, ſo Chriſtum und ſein Wort verfolget, als der ihr nicht will die Ehre thun, daß ſie ihn mehr ſollte ſehen predigen oder Wunder thun; und weil ſie ihn nicht wollen bey ihnen leiden, will er ihnen auch weit genug aus den Augen kommen.

Alſo haben wir die tröſtliche Verheiſſung denen Chriſten gegeben, ſo da geſchreckt werden durch den Tod und allerley Unglück, daß ſie können trotzen wider den Teufel und die Welt, und ſagen: Wenn du mich tödteſt, ſo tödteſt du mich nicht, ſondern hilfeſt mir zum Leben; begräbſt du mich, ſo reiſſeſt du mich aus der Aſche und Staube gen Himmel. Und Summa: dein Zorn und Toben iſt eitel Gnade und Hülfe; denn du gibſt mir nur Urſache und den Anfang, daß

---

[1] Denn weil ich, etc. "For because I am (go, or go and come) in a mortal state before their eyes, there is no cessation," etc.

[2] Ohne ihren Danck. See p. 338, Note 1.

[3] Also ist diss, etc. "Thus this is said by way of defiance to the shameless, wicked world, which persecutes Christ and his word, as [of] one who will not do it the honor to allow it to see (that it should see) him longer preach and work miracles."

mich Christus zum Leben bringet; wie er hier spricht: Ich
Lebe, und ihr sollt leben.

Ja, (spricht Fleisch und Blut,) ich muß gleichwol den
Kopf herhalten?[1] Ja, das schadet dir nichts (spricht
Christus); sie haben mich auch gecreuziget, erwürget und
ins Grab gelegt; aber, wie sie mich im Grabe und Tod
gehalten haben, so sollen sie euch auch darinnen halten.
Denn es heißt und soll heissen: Wie ich lebe, so sollt ihr
auch leben; das soll mir weder Teufel noch Tod wehren.
Diese Worte muß ein Christ lernen fassen und seinen
Christum also kennen in seinen tröstlichen Verheissungen,
ob ihm der Tod[2] den Stich beut mit seinem Spies, und
der Teufel seinen Höllenrachen gegen ihm aufsperret, daß
er nicht dafür erschrecke, sondern könne dem Teufel wieder
den Trotz bieten durch den Glauben auf diese Worte:
Weißt du auch, wie du den Herrn Christum auch gefressen hast und doch hast müssen wiedergeben, ja er dich wieder gefressen hat; also sollst du mich auch ungefressen lassen, weil ich in ihm bleibe und um seinetwillen lebe und
leide. Ob man mich drüber[3] aus der Welt jaget und
unter die Erden scharret, das lasse ich geschehen; aber
darum will ich nicht im Tode bleiben, sondern mit meinem Herrn Christo leben, wie ich gläube und weiß, daß
er lebt.

Es ist aber und bleibt wol eine hohe Kunst, solches fassen und gläuben, die ihnen schwer wird und manchen har-

---

[1] Den Kopf herhalten, "lay the head on the block," or
yield to execution. "Must I not" is to be appended in English to
such affirmatives with the interrogation point.  See p. 235, Note 5.

[2] Ob ihm der Tod, etc. "though death offer him a thrust
with his dart, and Satan yawn at him with fiendish fury." Beut
is obsolete for bietet.

[3] Ob man mich drüber, etc. "If man will on this account (on account of my religion) hunt me from the world and lay
(scrape) me under the ground," etc.

ten Kampf koftet, und dennoch nimmer gung gelernet kann
werden um unfers Fleifches und Blutes willen, welches
nicht kann des Schreckens und Zagens vor dem Tode ohn
feyn.[1] Doch muß es[2] angefangen feyn, und der Troft ge=
faffet werden.　Denn wo wir den nicht hätten, fo könnte
niemand bey dem Evangelio ftehen und beharren, weil
uns der Teufel fo mördlich feind ift, und die Welt fo
greulich zufetzet, und allenthalben fo zugehet, daß kein
elender, verachter Ding ift auf Erden, denn ein Chrift.
Darum müffen wir dagegen einen höhern, ftarckern und
gewiffern Troft haben, denn alle ihr Trotz und Macht ift.

20. An demfelbigen Tage werdet ihr er=
kennen, daß ich im Vater bin, und ihr in mir,
und ich in euch.

Wenn es dazu kommt,[3] (will er fagen,) daß ihr mich wer=
det fehen, aus dem Grabe und Tode wieder auferftanden,
und hinauf zum Vater gen Himmel fahren, und ihr folches
von mir predigen werdet: fo werdet ihr durch den Heiligen
Geift und euere eigene Erfahrung inne werden und erken=
nen, daß ich im Vater bin, und auch ihr in mir und wieder=
um ich in euch, und alfo wir mit einander Ein Kuchen feyn

---

[1] O h n [ohne] s e y n, obsolete *to be without*, governs the genitive like e n t b e h r e n.

[2] D o c h  m u s s  e s, etc. " Still we must make a beginning and
acquire confidence.　For if we had not this, no one could stand by
the gospel and hold out ; because the devil is so mortally hostile to
us, and the world so cruelly assails us, and on every hand things go
in such a way that nothing on earth is more wretched and despised
than a Christian.　Therefore, we must against all this have a confidence, higher, and stronger and more sure than all the insolence (defiance) and power of the world."

[3] W e n n  e s  d a z u  k o m m t, etc.　" When it comes to this
that," is a circumlocution like, " when it comes to pass that."　The
sense is the same as " When ye shall see me," etc.—E i n  K u-
c h e n, *all one.*　See p. 324, Note 1.　E i t e l.　See p. 10, Note 4.

werden: also, daß es eitel Leben sey, dadurch ihr in mir le=
bet, gleichwie ich im Vater und der Vater iu mir lebet.
Denn ich lebe im Vater, und solches Lebens, daß ich in eige=
ner Person den Tod erwürgt,[1] daß ihr müßt sagen, das
allein Gott zugehöret.

Darnach[2] auch werdet ihr sagen, daß ich in euch bin.
Denn wie mich der Vater auferwecket, und ich den Tod ge=
fressen habe: also will ich in euch auch den Tod fressen, daß
ihr durch den Glauben an mich des Todes Herren seyn sollt,
und nicht fürchten die Welt, Teufel noch Hölle und alle
ihren Trotz, daß ihr müsset alsdann sagen: Solche Kraft
habe ich zuvor[3] in mir nicht gehabt; denn ich müßte sowol,
als die andern, unter des Teufels Gewalt, des Todes
Schrecken und Macht bleiben. Aber jetzt habe ich einen
andern Muth, den mir Christus gibt durch seinen Geist, da=
ran ich spüre,[4] daß er bey und in mir ist, daß ich kann alle
der Welt, des Todes und Teufels Schrecken und Dräuen
verachten, und dagegen fröhlich und freudig trotzen auf mei=
nen Herrn, der droben bey dem Vater lebt und regieret.

21. Wer meine Gebote hat und hält sie,
der ists, der mich liebet. Wer mich aber lie=
bet, der wird von meinem Vater geliebet
werden, und ich werde ihn lieben, und mich
ihm offenbaren.

Er hat sie getröstet mit dem hohen Trost, daß sie sollen in
ihm und er in ihnen seyn, welches ist das Hauptstück der
Christlichen Lehre, daraus wir solchen Verstand haben,[5] daß

---

[1] Erwürgt [habe]. "That 1 have in my own person destroyed death so that," etc.

[2] Darnach, in a similar manner, or accordingly.

[3] Zuvor, before receiving the Holy Ghost.

[4] Daran ich spüre, "by which [courage] 1 perceive (trace)
that," etc. For the force of an in daran, see p. 80, Note 3.

[5] Daraus wir solchen Verstand haben, "from which
we learn," from which we have this understanding, viz.

wir nicht in, noch durch uns selbst gerecht und selig werden, sondern in Christo und durch Christum, der für uns alles ausgerichtet, das Gesetz erfüllet, Sünde, Tod und Teufel überwunden hat. Das werdet ihr haben (spricht er,) an mir, und darnach will ich auch in euch gepreiset werden, und werdets müssen bekennen und predigen in der Welt.

Es liegt aber alles daran, ob du solches[1] bey dir fühlest und findest, (wie er droben, V. 15, auch gesagt hat,) daß du diesen Mann lieb habest. Denn wo ihr solches wahrhaftig gläubet, so wird auch die Liebe da seyn, und werdet fühlen euer Hertz also gesinnet: So viel hat Christus, mein lieber Herr, für mich gethan, den Vater mir versöhnet, sein Blut für mich vergossen, mit meinem Tode gekämpft und ihn überwunden, und alles, was er hat, mir geschenckt; sollte ich denn ihn nicht wiederum lieben, dancken und loben, dienen und ehren mit Leib und Gut? Wollte ich doch ehe wünschen, daß ich kein Mensch geboren wäre.

Darum (sagt er) gehöret zum rechtschaffenen Christen, daß er mich von Hertzen lieb habe; sonst wird ers[2] wahrlich nicht thun. Das Hertz muß allein an ihm hangen, und nichts anders lieben noch fürchten.

Ist aber die Liebe da, so kann sie nicht ruhen noch feyren;[3]

---

[1] S o l c h e s, viz. an assurance that Christ has done all this for you. "Everything depends on this, whether, as he said above v. 15, you feel and experience this (i. e. have this confidence and trust) within you, so that this man becomes (is) dear to you."

[2] S o n s t  w i r d  e r, etc. "Otherwise he will certainly not do it," viz. obey and trust.

[3] F e y r e n. The word written fully would be f e y e r e n. The *e* in one of the last two syllables is always dropped. In the old language either of them was dropped; in modern German, the latter is always dropped and the former always retained. This rule applies to all verbs that have e r or e l before the termination e n, or to express it still more clearly, those verbs which have the derivative endings e r n and e l n. F c i e r n or f e y e r n, means, as a regular verb, to have a holy-day, to cease from toil.

sie fähret heraus, prediget und lehret jedermann, wollte gerne den Christum jedermann[1] ins Hertz pflantzen, und alle zu ihm bringen, wagt und läßt drüber,[2] was sie soll und kann. Solche Liebe wollte er gerne in sie treiben durch solche hertzliche Worte; darum spricht er: Wohlan, ich lasse euch diese Letzte,[3] daß ihr habt in mir alles, was ihr begehret, Vergebung der Sünde, den Himmel, des Vaters Huld und Gnade; allein sehet zu, daß ihr solches recht gläubet, so werdet ihr mich wohl lieb haben und halten alles, was ich euch gesagt habe.

Was sollen aber die wiederum haben, so solche Liebe zu ihm haben, oder, was geniessen sie derselben?[4] Das will ich ihnen (spricht er) wiederum thun: wer also heraus fähret, und sich erzeigt als einen rechten Christen, der wird von meinem Vater geliebet werden, und ich will ihn lieben und mich ihm offenbaren.

Wenn ein Christ angefangen hat, und nun in Christo ist, gläubet und lebt in ihm, und nun ihn lieb hat, fähet an zu predigen, bekennen und thun, was ein Christ um seines Herrn willen thun soll: so greiffet ihn der Teufel an und überfället ihn mit solchem Wolckenbruch, innwendig durch Angst und Furcht, auswendig durch allerley Gefahr und Unglück, daß er keinen Trost fühlet, und läßt sich ansehen und fühlen,[5] als sey Gott droben im Himmel, nicht bey uns, und habe unser vergessen. Denn er verbirget sich so gar,

---

[1] Jedermann, is in the dative, "every man's heart."

[2] Wagt und lässt drüber, etc. "It ventures and suffers (permits) for that purpose (for it) whatever it ought, or can."

[3] Letzte. See p. 279, Note 5.

[4] Was geniessen sie derselben, etc. "What benefit do they derive from it (what do they enjoy of it)? I will reciprocate the act (love them in turn). He who goes forth and shows himself a true Christian, will be loved of my Father," etc.

[5] Und lässt sich ansehen und fühlen, "and he looks on and feels as if," etc. Literally, "allows himself to look at it and feel."

als sey es aus mit uns[1] und wir keine Hülfe mehr von ihm haben: daß, wo er sich nicht erzeigte, und ließe seine Liebe spüren, so würden wir versincken und verzweifeln.

Aber laßt euch das nicht das Hertz nehmen.[2]  Denn es ist nicht also, wie ihr fühlet und euch düncket; denn ich habe noch andere und mehr Hülfe, die erste, andere und dritte dazu,[3] und will euch den Rücken halten,[4] daß ihr in der Noth, darinnen ihr dencket, ihr habt mich verloren, nicht sollt versincken, sondern wills machen, daß die Anfechtung, Schrecken und Noth dennoch euch in mir soll[5] lassen bleiben und wiederum mich in euch, ob ihrs wol nicht so eben fühlet zu der Stunde, wenn der Teufel wütet.  Er soll euch aber doch nicht fressen, sondern soll nur eine Versuchung seyn, ob[6] ihr recht gläubet und liebet.  Ja, ich will kommen, und mich so offenbaren, daß ihr in der Anfechtung spüret die hertzliche Liebe, so beyde, mein Vater und ich, zu euch haben.

22.  Spricht zu ihm Judas, nicht der Ischarioth: Herr, was ists denn, daß du uns willst dich offenbaren, und nicht der Welt?

Das ist fast die Frage, als sollte er sagen: Sollen denn wirs allein seyn, gelehrt, klug, heilig und selig?  Was will

---

[1] Als sey es aus mit uns, "as if it were all over with us." See p. 286, Note 1.

[2] Euch das Hertz nehmen.  See p. 285, Note 1.

[3] Die erste, andere und dritte dazu, "a first, second and third besides," i. e. I have more than one expedient; I can resort to another, a second and a third.

[4] Euch den Rücken halten, "support, protect or aid you."  This comes from one's putting his shoulders under another and holding him up.

[5] Dennoch euch in mir soll, etc. "shall still leave you remaining (to remain) in me, and me, in turn, in you," or shall still let you remain, etc.

[6] Versuchung seyn, ob, "a temptation or trial, [to show] whether, etc.

die Welt dazu sagen? Sollen denn so viel hochgelehrter, trefflicher, heiliger Leute, Priester, Pharisäer, und der beste Kern des gantzen Volcks, welches doch Gottes Volck heißt, und so viel trefflicher[1] Ansehen haben, denn wir arme Bettler, allzumal nichts und verdammt seyn? Was sind wir gegen ihnen, denn als lauter nichts? Solltest du nicht den hohen Leuten dich offenbaren, bey denen das Regiment, Gewalt, Ehre, und dazu grosse Heiligkeit und Gottesdienst ist, und da es[2] zu hoffen wäre, daß es von statten gehen werde? Was sollten wir elenden Leute ausrichten? Wer will uns gläuben oder zufallen?[3] Wir werden der Sache viel zu schwach seyn.

Das ist eben die Frage, daran sich noch alle Welt stößt, Gelehrt, Ungelehrt, Heilige und Sünder. Was ist es denn (spricht die Welt) um[4] diese neue Predigt? Ich sehe da nichts sonderliches; sinds doch eitel verachtete Leute, verlauffene Buben und Bettelvolck, so an dieser Lehre hangen. Wenn siehest du, daß grosse Herren, Könige, Fürsten, Bischöffe, etwas davon halten? Das ist das größte Argument und die stärckste Ursach, warum unser Evangelium nicht soll recht seyn: Wenn es wahr wäre, so hätte es Gott wol andern Leuten offenbaret. Warum sollens die hohen Häupter nicht wissen, die da können und sollen die

---

[1] **Trefflicher** is here in the comparative degree undeclined, whereas two or three lines above, it is in the positive and genitive plural. "Shall then so many (of) very learned, excellent and holy persons, priests and Pharisees, and the very flower of the whole people, which is even called God's people, and [who] have so much better standing than we poor beggars, all at once become (be) nothing and be condemned? What are we compared with them but mere nothing?"

[2] **Und da es**, etc. "and where it was to be expected that it would all go on well?"

[3] **Zufallen**, which generally means *to fall to one*, here means, *to take one's part, to join one's party.*

[4] **Was ist es—um.** See p. 247, Note 6.

Welt regieren und reformiren? Die solltens thun, so möchte es von statten gehen.

**23, 24.** Jesus antwortete und sprach zu ihm: Wer mich liebet, der wird mein Wort halten, und mein Vater wird ihn lieben, und wir werden zu ihm kommen und Wohnung bey ihm machen. Wer aber mich nicht liebet, der hält meine Worte nicht.

Lieber Judas (will er sagen), diese Sache ist also gethan,[1] daß man nicht muß fragen; ob König, Kayser, Caiphas oder Herodes, gelehrt und ungelehrt sey, sondern ob ichs sey? Das ist die Antwort auf die Frage. In dieser Predigt und Regiment, das ich will anfahen soll mir gleich gelten,[2] was in der Welt ist, einer wie der andere, ich will keinen aussondern, noch ausmahlen. In der Welt Regiment müssen wol solche Unterschiede seyn der Personen und Stände: ein Knecht kann nicht Herr seyn, der Herr muß nicht Knecht, der Schüler nicht Meister seyn, und also fort; aber damit habe ich nichts zu thun, und gehet mich nichts an. Ich aber will ein solch Regiment anrichten, darinne wir alle sollen gleich gelten. Ein König, der heut geboren und ein Herr ist über viel Land und Leute, der soll eben sowol kriechen in meine Taufe und sich mir ergeben, als ein armer Bettler, und wiederum soll dieser eben sowol das Evangelium hören predigen, oder die Sacramente empfahen und selig werden, als jener. Also will er die Leute allzumal

---

[1] Also gethan, *so constituted*, or so managed.—Sondern ob ichs sey, "but whether it is I [that am concerned in it].

[2] Soll mir gleich gelten, etc. "it will be to me indifferent what there is in the world [as opposed to my kingdom] one person as well as another [one will pass for no more than the other]; I will separate and sift out more," i. e. my religion is destined for all indiscriminately, and favors no particular classes, as the world does.

gleich und Einen Kuchen draus machen,[1] daß es ein ander Wesen sey, denn die Welt, führet, welche muß das Ihre auch haben und behalten, und Christus läßt auch gehen und bleiben; aber er ist nicht darum da, daß er solch Weltreich, sondern ein Himmelreich anrichte.

Darum antwortet er also dem Apostel Judä: Es wird nicht daran liegen,[2] was die Welt ist, sondern darauf stehets, daß ich dir gesagt habe, ich wolle mich dir offenbaren und denen, so mich lieb, haben; nicht, der eine dreyfache gülbene Crone oder scharlacken Rock trägt, nicht, wer edel, mächtig, starck, reich, gelehrt, weise, klug und heilig heißt, sondern, wer mich lieb hat, Gott gebe,[3] er heiße König, Fürst, Pabst, Bischoff, Priester, Doctor, Laye, Herr oder Knecht, klein oder groß; in meinem Reich soll aller solcher Unterschied aufhören.

### Und mein Vater wird ihn lieben.

Das ists, das wir nun oft gehöret haben, daß Christus mit hohem Fleis immer uns hinauf zeucht zum Vater, wider die leidigen Gedancken,[4] so Christum vom Vater scheiden und dem Hertzen einbilden: Ob ich wol an Christum gläube, wer weiß aber, ob mir der Vater gnädig ist? Darum will er uns immer in des Vaters Hertz führen, daß wir nichts sorgen noch fürchten sollen, so wir allein ihn lieb haben, und weit aus dem Hertzen werfen und reissen allen Zorn und Schrecken.

---

[1] Gleich und Einen Kuchen draus machen, "make them alike, and make one batch out of them." See p. 324, Note 1.

[2] Es wird nicht daran liegen, etc. "It will not depend on what the world is, but it rests upon this [principle, viz.] that I have said to you (or, as I have said to you)," etc.

[3] Gott gebe, *God grant,* i. e. "whether, in the providence of God, it be king," etc.

[4] Wider die leidigen Gedancken, etc. "against the wicked thoughts which separate Christ from the Father, and frame in the heart [the question] though I believe," etc.

Und hiebey (ſpricht er weiter) ſoll es nicht bleiben,[1] daß ich und der Vater ihn lieb haben, der da mich liebet, ſon= dern, wir wollen zu ihm kommen und Wohn= ung bey ihm machen ꝛc.: daß er nicht allein ſoll ſi= cher ſeyn vor dem zukünftigen Zorn, Teufel, Tod, Hölle und allem Unglück, ſondern ſoll auch hier auf Erden uns bey ihm wohnend haben, und wollen[2] täglich ſeine Gäſte, ja Haus= und Tiſchgenoſſen ſeyn.

**24. Wer mich aber nicht liebet, der hält meine Worte nicht.**

Hier haſt du kurtz die Welt abgemahlet und beſchrieben, was ihrer Art iſt, und was von ihr zu halten iſt, nemlich, -daß ſie Chriſtum nicht kann noch will lieb haben, noch ſeine Worte halten.

**24. Und das Wort, das ihr höret, iſt nicht mein, ſondern des Vaters, der mich geſandt hat.**

Wie kann doch der Mann alſo reden? Harte zuvor[3] hat er geſagt: Wer mein Wort hat und hält ꝛc., und jetzt ſpricht er: Meine Worte ſind nicht mein, ſondern meines Vaters. Wie ſind es denn zugleich ſeine und nicht ſeine Worte? Es iſt aber immer, daß[4] er ſich fleißiget, der

---

[1] Hiebey soll es nicht bleiben, " it shall not stop with this."

[2] Und [wir] wollen.

[3] Harte zuvor, *just before.* Compare the phrase, *hard by.*

[4] Es ist aber immer dass, " It is always the case that he takes pains (or, he always takes pains) to speak in such a manner (in the manner) that he may draw us to himself, and when he has drawn us to himself, then he flies (passes instantly) to the Father, so that when we hear him speak, we learn immediately to say [to our- selves], ' The *Father* says that to me *through* Christ ;' and [learn hence] to derive comfort, joy and love to him, so that [he can say] there is no other word of God to me or respecting me in heaven,

Weiſe zu reden, daß er uns erſtlich zu ſich bringe, und ſo wir zu ihm gebracht ſind, darnach flugs zum Vater zendt, daß, wenn wir ihn hören reden, alsbald lernen ſagen: Das redet der Vater durch dieſen Chriſtum zu mir! und den Troſt, Freude und Liebe gegen ihm ſchöpfen, daß kein auder Wort Gottes zu mir oder von mir im Himmel iſt, und auch die Engel kein anders hören, denn das Chriſtus mit mir redet.

Darum iſts gleich ſo viel,[1] daß er ſagt: Wer mein Wort hält, und: Die Worte, ſo ich rede, ſind nicht mein, ſondern des Vaters. Denn ſie gehen nicht von mir, und ich bin nicht der Anfang des Worts; ſondern der Vater hat mirs befohlen und mich geheiſſen, daß niemand ſoll zweifeln oder ſagen: Ja, Chriſtus prediget wol ſüſſe und fein, wer weiß aber, was der Vater droben ſagt? Er tröſtet mich wol, daß er mich lieb habe, und ſich mir offenbaren und bey mir wohnen will ꝛc. Ja, wenn es gewiß wäre? Wenn ichs vom Vater ſelbſt hörte, vom Himmel herab. Nein (ſpricht er), deß darfſt du nicht,[2] und würdeſt vergeblich darnach gaffen, ſondern ſollſt deß gewiß ſeyn, daß der Vater im Himmel kein ander Wort redet, denn das du aus meinem Munde höreſt, alſo, daß es wahrhaftig nicht mein, ſondern des Vaters Wort iſt und heiſſet.

25, 26. Solches habe ich zu euch geredt, weil ich bey euch geweſen bin. Aber der Tröſter, der Heilige Geiſt, welchen mein Vater ſenden wird in meinem Namen, derſelbige wirds euch alles lehren, und euch erinnern alles deß, das ich euch geſagt habe.

---

even the angels hear no other than what (d a s for w a s) Christ speaks to (with) me."

[1] D a r u m ists gleich so viel, etc. " So much is implied when he says, 'He who keeps my word,' and, 'The words,'" etc

[2] D e s s darfst du nicht. "That you do not need." D e s s gewiss, "sure of this."

Er eilet zum Beschluß, daß er will aufstehen und davon gehen zu seinem Leiden; denn diß hat er alles noch über Tisch geredt. Ich habe euch viel Gutes gesagt, spricht er, euch zu trösten und zu stärcken, daß ihr sollet unverzagt seyn und euch nicht betrüben meines Abscheidens. Nun das sind solche Rede und Wort, die ihr wol mit den Ohren höret, weil ich gegenwärtig bin; aber sie sind euch noch zu hoch, und werdets doch nicht verstehen, wenn ihr mich sehet von euch genommen, da wirds bald aus und vergessen seyn, was ich jetzt euch sage und tröste. Hernach aber, wenn da kommen wird der Tröster, den ich euch verheissen habe, der solls euch fein lehren, daß ihrs wohl verstehet und euch deß alles erinnern könnet, was ich euch gesagt habe. Sonst würde ichs umsonst geredt haben, und ihr alles vergessen, als denen es jetzt nicht zu Hertzen gehet, und nicht können begreiffen. Denn ihr seyd noch zu schwach von Fleisch und Blut, fasset nichts mehr davon, denn daß ihrs mit Ohren höret; darum muß der Heilige Geist kommen, der es euch ins Hertz drücke und weise durch Erfahrung, daß ihr verstehet, was ich gemeynet, und den Trost empfahet und fühlet, so ich euch gegeben habe.

27. Den Frieden lasse ich euch, meinen Frieden gebe ich euch; nicht gebe ich euch, wie die Welt gibt.

Das ist nun ein sehr tröstlich und lieblich Letzewort, daß er ihnen läßt nicht Städte und Schlösser, noch Silber und Gold, sondern den Frieden, als den höchsten Schatz im Himmel und Erden, daß sie kein Schrecken noch Trauren sollen von ihm haben, sondern rechten schönen, gewünschten Friede im Hertzen. Denn so viel, als an mir ist, (spricht er,) sollt ihr nichts anders haben, denn eitel Friede und Freude. Denn also habe ich euch geprediget, und bin mit euch also umgegangen, daß ihr gesehen und erkannt habt, daß ich euch

von Hertzen lieb habe und alles Gutes thue, und mein Va=
ter euch mit allen Gnaden meynet. Das ist das beste, so
ich euch lassen und geben kann. Denn das ist der höchste
Friede, wenn das Hertz zufrieden ist, wie man sagt: Her=
tzensfreude ist über alle Freude, und wiederum: Hertzeleid
ist über alles Leid.

Es ist nichts mit der Kinder= und Narrenfreude von
schönen Kleidern, Geldzählen, Wohlust, und Büberey; denn
dieselbige Freude währet einen Augenblick, und bleibet doch
das Hertz ungewiß und in Unfrieden oder Sorgen. Denn
es kann nicht sagen, daß es einen gnädigen Gott habe, hat
immer ein böses Gewissen, oder hat eine falsche Hoffnung,
die doch zweifelt: daß es doch immer bleibet in Unfriede
und Unruhe, vom Teufel getrieben, ob sie es gleich jetzt nicht
fühlen in ihrer tollen Weltfreude, so findet sichs doch, wenn
das Stündlein kömmt, daß der Unfriede angehet. Darum
habt ihr ja nichts mehr zu klagen, ich lasse euch den treff=
lichen, hohen Schatz, daß ihr könnt haben ein gut, fein,
friedlich Hertz gegen Gott und mir; denn ich lasse euch die
Liebe und Freundschaft meines Vaters und meine,[1] wie ihr
nichts anders an mir gesehen und gehöret habt, denn lieb=
liche, freundliche Worte und Wercke, und dieselbige nicht
mein, sondern des Vaters sind; darum habt ihr alles, was
ihr von mir begehren möget, ob ich gleich von euch gehe, und
ihr mich nicht mehr sehet.

28. Euer Hertz erschrecke nicht und fürch=
te sich nicht. Ihr habt gehöret, daß ich euch
gesagt habe: Ich gehe hin und komme wie=
der zu euch.

Da beschleußt er eben, wie er erstlich diese Predigt ange=
fangen hat, und will sagen: Weil ich nun von euch scheiden

---

[1] Meine, etc. "my (as you have seen in me and heard no other
than) affectionate and friendly words and works." This is harsh,
and hardly bears a literal translation.

muß, und nicht kann anders seyn, denn daß ihr um meinet=
willen müſſet in der Welt Unfrieden haben, daß euch der
Teufel mit ſeinem Anhang haſſet, verfolget und plagt: ſo
rüſtet euch dazu, daß ihr darum nicht erſchrecket noch ver=
zagt, ſondern getroſt und gutes Muths ſeyd, wie ich euch
anfänglich und bisher vermahnet habe durch mancherley
tröſtliche und herrliche Verheißung, und ſo viel Stücke er=
zehlet, die euch billig ſollen fröhlich und unverzagt machen,
daß ihr des geringen Mangels (daß ich leiblich von euch
gehe, item, daß ihr müſſet in der Welt äußerlich Leiden ha=
ben,) wohl und überreichlich ergötzet werdet. Laßt euch nur
das nicht erſchrecken, ob ihr ſehen werdet mich ſo ſchändlich
und jämmerlich gecreutziget, und ihr verſtreuet und in gro=
-ßem Elend und Jammer ſeyn werdet vor der Welt und eur=
em Fühlen nach; es ſoll nicht ſo böſe ſeyn, als ſichs läßt
anſehen. Denn ſolcher äußerlicher Jammer und Betrüb=
niß, Verfolgung und Plagen, ſoll nicht ewig währen, noch
ſtets bleiben; denn ich will wieder zu euch kommen und euch
erfreuen, beyde, leiblich und geiſtlich.

28, 29. Hättet ihr mich lieb, ſo würdet ihr
euch freuen, daß ich geſagt habe, ich gehe
zum Vater; denn der Vater iſt größer, denn
ich. Und nun habe ichs euch geſagt, ehe denn
es geſchieht, auf daß, wenn es nun geſchehen
wird, daß ihr gläubet.

Das iſt auch ein tröſtlicher Zuſatz. Was wollt ihr euch
bekümmern meines Weggehens? Ihr ſollt euch vielmehr
freuen. Denn wo gehe ich hin? Nicht in die Hölle, ſon=
dern zum Vater, in das herrliche, ewige Reich, und thue es
euch zu gute, daß ich auch euch zur Herlichkeit bringe. Dar=
um, wo ich nicht weggehen wollte, ſo ſollt ihr mich dazu hal=
ten und treiben, und euch dazu freuen und guter Dinge ſeyn,
daß ichs nur bald thäte.

Es ist aber eben also geredt, als unter denen, die ungerne von einander scheiden, als, Vater, Mutter und Kind, Mann und Weib 2c. Als da einer zum andern sagte, den er um des Evangelii willen verlassen müßte: Lieber Sohn oder Vater, Mann oder Weib, ich hätte dich wol gerne bey mir hier; aber du bist getauft und beruffen zum Evangelio. Wolan, kann es nicht anders seyn, so fahre hin in Gottes Namen; können wir uns hier nicht mehr sehen, so sehen wir uns in jenem Leben. Aber, wer kann solches thun? Die könnens wol, die ihre Kinder oder Freunde hassen, aber nicht die, so sich untereinander lieben.

Und zwar bekennet er hier selbst, daß er nicht gerne von ihnen scheidet, und sie auch nicht gerne von ihm, und müssen sich doch untereinander lassen. Darum redet er, gleich wie ein Vater zu seinen Kindern: Ich lasse euch wol nicht gerne; aber weil es seyn muß, so gebet euch zufrieden, und tröstet euch deß, daß ihr wisset, wo ich hinfahre. Denn ich komme nicht in Tod, noch zur Hölle, sondern in meines Vaters Schoos und Reich, daß ich euch auch dahin bringe, da ihr sollt wohl seyn. Darum sollet ihr euch ja freuen meines Gehens. Denn es ist nicht ein solch Scheiden, daß ich ewig von euch bleiben sollte, sondern, beyde, euer und mein Bestes, wie er hernach im 16. Capitel, 7. auch sagt: Es ist euch gut, daß ich von euch gehe. Denn es ist euch doch eine gewisse, ewige Freude, Herrlichkeit und mächtig Reich bestellet, dazu ihr sonst nicht kommen könntet.

Das ists, daß er spricht: Ich gehe zum Vater. Denn, zum Vater gehen, heißt nichts anders, denn aus diesem sterblichen Leben, (darinne ich habe dem Vater und euch gedienet, geniedriget unter allen Menschen,) das ist, aus dem Jammerthal und Gefängniß gegangen, in das herrliche, himmlische Schloß und ewige, göttliche Wohnung, da ich regieren werde zur Rechten des Vaters, und ein Herr seyn über alles, was im Himmel und auf Erden ist, welches ich

nicht kann thun in diesem Diensthause und knechtlichen We=
sen; ich muß zuvor meinen Dienst ausrichten, und mein
Leben daran setzen. Darum ist nicht besser, denn je ehe je
besser davon gegangen, daß ich gecreutziget werde, und dar=
nach verkläret, damit der Heilige Geist gesandt, und kund
werde, daß ich mich zur Rechten des Vaters gesetzt und mein
Reich eingenommen habe. Das sollte euer Trost und
Freude seyn, und sollets, beyde, mir und euch gerne gönnen,
wenn ihrs verstündet und mich vollkömmlich lieb hättet, wie
ihr hernach lernen werdet. Denn ich euch darum jetzt sol=
ches zuvor sage, daß ihrs hernach also erfahret und selbst
innen werdet, daß es die Wahrheit ist, und ichs treulich und
hertzlich mit euch gemeynet habe.

Deß setzt er nun Ursache, und spricht: Denn der Va=
ter ist grösser, denn ich. Als wollte er sagen: Das
soll auch ein grosser Trost seyn, daß ich komme in das grosse
Reich meines Vaters, da ich werde regieren, gleich dem Va=
ter, in ewiger Herrschaft über alle Creaturen rc.

Von seiner Verklärung redet er, das ist von dem Reiche,
dahin·er gehet, aus diesem Diensthause, daß er seine göttlich
allmächtige Gewalt und Herrschaft, welche er hat mit dem
Vater von Ewigkeit, offenbarlich einnehme, welches er jetzt
nicht kann thun nach und in seinem knechtlichen Amte, weil
er gesandt war in den Dienst und Demuth, darinne er sich
aller seiner göttlichen Herrlichkeit geäussert, (wie St. Paul=
us, Philipp. 2. 7, sagt,) und eines Knechtes Gestalt an sich
genommen: daß er demselben nach nicht allein kleiner ist,
denn der Vater, sondern auch geniedriget unter allen Men=
schen. Darum wollte sichs nicht reimen, daß er sich seiner
Herrlichkeit annehme, ehe und zuvor er solch knechtlich Amt
ausgerichtet hatte. Also ists von seinem gegenwärtigen
Amte, so er jetzt auf Erden führete, recht geredet: Der
Vater ist grösser, denn ich, weil ich jetzt ein Knecht bin;
aber, wenn ich wieder dorthin komme, zu meinem Vater, da

werde ich grösser werden, nemlich so groß, als der Vater ist,
das ist, ich werde in gleicher Gewalt und Majestät mit ihm
herrschen.

Solches habe ich euch gesagt, (spricht er,)
ehe, denn es geschieht, auf daß, wenn es
nun geschehen wird, daß ihr gläubet. Da
meynet er nicht allein diß letzte Stück, sondern, was er durch
das gantz Capitel geredet hat, als, daß er will ihnen die
Wohnung bereiten, item, daß der Tröster soll zu ihnen kommen, und Er samt dem Vater wieder zu ihnen kommen will.
Das sage ich euch wol jetzund;[1] aber ihr verstehets jetzt
nicht. Doch sage ichs euch darum, daß, wenn es nun so
geschieht, daß ihr alsdenn zurücke dencket:[2] Siehe, solches
hat er uns alles zuvorgesagt, da er von uns scheiden wollte; da sind wir wie die Stöcke gesessen, betrübt und er-
schrocken, und haben nichts davon verstanden. Nun aber sehen und greiffen wir, was er gemeynet hat ꝛc. Also werdet ihr denn gläuben, (spricht er,) ob ihr wol mich nicht
mehr sehet, samt der gantzen Christenheit bis an den Jüngsten Tag.

30, 31. Ich werde fort mehr nicht viel mit
euch reden; denn es kommt der Fürst dieser
Welt, und hat nichts an mir. Aber, auf
daß die Welt erkenne, daß ich den Vater liebe, und also thue, wie mir der Vater geboten hat: stehet auf, und laßt uns von hin-
nen gehen.

Die Zeit ist hier, daß ich davon muß,[3] und diß ist die letzte
Predigt, die ich thue. Denn der Teufel kommt, und zeucht
daher mit Juda und seinem Haufen, und will an mich und

---

[1] Jetzund obsolete for jetzt.

[2] Zurücke dencket, "call to mind [and say]."

[3] Davon muss, "must [go] away."

das Seine[1] ausrichten. Ich muß ihm herhalten, und ist
böse und zornig, er meynet, mich zu fressen; aber es soll
ihm so gerathen, daß es ihm soll den Bauch zureissen.
Denn er hat kein Recht noch Schuld an mir, ich habe es
nicht verdienet, und doch aus bösem, gifftigem Haß mich angreiffet und würget; er soll es bezahlen. Dräuet[2] also dem
Teufel heimlich mit scheelen Augen, sich selbst zu stärcken
wider seinen bittern Zorn, und die Jünger zu trösten (wiewol sie es noch nicht verstehen). Als sollte er sagen:
Wolan komm her, und versuche, was du kanst, friß und
würge, wie du willst. Aber du sollst an dem Bißlein[3] zu
käuen und zu schlingen haben, daß du davon erwürgen
mußt. Ich will dir wieder aus dem Bauche reissen, daß du
mußt mich und viel mehr, die du gefressen hast, wieder lassen. Und daß ich solches leide, thue ich nicht darum, als
wäre ich dem Teufel nicht starck genug, den ich oft ausge-
worfen und vertrieben habe, sondern darum, daß es soll
kund werden in der Welt, daß ich meinem Vater gehorsam
bin, und daß man an mir sehe und erfahre des Vaters Willen, daß ich euch durch mein Blut und Tod erlösen soll.

Also tröstet und ermahnet er sich selbst wider den leidigen
Teufel. Denn es gehet ihm nun unter die Augen, und be-
ginnet das Hertz zu treffen, daß er so gar jämmerlich soll
verlassen seyn, gelästert und aufs schändlichste gehandelt
werden; aber es schadet nicht. Laß nur hergehen, weil es
der Vater will, daß der Teufel soll überwunden und ge-
schwächt werden, nicht durch Macht und Kraft und herrliche
Wunderthat, wie zuvor durch mich geschehen ist, sondern
durch Gehorsam und Demuth, in der höchsten Schwachheit,
Creutz und Tod: daß ich mich unter ihm werfe und mein

---

[1] An mich und das Seine, "do his work on me."

[2] Dräuet. "He thus threatens Satan shly with leering eyes," etc.

[3] An dem Bisslein, etc. " But you shall have in the mor-
sel something to chew." Biss, *lit.* Bisslein is a diminutive of
this.

Recht und Macht fahren laſſe, aber eben dadurch alle ſein
Recht und Macht ihm wieder abſchlage und gewinne, daß er
auch an euch kein Recht und Macht habe, weil er mich ohne
alle Schuld angreiffet und ermordet, und alsdenn vor mir
muß weichen und fliehen, ſo weit die Welt iſt, durch ſeine
eigene Schuld verurtheilt und verdammt. Das ſoll als=
denn in aller Welt geprediget und offenbar werden, daß ich
ſolches gethan habe, nicht aus Unkraft oder Ohnmacht, ſon=
dern aus Gehorſam des Vaters, den Teufel alſo zu über=
winden, daß dadurch ſeine Ehre, beyde, ſeiner göttlichen
Gnade und Güte gegen uns, und ſeiner allmächtigen Ge=
walt wider den Teufel, gepreiſet und ausgebreitet, und die
Chriſten dadurch getröſtet und geſtärcket, und alſo des Teu=
fels Reich gantz und gar zerſtöret werde. Amen.

---

## COMMENT ON PSALM 118, V. 1.

**Danket dem Herrn, denn er iſt freundlich
und ſeine Güte währet ewiglich.**

Dieſer Vers iſt eine gemeine Dankſagung für alle Wohl=
that, ſo Gott der Herr erzeigt aller Welt täglich ohne Unter=
laß, in allen Dingen, beide guten und böſen Menſchen. Denn
das iſt der heiligen Propheten Weiſe, wenn ſie Gott in ſon=
derlichen Dingen loben und danken wollen, ſo fangen ſie hoch
an und holen es weit, loben ihn zugleich ingemein, in allen
ſeinen Wundern und Wohlthaten. Alſo hie, weil dieſer
Pſalm ſonderlich Gott lobt um die höchſte Wohlthat, der
Welt erzeiget, nämlich um Chriſtum und ſein Reich der
Gnade, der Welt verheißen und jetzt erzeiget, fängt er an
mit gemeinem Lobe und ſpricht: Danket dem Herrn: denn
er iſt ja doch ein herzlicher, gnädiger, frommer, gütiger Gott,

31

der immer und immer wohlthut und eine Güte über die andere mit Haufen über uns ausschüttet.

Denn du mußt diese Worte: „freundlich‟ und „feine
Güte‟, nicht so kalt und roh lesen, noch darüberhin laufen,
wie die Nonnen den Psalter lesen, oder wie die Chorherren
und Chorschüler solche feine Worte blöcken und heulen in
ihren Kirchen, sondern denken, daß es lebendige, treuliche
und reiche Worte sind, die Alles und Alles fassen und einbilden, nämlich daß Gott freundlich ist, nicht wie ein Men sch,
sondern der von Grund seines Herzens geneigt und günstig
ist, immer zu helfen und wohlzuthun, und nicht gerne zürnt
noch straft, er müßte es denn[1] thun, und werde überhaupt
dazu gezwungen und gedrungen durch unabläßliche, unbuß-
fertige und verstockte Bosheit der Menschen, daß, wo er zürnen muß und strafen, da könnte ein Mensch nicht so lange
harren, sondern strafte hunderttausendmal eher und härter,
denn er thut.

Und solche freundliche und gnädige Gunst beweist er über
alle Maaßen reichlich und gewaltiglich, mit seiner täglichen
und ewigen Güte ; wie er hier spricht : Seine Güte währet
ewiglich, das ist : ohne Unterlaß thut er uns immer das
Beste, schafft uns Leib und Seele, behütet uns Tag und
Nacht, erhält uns ohne Unterlaß bei'm Leben, läßt Sonne
und Mond uns scheinen, und den Himmel, Feuer, Luft und
Wasser uns dienen, aus der Erde Wein, Korn, Futter,
Speise, Kleider, Holz und alle Nothdurft wachsen, giebt
Gold und Silber, Haus und Hof, Weib und Kind, Vieh,
Vögel, Fische, Summa, wer kann es Alles erzählen ? Und
dieß Alles die Fülle[2] und überschwänglich alle Jahre, alle
Tage, alle Stunden, alle Augenblicke.   Denn wer kann al-
lein die Güte rechnen, daß er Einem giebt und erhält ein
gesundes Auge oder Hand ?   Wenn wir krank sind oder

---

[1] E r  m ü s s t e  e s  d e n n  t h u n, “unless he is obliged to do it.‟
[2] D i e  F ü l l e.   See p. 235, Note 8.

deren Eines entbehren müssen, so sieht man allererst, was
für eine Wohlthat ist, ein gesundes Auge, eine gesunde
Hand, Fuß, Bein, Haupt, Nase, Finger haben, item, was
für eine Gnade sey, Brod, Kleider, Wasser, Feuer, Haus
haben rc.

Und wenn wir Menschen nicht so blind und der Güte
Gottes so überdrüssig und unachtsam wären, so ist freilich
kein Mensch auf Erden, er hat so viel Güter an sich, wenn
es sollte zum Wechseln kommen, er nähme kein Kaiserthum
noch Königreich dafür, und wäre dafür derselbigen Güter
beraubt. Denn was kann ein Königreich für ein Schatz
seyn gegen einen gesunden Leib? Was ist aller Welt Geld
und Gut gegen einen Tag, den uns die liebe Sonne täglich
macht? Wenn die Sonne einen Tag nicht schiene, wer
wollte nicht todt seyn? Oder was hülfe ihn alle sein Gut
und Herrschaft? Was wäre aller Wein und Malvasier in
aller Welt, wenn wir sollten einen Tag Wassers mangeln?
Was wären alle hübschen Schlosser, Häuser, Sammt, Sei-
den, Purpur, goldene Ketten und Edelgesteine, aller Pracht,
Schmuck und Hoffart, wenn wir eines Vaterunsers die Luft
lang[1] entbehren sollten.

Solche Güter Gotter sind die größten und allerverachtet-
sten, und darum, daß sie gemeine sind, danket Gott Niemand darum, nehmen sie und brauchen derselbigen täglich
immer so dahin, als müßte es so seyn, und wir hätten ganz
Recht dazu, und dürften Gott nicht einmal dafür danken.
Fahren dieweil zu, haben das Herzeleid zu thun, sorgen,
hadern, streiten, ringen und wüthen, um übrig Geld oder
Gut, um Ehre und Wolluft, und Summa um das, welches
solchen obgenannten Gütern nicht das Wasser reichen
könnte, und uns auf's hundertste Theil nicht so nütze seyn

---

[1] Eines Vaterunsers—lang, " for the space of the Lord's
Prayer, i. e. as long as it would take to repeat the Lord's Prayer.

mag, sondern vielmehr uns hindert an dem fröhlichen und friedlichen Brauch der gemeinen Güter, daß wir sie dafür nicht erkennen, noch Gott darum danken können. Das macht der leidige Teufel, der uns nicht gönnen mag, daß wir Gottes Güte und der reichen täglichen Wohlthat brauchen noch erkennen könnten, wir wären allzu selig.

Siehe, nun sage du, wie viel sind wohl Leute auf Erden, die diesen Vers verstehen? Wahr ist es, kein Bube ist so böse, wenn er in der Kirche solchen Vers singt oder sonst hört, er läßt sich dünken, er verstehe ihn überaus wohl und habe ihn nun bis auf den Boden ausgesoffen, der doch sein ganzes Leben lang nie daran gedacht noch gedankt hat für die Milch, die er von seiner Mutter gesogen hat, geschweige denn für alle die Güte Gottes, die ihm Gott sein ganzes Leben so unzählich und unsäglich erzeigt hat, daß er wohl alle Stunden allein seiner Undankbarkeit halben mehr Sünde gethan hat, denn Laub und Gras im Walde ist, wo Gott ein Wucherer wäre, und wollte genaue Rechnung fordern.

Darum sollte dieser Vers billig einem jeglichen Menschen täglich, ja alle Augenblicke im Hertzen und Munde seyn, so oft er äße, tränke, sähe, hörte, röche, gienge, stünde, oder wie, wo, wenn er seiner Glieder, Leibes, Guts oder einiger Creatur braucht, damit er daran dächte, daß wo ihm Gott nicht solches zu brauchen gäbe und wider den Teufel erhielte, so müßte er wohl entbehren, und daneben sich ermahnte und gewöhnte zu einem fröhlichen Herzen und lustigen Glauben gegen Gott mit Danksagung für solche seine tägliche Güte und sagen: Wohlan, du bist doch ja ein freundlicher, gütiger Gott, der du ewiglich (das ist: immer und immer, ohne Unterlaß) mir Unwürdigem und Undankbarem so reichliche Güte und Wohlthat erzeigest; Lob und Dank müssest du haben.

Und das dient auch dazu, daß man damit sich trösten kann

in allem Unfall. Denn wir sind solche Zärtlinge und so
weiche Märtyrer, wenn uns nur ein Bein wehe thut oder
ein kleines Blätterlein auffährt, so können wir Himmel und
Erde vollschreien mit Klagen und Heulen, Murren und
Fluchen, und nicht sehen, wie gar ein geringes Uebel solch
Blätterlein ist, gegen die andern unzähligen Güter Gottes,
die wir noch voll und ganz haben. Gleich als wenn ein
König unsinnig werden wollte, daß er einen Pfennig verloren hätte, unangesehen daß er schier die halbe Welt hätte,
mit unzähligem Geld und Gut, und wollte darüber martern,
veitstanzen und pestilenzen,[1] Gott schänden und mit andern
Flüchen herausdonnern, wie jetzt die Marterhansen[2] mit
Fluchen ihre Mannheit beweisen.

Nun läßt doch der fromme Gott solche geringe Uebel uns
allein darum widerfahren, daß er uns damit stärker aus
dem tiefem Schlaf erwecke und treibe dahin, daß wir lern-
ten dagegen ansehen die großen unzähligen Güter, die noch
vorhanden sind, und was es werden sollte, wo er seine Güte
gar von uns wenden und nehmen wollte. Wie der fromme
Hiob that, da er sprach: „Haben wir Gutes empfangen
vom Herrn, warum wollten wir das Uebel nicht leiden?"
Siehe, derselbe kounte dieß schöne Confitemini und diesen
Vers gar fein singen und sprach: Wie es Gott gefällt, so
gehe es, des Herrn Name sey gelobet rc. Er fällt nicht allein auf das Uebel, wie wir Puppenheiligen thun; sondern
behält vor Augen alle Güte und Wahrheit des Herrn, tröstet sich damit und überwindet das Böse mit Geduld.

Also sollen wir auch alle unser Unglück nicht anders ansehen noch annehmen, denn als zündete uns Gott damit ein
Licht an, dabei wir seine Güte und Wohlthat, in andern unzähligen Stücken sehen und erkennen möchten, daß wir uns
dünken ließen, es wäre solch geringes Uebel ein Tröpflein

---

[1] Veitstanzen und pestilenzen, "act like one with
St. Vitus's Dance, or in the pestilence."    [2] Cowards, jacks.

Wassers in ein großes Feuer, oder ein Fünklein in ein gro=
ßes Wasser gefallen, damit der Vers uns bekannt und lieb=
lich würde: „Danket dem Herrn, denn er ist ja doch freund=
lich und seine Güte währet ewiglich."

Summa, wir können gegen Gott kein größeres noch besse=
res Werk thun, noch edleren Gottesdienst erzeigen, denn
ihm danken, wie er selbst sagt, Ps. 50.: „Das Dankopfer
ist meine Ehre oder Gottesdienst, und dasselbe ist der Weg
dazu, daß ich mein Heil sehen lasse." Solches Opfer ge=
fällt ihm über alle Opfer, Stifte, Klöster und was da seyn
mag, wie er sagt Psalm 59. · „Ich will den Namen Gottes
loben mit meinem Liede, und will ihn hoch ehren mit Dank.
Das wird dem Herrn besser gefallen als ein Farren, der
Hörner und Klauen hat."

Wiederum, gleichwie Gott loben und dankbar seyn der
höchste Gottesdienst ist, beide hier auf Erden und dort ewig=
lich; also ist auch Undankbarkeit das allerschändlichste Laster
und die höchste Unehre Gottes, welches doch die Welt voll,
voll, voll ist, bis an den Himmel hinan. Aber Gott ist so
ein gütiger Herr, wie dieser Vers singt, daß er um solcher
Undankbarkeit willen dennoch nicht abläßt noch aufhört wol=
zuthun, sondern, wie er hier sagt, seine Güte währet ewig=
lich, läßt immer für und für seine Sonne aufgehen, beide
über Gute und Böse, und läßt regnen beide über Dankbare
und Undankbare, Matth. 5. Giebt Buben wohl so viel
Güter, Kinder, Gewalt als den Heiligen, und viel mehr,
behütet vor Krieg, Pestilenz, Theurung und allen Plagen
des Teufels. Das ist und heißt eine göttliche Güte, die um
keiner Bosheit willen abläßt oder müde wird. Ein Mensch
vermag solche Güte nicht. Denn Undankbarkeit kann kein
Mensch leiden, und sind Viele darüber rasend, toll und un=
sinnig geworden, wie die Historien von Timon schreiben.
Es ist menschlicher Natur zu schwer, Wohlthun und eitel
Böses dafür empfahen.

# INDEX TO THE NOTES.

The first figures refer to the page, the second to the notes.

Decken, Deck, Deckel, p. 25, n. 3.

Dein, genitive for deiner, p. 46, n. 4.

(An) dem dass, p. 280, n. 1.

Denn, *then*, p. 214, n. 2 end— for als, *than*, p. 5, n. 3 — p. 8, n. 4—after nicht, p. 19, n. 1—after kein, p. 97, n. 2—*except*, after es sei, sie haben, etc., p. 37, n. 2—p. 73, n. 5.

Dennoch, p. 66, n. 5—p. 16, n. 3.

Der, for derer, p. 4, n. 2—p. 106, n. 5—p. 115, n. 1 end—der, *he*, more emphatic than er, p. 243, n. 4—p. 284, n. 2 — der (with der understood), *he,who*, p. 39, n. 1—p. 43, n. 4 — p. 48, n. 1—p. 61, n. 6—der der distinguished from der wer, and derjenige welcher, p. 14, n. 5—p. 35, n. 4.

Dergleichen, p. 4, n. 2.

Derhalben, p. 8, n. 2. Derohalben, p. 217, n. 1.

Derjenige welcher, p. 14, n. 5.

Dess, for dessen, p. 4, n. 2— p. 126, n. 2.

Dessgleichen, p. 4, n. 2.

Desshalb, p. 246, n. 4.

Dess viel, p. 231, n. 6. Compare p. 241, n. 1.

Desselben ungeachtet, p. 318, n. 2.

Desswegen, p. 217, n. 1 — p. 246, n. 4.

Deuten, p. 244, n. 5.

(Aller) Dinge, p. 183, n. 3.

Dichten, p. 4. n. 1 — p. 73, n. 2—Dichten und Trachten, p. 4, n. 1.

Die, *those*, p. 7, n. 3—p. 19, n. 3.

Diessmal, p. 6, n. 1.

Dieweil, p. 26, n. 2—p. 104, n. 1—p. 106, n. 4.

Ding, p. 58, n. 3 — p. 26, n. 1— p. 254, n. 3—p. 275, n. 3.

Doch, p. 66, n. 5.

Dorf, p. 27, n. 2.

Dort, distinguished from da, p. 223, n. 2.

Dräuen, for drohen, p. 95, n. 1—p. 155, n. 2.

Dranseyu, p. 319, n. 3.

Drinnen, p. 71, n. 4.

Droben, p. 42, n. 1.

Dunkel, p.74, n. 6.—Dunkel, p. 254, n. 3.

Dünken, p. 22, n. 3.

Dünne siehen, p. 233, n. 4.

Durch, p. 126, n. 1.

Durchgöttem, p. 331, n. 2.

Durchlauchtig, p. 92, n. 3.

Durchtreiben, p. 253, n. 2.

Dürfen, p. 54, n. 4.

Durst, *daring*, p. 336, n. 3.

Düster, p. 254, n. 3.

E.

E, final omitted, p. 5, n. 4 — p. 6, n. 3.

Eben, p. 171, n. 3 med.

Edel, p. 221, n. 7.

Eher, p. 57, n. 2.

Eigen with the genitive, p. 3, n. 5—p. 119, n. 2—with mein, sein, etc. p. 216, n. 2. Comp. p. 214, n. 2 end.

Eigentlich, *properly, literally*, p. 45, n. 3.

Ein, when an adjective, p. 165, n. 3 — when it goes before an adjective, p. 267, n. 3.

Ein um den andern, p. 116, n. 1.

Einblauen, p. 321, n. 2.

Einbilden, p. 289, n. 1.

Einfall, p. 291, n. 1.

Einfallen, p. 242, n. 1 end.

Einig, for einzig, p. 93, n. 2 —p. 149, n. 1—p. 210, n. 2—p. 251, n. 5.

Einerlei, p. 77, n. 2. Compare, p. 3, n. 4.

Einmal, p. 48, n. 2.

Einnehmen, p. 26, n. 5.

Einrichten, p. 50, n. 2.

Einsetzen, p. 164, n. 4.

Eitel, p. 10, n. 4—p. 82, n. 1.

Elend, p. 44, n. 4.

Ellipsis of verbs, p. 35, n. 3.

H.

END.